French North Africa

French North Africa

The Maghrib Between Two World Wars

JACQUES BERQUE

Translated by
JEAN STEWART

FREDERICK A. PRAEGER, *Publishers*
New York · Washington

BOOKS THAT MATTER

Published in the United States of America in 1967
by Frederick A. Praeger, Inc., Publishers
111 Fourth Avenue, New York, N.Y. 10003

Originally published in France as
LE MAGRIB ENTRE DEUX GUERRES

© 1962 by Editions du Seuil

English translation © Faber and Faber Ltd., in London, England, 1967

Library of Congress Catalog Card Number: 65-20083

Printed in Great Britain

Contents

7

Stages of Historic Enlightenment
Enduring Factors in Maghrib Life

CONTENTS

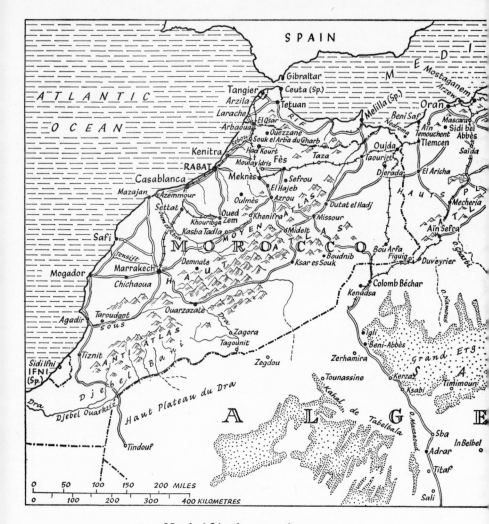

North Africa between the two wars

Preface

I n the preface to *The Arabs: their History and Future*, I apologized
for having divided what was indivisible. By considering only the
Arab East, I restricted the scope of my enquiry; a sequel on the
Maghrib seemed imperative. Here it is. But it is open to a similar
indictment, since it deals with the Maghrib of a past epoch. I have
thought it possible, in fact, to isolate the period between the two world
wars – from 1918 to 1939 – and to make this the basis for a further study
of the independent Maghrib.

A more orthodox procedure, no doubt, would be to wait another
thirty years before discussing this interwar Maghrib. By then, archives
will be accessible, documents will have been collected into series, and
monographs written covering all questions. Once wounds have been
healed and sorrows forgotten and passions have died down, the historian
will be able to consider this period with the serenity which the study
of the past often brings.

Could I hope to claim such serenity? Or could I attain only an illusion
of serenity, by a costly and forcible 'pacification' of my own mind? As I
write these words, many who lived, happily or unhappily, through the
interwar period, are still among us. I have shared in their existence,
through physical proximity, family relationship, professional activity,
acquaintance or intimate friendship. I have met many of the men and
lived in most of the places discussed in the following pages. Yet I have
not merely indulged in recollection. I have had recourse to memory only
in order to bring life to my documentation, which is derived either from
the writings of the period or from evidence whose origin I cannot, for
obvious reasons, always cite, but for whose authenticity I can vouch.

This familiarity with the subject offered advantages and disadvantages.
The main disadvantage was that I had to depend on my own researches
to an excessive degree. In this matter, academic studies provide neither
enough detachment nor enough mutual assistance. The period is too

close to us, and inevitably subject either to spurious indignation or to discreet neglect, and has inspired practically no investigations. As far as politics were concerned, indeed, I had the benefit of Ch.-A. Julien's analysis. But for other fields, and particularly that of economics, to what could I refer?

Economists had not yet begun to use the methods or even to ask the questions that have sprung up in men's minds during the past twenty years. Anticipation, had they been capable of it in this matter, would have been useless to them, for lack of an adequate social interpretation. In fact, the ethnography of North Africa was out of date and its sociology conventional. Such an approach neglected the specifically historic elements of reality. Because of these deficiencies I am still deprived, on many issues, of the right to draw conclusions. The *petit peuple* of the towns and the rural worker are described here, but no more; I have merely indicated their position with respect to major happenings, without feeling entitled to integrate them into the systematic construction of which some day they may, or will, form the essential part. One must avoid degrading useful schemes of analysis and judgment into stereotypes. For instance, the history of the class struggle in North Africa, although referred to at several points in this book, cannot be seriously studied until we have at our disposal a greater wealth of material and more direct instruments of research.

Should I have postponed synthesis on this account? But the sociological interest of my undertaking lay precisely in reconstituting a whole, and giving their right proportion to different elements, studied from the point of view of their mutual function and significance. Fortunately, in this task, despite all the difficulties inherent both in the proximity of the period and the inadequate documentation, I enjoyed the benefit of valuable co-operation, thanks to the constant contact I have maintained with the people of Mediterranean Islam. An Egyptian essayist rightly remarked of my last book that it seemed intended for the Eastern as much as for the Western reader. This struck him as unprecedented! Is the attempt over-ambitious? My study, thus conceived, requires its object to become an interlocutor, both critic and participant. This involves risks, no doubt. For instance, the risk of being frank and causing offence. But even that is a change from the orientalist's usual isolation. A dialogue, free from illusions but not lacking in warmth, reveals the meaning which a society ascribes to itself, and perhaps the direction in which it is going.

And that means the direction in which we are all going. For in this world of mutual exchange and conflict, the convenient division between observer and observed is no longer valid. No less than the antagonisms of contemporary politics, the differences that analysis spotlights, and that form the basis of self-awareness, all finally remind mankind of its unity.

This partly deliberate, partly involuntary adherence to the matter
of my study, while obliging me to concentrate on the specific character
of particular environments, moments and phenomena, required by way
of compensation some concern with theory. The 'case' of North Africa
suggests general problems: first and foremost, that of the nature and
limits of the Colonial system as it exists in fact. This is the essential
problem of our time. The way we solve it will determine the analysis and
practice of decolonization–which means the imminent course of the
world. And the North African scene between the two wars, during the
apparent apogee of French imperialism, provides a fruitful field for the
study of this problem.

Now that we know how the system ended, it is easy, perhaps too easy,
to say whither it was leading. But in relation to that central theme,
people and events and things did not operate on the same level or become
equally involved. The relationships varied and at different levels might
be those of concrete determination, of logical sequence, or merely of
configuration. They might on the other hand be compensating relationships, or else ones that seemed irrelevant and even gratuitous. Hence
the need to distinguish various degrees of function and significance.
'Social' history, in order to deserve its name, should aim not only at
reconstituting facts or even aggregates of facts. It cannot rest content
with merely collecting data, nor even with setting forth laws. From these
aggregates, these data, these facts and laws, history must reconstitute
a *whole*.

Now it is through, and in, phenomena that this global reality becomes
manifest to us, becomes part of us. Research, which concentrates on
series and lines, symmetries and regularities, can only apprehend these
by way of what is apparent and contingent. It cannot dismiss eye-
witness accounts of events. How could it be otherwise? Life is that
through which the idea takes on a body and the body takes on a meaning.
Life integrates the vast world with the most fleeting human action,
combines the constant and the ephemeral, the trivial and the profound.
And life cannot be dissociated from events, even though these may wear
a purely picturesque and anecdotal appearance. For after all, the event
is what affects us, if it does not actually make us what we are. It is the
tip of a cone which leads to the broadest and most all-embracing
concepts.

It goes without saying that life, by reason of its essential plurality, is
more easily felt than understood by those who are living it. For the
individual or for the group, it may seem fair or unfair, happy or unhappy.
At any moment, it qualifies itself; but time calls all qualifications in
question. Our present obscures what preceded it; it emits smoke-screens
like those that used to trail behind old-fashioned steam-engines. To
remember the past means to requalify it in relation to ourselves. It

means–too often–judging 1930 in terms of 1960. A convenient, but arbitrary process. Under the cloak of dogmatism, it runs the risk of agnosticism, which denies all objectivity to the past. It thus goes contrary to what we expect from history.

True, when the sequence of events takes place amid sufferings, and is accompanied by a renewal of moral values, as happens in times of revolution or indeed of decolonization, much strength of mind is needed to avoid the facile hindsight with which, watching the epilogue of a drama, we recall the second act. But in order to bring to life the historic moment *as it was*, not as we want it to have been, it is necessary to retain its essential flavour, its availability. Thus the historian must assume a kind of forgetfulness of the actual sequel which he knows beforehand. This is merely a feint. But it makes it easier for him to recognize the way things and people were moving.

They were moving–and we are moving today–towards one possible alternative rather than towards any other. And this, I believe, is the possibility of ever greater freedom. But if I am right in believing this, it will not be enough to show it deductively by collecting more or less complete data in support of a postulate. It will be necessary to recover the indications of this movement in reality as it was lived. This attitude will be quite as legitimate as that of the economist concerned with extracting cycles, tendencies, and numerical relations between facts. In his case as in our own, what matters is to discover a meaning, a direction. Only the process is more serious and more risky in our case than in his.

What we are dealing with is not only facts and the quantitative relations between them, but their quality, their subtle flavour. If it is true that there was 'something rotten' in the stage of North African colonization that we are now considering, this must surely have shown itself by certain signs at the time. Misery that was only too real, disappointments that were only too well founded, a growing incapacity on the part of the authorities already struck the clearsighted observer and from time to time produced dramatic explosions. But these vices, or contradictions, which our present analysis reveals, at the time scarcely disturbed the solid-seeming, and to some extent prosperous, order that reigned in North Africa. They were vices and contradictions only in despite of existing reality, and in relation to a potential reality.

Today we are too apt to reconstruct the former of these two realities in terms of the second, which we deserve no praise for anticipating, since it has already occurred. The operation has a certain didactic value. But it displaces the real problem, which is not to refashion the past according to its consequences, but to state precisely the real relations between the two. Doubtless the catastrophe that eventually engulfed the old Maghrib is being subjected today to retroactive condemnation. There must surely have existed within that period some mysterious vice that the two sides should depend on to explain their uprising in the one case, and their dispossession in the other! But it was surely from more concrete, yet slighter, indications that, at the time, the direction of future developments must have been revealed.

The defeat of the colonial system was heralded by an almost imperceptible, but eventually irresistible, alliance between the forces of morality and those of efficiency, conspiring to misinterpret its successes and to aggravate its vices and its contradictions. The process most frequently escaped analysis. But it cropped up in people's lives. The revolution was ahead of men's awareness of it. But beneath the joys of that time we hear a note of bitterness; behind its miseries, a note of expectation. Paradoxically, dark shadows overcast a scene which should have been green with all the wealth of its plant-life. A subtle, uneasy shift in the tone and accent of life, a sense of inauthenticity, betrayed injustice under the cloak of order, and disease under that of health.

If these things have been observed and interpreted correctly, the Maghrib between the two wars—that triumph of colonial achievement —was fostering its own downfall. It bore within itself, as the philosopher would have said, its own negation. This engendering of death was taking place under our eyes, within us and all around us, concealed maybe in the delights of action, the ripening of fruits or the beauty of women. And meanwhile, a different future was taking shape, destructive yet creative; once again, life was to prove the stronger.

Kairouan, 1st July 1961

11 November 1918

On 11 November 1918, a detachment of French troops was encamped in the neighbourhood of Arbaoua, in Northern Morocco. When the armistice was announced, they fired a few volleys over the lands under Spanish influence. In a village of the High Plateaux of Oran, the school closed; the children, European and Muslim, streamed in procession through the streets. In the gloomy playground backing on to a disused graveyard, only two pupils were left; the administrator's son and the Qadi's. However, they were to get plenty of other holidays in the ensuing months. Throughout North Africa, the celebration of victory unleashed wild excitement. In Algiers, in the Rue d'Isly, crowds clambered on the platforms of trams, or cheerfully overturned the electric motor and its trailer; they pulled down shop-window blinds and tore up fences. There was much singing and dancing and some raping: a vast, shocking display of joy, if the terms are not incompatible. For the demobilized men were coming back, bringing the problem with them.

For ex-soldiers of both breeds, coming back was a severe ordeal. War had seemed to them like a kind of divine judgement. The sons of these two military nations returned home with rival feelings; the French with the sense that this land contained their manifest destiny; the Arabs, that they had earned rights, for had they not, in this war, been part of France, fought her foes bravely and loyally? Now, the heroes returned to find a land already shaken by formidable currents of world opinion. Disappointment quickly followed. The readjustment between the pre-war and the post-war world looked like being difficult. Nobody realized yet –presumably through being unused to such things–that a victor earns only a single right: the right to remake himself, to become something different. His former self is doomed, and must be replaced, with all his feelings, his attitudes, his whole moral code. But among the victors, self-confident through preponderance, very few had enough courage or enough prudence. Those who came home full of hope, particularly the

Muslim soldiers who had seen terrible things, soon realized that everything was beginning again as it had before. With an ironic contrast
between war and peace, everything was reverting to the accepted
colonial way of life. In the three countries of the Maghrib things
resumed their course. And this continuance was as intolerable to self-
interest as to justice.

At the end of the first world war, North Africa still contained regions
that were not completely distinct, but intact in the sense that they were
not subject to the central power. In Morocco, where large stretches of
them still existed, they were known by the traditional name of *siba*, which
we interpret as 'dissidence', although it may possibly mean the 'free
flowing' of things.

Let us trace a diagonal between Tafilalt, the cradle of the ruling
dynasty, and Rabat, seat of the French protectorate, and another
cutting it at right angles towards the middle.[1] This second line–running
from the confines of the Anti-Atlas, whence, according to legend, the
mahdi will some day appear, to those of the Eastern Rif, at which the
Spaniards kept nibbling, with scant glory to themselves–crosses the
high pastures of the Middle Atlas. It thus connects three unsubjugated
regions: that of the Shleuhs, that of the Imazighen and that of the Rifis:
the human substructure of North Africa. Whereas some of their brothers,
such as the Kabyles from Jurjura, the 'Ibadis from the Mzab, go in for
unspectacular adaptation[2] and compromise within limited sectors, these
others maintain proudly by force of arms their resistance to change and
their adventurous, if aimless, freedom. Two-thirds of Morocco are thus
in a state of *siba*; whether through conviction of final victory, only to be
granted by a Berber providence, or through the defiant attitude of
desperate men. Two warriors captured at Sefru were taken before the
investigating officer: 'If I let you go, what will you do?' 'We shall kill
you.' At a sign of the huge *sha'ush* (guard)[3] Zammuri, they were taken
away; two shots rang out. Elsewhere, in lands that seemed to have lain
untouched for centuries, curious relationships were formed, with a kind
of Homeric freshness. The 'Frenchmen's Makhzen' kept on growing,
even among the tough men of the Rif and the treacherous Jebalas. In
1920 an army column concentrated on 'Ain Defali, went up the Rdat
valley, occupied Wazzan, where Lyautey marched in on 7 October

[1] This historic centre of Morocco would lie in the region of the *zâwiya* of
Dila', thus further explaining the latter's importance in the seventeenth century.

[2] The whole Moroccan school resumes and amplifies, on this point, theories
long accepted in Algeria with regard to the Kabyles. The result had been, in
ethnology, Masqueray's 'romanism'; and in politics, certain far more questionable attitudes. Cf. Ageron 'La France a-t-elle une politique kabyle?' *Revue
historique*, 1961, pp. 311–51.

[3] *Sha'ush*, or *chaouch*, used as a generic term to describe a variety of subor-
dinate Muslim officials: porters, orderlies or guards.

and was welcomed by the Shorfas (shurafa'). Gone were the days when mystic brotherhoods whetted popular feeling against those in power.

In these apparently new regions, the conqueror saw reserves of white barbarians, the last of the Mediterranean world, and assumed with satisfaction that he could mould this vigorous humanity as he chose. These remote cousins of the Ancient Gauls were reliable allies; in any case they were very different from the Arabs of the plains, indeed from Muslims in general. In short, they could be reclaimed. Officially, they were reclaimed on behalf of the Sultan. Note that this was known as pacification or penetration, not as conquest. Ostensibly, the only conquest sought was a moral one. 'A doctor is worth a battalion': the sinister formula might have derived from a Clausewitzian adage, 'civilization is a form of warfare'. In any case, the *baruds* (conflicts) did not always confine themselves to being 'honourable'.

The prevalent form of rule among the Shleuhs of the South was tyranny; their public life oscillated traditionally between this and an elementary form of democracy. Possibly as a result of the unaccustomed shocks to which, ever since 1830, the societies of the Maghrib had been subjected, fragmentation was on the increase. The confederation had broken up into groups and these into smaller groups, clustered around their chiefs. That is why the caïds Anflus, Mtuggi, Gundafi, Glawi, Laiyadi, securely self-confident, controlled the regions from the ocean to the foothills of the Middle Atlas with a network of rapacious intrigues, an excellent bargaining basis. They held, or they sought to hold, the major passes of the Atlas range. And they overflowed on to the river Sus and the Anti-Atlas, where Justinard, as outpost, had held Tiznit since 1916.[1]

In certain cases, where direct contact prevailed, the initiative of individual officers won the enthusiastic support of the native group. There was much display of fine personal qualities; this happened at every stage of the Bureau's[2] progress, so long as intermediaries, bureaucrats and parasites did not interfere to ruin the fine individual gestures and give back its prosaic character to the occupation. The achievements of the Affaires Indigènes, which often proved enduringly successful, stand midway geographically, chronologically and morally between heroic encounters and self-interested exploitation.[3] Behind the conquerors, here strengthened by the allegiance of the Sharifs, the country

---

[1] Cf. his moving little book *Le Caïd Goundafi*, 1951. Justinard may later have been a victim of intrigues by al-Glawi, jealous of the other 'great Caïd'.

[2] Bureau Arabe, i.e. military unit of administration. This nomenclature dates from Bugeaud's days in Algeria. It was commonly used by the French in Morocco too.

[3] Cf. the article by V. Monteil, 'Les Bureaux arabes du Maghreb (1833–1961)', *Esprit*, Nov. 1961.

began to be organized. A special Bulletin, in 1920, specifies meticulous details about different Moroccan towns: for instance we read of the regulations for the Rabat fire brigade, a decree on moral conduct at Azemmur; we learn that Casablanca rejects the concessionary system for electric energy, and that a welfare society has been formed at Fez. Everywhere, municipalities were concerned with supplies, with administration, with leisure, and with organization in every sphere. Meanwhile big business, like the administrative order, settled in under cover of impressive pageantry.

Morocco renovated in this way can be contrasted with Tunisia where colonial enterprise seemed already tired. Although the war had more or less spared the Regency, a grave problem was facing the French here: that of a demographic setback, the risk of being overrun by Italians. With the advent of Fascism in Italy, the danger increased. While towards the West, in the province of Oujda and around Oran, the Spanish tradition lingered only in the form of folklore and even ended up as proud French nationalism, and while the Italians and Maltese of Constantine were subject to the same process of assimilation, in Tunisia Italy cheerfully asserted her priority in this Mediterranean synthesis.

According to Rodd Balek,[1] there were in Tunis, for every forty-nine French lawyers, nineteen Italian ones and thirteen Muslim students; for every ninety French doctors, sixty-five Italian and ten Muslim ones. These figures in themselves reveal the unusual character of the whole, with its close competition between European rivals and natives. At the same time, in the political struggle and in social maturity, Tunisia was about a generation ahead of the rest of North Africa. As early as November 1919 Shaikh Tha'alibi had published in Paris his pamphlet, *Tunisie martyre*. He appealed to the constitution formerly laid down by a bey, which had just been duly recognized as valid by a couple of French journalists. In February 1920 was founded the Destour party, *Hizb al-hurr al-dusturi*. It set out with a radical programme aiming at independence, but transformed this the following year into reformist complaints.

The conflict between intransigence and compromise, which characterized the whole story of this opposition movement, is peculiar neither to this country nor to the colonial era. But perhaps the greater flexibility shown in these transactions may have helped to safeguard something essential. If intransigence sometimes promotes progress, it is also conducive to dangerous tendencies, for instance to metaphysical quibbling. The Muslims were torn between two perilous options. Purity may play into the enemy's hands, but expediency corrupts ... And this moral, well-nigh theological uncertainty was further complicated by a growing trend towards political and social commitment in the modern sense.

[1] *Afrique française*, 1920, pp. 128 ff., 168 ff., 194 ff., 226 ff.

This type of effective action would surely cost the old believers yet another renunciation.

On 15 September 1920 Tunis witnessed a sensational demonstration about the cost of living. The initiative came from certain French liberals. One of the speakers, Durel, a schoolmaster, climbed on to the platform. He stood silent for a moment, his head bent, his loose tie floating in the wind. As soon as he spoke, a sympathetic thrill ran through the audience. He was followed by a Tunisian, the general secretary of the Tramway Workers' Union. For at that time Muslims and *petits blancs* joined hands on certain issues. Nobody suspected that the latter would eventually transfer their allegiance to the establishment. The left wing, in the bright haze of their hopes, confused national emancipation and social freedom. In the long run, they were not so far wrong. The fact remains that in 1920 there seemed no danger of a serious rift between nationalism and that socialism which fervent apostles had begun to propagate in North Africa.

The masses were beginning to stir of their own accord. There was the anger of workers back from the front who could not find employment:[1] the rise of prices: harsh taxation. And, without resorting to violence, the mob sometimes expressed itself in symbolic gestures. One day in 1920 an Italian motorist, who had nearly knocked down an old Moorish woman, was in danger of being hacked to pieces; a Tunisian driver got off his tram to join the fight. The cafés of Bab Menara and Bab Jdid had no wireless in those days, but customers clubbed together to subscribe to a newspaper and hire a public reader, to whom they listened while enjoying highly uncanonical drinks. The Young Turks met at the Japanese café in the Avenue Jules Ferry, the Socialists and, presently, Communists at the Café de France. Militants such as Louzon and Finidori dispensed the new ideology. Strikes broke out, including, in the space of one or two years, a tramway strike in Tunis, an unsuccessful miners' strike at Gafsa, a token strike of railwaymen in 1920, which also led to retaliatory measures, and, finally, the great strike of flour-mill workers, which frightened everyone, although it, too, turned out badly for the workers. At the Labour Exchange there was a gathering of a hundred or two hundred workers on 6 November 1921, chiefly Tunisian and Italian, for the Frenchmen involved were militant trade unionists or journalists. The men were asking for an eight-hour day. The military authorities managed to get some bakeries going, and flour was fetched from Marseilles. At the Labour Exchange, Durel reported on his negotiations with the Resident-General: they had failed. At any rate, he promised, there would be no victimization. This was something of a euphemism. . . .

[1] Cf. Augustin Bernard, 'Le placement des démobilisés de l'Afrique du Nord', *Afrique française*, 1919, p. 208 ff.

Among the Tunisian bourgeoisie, the protest movement grew. In 1920, two delegations reached Paris: one in July and the other in December. They were received by important statesmen; on their return, however, they had short shrift from the Colonial authorities. Their social origin is worth closer study; they included, for instance, Ahmad Sakka, born in 1892, son and nephew of caïds, a man of good family; he had studied in France, first at the Lycée Carnot and than at the École de Droit; he served his term in the office of Maître Guellati, and finally, back in Paris, had won the sympathy of the Socialists. By the side of this Westerner, we find figures from the old Tunis, such as Farhat bin 'Aiyad, scion of a famous family now ruined, and Muhammad Riahi, whose forebears were city marabouts, but who now held a humble post in the Waqf ministry. The connection is obvious between political demands and the resentment of a class that had seen better days. In contrast, we find others who are going up in the world; Shaikh Salah bin Yahya, of Tha'alibi, a Mozabite who had come from the Pentapolis about 1910, and had adapted himself readily to the Great Mosque. This pious man found his chief difficulty was dealing with his 'Ibadi brethren from Jerba, subtle argufiers and thrifty tradesmen. The great city had already begun to attract new appetites and to mingle the names of *parvenus* with those Turkish and Andalusian names that spoke of bourgeois dignity and the nostalgia of history.

The picture would not be complete without a glance at the secondary towns. Sfax was entirely dependent on the olive oil trade. Loans in anticipation of the harvest, proscribed by Islam but generally practised, were advanced on the security of women's jewellery. Agricultural cycles, speculation, feminine initiative, internal equilibrium and family ambition had all from time immemorial played their part. Meanwhile, new practices came to the fore. Colonial intervention had enormously increased the area devoted to olive growing.[1] It had also created needs and habits. In the spring of 1920 a clandestine Stock Exchange opened where all sorts of transactions in stocks and shares and in real estate went on. The story ended with the ruin of a number of well-known tradesmen. A permanent conflict divided the new rich from the ancient hierarchies, and both of these from the foreign entrepreneur. The latter, enjoying technical superiority and the protection of the law, was at a disadvantage through his inferior adaptation to his environment. Hence arose many disputes. In October we hear of the adventure of a certain managing director of the Omnium—one of those societies whose very name proclaims their lucrative multivalency. On his concession he discovered a Bedouin hunt in full cry, with a pack of gazelle-hounds. Here was a classic contrast between two ways of life: the capitalist firms versus the patriarchal hunting-party. On this occasion the

---

[1] Initiated by Paul Bourde.

European, in spite of having killed some dogs and fined the huntsmen, was able to hush up the matter. The local inhabitants had to resist by what crafty means they could. At Sousse, a Muslim broker opposed with violence the carrying out of an order relating to a huge domain occupied, as was often the case, by tenants without legal title. He had acquired by craft the tenant-farmers' rights, to uphold them against those of the original proprietor and his European buyer. When the latter appeared armed with his title-deed and an order from the courts, the broker's henchmen prevented him from taking possession. In the end, it was the tenant-farmers who were jailed. Meanwhile, however, at Suq al-Arba' in the North, an assembly of *colons* had analysed with perspicacity the dangers in store for agriculture, and had decided to embark on mechanization.

When things are on the move a number of shocks are inevitable. It may be new customs, or new techniques, or colonial competition that provide the decisive stimulus. But on each occasion the old way of life disintegrates a little further. The construction which arises from its ruins cannot wholly replace the past: whence a tremendous heterogeneity of people and things and situations. Such an aggregate includes reactionaries and pioneers, crooks and creators. The slightest incident is directly or indirectly connected with the major facts of the period. On the one hand the ruin of pastoral agriculture and the expansion of the use of machinery, on the other the inequality of wealth, of ways of life, of status, and the advantage taken of that very inequality by speculators; and finally, social or political indignation. And as a background, world-wide upheavals from which Tunisia could no longer be isolated. The colonial system which, at its outset, had made use of these widespread trends, began to find them disturbing; it sought to limit the effect of the forces which had formerly borne it to power.

In Algeria, a land much given to quarrels over identity, argument was rife about 'status'. From time to time, there were parliamentary rows between progressives and conservatives: Moutet and Morinaud, for instance, in 1920.[1] Parliament decided against any sudden change. And yet, as a result of Clémenceau's personal efforts, one reform had been passed. The law of 4 January 1919 revived the old *jama'a*, that basic reality of the whole Maghrib. It was granted, or rather it had restored to it, a share–albeit a very modest one–in public affairs. Its elected president, even if he owed his position largely to the influence of the Administrator, was henceforward a rival to the caïd. In the *communes de plein exercice*[2]

[1] The debate lasted from 23 Dec. to 30 Dec. 1920. The *colons'* party implicated Ch.-A. Julien who, at the Congress of Tours, had indicted Algerian colonization.

[2] A municipality closely copied from the French model, and generally set up where the European population predominated.

he could take part in electing the Mayor. It seemed little, but it meant a good deal – enough to promote fears of insurrection. Only the Jacobin ruthlessness of 'Tiger' Clémenceau could get the reform passed. It still had to be applied.

In 1919 the Place du Gouvernement d'Alger, called in Arabic the 'Square of the Horse' after the statue that stands there, was still entitled to its French appellation. For not far off, in the Rue Bruce, the Old Palace housed practically every Government department. A dark staircase led up to a vestibule on the fifth floor where a vast map of Africa adorned the wall, dating at least from Colonel Flatters' day; this was the Direction des Affaires Indigènes (the Department of Native Affairs). The Archbishop's palace was a house in Berber style, elegantly corbelled. The Consular palace was close by. The square itself, built over vaults, had thrust the Fisheries Mosque deeper into the ground, as one system supplants another. It opened splendidly on to the street; of its three built-up sides, one was occupied by the Hôtel de la Régence, with its drooping palm-trees, and the old-established bookshop of Bastide-Jourdan;[1] the other two by cafés where, all day long, a truculent and furtive crowd discussed the sheep trade, love affairs and politics.

The heroes of the preceding generation had left the stage:[2] at Rabat, a few months previously, Colonel Berriau, who had championed the Bureau Arabe under Lyautey; in Tunis, le père Roy, who for several decades had dominated the General Secretariat. This sometime post-office clerk had been adept at intimidation, manoeuvres and secret discussions. In the dusty attics of the Old Palace, Dominique Luciani, an Arabic scholar and a philosopher, was preparing to retire. His successor's name was already being mentioned: Mirante. In town halls, in the Délégations Financières as well as at Government House, certain issues were being unwillingly recognized which were to occupy the forefront of the stage during the whole interwar period. Thus Algeria witnessed electoral struggles which were made more bitter by tortuous intrigues in the background.

Let us glance at one of the newspapers of the time, the one most concerned with the 'native problem', the *Akhbar*. Victor Barrucand, a former Symbolist poet, had published under his joint signature – and, so they say, exploited – the manuscripts of Isabelle Eberhardt.[3] What vistas this calls up! 'Ain Sefra, Lyautey's 1903 team, Southern Oran, the venture into the heart of the Sahara . . . This number of *Akhbar* (22 January 1919) discusses Clémenceau's reform, as everyone else was doing. It approves of it. It inveighs against many opponents such as

---

[1] Which published many works by Algerian orientalists. It hides discreetly behind the Café d'Apollon, another important place in Algiers during the colonial period.

[2] *Akhbar*, 1 Jan. 1919. On Roy, see *Akhbar*, 19 June 1919.

[3] Mallebay accuses him of plagiarism, *Annales africaines*, 10 Jan. 1920.

Bailhac[1] who, when he speaks of an 'awakening Algerian consciousness', means that of the *colons*. Barrucand also joins issue with Jean Mélia,[2] champion of total assimilation. His position is thus a complex one, often changing like the situation itself, and suspect to many people. Abbo, President of a Mayoral Congress held in May 1920, denounces the Reforms on patriotic grounds. An opposing Congress demands native representation in Parliament. We read of one quarrel that almost led to a duel,[3] and of manoeuvres, surreptitious or brazen but in either case controlled by the Administration. A list of Muslim candidates, as strongly oppositional as the times would allow, won the municipal election. But another election, that to the General Council, was annulled; one successful candidate had been the Amir Khalid, grandson of Abdel-Kader ('Abd al-Qadir), who was accused of having brought inopportune feelings into play.[4] In these controversies, religious arguments are freely flung about: 'the marabouts are behind you,' or even sometimes, 'the marabouts and the freemasons are behind you.'[5] On the other hand, military decorations and honours are flourished. The Amir Khalid had plenty of these. He was often to be seen amid crowds of friends in one of the cafés of the Place du Gouvernement. The Russian wife of another Algerian notability, Dr. Benthami, painted a portrait of him which was much talked about: a haughty face with dreamy eyes, against a background battle scene . . .

He was a romantic figure.[6] But the quarrel was not a romantic one.[7] It spread far beyond the bounds of Algeria. The slightest, most contingent fact in North African history can be connected with infinitely wider phenomena. The world was in a state of panic then, in the throes of a financial crisis. On 1 August 1919, the important English journal the *Economist* headed its leading article with a single figure: '8 per cent.' The Bank rate, traditionally low in England, had soared up several points.[8] England was unprecedentedly short of capital; France even more so. The ravages made by war in the finances of these two nations had created a boundless need for available funds. In general during this period both countries were to seek compensation from their overseas

[1] *Echo d'Alger*, 7 Jan 1919; *Akhbar*, 13 April 1919.
[2] *Akhbar*, 27 Feb.1919.
[3] *Afrique française*, 1920, pp. 249 ff.; *Ikdam*, 4, 11, 18 June 1920. As seconds to this duel, which fortunately did not take place, Khalid had summoned Maître Qa'id Hammud and Muhammad bin Rahhal (about whom more later, cf. p. 75).
[4] *Ikdam*, 5 March 1920.
[5] *Ikdam*, 8 Oct. 1920.
[6] Cf. his portrait in the Amir Khalid's pamphlet, *La Situation des musulmans d'Algérie*. Amir Khalid, like Shaikh Tha'alibi, somewhat mysteriously left the Maghrib for the Middle East.
[7] Strikes, street fights, rise in the cost of bread from 15 to 17 sous per kilo.
[8] B. de Jouvenel, *L'Économie mondiale au XXᵉ siècle*, p. 112.

revenue. Whence the new value assumed by what was beginning to be known as the Empire. This shift of interest involved an increased influence of the metropolitan power on these territories; protectionism, discriminatory measures, the abandonment in economic matters of the liberal tradition, which indeed was somewhat obsolete . . . Correspondingly, the policies of the imperial power were to be increasingly subject to financial considerations, almost indeed to the hazards of the bankers' game. They would have done better to consider the real entity underlying the fiduciary and abstract aspects. But in France as in England the economic system that won the day was no genuine economic system. These countries, in the throes of reconstruction, neglected the concrete in favour of its image. They were to pay a high price for this selfishness armed with pseudo-orthodoxy, but constantly contradicted by the facts. Whereas they were concerned with increasing production, what broke out was a crisis of over-production. In June 1920 it brought about the collapse of prices, and the consequent collapse of the European exchange.[1]

Besides these general effects of the world situation, there were others peculiar and apparently more favourable to North Africa. The war had intensified North African trade with the parent state and its allies. It had made abundant funds available, particularly to the *colons*. It had bequeathed to Tunisia a considerable merchant fleet, which could be used, for instance, to carry phosphates to Great Britain. It had opened new trade channels for mineral ores. But this prosperity remained more or less in suspension externally. Tunisia, moreover, differed from the other two countries of the Maghrib by the less independent character of its trade as well as the more precarious structure of its investments. From the point of view of finance, Tunisia cannot be compared with Algeria, nor, above all, with Morocco. Algeria had grasped the importance of finding on the spot an answer to local economic needs; she was not to achieve this until 1939. But the aim she envisaged, and strove towards with some success, was the equipment of her territory. In 1920, the sum of 500 million francs allotted to this purpose in 1914 by the Délégations Financières was felt to be inadequate. Algeria was already concerned with establishing a circuit between production and trade, and envisaged a policy of dam-building, hydraulic works and agricultural loans. The emphasis lay on equipping the land as a solid basis for construction that was felt to be stable and considered to be legitimate. In Tunisia, it lay rather on the great concessionary societies, in other words on speculative profit. Morocco combined these two attitudes and even surpassed them in the deliberate, intensive and almost ostentatious character of its effort.

[1] Id., ibid., pp. 129 ff.; cf. also C.-J. Gignoux, *La Crise du capitalisme au XXᵉ siècle.*

It has been estimated that the total capital invested in Algeria and Tunisia, taken together, was tripled between 1907 and 1919.[1] By 1919 it amounted to 3,000,000,000 francs. How was this sum distributed in detail? Out of the whole, 790 million consisted of loans, indicating the predominance of support from the parent state and of impetus from the centre; insurance companies and banks alone provided 400 million, to which we may add 1,000 million from transport interests, a fact in itself indicative of social evolution; the inclusive sum from these two sources being 1,400 million, half the total investment! Moreover, the liquid assets in circulation were sufficient, during this period of equipment, for the Trade Association of Algiers to seek to create a securities bank.

This dynamic and relatively coherent character of North African policy contrasts favourably with certain aspects of the parent state's economy.[2] Things were very different on the two shores of the Mediterranean. By 1919 every financial company and every undertaking in the Maghrib had decided on enormous capital increases. The Crédit Foncier increased its capital from 70 to 125 million francs; the Algerian Company from 70 to 100 million francs. An entirely new firm of Moroccan investment, the Paris-Maroc, which built at Casablanca that huge block called the Excelsior, in which many business deals were done at the time, increased sixfold its initial holdings of 5 million francs. The Bastos Society of Algiers, cigarette manufacturers, raised theirs from 3,300,000 francs to 10 million. Actually, we find that the profit on this initial capital of just over 3 million francs, in 1918, was 855,000 francs: about 20 per cent of the initial contribution. The Franco-Moroccan Omnium rose from 3 to 10 million francs; and we might go on indefinitely enumerating examples of this optimism in enterprise,[3] which was to prevail over any sort of conservatism.

The keenness with which profit was sought, thus set in the context of the time, seems to have acquired a sharper flavour from the precariousness of the world situation, and a fresh zest from the difficulties of the parent state. It played a prominent part in the progress of events. On the other hand it provided a legitimate source of indignation to many of the dispossessed. These had suffered and were still suffering from the impact of modern economic methods, which were entirely European, on traditional ones, which were at the time strictly indigenous. Hence much bitter resentment. Any period of drought brought crowds of destitute *miskin* out on to the roads; there is something extremely painful about the official use of the term.[4] But these vagrants did not merely arouse

[1] *Revue des valeurs de l'Afrique du Nord*, 20 Feb. 1920.
[2] V. Demontès, *L'Algérie économique*, 1922, vol. I. p. 19.
[3] Details taken, once again, from the useful *Revue des valeurs de l'Afrique du Nord*, a bulletin published by the Crédit Foncier d'Algérie et de Tunisie. Wider and more specialized studies are of course needed.
[4] *Ikdam*, 5 Nov. 1919 deals with the *miskin's* daily life.

compassion; they caused terror. For they went pilfering through the countryside, robbed when they had the strength, and died of infectious diseases, which imperilled public health. Hence, besides some harrowing pictures of starvation, we find in the newspapers of the time many complaints of insecurity. The various elements of the population reacted differently to the poverty that aggravated their mutual tension. Which was responsible for the famine, the failed harvest of 1920 or the revival and expansion of European agriculture? The break-up of traditional society under Western influence provoked many conflicts. If these did not necessarily break out openly, they found an outlet in symbolic impulses. The Algerian press repeatedly mentions cases of the desecration of graveyards.[1]

But the legislative authorities were never slow to take repressive action. From 1919 onwards they invented new regulations and special procedures every time the opposition allowed them to. In Tunisia the same thing happened. The preparatory statement of the Beylical decree of 8 September 1922, on the transportation of habitual criminals to Guiana, ascribes the increase of crime to the decadence of traditional society: the new development of transport, the growing economic pressure, the weakening of the caïd's powers, the intensification of repressive measures. The break-up of traditional groups is clearly seen; vagrancy, like other offences, developed in proportion as the old bonds of solidarity were dissolved and the whole of society moved forward into the Iron Age. But from this we promptly shift to a general view, showing whole populations driven by laziness and the hope of plunder towards the seaboard region and the fertile plains. Thus the nomad, the transhumant, in fact all those who escaped from the attraction of colonial agriculture, saw their *raison d'être* questioned. By 1920 the question was openly discussed in official documents – not always with equal frankness, yet never wholly dropped.

It is paradoxical that at the very moment when William Marçais was discovering at Takruna the original nature of village groups and their languages, and French penetration into Morocco had brought into being not only the 'lords of the Atlas', to use the Tharauds' term, but above all non-nomadic peasants – builders of barns and diggers of drains – people still thought of the men of the Maghrib as geographically mobile but socially static. Scholars from Rabat, studying the monumental reliefs of the Almoravid, Almohad and Merinid empires, none the less persisted in denying any tradition of political unity to the land. The fact is that any system needs an explanation, needs its own explanation. But this system, which should have been founding the future, could account for nothing but the past. Thus the colonial power refused to give up its Khrumirs. Like military theorists endlessly preparing the last war and

[1] *Ikdam*, 8 Oct. 1919.

neglecting the next, it set up its victory over antiquated forms as a practical prescription, almost as a scientific doctrine.[1] And including itself in this paradox, it invoked pioneer virtues in support of a process of stabilization.

[1] French experience in North Africa, which was already out of date, was to prove a fatal guide in the administration of France's mandate in the Levant.

Part I

Assessment of the Situation

CHAPTER I

The Dispute Over Fundamentals

The most provocative symbol of the colonial epoch in the Maghrib is that of the tiled farmhouse, a cheerful dwelling standing amid vineyards. It aroused the most violent, and violently opposed, reactions from Frenchmen and the people of the Maghrib. The fact that it was surrounded by more significant forces matters little; it implied all the rest. Banks, military camps, factories and schools may have played at least as important a part, but none made so deep an impression on everyone's feelings as this French farmstead, this heraldic emblem on African soil.

Two nations sought legitimacy through their ownership of the land. The French, because they were exhausted from the ordeal of the Great War and had transferred to the other side of the Mediterranean the hopes that seemed doomed to failure at home. Influenced by his longing to take root, as well as by his belief in the gold standard, the Frenchman's concept of his traditional being took the form of a somewhat short-sighted avarice. He could not resign himself to the inflation, or to the mobility, of the post-war period. He transferred to North Africa his longing for something settled and permanent. As for the people of the other nation, they had lost a vast portion of their property[1] from the Moroccan

[1] We ought here to be able to consult some general critical study of expropriation, in its direct and disguised forms. None exists. Let us merely note two points. In 1921, in the Tadla, an inventory of lands suitable for colonization included a no-man's-land at the intersection of the Bani Khiran Urdigha and Sma'ala tribes. After various difficulties, reflected in press campaigns, 1,000 hectares were allotted by way of compensation to the 'Elders of Oued (Wadi) Zem'. This levy (1926) was made chiefly at the expense of the Sma'ala tribesmen. Is there not some connection between this and the events of 1955? (Cf. *Renseignements coloniaux*, 1930, p. 5). In Algeria, at the Session of the Délégations Financières of 11 May 1928, the Arab section put forward a motion against the expropriation of native lands for purposes of colonization. The Governor-General protested, and 'demonstrated' that between 1904 and 1928 only 310 hectares had been levied! The delegate Sisbane withdrew the motion (*Afrique française*, 1928, p. 298). Now, just at the same period, the Aulad Diyab were evicted from the

35

Chaouia to Cape Bon in Tunisia, and were in danger of losing still more: it was in any case the best portion of it, or the most exploitable portion, that they had lost. Their hearts belonged to the land, and they yearned for what they no longer had, watching it bear fruit in unguessed-at forms.

The land and life of the Maghrib, then, were dominated by the conflict between those who sought to take root and those who hoped to recover their own. The necessity of avoiding the blatant forms of violence, of observing rules, of using guile, rendered it even more acute. The first step was invariably procedure. True, the end was invariably production. The ownership and exploitation of the land thus played a considerable part in the legal and economic system. But these developments, and the whole mass of activities, feelings and concepts brought into play[1] could not conceal a more basic quarrel. This only emerges clearly when one considers vast geographical ensembles and great historic unities. The physical and social reality of North Africa at that time must be seen as, simultaneously, the object, the result and the agent of a considerable process of *appropriation*. The word must be understood in both its senses, as taking possession and as adaptation. Energies are poured forth over a given area. They modify it, they are modified by it. Technical exploitation, investment, population movements, are so many forms of energy affecting the land. But this land does not remain inert. It contains undying forces both material and human. Hence a complex process of exchange, involving the whole effort of one nation to control another nation, each seeking foundations in this soil, even more than food. The variation in the rural scene by no means circumscribes the conflict, but it provides its most tangible image.

The Land

One might define the traditional Maghribi domain as a social centre, a home, spreading outwards into space.[2] The land clings round the

Constantine region. Their protests only resulted in a measure of administrative internment, although the scandal was brought to the notice of the public by an ex-officer named Budiaf (1926). In Tunisia, we might mention the notorious affair known as the 'Five Tribes Case', in the district of Sfax: persistent encroachment, by the Bil Garwi family, on lands which had initially been held collectively. But what is characteristic of the period is that these abuses, although they involved acts of violence to a considerable extent, remained most frequently legalistic, if not even legal. . .

[1] Which confirms the importance of law and jurisprudence concerning real estate, in the three North African countries. Already in the Maghribi *nawazil*, the chapters relating to agriculture were of great importance. I understand from Charles Saumagne that real estate law also occupied a considerable place in the Latin epigraphy of North Africa.

[2] I must refer here to my article, 'Droit des terres et intégration sociale au Maghreb', *Cahiers internationaux de sociologie*, vol. XXV, 1958, in which these ideas are developed.

nucleus of power, wealth or saintliness. When men's efforts are increased, the result is those vast estates: local manors, *habus*[1] that control a whole region, or Maraboutic apanages. These spread towards indefinite boundaries until they encounter a competitor. Their rights consist in the virtuality of rights, the hope of expanding the *'amir* (the cultivated area) into the *ghamir* (the waste land) by prevailing over the neighbour's forces. A landed proprietor of this sort would seek guarantees not in precise limitation, nor in individual technique, but in his own title. Thus besides the varying density of population, which accounts by and large for the distribution of tenures, we have another factor: the relative power of a symbol, of a name. While a tendency to restriction prevails wherever the irregularity of the terrain, the small scale of cultivation, or quarrelsomeness have led to social concentration, the inverse conditions are favourable to other forms of property. These, whether known as *latifundia, habus*, or collectives, are characterized by rivalry between the community of inhabitants and the authority of the lord or governor. The vast stretch of lands, with low or unevenly distributed rainfall, between the lower steppes of Tunisia and the High Chaouia of Morocco, by way of the high Algerian plateaux, has always formed an object of controversy between jurists. For it is the scene of a constant alternation between these various types.

When authority is relaxed, the peasant seeks, individually or collectively, to get back the soil. On the other hand, the ruler asserts his rights, whenever he has the opportunity, as against the rights of those who are ruled. His rights may remain unspecified, in which case they do not conflict with the existence of local groups. But they may become imperative; and then we see the land being broken up, its inhabitants shifted about. Of course the pressure of the individual is never absent, any more than is the pressure of the community. Their conflict and their compromise affect the aspect of the landscape, the type of cultivation, the size of the fields. But all this is difficult to interpret. A thousand small plots welded together honeycomb-fashion may imply bitter quarrels over suburban land or, on the contrary, a concerted effort at irrigation. When buildings spread over the waste land that surrounds them as in some big Moroccan *'azib*,[2] this may reflect either the growing prosperity of the landlord or else slackness in developing the land. Hence the ambiguity of many of these forms. Where land is concerned, several orders of things are always involved: man's material enterprise and nature's resistance, the economic system and the moral code, a kind of alternation between the individual breaking free from the group and the group holding back or taking back the individual. It was in such a context that French rule affected the rural areas of the Maghrib. Even without intervention from the *colon*, France mobilized North African space and precipitated

---

[1] *habus*: pious foundation.
[2] *'azib*: manorial domain.

decisions on rights in abeyance. She equipped and diversified the rural scene even before taking possession of it.

A hundred years or more of juridical argument about agrarian laws only reveal the extent of the movement. Tunisia offers the widest gamut of experience, with its collective farms–which had to wait till 1936 for legal defiinition–its *habus*[1] covering half the country, its huge domains, the whole being contended for between the modern agriculturalist, the traditional occupant and the legal owner. In Algeria, the *Senatus consultum* of 1863–an equivocal instrument, since it simultaneously consecrated tribal ownership and yet, by way of 'partial enquiry', sanctioned private alienation of it–also included, in anticipation, the rural commune. In Morocco, collective tenure, sometimes covering enormous areas, led to a similarly equivocal situation, since it originally proved of service to the Colonial authorities and eventually, on the eve of the second world war, appeared to them as a serious hindrance.

Now the delimitation of ownership of the land, like the exploitation of it, is a cumulative process. The joint effects of judicial disputes, of delimitations, of cadastral surveys, of 'Francisation' in Algeria, of immatriculation in Tunisia and Morocco, led to an increasingly clear partitioning of small plots, duly registered. But this competitiveness was also productive. The ultimate rights were determined less by the title held than by the work achieved. The development of the land as against the legitimate ownership of it: these were the extremes between which tribunals, administrative investigations, the whole French legal system professed to effect a conciliation. And where in addition the European way of life was long established, in the oldest and best-looked-after lands where the red-roofed villages stood, and the 'olive-trees of justice'[2] grew, a new agrarian order reigned, sure of itself and organizing its past as well as its future.

For the *colon* needed precedents for his field. In that much-disputed, much-adulterated land, he found therein a way–comparable in this respect to institutions and standards and creeds–to legitimize it. His 'favourite field', since love distinguishes between its objects, 'is slightly undulating towards the West, and flat as far as the road that limits it to the East. It consists of dark earth, lying shallow on a soft chalky subsoil. Of course it needed much cultivation, the clumps of dwarf palm trees had to be dug up and vines planted in their place.'[3] This represents a certain period of Algerian history. 'If some day you pass along that road

---

[1] For the mobilization of which the Tunisian Service Foncier enacted the Decree of 1926, whereby quarrels between claimants and *enzelists* (with regard to a right of occupation, dividing eminent property) were submitted to arbitration by a mixed Tribunal. This law was to be democratically applied by Commandant Valentini, Ch. Saumugne, H. de Montéty and President Labbe. Cf. H. de Montéty, *Une loi agraire en Tunisie*, Caors, 1927.

[2] The phrase is Jean Pélegri's.

[3] Marcel Florenchie, *Terre algérienne*, pp. 51 ff.

you will still see on the upper part of the field three fine fir-trees, the remains of a spinney that had to be thinned to allow vines to grow.' The battle between vineyard and forest . . .

The *colon*'s field is the *arriviste* in agrarian history. But it was a fine field, with nothing harsh about it; well-tilled, level ground and docile crops. The wild woods of the Maghrib had become a mere memory, but persisted on the land of the Maghribi farmer. The fellah had not finished clearing away stones; he left a few clumps of jujube trees, piously skirted by the plough, to subsist in the fallow land, like those tufts of wool that the shearer leaves standing on a ram's loins. His boundaries were not imposed on the landscape, but merely hinted at. They were always ready to extend towards the horizon, when the strength of his teams was matched by the fertility of his wandering herds, but they were equally ready to contract in face of natural obstacles and risks.

These risks threatened everybody. During the twenties the fellah and the *colon* alike were helplessly subject to the vicissitudes of the climate. For both, potential prosperity could be foretold as early as February by the look of the shoots, and confirmed when the ears were formed. Ominous signs, on the other hand, might herald famine for the fellah and bankruptcy for the *colon*. In a dry winter the stock-breeder could envisage his animals' bones strewn about the roadway; the harvest would be so poor that the grain would have to be picked by hand. Even the blades of the prickly pear would begin to shrink. Then the fellah, his nostalgia sharpened by hunger, would recall the good years, '*am saba, kimiya*,[1] when the *shebka*, the basket of woven esparto grass, would return, heavily laden on a beast's back, towards the village. And the *colon*, terrified by the prospect of the bailiff's summons, would remember the cheerful clatter of the flour mill, with the fine dust dancing up above the sacks of grain . . .

Recourse to Mechanical Energy

The *colon* was to seek his security against the uncertainty of the climate, and his unquestionable advantage over the traditional farmer, in what was then a new form of energy: mechanized ploughing and harvesting.[2] Already for a long time the railways, and more recently motors on the roads, steam engines and winches in the fields, had shown that discrepant development of methods of which European economy took advantage. Henceforward there was no going back; in agriculture,

[1] Literally 'a work of alchemy', and the phrase is always followed by *t-bârek Allah* (in Moroccan dialect).

[2] We have no systematic study of mechanization in North Africa comparable to that of Gabriel Saab about the Middle East. In Morocco there were keen discussions, echoed in the Press, on the relative advantages of mechanical or animal traction. There are useful observations on Tunisia in Poncet's *La Colonisation et l'Agriculture européenne en Tunisie depuis 1881*, 1962.

modern methods broke with the past, and the farm broke with the land around it. Perhaps some materialistic computer might have reckoned up all the forms of energy being used at that time by the colonial régime in its conquest of the Maghrib. And not only in tangible forms; speed, lighting, pressure and traction, percussion and heat–but under more abstract forms: finance, technique, administration. We have not yet reached the point when such reckonings can be made. Lacking the basis of an economic history, the sociologist can only make random observations, and unfortunately his questions go far beyond the answers which specialists have hitherto provided.

Doubt arises at once. Mechanization and motor-power played an effective enough part in North Africa in accentuating the divorce between the two economic systems and cutting the rural population in two, so to speak. But on the scale of world development at that time, did the energy thus being applied to the country produce results (apart from these disjunctive ones) commensurate with the ambitions of the system? In other words, did its concrete contribution compensate for its serious social consequences?

The Trans-Saharan Railway was much talked about; but only under the Armistice régime did a section fifty kilometres long–the first and last–begin to function. The Casa-Tunis railway junction waited, somewhat mysteriously, until 1933 to operate. Between 1919 and 1939 the number of engines in use on Algerian railways only increased from 489 to 644, which scarcely corresponds to the rhythm of a 'new country'.[1] It is true that the Tunisian railways, admitting a deficit between 1929 and 1939, attribute this in part to competition from the motor car.[2] The number of cars in circulation here, in fact, shows the same increase as in the rest of the world, with the same fluctuations.[3] In 1952 Algeria, wishing to assess the average age of cars in use, discovered that a great many of these dated back to the optimistic spending spree of 1930.[4] At the end of 1931 Algeria registered 11,000 lorries, 2,666 buses, 79,466 private cars, 8,589 motor-cycles and sidecars.[5] In Tunisia, the imports of petrol rose to 3,000 tons in 1920, and over 21,700 in 1928; of paraffin oil, 24,837 tons in 1934. Imports of gas-oil rose from 1,091 tons in 1921 to 5,582 in 1926, then to 24,792 tons in 1936. To which one should add, in 1938, 3,500 tons of fuel oil. The total of mineral oil

[1] These figures were provided by the General Secretariat for Economic Affairs of Algeria, through my friend the late Salah Buakwir.

[2] *Les Chemins de fer de la Tunisie*, 1931; *La Situation déficitaire des Chemins de fer tunisiens*, Dec. 1947. Some of my information I owe to the engineer Tixeront.

[3] Extract from an unpublished Tunisian note. Cf. also report of the *Sous-commission d'études économiques*, 1932, vol. II, pp. 87 ff.

[4] Extract from an unpublished Algerian note.

[5] Hoffherr and Mauchasse, *Bulletin économique du Maroc*, April 1935, p. 109.

imports, which show a growing superiority over those of coal, rose from 50,000 metric tons in 1920 to over 250,000 in 1928 and soared to almost 550,000 in 1932.[1]

Meanwhile the roar of the tractor was heard in country places. Tractors and pumps were the forms of motor energy most directly profitable to agriculture. Between 1920 and 1925 a thousand tractors were sold in Tunisia, and between 1926 and 1930 three thousand, as well as 750 combine harvesters. By 1930 the number of machines functioning efficiently in this country was reckoned at 2,500 tractors and 750 combine harvesters.[2] In Algeria the graph is even more instructive. In 1931 there were 5,330 tractors, mostly consisting of wheeled vehicles of less than 25 h.p. Of these, 92 per cent belonged to the *colons*. The trade was severely affected by the crisis in vine-growing and agriculture. Imports dropped from 6,816 tons in 1931 to 2,456 in 1936. They rose again to 6,300 in 1939. But in the meantime needs had evolved. If the total number of vehicles (5,600) was the same in 1939 as in 1930, their capacity had increased two- or threefold: more than 50 per cent of these machines were equipped with caterpillar wheels, and their power was up to or over 30 h.p.[3] Economic concentration had thus acted in favour of the big European landowner. The same happened in Morocco, where 3,620 tractors were in use. These figures are relatively low, the surface area per tractor being far greater in North Africa than is usual in France.

These facts, although connected with our argument, provide only a very partial answer to the initial question. We need to specify in detail the various uses to which energy can be put, and to calculate the evolution of the average quotient of energy per head of the population. The best we can do, in the absence of any synthesis provided by a qualified technician, is to point out a few significant facts.

In Algeria, between 1928 and 1939, production in kwh rose from 102,439,748 thermal kwh and 13,008,782 hydraulic kwh, i.e. a total of 115,448,530 kwh; to 223,659,377 thermal kwh and 59,337,552 hydraulic kwh, i.e. a total of 281,996,929 kwh. The consumption curve fluctuated between 1931 and 1939 somewhere around a total thermal balance-sheet equivalent to 750,000 tons of coal, showing no tendency to increase.[4]

In Tunisia, between 1932 and 1939, there was a slight rise, from 300 to 400,000 tons of coal-equivalent.[5] The electrification programme,

---

[1] Extract from an unpublished Tunisian note.

[2] Ch. Coupin, 'La motoculture en Tunisie et ses tendances actuelles', in *Congrès d'agronomie du Cinquantenaire*.

[3] Extract from an unpublished Algerian note.

[4] Extract from a balance-sheet drawn up by the Algerian Service des Mines. Cf. also Fontaneau, *L'électrification de l'Algérie*.

[5] Claude Zarka, 'Quelques aspects de la création économique en Tunisie', *Cahiers de l'I.S.E.A.* (Institute de Science Économique Appliquée), no. 12, 1959, pp. 153 ff.

exclusively realized in central power stations, only affected public services: lighting and tramways.

Prospects were brighter in Morocco, which in addition made greater use of water power and thus tended to diminish its dependence on external sources. From 1926 to 1934 its production rose from 20 million to over 100 million khw (exclusive of losses).[1]

But these figures are definitely low. In 1933, the annual average of individual consumption in comparison with France can be set out as follows:[2]

	Energy derived from liquid combustibles (in tons)	Energy derived from solid combustibles (in tons)	Electric energy (in kwh)
Algeria	1 per 25 inhabitants	1 per 10 inhabitants	27 per inhabitant
Tunisia	23	12	18
Morocco	39	26	22
Whole of N. Africa	28	14	23·5
France	8	1·5	370

Furthermore, within these meagre averages we should distinguish between the European sector, which is mechanized, and the native sector, which depends for the most part on animal power and even on human strength. Two expressions, which have a harsh ring, bear witness to this. One is the consecrated term 'unspecialized labourer', almost exclusively applied at that time to the North African worker. The other, combining realism with gallantry, is a proverb of the Moroccan Jebalas, which defines woman as *fi'n-nhar dabba' fi'l-lil shabba*: 'a beast of burden by day, a beauty by night.' A circuit is thus established between the exploiters and the exploited (who also exploit one another), between the entrepreneur's efficient use of his machines and the 'usability', so to speak, of the masses.

The working masses were sometimes engaged on large-scale public works, such as the Algerian dams, or that harbour at Casablanca whose sinuous jetty, while it reflects, as has been ironically said, 'the curve of uncertainty,' none the less protects a considerable expanse of water, or the forester-controlled woodland which actually sometimes had only a

[1] J. Dresch, 'Les courbes de l'apparition des soubresauts de la crise marocaine', *Bulletin économique du Maroc*, Jan. 1936, p. 4.

[2] Hoffherr and Mauchasse, 'La consommation des diverses sources d'énergie en Afrique du Nord', *Bulletin économique du Maroc*, April 1935, pp. 113–14. According to G. Spillmann, in *Industrialisation de l'Afrique du Nord*, 1952, p. 30, Algeria, Tunisia and Morocco produced in 1939 respectively 272, 159 and 71 million kwh of *dear* electricity.

potential or nominal existence. The administrator, the officer, the native chief moved about at their tasks in everyday and visible reality; around them many other figures, the mounted postman, the roadmender, the travelling *mukhaznis*[1] in their blue burnous, on their trotting horses, and the colonial doctor who, on market days, would gather around him clusters of patients like some latter-day magician. And all these scenes, which formed part of everyday life, were interrupted here and there, particularly in a dry year, by the Bedouin horde travelling northward, the men walking with springy step, their arms bent back to clasp the bludgeon held behind their necks, the women in red dresses, the swaying palanquins . . .

But although European initiative extended to many other spheres besides the vineyard and the cornfield, and although wild nature still reigned over millions of acres, defying the advance of modern methods, agricultural activity was still the issue that aroused the most violent reactions. Perhaps this is because the settler always establishes such direct contact with the landscape, which he breaks up and then reconstructs. Let us return to the idea of a form of energy flung against the soil which grasps and penetrates it; an ambiguous action, simultaneously destructive and productive, and provoking the keenest emotions. There is an element of passion in the relation between the cultivator and the earth. According to a symbol as old as the world, he experiences a sensual excitement when he thrusts the ploughshare into the soil. Hence the boundless bitterness of the fellah who, at ploughing time, goes past the fields that have been taken from him or lie neglected. This bitterness was one day to turn into anger.

For a long while, at least ten years after the first world war, land settlement constituted the acknowledged end of the French system in North Africa. Thus, according to an official handbook of 1922, 'the process of settling on the land has always been the dominant concern of our Algerian policy. Despite the variations and uncertainties imposed by circumstances, it has been pursued continuously and tenaciously', though not without some incoherence. The administrative account carries solicitude to the point of studying what sort of headgear the immigrant should bring with him. It advises 'a broad-brimmed hat of which the crown does not rest directly on the head'; felt is 'a little too heavy, elder-pitch or cork are more commonly used. Extreme bodily cleanliness is recommended, for personal neglect is the source of many evils.'[2] A useful maxim . . . Viollette himself, when courageously indicting the great landowners, felt bound to praise the small settler by way of contrast:[3] modest, deserving, bemedalled, a democrat, almost an anti-clerical: in short, the typical voter from the Midi.

[1] *mukhaznis*: a sort of militia attached to the local administration.
[2] Pamphlet issued by the Governor-General.
[3] *L'Algérie vivra-t-elle?* 1931, pp. 9 ff.

Morocco held many attractions in 1910. Immigrants poured in at the rate of four to six hundred a month. Naturally this aroused considerable uneasiness. In 1919 Lyautey, back from Tafilalt, found Western Morocco in a state of great agitation. The newly-demobilized men, their appetites whetted by the prospect of exploiting a new country, turned against the veteran hero. Such boldness, confident of impunity, was in strong contrast with the respect shown to the 'jininar', the General, by Muslim crowds. The contrast was to be intensified. The administrator, a potentate for the native population, too often played the part of complaisant demagogue, or even electoral agent, where Europeans were concerned. In 1919 the Agricultural Chamber of Rabat abdicated in protest against the creation of a Moroccan section. Lyautey was obliged to persuade and pacify.

At Tunis in 1921 the Consultative Conference was the scene of sharp debate between the French and Tunisian sections. The idea of a fund for land purchase by natives was rejected as an outrage against French prestige. A meagre credit was granted, however, towards popular education in agriculture. According to a significant distinction, production was the *colon*'s business; the fellah, at best, must be his docile imitator.

What could the fellah offer in opposition to this formidable dynamic force, weighted by technical mastery and backed by the law?[1] Aggressiveness, no doubt: infringement of pasture rights, pilfering here and there. But, above all, evasion: physical, in the form of emigration; moral, in the form of idleness. His whole tradition favoured this attitude. His system was characterized by a reversal, paradoxical in our eyes, of the relation between his work and his wages, which included a large proportion of 'casual earnings'. His aim was less to produce than to survive and perpetuate himself. He sought in things eternal an alibi for the daily round. The rural group, near neighbour to the settlers' village, withdrew into a sort of internal void.[2] Here the fellah took shelter, holding himself uncommitted: long days of rest, festivities, wanderings and meditations. Thus he exercised his private being. Explosive phases alternated with the phase of withdrawal and introversion. But they were rare, indefinitely restrained or severely repressed. The group could still escape towards the oil wells or the factory in the big city. The individual could still proliferate.

The village of Renault,[3] not far from Mostaganem, overlooks a plain of heavy soil, cut out of the mountain of Dahra, where battles were fought against a *mahdi*, 'master of the hour', in the latter days of Bugeaud.

---

[1] Which finds full expression in the three volumes published by the *Congrès de la colonisation rurale* (held at Algiers for the Centenary, 26 to 29 May 1930).

[2] Cf. p. 152 ch. II.

[3] I quote again from Marcel Florenchie, *Eux et Nous*, p. 130.

A centre was founded here in 1874; and the descendant of one of its pioneers has told us about it.

He observes a subtle connection with nature in his Muslim neighbour and acquaintance: 'The Arab withdraws during the winter, escapes at the end of spring. It seems as though the approach of harvest time excites him strangely. . . . The Arab is attached to his garden, as may well be imagined. Close beside it, preferably on rising ground, he builds a hut of branches and thatch from which he can keep watch. This is generally the responsibility of one of his children, for he devotes himself entirely to his task of harvesting, and to the even harder one of treading the grain, for his neighbour, whose farm is mechanized.' For the peasants are becoming a proletariat. This upheaval reflects the shift from a traditional mentality to a modern one. 'No effort is too great for him where corn is concerned. Exhausting days with the sickle, transport to the thresher, with the ears carried in baskets slung across mules' backs, are the easiest part of his task; it is on the granary floor that the fellah's quiet patience is most wonderful. . . . The labourers' joy breaks forth at the sight of full ears and tall wheat.' But unfortunately they have had to borrow largely. When the accounts are done, they discover how little is left. First famine, then a drop in the market price of grain; the fellah has to borrow once again. Despite his economic misfortunes, he possesses the virtues—or weaknesses?—that his neighbour the *colon* allows him: his 'insouciance', his 'obligingness', his 'fatalism', his sense of 'fraternity', and above all his religion, which every year brings some hundred thousand folk together at the great *mausim* (festival) of Inkerman.

The inner life of the group was thus occupied with ritual practices and repeated contact with the holy men of the tribe, with the united hopes of man and his land. But gradually alien things came to replace these. And here our witness shows a certain lack of perspicacity. Already in 1934 he had met workers in the village street who had returned from France. He had learnt from the postmaster what substantial sums were received weekly by the families of those who had emigrated. But this first-hand observer, so sensitive to everything that concerned the land, did not realize, any more than the administrator or the ethnologist, that a tremendous change had taken place during the thirties. He comments, rightly, on the robust tenacity of this self-enclosed human community. But he still stresses its incompatibility with modern economic methods, its almost ritual specificity, which the very presence of Europeans was already destroying. For the social and moral configuration of the peasantry was altering, more or less actively in different regions, but increasingly everywhere. Their inner life, devoted to self-exercise and uncommittedness, was developing aspirations akin, and therefore opposed, to those of the European group.

Little by little, the fellah or the worker became aware of the precise, hard and painful relationship between time, profit and efficiency. Even

45

in the matter of belief, they tended to turn from religious faith to politics, that other form of hope. Thus if during the whole interwar period there existed any stable relationship between the *colon* and the fellah—the one a conqueror, the other repressed or proletarianized—and if that very inequality, upheld by official myths, was aggravated by the disparity of methods used, the final situation was different from the initial one. In the relatively brief period of time we are dealing with here, a new peasant type had arisen in many regions of the Maghrib.[1]

The Scope of the First Efforts

The colonist brings the force of his efforts to bear on successive levels of a country's life, moving on when these are exhausted and also when his own demands, or the resistance he meets with, increase. He goes on to deeper levels, according to the familiar ways of colonization: the propagation of techniques, persistent appropriation, and both used together in assault.

The victims of the attack, meanwhile, do not remain inert; they try to repel or defy the force that is penetrating them. Their reaction varies according to the nature, the age, the degree of the aggressive elements. If the colonial power divides them in order to rule over them, they divide it, as it were, in order to resist it. After the liquidation of tribal conflict, they accept political allegiance, modifying or limiting it as far as possible. They insist on respect being paid to their faith and their women; on these points they would sooner die than yield. This is acknowledged, and duly allowed for. On the other hand, they accept the culture which is somewhat grudgingly offered them. They do not so much learn from it as adapt themselves to it. They pay the price for a belated and devastating accession to industrial civilization, and they pay it not unwillingly. But in certain spheres they yield only to force. This is the case with landed property. For a whole century this was defended and attacked with equal stubbornness.

At the period when my study opens, about 1919, French domination, even in the most forward regions, demanded approval of the civil order which it was imposing on the bulk of the country step by step. For instance, in Morocco there was no repetition of the shocking excesses of the first Algerian colonization, nor the deplorable results of the law of 1873; nor even of the ravages inflicted by the Tunisian law of 1898 on the *habus*. In the whole of North Africa, the advance of European ownership and the retreat of the native proprietor took place in a civilized, legal, and therefore somewhat hypocritical fashion. If, by and large, the legislators conspired with the administrative and judiciary authorities to favour the expansion of the *colon*, there were also counter-

---

[1] This essential figure will recur throughout this book.

currents and protests, and even courageous champions of equity here and there. Muslim opinion will never forget them.

In fact, encroachment, even with legal support, represents a regressive stage of French occupation. It can be defined as the abuse of one-sided human relations. This abuse proves as dangerous to whoever practises it as it is fatal to whoever endures it. The reasons for its failure lie in its anachronistic character, and in its lack of respect for constructive methods. This is one of the shameful sides of the colonial system. The very idea of it is so shameful that public opinion in general, and decent people almost everywhere, have deplored it. But this has not brought about its total disappearance. If protests from the native population, and the French magistrature, restricted excesses in the realm of land tenure, these excesses continued, or were even intensified, in other spheres (for instance, in that of the administration of native affairs, where they reveal not so much the primitive nature of the system as its obsolescence). In regions which had been brought under control a long time ago, the extortion which was inherent in the caïdal administration—with a few honourable exceptions—had long since ceased to be 'feudal'. It was now merely an abuse, which would in the long run prove destructive to the régime that practised it. Whoever exploited the native, or took advantage of racial preponderance, whether by administrative measures or by a judiciary decision, was taking part, more or less, in that very ancient economic system whereby man eats man. *Kla*, to eat, is the expressive word in the Moroccan dialect for 'to act unjustly'. Moreover, such cannibalism could take politer forms. Privileges, sinecures, nepotism, improper concession of lands or prebends were all forms of that exploitation of man which eventually always recoils against the exploiter. Abuses, in North Africa, are the reactionary form of energy, and its most easily available solution.

To some extent, the colonists adapted traditional methods such as the cultivation of cork and esparto grass, the collecting of medicinal plants, eggs, snails and so forth.[1] Extensive stockbreeding,[2] cultivation by the *Khamis* (sharecroppers) system,[3] agricultural co-operation without technical innovation: such practices are as it were tangential to

[1] Which yield considerable results, even by modern standards, but which belong to the old practice of 'collecting', so long as they are not exploited industrially. The question was raised by the Colons' Delegation at Algiers on 24 May 1921. Cf. also *Procès-verbal des délégations de colons*, 17 June 1927.

[2] A long comparative study by J.-L. M., 'Le cheptel de l'Algérie', in the *Dépêche algérienne*, 2 Sept. 1930: '. . . Among European settlers the improvement of domestic species was held back for a long time by impatient disregard for the milieu and for proper feeding, by a failure to understand the laws of heredity, and by unthinking trust in prejudices. . . . Thus Algeria is still short of mass-produced engines, milk-cows, etc.'

[3] *Khamis*: system whereby tenant-farmers receive one-fifth of their produce as salary.

the soil, devoid of creative impact. Their share–it is enormous–has not been adequately stressed by the economic historians of North Africa. But it is only fair to say that thinking Colonials held them insufficient. Modern agriculture, by choice and from necessity, must go beyond these limitations. But it insists that its technical superiority must go hand in hand with administrative privilege. A temporary advantage, but a weakness in the long run. A confusion of levels, one might also say.

Between 1925 and 1930 we can still find in Morocco, in the Chaouia, in the Gharb, in the Tadla, shocking examples of this first generation of agriculturalists. A golden age for the middleman and the lawyer. The middleman was often quite unscrupulous. He seemed to propagate himself by thrusting into all the interstices of this society, in every crack he could discover, not exactly roots or creepers but human contacts, *ash'ab*, associates, accomplices, acolytes. In 1928, in the *suqs* of Had-Kurt, one might have seen one of these middlemen, a well-known figure; surrounded by clients, he eclipsed the neighbouring caïd. His friends silently deposited around him, in his *guitoune* (for, like the caïd himself, he set up a tent), a dozen dishes covered in Moroccan fashion with conical lids of woven straw. He was not so much concerned with executing contracts as with exercising patronage. Many of his purchases were no more than manoeuvres and threats, *ballons d'essai*. He would acquire an unspecified share of some property; then his tractor, or rather that of the settler to whom he had already resold the property, would appear on the disputed soil. After a series of long controversies, the estate would settle down, like sediment at the bottom of a witch's cauldron.

Naturally this type of man has no connection with agriculture. To return to our original metaphor, he acts at a superficial level, his impact is feeble, if his shrewdness is unquestionable. The true *colon* despises the broker and the contact-maker, from whom he differs so widely, in his way of life, his habits and even his physical appearance. Even if he has not originally sprung from farming stock, the settler feels his peasant instincts stir at contact with the soil. He digs deep into the earth, literally as well as figuratively. His interest impels him to outclass, as well as to supplant, the extensive agricultural methods of the fellah. His honour, as well as his historical achievement, lies in having altered the landscape of the Maghrib, increased its total production, and successfully accomplished some remarkable botanical adaptations, in collaboration with Government agronomists: hard wheat and citrus fruit among others. His ploughing technique was renovated between 1920 and 1925. The triple ploughshare which broke up the plain of Bel Abbes was replaced by the disc-plough imported from America. The tractor traced its long furrow on the plain, while the wives and children of the ruined fellah sometimes threw themselves in front of it in a dramatic gesture of protest. It tore up the *sedra*,[2] thickets of which betokened a rich soil,

[1] Wild jujube tree: *zizyphus lotus*.

48

while the processes of surveying and demarcation were being carried out. An unforeseen wealth, the result of the deposit of ages, could then be raised from strata in the soil which the fellah had not been able to reach. The victory of speed and depth in agricultural methods, due to an increasingly systematic use of large-scale implements, could increase the yield of the soil threefold. This irresistible movement absorbed everything around it. At the confluence of the Warga and the Sebu, a couple of Spanish settlers, on their own, cultivated the whole region. A few years later, the Aulad Khalifa faction retained, by way of pasture, only the grass verges by the roadside. This situation may be justified in terms of sheer production, but in human terms it is disastrously negative.

The triumph of technique appears complete. Mechanized agriculture can defy the bad weather of autumn which makes the clayey soil, the *tirs* or *dehs*, so hard to plough. It deals with sowing, harvesting and threshing in the minimum amount of time. It thus cancels out certain hazards of the North African climate: prolonged drought at the end of the summer, or rain beating down the sheaves. By speeding up processes, it enables some of the risks to be avoided, while by plunging into the depths of the soil it reaches wealth hitherto untapped.

The region of Petitjean[1] in the Gharb bears witness, pre-eminently, to this revolution. Already in 1920 it had formed its first co-operative, making use of mechanical ploughs and threshers. Petitjean, not far from the tomb of Sidi Qasim, consisted at that time only of a *zawiya*, or religious centre, dedicated to that saint, plus a *qasba* or fortress of Bwakher, the 'Sultan's Black Guard', established by Maulay Isma'il. A settlement plan was applied in 1916. This was one of the first regions to be developed in Morocco, and also one of the most optimistic. Not far off was Tselfat with its hydrocarbon, which gave rise to such high hopes. Another and more wholly propitious circumstance was that the Tangier-Fez and the Rabat-Meknes railway lines crossed at Petitjean, which became an important station, with engineering workshops, a body of workmen, and presently a Union movement which was to play its part in the country's progress. In 1920 a second plan was launched. It encroached deep into the *guish* or tribal territory of the Sherarda. The men of this tribe owed military service to the old Makhzen, in return for exemption from land taxes. The modern version of this privilege was that the State laid claim to their property. This official takeover gave rise to interesting developments of the land. But it turned the old-time warriors, far and near, into proletarians. And very soon there arose, in the suburb of Kabbar, La Caprière, a rural shanty-town, perhaps the first of its type.

Today Petitjean, which has become Sidi Qasim again, has over 15,000

[1] Besides personal recollections, I am indebted to an unpublished study by M. Le Coz.

inhabitants, of whom 12,000 are Moroccans. Among these half are Sherarda, 20 per cent sprang originally from neighbouring tribes, and 20 per cent are men from the South, who began to pour in from 1935 onwards. Townsfolk from Fez, too, had come early on to take advantage in their own way of these new commercial possibilities. They congregated in the bourgeois district of El-Mers (Al-Mars). It is certainly a strange story: the village founded on hopes of hydrocarbon and then of land settlement now became an important rural centre. Continuity was ensured by agricultural technique, which completely renewed the landscape by replacing the previous meagre crops by olive and orange groves, by huge fields of hard wheat and of peas destined for drying, where the whirr of diesel engines can be heard.

Nature's Answer

In other cases, the modern system lost the battle. The traditional relationship of the fellah with his milieu, poverty-stricken though he was, was one of equilibrium. And above all it imposed no burden on the community. In a milieu which, indeed, was very different from grain-growing areas, in the western High Atlas, an average of 250 litres of water satisfied, over a period of eight hundred years, the needs of the small community of Seksawa, which had its historic hour under the Almohads and the first Merinids. Lower downstream, the same quantity of water seemed barely sufficient, in 1950, for the handful of settlers in Shishawa. The fact is that the efforts of the *colon*, while tending to introduce a dynamic disequilibrium, cause a disturbance in the relations between man and the soil which only a constant renewal of technique, close administrative attention, generous subsidies and unremitting energy can turn to good account. Failing these, ruin is bound to come. That is why colonization experiences so many failures. The land takes its revenge for the challenge flung at it.

South-west of Oran, Saint-Denis-du-Sig,[1] a classic case of colonial misfortune, numbers today 10,000–15,000 inhabitants. Its plain covers some 20,000 hectares, at an altitude of about 40 metres. It still comprises three levels of natural vegetation: the respective habitats of the mastic tree, the jujube tree and salsolaceous plants, for the salt collects in the low-lying ground. The Habra and the Sig form, by their confluence, the Macta, scene of a historic battle which today seems prehistoric. During the whole of its life the village has suffered simultaneously from lack and excess of water. It has to depend on irrigation derived from the Shorfa dam. But the rising of the salt, due to the humidity of the marsh-land, lays waste its territory. If we were to end this story in 1939, as our subject requires, we should have to assume a definite defeat.

In 1841 Colonel Charras, founder of the village, had designed it as

[1] G. Gaucher and P. Simonneau, *Terres et Eaux*, 1951.

a square. And its layout is still quadrangular; in the centre we find a square with a garden, the town hall, the '*colons*' house', the church and the mosque. It looks quite European at first sight. In 1921 its population consisted of 3,126 Frenchmen, 2,813 foreigners (chiefly Spaniards) and 5,000 Muslims, out of a total ten thousand. In 1926 the figures were respectively 3,000, 1,308, 5,000: total 9,672–the population had shrunk. In 1931, 3,000 Frenchmen (their number remained stationary), 1,400 Spaniards, but already over 6,000 Muslims. These had begun to congregate in what was known by an unfortunate name, the 'negro village'. Saint-Denis-du-Sig failed to develop. It was worsted in its battle with the soil. It succumbed before the rising tide of salt, to which a well-known farm in the neighbourhood, known as 'Tamarisk farm', bears dramatic witness.

In 1856 this farm cultivated an estate of 456 hectares. The owner was a Frenchman, living on the land, which he exploited with the help of Spanish and Muslim workers. He grew prosperous. But in 1903 the saline tide rose abruptly, and the balance was disturbed. In 1910 it made further inroads. Only the south-western part of the estate could still be cultivated. The pioneer went back to France. His Spanish bailiff, son of one of the original labourers, succeeded him. The value of the estate dwindled daily. In 1920 the bailiff himself left the village. Development ceased. Halophytic plants and dusty tamarisks invaded what had once been ploughland. The buildings crumbled. In 1940 four date-palms marked the site of the former farmstead; things had reverted to their pre-1856 state. Now there is nothing there but a patch of barren ground, where cattle might be raised, worth at most 500 francs per hectare, in spite of successive devaluations. A Muslim has bought it back.

In about 1934 the village had to give up growing cotton and citrus fruit, and fall back on the cultivation of olives. Meanwhile the *colons* had left, some returning to France, others settling in Relizane, or Perré-gaux, or even in Morocco. True, after 1940 a better adaptation of soil science and an intensive use of credit gave the place a new lease of life. But in the period that concerns us, we have to admit a defeat, involving, as might have been expected, the ecology of the soil and the unequal resistance offered by human groups.

Even prior to the war of 1914, the region of Sersu had been put under cultivation. But after a few years of success, the yield began to drop. It was then realized that the initial fertility had come from the age-old manuring of the soil by herds during transhumance. Now it so happens that the practice of intensive cereal culture conflicts with transhumance and starts off a fatal rivalry between the tilling of the soil and the rearing of stock.[1] Elsewhere, on the high plateaux around Constantine, it was

[1] There is an important study of this question by Commandant Lehuraux.

found that deep techniques made the water rise by capillarity, thus covering the soil with a chalky crust. Agronomists countered these various risks with admirable and unremitting scientific efforts: experiments with new techniques, research into new plants, even a botanical revolution in the case of wheat. The excellent collection of the Society of Algerian Agriculturalists[1] gives some idea of these efforts, to which researchers such as Laumont in Algiers, Caillou and Boeuf in Tunisia and E. Miège in Morocco have contributed. Thus the Agronomic Research Institute of Rabat, created by Miège in 1919, has resolutely studied the introduction of new varieties and ways of increasing their yield. It has succeeded notably in the case of soft wheat, as a result of botanical experiment on over 10,000 specimens.[2]

Does this imply that climatic hazards have been entirely mastered? The report of a banking administrative council, in 1924, indicates that a heat wave suddenly caused the failure of a wheat harvest which had promised well, and made it drop from ten million bushels for Algeria to only five million, while barley dropped from ten to four million.[3] In spite of all his efforts, the North African farmer is still the *fortunatus agricola*, by which we must understand not 'fortunate' but 'in need of luck', requiring the co-operation of unforeseeable assistants. Could things be otherwise? His labours stand midway between nature and the civil community, both unorganized. On the one hand lie uncontrollable forces, on the other the hazards of commercialization. Nor must we forget all the middlemen: carriers, wholesalers, brokers, forwarding agents, metropolitan buyers.[4] In such a system, man cannot succeed in regulating the passage from the natural beginnings to the social end; bent on individual profit, he resents any rationalization. For this would imply a return to objectivity, and would call too many things in question.

Science, then, could not carry things to their conclusion. In vain did assiduous researches combine, in the study of variations in yield, the computation of probabilities with that of genetic characteristics. The yield dropped,[5] because technical methods had worn out the soil. And nothing could be done about that. The consumption of super-phosphates had followed the course of mechanization. Belatedly, it became evident

---

[1] Of which J. Homolle has published a most useful index.

[2] Unpublished notes by E. Miège.

[3] *Compagnie Algérienne.*

[4] The question of a slump, particularly in cereals, recurs constantly in the debates of the Délégations Financières and in the Algerian press. E.g. *Non colons*, 17 May 1930, p. 103 (Ch. Lévy); Pionnier, *Presse Libre*, 6 Nov. 1834.

[5] Between 1900 and 1932 the wheat-growing area of Algeria remained stationary (respectively 1,438,464 ha. and 1,495,100 ha.) but the yield dropped from 6,8 to 5,4 quintals. The highest yield, 8,4 quintals, was in 1920. But production dropped as a whole. (Marcel Donon, senator, in *Documents parlementaires, Journal officiel*, 1932, Annexe 847, p. 1218.)

that chemical restitution does not compensate the soil for the disappearance of humus, and that the clearing of the land may encroach on basic reserves. Many complaints were made about the goats that ravaged the grassy slopes and liquidated what was left of the forest.[1] Other critics blamed the tractor, and the drastic measures resulting from its use.[2] The debate continues to this day. At that time, indeed, people were not greatly concerned about the deterioration of the soil.[3] A few timid measures were taken, however. In Tunisia, in 1926, when Cap Bon was in danger of being overrun by sand, a perimeter of fixation was created.[4] In Algeria, in 1929, in the region that lies between Cassaigne, Renault and Tenès, what we should now call a rehabilitation project was begun.[5] But these were the only endeavours in that period. The problem of the relationship between society and nature was not then envisaged with the breadth, precision and the dismal wealth of experience which we bring to it today.

Natural resistance is thus encountered, and it may be positive or negative, gentle or violent. Countless physical or moral elements contribute to this. The old revolt of the Maghrib may have died down, under its tribal form; but mud silts up in the first Algerian dams, the vagaries of the weather threaten the colon as much as, if not more than, the fellah; periodic plagues, of locusts for instance, remind the country of its desert origins, not to mention the wheat-bug and the meadow-rat. At harvest time the pretty sparrow can prove a fearful pest, against which there is no remedy but the age-old *twiza*, or mutual aid system. True, these are constant factors, from which these nations, once emancipated, will still have to suffer as they did under the French régime. But colonization, which is only justified by efficiency, wastes its persistent, well-equipped and sometimes talented labours, for its assault on the natural milieu is more violent, more insolent than that of the peasant tilling his own plot. Colonization seeks to win too much and too quickly. This makes its techniques ruthless. It seems to be flogging Nature on. The onslaught of these new forces on the old land and its people called forth, in opposition, a confederacy of men and things which could only be countered with another confederacy; which is why the State, the financier and the landowner had to support one another. And why, also, the *colon* came— to a degree far beyond his economic and social significance and his human value—to symbolize French rule in the Maghrib.

[1] A classic theme of the Service des Eaux et Forêts.
[2] J. Poncet has usefully, but with occasional exaggeration, stressed the destructive results of motorization.
[3] Yet the regression of woodlands was noted with alarm, *Procès-verbal Délégations financières*, 17 June 1927 pp. 283, 286. In Algeria at that time offences against the forestry laws numbered 45,000 per annum!
[4] Decree of 5 July 1926.
[5] Cf. Berlureau, *Echo d'Alger*, 29 Jan. 1928.

Contradictions

The qualities of enterprise, energy and efficiency which achieved unquestioned results were matched by faults inherent, of course, in the system rather than in individual men. A tendency to take the easiest way too often meant that the prospect of quick returns prevailed over long-term creative prospects. If colonization displayed a certain capacity to develop, it made excessive use of State assistance in its efforts. This not only detracted from its merits but also, and above all, limited its powers of adaptation. If the introduction of new forms of haulage between 1921 and 1925 partly solved the problem of climatic risks and that of excessive subdivision of the land, if botanical research and experiments on productive varieties frequently resulted in successful analyses, these positive achievements were jeopardized by a system inclined to, and possibly dependent on, protectionism; this same protectionism, acting in the interests of the vine-growers of the South of France, recoiled disastrously on those of North Africa. Their vineyards were restricted, then banned, and even uprooted[1] (1935); which reveals the contradictions inherent in this economic system. Competitive over-production or, conversely, the disastrous effects of hasty planting, ruined old vine-growing estates. There was a real collapse at Telagh, near Oran.[2] True, widespread efforts were made to alter the situation. North Africa took her revenge on citrus fruits and on early vegetables, which were almost exclusively European products. The duty-free import into France of Colonial produce, including an incidental quota of hard wheat, representing as it did the sale of Arab labour at French prices, resulted in a paradoxical reversal of the market after 1930; the *colon* now, commercially speaking, was colonizing the parent state, just as this had colonized North Africa for him.

State aid unfortunately came to be identified with the industry of the *colons*. Thus the Moroccan budget proposed for 1926 allowed a credit of a million and a half towards the cultivation of fallow land, a discreet way of helping the settler as against the fellah, who generally lets his land 'sleep' (*raqda*) every alternate year. In Algeria, to which this improvement spread, we find in 1924, in the Algiers district, 47,000 hectares of 'European' cultivated land as against 19,000 hectares of 'native' land. In Oran, respectively 229,000 and 58,000 hectares; 55,000 and 29,000 hectares in the department of Constantine. The average per cultivator came to 31, 43, and 49 ha. according to the department, for *colons*; only 4, 5 or 6 ha. for fellahs. The difference is instructive.[3] The law of large numbers and large masses made the privilege even more glaring.

[1] Much was written about this at the time, though without awareness of the 'contradictory' aspect.

[2] Saint-Germes, *Économie Algérienne*, 1950, pp. 100 ff.

[3] *Revue des valeurs de l'Afrique du Nord*, April 1924 and May 1926.

It thus appeared, as early as 1931, at the seventh North African Conference[1] that increasing recourse would be had to credit, the only way
not only to promote modern agriculture but even, in certain cases, to
salvage it. Each of the three countries pursued an individual line. If
Algeria inclined towards mutual assistance, which despite organizational
successes remained subservient to the chiefs, Morocco chose a form of
preventive credit, demagogically inflated, while Tunisia too frequently
resorted to disguised forms of relief.

In 1930 Morocco established a Federal Bank, because the colonists
were in debt to the tune of 145 million francs, of which 27 million were
described as 'abnormal paper', or, in bankers' jargon, bills that were
protested or whose maturity was in abeyance. Hoffher, who at that time
wrote an apposite but discreet account of the Protectorate's economy,
pointed out that between 1916 and 1931 loans to native borrowers only
amounted to 106 million, which is a small sum for 600,000 cultivators.[2]
In fact, credit more and more became the means by which the colonists
tried to survive in a hostile milieu. Thus the accounts of a regional bank
include: total amount of loans to victims of disasters–floods, 27–8:
sirocco, 29: locusts, 30; together with loans of land, loans on mortgage
etc.[3] If we took such statements seriously we should think that North
African agriculture consisted of a series of shipwrecks and refloatings.
Fortunately this was not the case. But its technique, while forcing its
way into the countryside and creating concrete wealth, also proved
increasingly subject to financial bondage.

And while its own preaching of productivity was increasingly contradicted by this enslavement to a rapacious abstraction, we must also
note the growth of its land-hunger. It sought, as it were, to make the
property of the native population pay for its own uncertainty. Neither
technical innovation, nor the adaptation of collective methods (protectionism, credit) enabled it to ensure its survival except at the expense of
traditional agriculture.[4] It sought to enlarge an already over-vast domain chiefly by the absorption of lands that had long lain fallow, from
which cultivation would bring forth latent treasures. By a strange paradox, the colonist, having acquired a legal position and almost a legitimate
title, nostalgically yearned for the good fortune of those adventurous
pioneers who had broken the ground. And this aspiration was all the
more dangerous because of the swift increase of the surrounding
population.

---

[1] Held at Tunis.
[2] *L'économie marocaine*, 1932, particularly pp. 125–9.
[3] *Bulletin de la Chambre d'agriculture de Rabat et d'Ouezzan*.
[4] Augustin Bernard, 'Le placement des démobilisés de l'Afrique du Nord',
Afrique française, 1919, p. 208, has an instructive comment: 'In North Africa
the land has never lacked colons. The colons have lacked land! Cf.' ibid., J. Saurin's
strange concept of colonization by grafting (p. 210).

For a long time French writings published in the Maghrib were concerned only with the manpower crisis. The *colons*, for whom low
wages were vital, protested against the emigration of workers to the
parent state, both from Algeria and from Morocco. This great problem
caused widespread anxiety for some twenty years.[1] It was the favourite
hobby-horse of all Parliamentary critics of the Government. Their
remarks ring strangely in a country now crippled by under-employment!
We may remember that in another African country, Egypt, similar
preoccupations were felt about 1910, after perennial irrigation was made
general. There came a moment when economists feared a shortage of
manpower to cultivate the soil. Today the situation is reversed. Nothing
reveals the movement of history so vividly as such reversals. By a cumulative result of a series of widely differing factors, Algerian demography
began to pick up after 1930, and its rate of increase grew even greater
after 1935. The dispossessions resulting from European appropriation
were thus augmented by those involved in the indefinite dividing-up
of an inheritance: eviction was aggravated by the worsened conditions
of all categories of native life. The small-scale fellah farmer realized that,
with less than ten hectares, he was working at a loss. As soon as he had
broken free of group control, he found that it was to his material advantage to go elsewhere, either as farm labourer or, better, as factory worker,
as casual labourer, or even as unemployed worker on the outskirts of the
city. From 1935 onwards particularly, these uprooted peasants flocked
into the urban areas. History was accelerated thereby.

Having intensified its appropriation, altered the landscape and produced a type, industrialized agriculture was suddenly seen by everyone –
including its beneficiaries – as the creator of a tempting vacancy. For the
demographic growth of the Muslims intensified the challenge flung by
the settler's farm at the rest of the country. The islet of well-cultivated
land, sparsely populated – by autonomous fellahs, that is – contrasted
more and more dangerously with the teeming 'reservations'. The *colon*
had intruded as a third party in the centuries-old rivalry between the
city and Bedouin life. And this third party was a stranger, an expropria-
tor. He had taken possession of lands of which many others considered
themselves dispossessed, possession and dispossession being the two
faces of the same phenomenon. And now this modern agriculture,
brutally thrust into the landscape, began, after a certain stage, to lose
much of its offensive force and its concrete claims. What was now most
obvious was not its capacity to conquer, but the extent of its occupation;
not the trees it had made grow, the buildings it had put up, even the
wages it paid, but the immense extent of the areas where it diminished

---

[1] Cf. *Renseignements coloniaux*, 1920, p. 357 (Algiers Chamber of Commerce),
p. 423 (Constantine Chamber of Commerce, Assembly of Agriculturists of Al-
Affroun); Aug. Bernard, 'La main-d'oeuvre dans l'Afrique du Nord', *Renseignements coloniaux*, 1931, p. 108, etc.

the number of cultivators, even if it increased the number of workers, as conventional economists strive to prove. Whether or not they are right, the Maghribi peasant refused to accept the system. The human emptiness of the *colon*'s domain contrasted with its prosperity. The exact opposite prevailed among the surrounding peasantry: a growing mass, growing ever poorer. The contrast was pregnant with danger . . .

The picture must be qualified, of course. The relative impoverishment of the fellah, the growing rift between small and great, seemed in certain regions to be favourable to the progress of the middle-sized cultivator, in whom the Administration took an interest. We lack precise facts from which to judge this. We shall also have to wait until special studies have been made before we can understand in detail a movement which, taken as a whole, is unmistakable. An antagonism existed between colonists and peasants, which was aggravated and not abated by time. The State had been forced into solidarity with the privileged landowner. European agriculture, not content with uniting two forms of energy–finance and technique–seemed to have taken over a third, that of the law and its applications. Finally, it incurred all the gathering bitterness resulting from an evolution which was far greater than itself: the movement of men, in North Africa as in the rest of the world, from the cosmological to the technological way of life. True, agriculture was by no means responsible for this evolution. But since in many respects it was both its instrument and its beneficiary, there is little to wonder at if the symbol of which it took advantage recoiled against it one day.

Its arrogant achievements–a fine, well-built homestead, substituting regular planes and gleaming woodwork for the irregularities of the African landscape–required an energetic combination of factors. The *nec plus ultra* was the creation of a local wine: Mornag, Toulal, Staoueli, or the success of some particular variety of citrus fruit, or else the invention of some kind of soft wheat. But in order to protect itself from the outside, the system had to live in artificial isolation. The way things were going favoured this. In the twentieth-century world, ever more compelling needs of production and consumption forced legislators to establish broad groups and use large-scale methods. This is indeed noticeable in North Africa; but here, the expansion of undertakings of general interest contrasts with the selfish individualism of their intended purpose.

Apart from any moral consideration or political judgement, there is something terribly weak about a system that shows such disregard for the whole rural humanity of North Africa, and mobilizes so many collective means to create, in the end, at best only a freak landscape, and to enrich only a minority.

Wealth from the Subsoil

A few perspicacious minds recognized the danger in time. They therefore sought to create in the Maghrib a wealth unconnected with agricultural quarrels, indeed capable of uniting in a common project the two rival populations. This wealth might come from the subsoil, and it might be sought from two sources: water and minerals.

In fact, from 1930 onwards North Africa became increasingly dependent on hydraulics. She hoped for salvation by water. Irrigation would not only bring new life to the land, it would re-create it, and rivalry with the indigenous population would thereby be averted. Hydraulic engineering requires small plots; it demands much work, rather than much space. The energy and efficiency shown in the undertaking constitute a claim that can scarcely be called in question. Again, with mineral wealth, which seems to spring from nothing, nobody is robbed, while the enterprise pays for itself and provides increased employment. 'But farmers did not seem to realize at all the advantage they would gain from the development of the mineral industry in Africa.'[1] A few pioneers, rising above the speculative empiricism which had hitherto been dominant in this type of exploitation, understood what powers of renewal were latent in the subsoil of the Maghrib, and particularly in that of the Sahara. Eirik Labonne was one of these few.

Historical analysis, concerned with discovering stages and rhythms, must be careful at this point not to neglect continuity. Work with water and work with mines have always formed part of European activity in North Africa. Mining, indeed, has attracted large sums of capital. It played a part in the economic conflicts of the parent state and of the world which agriculture could not. But perhaps we can distinguish in this development, as in that of land settlement, a logical progression.

Whether we are dealing with water or with phosphates, iron, lead, etc., the whole story must be looked at from two points of view, like so many other categories of things and of people. On the one hand, from that of profitable development, and on the other, from that of the law. On the one hand, we have intensified exploration in depth; on the other, the granting of permits for research and exploitation. Hence arise several series of problems, technical and legal, superficial and profound, which the Colonial State had to face, and which it solved with varying success.

This is not the place to retrace the long chronicle of the mining industry of North Africa.[2] Begun in 1845, it employed 42,000 workers in 1938, and produced 1,300 million francs' worth of minerals of which phosphates were the most important, with iron in the second place. The

---

[1] E. Jussiaume (E. Labonne), *Réflexions sur l'économie africaine*, 1931, pp. 50 ff.
[2] From a copious bibliography I mention only the brochure by G. Bétier, 'Les mines et les carrières', from the volume *Algérie et Sahara* (*Encyclopédie coloniale et maritime*).

'mining fever' had broken out in the province of Constantine towards the end of the nineteenth century, fanned by the profits from the phosphate mining works at Tebessa. It died down in Tunisia and Algeria, but revived sharply in Morocco. There were some brilliant successes, for instance with phosphates in Khouribga and then at Louis-Gentil; some disastrous failures, such as the coal mines of Kenadsa; a suspicious fiasco over all oil-wells; dazzling hopes encouraged by the discovery of manganese and cobalt in the High Atlas ... In general, except for the B.R.P.M. (Bureau de Recherches et de Participation Minières) there was a lack of dynamism and of consistency. The most reliable visions, such as those of Marcel Soignac in Tunisia, remained unrealized, since the speculator's point of view prevailed over the producer's. How could it have been otherwise? Except for the pioneer whose comments I have quoted, nobody yet saw the potential benefits, for construction and for integration, inherent in the extractive industries.

These are the broad lines that a more specialized enquiry would complete with useful corrections and precise details, without, I believe, altering the basic conclusions to be drawn from the picture. Commercialization of the mines, it seems, was considered all-important. At best, this was organized on the North African scale, as happened with phosphates from 1933 onwards.[1] More frequently it followed the hazards of the London and New York markets. In the absence of any plans for equipment and industrialization, the mines, without organic connection with the country, were subject to the vicissitudes of international finance. It is significant that the graph of production in Algeria follows closely the fluctuations of capitalism. 'The evolution of these stock exchange prices does not mean that firms had stopped growing rich, but simply that cyclical circumstances reduced their capacity for expansion. These investments ceased to interest speculators.'[2]

Thus, apart from the endeavours which will be discussed presently, we find no signs at this period of any attempt to go deeper into the data of the milieu, nor to integrate the economic with the human aspects.

Were things any better with respect to water power and hydraulics?[3] Already in 1851, in the French Chamber, Lamoricière had defended the concept of water as public property. And Morocco, long afterwards, was also to consider that water belonged to the State, without prejudice

[1] Agreement of 22 August 1933, resulting from competition and from the hazards of world finance (unpublished note by M. Solignac).

[2] Unpublished study by M. Hincker.

[3] At least half of the first volume of V. Demontès' *L'Algérie économique*, 1922, is devoted to irrigation. Cf. also *Renseignements coloniaux*, 1928, p. 111, concerning the Congress on Water organized by the General Confederation of Algerian Agriculturists; R. Martin, *Les Grands Barrages et l'Irrigation en Algérie*, special number of the review *Chantiers*, Algiers.

to earlier rights. This implied public enquiry, with presumption in favour of the State, but also the State's duty to analyse, investigate and regulate.[1]

The most difficult problem arose in Tunisia, on account of climatic conditions.[2] However, until about 1930, only the most superficial prospecting was undertaken, chiefly with a view to catching and storing water for supplying cities. Scientific investigation had to wait for the thirties. Then began the systematic study of the 'water cycle'. This brought together the most diverse branches of learning. Thus it was discovered that a constant exchange takes place between the evolution of the underground water level and that of the crops grown on the surface. History became involved with hydro-geology. It now appeared possible to activate the vital circuit by working on selected factors. The Algerian experiment with large dams was therefore avoided, not only because they would make the cost of water very high but chiefly because they were not 'populating'. Now besides the economic income from water there is what one might call its human income, namely the number of people that can live on a continuous outflow of one litre per second. This number may be less than one and in some cases as high as ten. Thus, in view of the active conservation of water and of 'hydraulics in the interest of population', there was some opposition to such large-scale projects as barrage-reservoirs, and an insistence, above all, on well-boring.

For too long a time, these wells had been profitable only to the *colon*. Now the necessity of interesting the fellah in these enterprises had always been imperative, but had never been admitted. The results obtained by certain administrators such as Penet, at Tozeur, had even, for a long time, excited controversy between engineers, who were generally contemptuous of them, and more empirically-minded people who were conscious of the basic human situation. Two points of view were thus in conflict, whereas for any long-term success their co-operation was necessary. If the engineer Gosselin won the day by instituting 'groups with hydraulic interests' (decree of 30 July 1936), his adversaries held up the execution of his programme after two years. In return, he accused the micro-hydraulic methods pursued by the Service du Paysanat, especially from 1936 onwards, of technical naïvety and financial extravagance. Other technicians, finally, pointed out that in both cases the power of the Administration proved paralysing[3] and that better observation of traditional practices, particularly the control of streams, would

[1] Passeron, 'Statut des eaux souterraines dans les Territoires du Sud', *Renseignements coloniaux*, May 1930, a sequel to the interesting researches of H. Bruno in Morocco, Moulias in the Sahara, etc.

[2] M. Gosselin, *L'Hydraulique en Tunisie*, Tours, 1941; 'L'inventaire des ressources hydrauliques de la Tunisie', *Annuaire des Ponts et Chaussées*, nos. 5-6, 1951.

[3] Or too favourable to the *colons*, as at Ousseltia.

have been more effective. Nevertheless, shortly before the last war, under the impulsion of Eirik Labonne, a 'plan of rural equipment' was set out, a synthetic conception which was actually put into practice at Kasserine. But the promulgation of the decree was delayed until 31 July 1941, and it collapsed during the catastrophic régime that followed the Armistice. When resumed later, it was considerably weakened.

Let us go back to the mines.[1] Anxious to secure important budgetary returns in order to relieve private enterprise, the Moroccan Protectorate had, as we should say today, nationalized its phosphate mines. Thus it precociously inaugurated a form of State control which still exists. Legislation about water, as about forests, abandoned the Metropolitan precedent and inclined towards a domainal system. Morocco had a conscientious colonial system at that time. Abundant capital went together with official energy and friendly relations with the Makhzen.

It was in a somewhat tenser atmosphere, that, in 1928, legislation took place concerning the Bureau de Recherches et de Participation Minières. The speculative anarchy then rife among prospectors was controlled for the first time, while a policy of co-operation enabled the Resident to arbitrate between rival groups, and above all to direct activity towards sectors it considered of national interest. The originator of these new ideas, Eirik Labonne, then Secretary-General of the Protectorate, not only showed astonishing foresight—he was in advance of his whole generation in referring to the wealth of the Sahara—but he also anticipated the theory of 'poles of development'. These two ideas, which were extremely bold for their time and are still largely valid for the future of the Maghrib,[2] were met with derision or indignation. The violence of this reaction might well surprise us, if we did not take into account what a fundamental change this initiative involved.

Eirik Labonne saw, no doubt, that the *colon*, who had hitherto been omnipotent (and who was to remain so to the end) depended on precarious foundations: his investments and his technical equipment were inadequate for any large-scale undertaking, he had suffered setbacks in the matter of manpower, while the challenge he had flung at the land and its people could not be maintained. Without recognizing as clearly as we can today the element of paradox and injustice in such a primacy, the economist proposed to substitute for it other modes of action and even another sort of presence. He sought to replace land settlement by electrification. The electricity was to come from the coal mines of Jerada, the lignite mines of Cap Bon, and above all from the great dams. The subsoil

---

[1] Mauchassé, 'La participation de l'État à l'activité minière au Maroc', in *L'Industrialisation de l'Afrique du Nord*, 1952, pp. 163 ff.

[2] Apart from the BRPM (1928) a certain number of analogous mining organizations were founded in North Africa between 1939 and 1948.

thus pressed into service—whether through mining or hydraulic developments—would provide sources of energy from which the French and the
people of the Maghrib would benefit together.

At the same time, or a little later, other attempts were made, in a
slighter and more superficial fashion, to deal with the difficult problem
of wresting from the privileged class the benefits of collective efforts. In
Algeria the engineer R. Martin, the creator of a new series of great dams,
envisaged the recovery and the distribution among the peasantry, both
European and indigenous, of part of the profits gained from irrigating
vast areas of land. Without being as fundamental as the electrification
project, no more in fact than a timid attempt at distributive reparation,
this suggestion was none the less condemned. Since the 'Martin Decree'
had unfortunately been passed under the Vichy government, its abrogation became a 'democratic gesture'.[1]

These setbacks seem to have aroused no interest in the mass of the
Muslim population or the partisans of reform. The latter, indeed,
undoubtedly considered that such controversies affected only the preponderant group, whereas in reality they involved a whole shift of values.
An energetic policy with regard to hydraulics, if carried through so as
to transform the ecology of North Africa, might have had decisive
results. It still conditions any project of national construction in the
Maghrib. No doubt the plans were tainted with 'technocracy'—a favourite word of the time—even with a certain apparent contempt for those
whom they affected. And so even his rejection by the ruling group did
not reconcile Muslim opinion to Eirik Labonne, either in 1928 or later
on, during his brief proconsulate in Morocco.

It was presumably still too early, or already too late. Under the Second
Empire, Saint-Simonian inspiration had effectively coincided with the
views of the Bureau Arabe. Only another such coincidence could have
maintained these high technical ambitions in that context of French
strategy in which Labonne had conceived them; and not for long. For
such a break-through towards the depths of the soil of the Maghrib
could not possibly be accompanied by a psychological or social break-
through of the same depth and significance, which would have revealed
and set free the dangerous forces of 'the underground'.[2] Moreover, as
the so-called 'native' policies—the only ones that were being considered—
became obsolescent, and as economic problems acquired world-wide
significance, the two lines of development began to diverge irremediably.
Reduced to incoherence by the opposition between the successful and
the less successful colonists, contaminated by the anachronistic character
of the régime, such attempts—with which we may compare that of the

---

[1] Independent Tunisia applied a similar principle in the Office of the Mejerda.
[2] 'The grotto' is the metaphor suggested in G. Buis' book, as in Kateb Yacine's
Nedjma.

Moroccan S.M.P.[1] in 1945–did not fully succeed either at the time we are considering, or after the second world war. The whole colonial period, except for scattered efforts, hostile reactions[2] or reformist velleities, remained loyal to the symbol of the red-roofed farmhouse.

This symbol, although lucrative to individuals, proved costly to France and to Africa, and the cause of its failure lay in its very achievements. French energy, confined to the superficial strata of the soil, was forced to compensate by expansiveness for what it missed in depth. The settler's claim to several million hectares of the best land in North Africa, although justified by production, was in direct conflict with the peasants' right to their land, and drove the uprooted masses to seek an outlet for their energy in the outskirts of the towns. Thus the proletarianizing of the city[3] went hand in hand with the colonizing of the countryside. And just as the latter had failed to grant the traditional peasantry any scope for free co-operation, so there was to be no real co-existence within the city; the political situation was to admit no middle term between the two extremes. Now for a whole generation, even before the final upheaval, Europeans had begun to desert the *bled*,[4] as though to make the symbol of the farmstead even more oppressive. And when the contradiction reached its height, the insurgence of a landless population for the reconquest of their depopulated land was to be seen.

[1] Secteur de Modernisation du Paysannat.

[2] These are frequently inspired by the same symbol in an opposite direction.

[3] Paradoxically, the urbanization of the Muslim population coincided with the slowing-down of their urban building, from 1931 onwards, in Algeria. Cf. *Travaux nord-africains*, 15 Jan. and following numbers.

[4] Fears expressed as early as 1924 by Augustin Bernard, 'La colonisation française en Algérie et le decret du 9 sept. 1924,' *Afrique française*, 1924, p. 638. J. Casenave depicted the exodus of *colons* towards the towns in the *Dépêche algérienne* of 16 Feb. 1931.

CHAPTER II

The Conflict Between Things and Symbols

In the Haouz region of Morocco, until quite recently, custom required the native chief, at the approach of each season of the agricultural year, to present the Administrator with a register of *twizas*.[1] This form of mutual aid, in which European scholars recognized 'an archaic form of exchange',[2] had long since caused to be either bilateral or 'sociological'. It was purely a kind of organized imposition. The right to forced labour for irrigation, ploughing, harvesting, etc. had become a perquisite of office and even sometimes a personal and transferable privilege: the caïd might sell the use of this man-power to a third party.[3] With more laudable aims though in equally primitive fashion, the tribal organization supplied the Bureaux with a labour force. This provided a great many roads, *burjs* (forts), wells, irrigatory canals, such equipment in short as official technicians could never have produced. And where Berber democracy had not been crushed by the 'great caïds', that group kept strict control over this work, husbanding its human resources in a way that matched the whole administrative system. For the officer in charge was only a distributor of manpower. Hence his amazing ecological adaptation. Primarily a horseman with no mechanical means at his disposal, working at the humblest level, this usurper, often a just man and sometimes an impressive figure, fitted into an order of relationships which any technical progress, such as the use of the motor car, was to endanger and eventually to abolish.[4]

Now this 'Arab bureau', *Ibiro 'arab*, as it was naïvely called from one end of North Africa to the other, meaning the authority in charge of Native Affairs, Civil Control, or the mixed commune, was a typical

[1] *twiza*. Originally 'mutual aid undertaken by a group, to perform some task of general or private interest, on a reciprocal basis.'

[2] R. Maunier, following Mauss.

[3] Observed at Shishawa in 1948.

[4] This dialectic relation between man and the machine takes on a tragic character in G. Buis' novel, *La Grotte*: the hero is killed as soon as he rides his horse again.

64

feature of French intervention in this country, and the one which proved most acceptable in its time and place. True, at the period under discussion, the system only functioned fully in the forward marches: the High and Middle Atlas, the Southern Territories; elsewhere, only degenerate forms of these bureaux remained.[1] And a decadent version of the system, varying according to zones and periods, the aptitude of individuals and the intensity of problems, constituted the background. It was connected, by historical and logical links, with the material processes described in the previous chapter. And it was not by chance that at the furthest extreme from this type and its setting, in a city such as Tunis, where the régime was already out of date, the masses, crushed by modern economic developments, were stirring in political opposition under the leadership of insurgent intellectuals. Bureaucratic Residents, whether wily, like Lucien Saint, or authoritarian, like Marcel Peyrouton, failed to take into account these new forces. Already the inefficiency of their rule was only palliated by its use of the police and the army.

Thus at the two extremes of the colonial system we find in perfect antithesis the humble rural office and the central bureaucracy. In the one case, success was achieved at an elementary level, the Frenchman reaching an understanding with the inhabitant of the Maghrib, if not an appreciation of the latter's culture and history. In the other case, the manoeuvres of official 'native policy' were soon rendered outdated, in relation to the forces that emerged from the colonial phase, by the action of young leaders. And in between, all the other forms of French activity, disturbed in various ways by the materials and modern transformation of the country.

The Decline of the State

During the whole interwar period, France's power dwindled in proportion to the growth of her appetites and her responsibilities.

She was forced to increase her demands on her colonial empire at the same time as these were being fiercely challenged. She asked for more than she received, she promised more than she performed, she undertook more than she could accomplish. Although in the three Maghrib countries she enjoyed an established situation, with all the advantages and risks that this implied, she would not refrain from intervention. Whether by means of military penetration, economic concentration or administrative drive, she invariably made demands. France seemed permanently to play the part of the 'plaintiff', to use a term of Muslim law, *al-mudda'i*. and this laid on her the onus of initiative, procedure and responsibility.

[1] Such figures suggested to Montherlant the term 'useless service'. The brochure by Colonel Materne, *Derniers Conseils*, 1937 (a sort of *vade-mecum* for the Colonial officer) reveals, better than any study could do, the nature of the system. It abounds in wise saws expressing a traditionalist attitude.

Meanwhile the great mass of the Muslim people, although visibly stirring into life, remained on the defensive for a long time; their attitude was secretive and reserved.

In 1919 it was somewhat paradoxical for France, bled white by war and longing above all for peaceful enjoyment and security, to assume such an attitude in North Africa. The capitalistic profit-motive brought forward entrepreneurs and explorers, educators and administrators.[1] But these duped heroes had to stand surety for the gains made by the vinegrower, the banker and the speculator. For the selfishness of the ruling power increased with its sense of vulnerability. Already, over most of the country, its strength was used not to dare, but to hold on. It hoped to live on its past glories, whereas it was less the audacity than the offensive nature of French ventures that, more and more, became evident to the Maghribi.

With their wounded pride, their chivalrous tradition, their insatiable virile honour, they found it hard to submit. They knew they were being untrue to themselves in so doing. Their warlike instincts barely dormant, they found themselves forced to obey, not as victims indeed but as shattered victors.

This double paradox can already be perceived, underlying all the end-of-war rejoicings. Divergence could only grow between France and the peoples of North Africa. These expected the future to bring about a change in their political, social and moral situation. The Europeans, on the contrary, were concerned only with profits and productivity. It was going to be hard, indeed, to bring together these two lines of fate. The chronicle of the years ahead was to be marked by provisional successes or failures for either side. But success or failure, and our verdict on the men and actions in the foreground, were to depend on how far they advanced the endless effort towards this impossible union. At a level far deeper than events or policies–official or oppositional–great forces, over great areas and in broad rhythms, were conflicting and interpenetrating. Now although these split up into a multiplicity of facts, beings and situations, the sum of the various factors is a simple one. There is a hidden side, and a side which is visible. Among men and things, some are indigenous and some are foreign. The construction of a country, the promotion of a consciousness were to depend on this rivalry, the extent of which few people assessed at the time.

It is true that in the immediate post-war period these redoubtable forces were by no means evident. The colonial power, although its energy was failing, could still maintain a hold over this land where violence was latent. It still had in its favour the inequality of two cultures, two economic systems, two ways of life. This inequality, which none

---

[1] Cohen-Hadria, *Souvenirs inédits d'un témoin socialiste*, gives a shrewd account of the life of the opposition movement in Tunisia.

contested, and which functioned to the profit of the French régime, sanctioned it in the eyes of its beneficiaries and even, to some extent, in the eyes of its victims, who were also its 'object'. This sort of acceptance may, in retrospect, seem surprising and even shocking. But we must look back to 1920. Any plea for justice, any demand for reform were considered extremist at that time. As such, they were considered subversive by authority and by the majority. Few movements consciously rejected this state of tutelage. None the less, national hopes had already begun to spring up. Tribal resistance in the West, the Destour's demands in the East were manifestations of this, incongruous indeed–the one primitive and the other precocious, the one a movement of highland barbarians, the other of middle-class townsfolk–yet none the less significant. In the pamphlet 'Tunisia's Martyrdom', the arguments are less remarkable that the foresight. Lyautey already spoke of 'inevitable aspirations',[1] of the future emancipation of the nation. But the fact that he had little following in Morocco, and that in Tunisia and Algeria these early movements met with almost total failure, is not due solely to repression or to the astuteness of the administration–the main cause was probably the still unimpaired strength of French prestige.

Prestige on one side, humiliation on the other, boldness and conservatism, profits and losses, enthusiasm and failure, all still held together, by virtue of authority and custom, so as to give the illusion of an adequately integrated whole, or one in process of integration. Nobody had serious doubts about the future of a French Maghrib–least of all the geographer E. F. Gautier, a perspicacious scientist, but a man of his time.[2] On the contrary, it seemed that energies which were failing elsewhere found fresh vigour on the soil of North Africa. No doubt, more clear-sighted observers might have recognized the dangers inherent in this state of things, due to the injustice of what had been done and the exorbitance of what had been hoped for. But these dangers were not perceived by the majority. The rival excesses of sectarianism and opportunism crippled an opposition which, it is true, was fighting against superior odds, and detracted from its perspicacity. To many nationalists or socialists the continuance, if not of the Colonial régime, at least of French tutelage, seemed assured for a long while to come. The proud man's submission to the conqueror, the starving worker's docility towards the entrepreneur, the defenceless peasant's conflict with the *colon*, the admirable self-sacrifice of the sharpshooter, the more or less lucrative resignation of a dispossessed élite; these are the attitudes most in evidence. While, according to the 'Key of Dreams' consulted by the

[1] In the circular of 18 Nov. 1920; which seems never to have been applied, except by General Méric on 16 Jan. 1956!
[2] *L'Algérie et la Métropole*, 1920, pp. 217 ff.; still worse ten years later, in *Un siècle de colonisation*, 1930, pp. 233 ff.

housewives of Algiers, 'to dream of Arabs means good luck'. So, for the moment, there were only 'white' Arabs, whose whiteness was indeed wearing visibly thin. As for the 'black' Arab, *ad hoc* institutions kept him well under control: the fine regiments of the Legion at Bel Abbes, or the Senegalese; a host of civil and military administrators, a substantial police budget, penitentiaries (model or otherwise) and, more subtly, a rulers' policy which knew how to strike, but also how to compromise, to smile and sometimes to understand . . .

The Semantics of Colonialism

As I write these words, my attempted analysis comes after a long series of similar efforts. These began when the French first settled in the Maghrib. They reflected the observer's anxiety in face of the problems of action. To understand, to explain, to penetrate, these were the accepted methods for taking possession of positive realities. Now this attitude of the French encountered a corresponding eagerness on the part of the Islamic populations. The rational ardour of the French was matched by the Maghribi enthusiasm for casuistry, decadent indeed and enfeebled by its detachment from reality, but still lively. The inhabitant of the Maghrib is a jurist and a litigant, by ancient tradition, and, still, in present-day behaviour. He sought, in the new things that were taking shape before his eyes, reasons for submission or rejection. He did so with an ardour which his subjection made all the keener.

After the war, this urgent need possessed the generation then reaching maturity. The first 'advanced' Arabs made their appearance, influenced by the argumentative tradition of their race, by political controversy on the French pattern, and by the first international discussions about national emancipation. On the French side, the first doubts were felt; socialism began to express itself, to the horror of those in power and in possession. Now the actual state of affairs surrounding the controversy was far from clear; for those of the 'old school' it was either a 'mystery of iniquity' or a reminder of those more or less irrecoverable 'good old days'. But already most criticisms, or replies to criticisms, were based on logic. The impatient arguments of the 'rational' were met by the prudent arguments of the 'reasonable'; it was merely a family quarrel!

The temperament of the opponents and the movement of the period thus combine to fill the chronicle of events, down to its most trivial details, with arguments and justifications. Thus began, or continued, that long legal battle, the French colonial system: a system in which those in power stood by their rights (positive and even moral) and the plaintiff appealed to justice, equity and logic, while neither made reference to the strength of irrational or factual elements. This is surprising, for whereas many reasons were put forward in favour of French appropriation on the one hand (treaties, the need to 'reform', to spread civilization, etc.)

and of national repossession on the other (revealed truth, the right to dispose of oneself, the great principles of 1789), both parties derived their greatest strength from mutual misunderstanding. Everyday speech seems to have been aware of this, when it contrasts the 'brute force' of one side with the 'force of inertia' on the other.

Although prevalent everywhere, and affecting more or less every situation and every individual, as is normal in a society in a state of violent transformation, this quarrel did not by any means break out with equal sharpness everywhere. In Algeria, in Tunisia and more recently in Morocco, mutual concession and uncommon understanding have been attained at certain levels; then the challenge which, in other sectors, aroused such violent passion, remained unspoken and pointless. Both sides envisaged public order as a matter of French initiative, even when they rebelled against it. Modern culture was also unanimously attributed to Western influence. Old believers resented this, but the young increasingly saw in it a means of progress, at any rate a weapon. On the economic plane, another agreement was reached. The expansion of industrial civilization went on. True, its oppressive force was greater than its power to persuade. But it all amounted to a state of fact, which nobody actually called 'legitimate', but which everybody acknowledged and outwardly accepted.

Only, beneath these levels of agreement, other levels can be guessed at whose existence fills us, like the men who lived through those times and observed them, with a certain anxiety and dismay. On all sides, we find a sense of some occult force underlying action. Truths openly averred, official truths, were met with others, whispered and confidential; the underside of the cards. And the language has a wealth of terms to express them, from the classical *dasa'is*, 'intrigues', to the dialectal *tahramiyat*, 'manoeuvres', or the metaphorical *na'ura*, 'devious ways' (derived, possibly, from the image of the *noria*).[1] Those who deplore or denounce the suspect obscurity of the Colonial order blame the 'administration' (the word is preferred to 'state') and accuse the French, not of inconsistency but of Machiavellism, which seems very odd to us today. The Director of Native Affairs, the Pasha devoted to the French régime, in fact almost all the leading figures of the time were indeed considered as the agents of some occult power, rather than as intriguers, oppressors or exploiters. The Maghribi suspected black magic behind the forces that were gradually taking hold of his material existence and which therefore seemed to be irresistible and immeasurable. Meanwhile the European, even when his position was secure and satisfactory, saw plots and conspiracies everywhere. So, while the old Colonels devoted themselves to etymological research and found connections between the Berber language and Caucasian, Japanese, Basque or Amerindian idioms,

---

[1] *noria*. A time-honoured expression in the Maghrib. A primitive kind of pump by means of a water-wheel.

retired administrators were composing novels on the theme of insurrection. This insurrection was so far only a mythical one. But the myth reflected fear. Wise men exhorted their compatriots: 'Beware!' *Rodd Balek*; this even became the pseudonym of a high official, author of several studies of Tunisia in the twenties. And no doubt these studies are over-subtle, seeking to be realistic and adroit yet they are none the less of great sociological significance, revealing the anxiety aroused by a mystery–or by unyielding reality.

If both sides shared this feeling, in spite of all that in practical life brought them together and gave them experience of one another, it was because, notwithstanding constant contact and the inevitable display of ordinary virtues and faults on either side, they felt it impossible to know one another. The closer life, with its average joys and misfortunes, drove them together, the more strongly they felt the difference dividing them, the antagonism of their relationship, and rather than seek the reasons for this, they proclaimed themselves insoluble to one another. Common opinion deplored their 'mutual incomprehension'.[1] In this conflict between historic consciousness and the opaque nature of things, beings and situations, the French and the Maghribis had to admit that they were, to some extent, a mystery one to another. Their mutual relation was, at the same time, one of aggressive awareness and one of defensive obscurity.

A country in process of integration and disintegration, a Colonial country such as that which I am now studying, is a mass compact of sufferings and joys, of iniquitous deeds and just claims. Its deepest tendency cannot be discovered, save as a working hypothesis. For it has not, as yet, developed a clear intention. It is still in a state of being rather than in a state of consciousness. If we attempt to analyse it, we are struck by the vision of two forces, whose effects cut across one another: forces different in age and in destiny. The combination of them, which we recognize and can trace everywhere, or almost everywhere, produces that scene of mingled catastrophe and splendid creativity–life in North Africa in those days. How far that life overspills the systems that occupy the forefront of the stage!–whether that of the French administration superimposed, here and there, on a *Makhzen* or a *Beylik*, or else those rival systems, early Tunisian nationalism or early Socialism; all these systems, however basically unequal, have in common their inability to account for the real conflict.

The inadequacy of the hypotheses proposed sends us back to the basic data. Consider the Maghrib geographically. Its divisions corre-

---

[1] Thus *La Tunisie Française* and *La Voix du Tunisien* argued on this theme in November 1932. In a brochure published in 1922, the Algerian journalist Rouanet collected the articles from the *Dépêche Algérienne* on problems of racial understanding and co-operation.

spond to different stages of progress in action and knowledge. The 'Southern Territories', the 'Military Territories' were both a relic of primitive society and a field of manoeuvres for the advance guard of colonization. They were to retain this character, more or less, until the end. There were also in the North zones where the two sides confronted one another in more prosaic fashion; they were known, significantly, as 'civil' or 'mixed'[1] zones. There were, finally, the Europeanized capitals, with 'holy hills' commonly, though mistakenly, believed to be the seat of fateful decisions. And the University of Algiers itself, where North-African enthusiasm for the Middle East flared up for the last time before 1930, does not provide us with any general explanation.

Colonization imposed on the country not only its authority, but a whole set of descriptive symbols. These replaced and repressed an ancient system, affecting towns and villages, pastoral and agricultural lands: a whole cycle of politics and piety. The ancient signs were absorbed back into the land, as those of European civilization spread. But even in our own day they have not entirely disappeared. From 1919 to 1939, we can glimpse only a moment of the process: an unfinished process, but revealing hidden depths . . .

Daily life was full of these symbols, or signals, which the critic must take into account just as much as those that express politics or the arts. Some of them refer to constant factors of the milieu. The church steeple rising up over the village square, while the marabouts dotted over the countryside and the fresh whitewash on the mosque defy it uncompromisingly. There are minarets: the one at Ghardaia, about which 'Ibadis and Malikis argued fiercely in 1930. Or the one that was driven underground in the Place du Gouvernement at Algiers, to make way for an equestrian statue. Or those which the statue of Cardinal Lavigerie challenges from the Porte de France at Tunis, and which fling back his challenge. Then there are military symbols: parades, fanfares, the Mausoleum of Remembrance, the column dedicated to the dead of the African Army, that towers over Algiers, the monument of Sidi Brahim adorning the Place d'Armes at Oran. And the bugle calls echoing from the old walls of the Meshouar (Mishwar) at Tlemsen, drowning the voice of the muezzin . . .

Other symbols represent social rise or fall. For instance the boat leaving 'for France' in the summer, loaded with the wealthy or those who aspire to wealth. More and more, the possession of a car. And before long, air travel; there was quite a sensation in the Press when a few Tunisian ladies took their first flight. Meanwhile the lower orders began

---

[1] The name familiarly given to the hill on which the Governor-General's Residency stands in Rabat. In Tunis, the Residency characteristically forms part of the European sector of the town. Equally characteristically, the seat of the Algerian Government was in a Berber building and surroundings, until it was transferred to the Centenary building.

to visit seaside resorts, which themselves were graded in a hierarchy.[1] Finally, the great mass of the people, enjoying no summer holiday but remaining in the *bled*, found refreshment only in the water from their stone jars.

Of course, a wide variety of factors are involved in the European's appropriation of the country's symbols – of which the naming of villages and streets is only one instance. Competitive greed plays its part, and a considerable one. But it is not the only motive.

The newcomer, confronting this reality, seeks out that part which remains hidden from him. The conquest of *things* only sharpens and makes desperate his compulsive longing to conquer the *person* opposing him. In so far as my opponent resists me, he is a person; in so far as I can grasp him, and imagine I have enslaved him, he is an object. I seek, literally, to *appropriate* this 'native' and all that belongs to him: his food, his field. But there is always some part of him that escapes me, even though he has become my servant, my batman, my workman, my *fatma*.[2] He resists alienation, maintaining his personality in regions of himself to which I have no access: his faith, his sexual life, his ever-watchful aggressiveness, his hope. And what is that element of obscurity that, despite the triumphs of my administration, baffles my science, my agriculture, my planning in every sphere – that which I cannot penetrate nor possess, that which I covet and vainly long for? Is it a last remnant of 'barbarism', or a last refuge of human liberty?

The Colonial debate, at that time and in that country, can thus be interpreted in terms of reciprocal knowledge and action. It took this form because the French aimed at being ubiquitously present, because French logic required it of them in spite of themselves, and because the men of the Maghrib maintained their cause unfalteringly, while the very progress of public order, administration and, to some extent, education sharpened the debate by providing, at least in part, a common language.

From Islam as Refuge to Islam as Revolution

The criterion of good sense and plausibility was alleged by both parties whenever the question of reform arose. 'Reform' is an ambiguous word; it may be used to justify further colonial intervention, or on the contrary serve as prelude to more radical demands. In fact, many years were to elapse in the Maghrib before it became clear that reforms must weaken

[1] Particularly since it was not until the Popular Front that town councils took the trouble to build public swimming pools or to organize adequate transport to nearby resorts.

[2] A generic name unfortunately given to Muslim maidservants.

the power of France precisely in so far as this stood for normality and order. So long as it had that reputation, it retained a considerable flexibility; conservation implied reform, or self-reform, for it. But few Frenchmen realized this. And once the opportunity was past, there came a moment when any reform must endanger their achievements. In any case all reforms, of whatever sort and origin, whether representing concession or the demands of the opposition, a mere battle of words or a serious plan for the future, were always put forward as a rational effort, conducive to the best interests of both parties and bound to convict the adversary of absurdity.

But gradually this privilege of reason shifted its ground. Lyautey's policy in the twenties had known how to respect the individuality of the other, leaving it a kind of refuge, like that *hurm* of Maulay Idris into which, in spite of flatterers, the Marshal had always refused to enter. But soon the significance of the *hurm* had altered. And the pre-colonization Arab who still lingered there felt himself hounded, driven out of all his successive hiding-places by a hostile effort backed by the mighty weight of modern times, and, simultaneously, ashamed of the retreat to which a pretence of submission had relegated him. And that is why his destiny gradually became intolerable to him. The higher he rose, the more clearly he perceived and analysed, the more deeply he was shocked by these very limitations, or protections, and the more he realized the arbitrariness of a situation originally attributed to fate, *maktub*.

True, throughout this conflict we meet cases of naked revolt, a kind of disinterested refusal: what, in the mountain districts, they called '*barud* (battle) of honour'. The tribes of the High Atlas, on such occasions, used the verb *raffada* in the sense of 'armed refusal'. The word paradoxically combines echoes of our 'refusal' and the memory of *Rafid*, an old Berber heretic. An unquenchable hope enabled one small tribe, in a corner of the Sargho,[1] to brave the greatest military power of the time (1933). Such gestures and utterances were constantly being noted by European observers, even in the quiet back streets of Salé or the markets of Mitija. And one such resistance movement achieved military fame, possibly on an international scale: that of 'Abd el-Krim in 1925. But how many others seem to us, in retrospect, crazy or merely formal, and derive their whole value from their basic attitude of refusal! Now this same refusal, as superior forces broke it down, took refuge in a side of life that formed its surest repository: namely religion. Islam, correspondingly, withdrew into the fatal retreat of the *zawiya*, of popular mysticism and xenophobic piety. This was how, in the eighteenth century, maraboutism and the Brotherhoods had developed. They retained their vitality until 1930. Thus protected by its very remoteness,

[1] Where Bournazel fell, on 28 Feb. 1933; the end of an epoch.

religion offered a merciful refuge to crushed resistance movements, unappeased angers and anachronistic violence. For believers, whom their sons tended increasingly to disavow, it raised a rampart against the advance of enlightenment, still identified with that of the foreigner. It distilled the unknowable element of the Maghrib and its most intimate rebellion.

Thus, when General Alfau occupied Tetuan in 1913, Sharif Tuhami al-Wazzani, a holy man, 'sufi by inheritance', took refuge from the disasters of the time in his *zawiya*.[1] Such, indeed, is the title of the book in which he relates a spiritual odyssey, wonderfully protected, or so he thought, from the malady of the times. The Maghrib still contains such types. Ibn al-Muwaqqit, his compatriot, seeking a dream city, returns to his home town, Marrakesh. What abuses need reforming there! What vicious practices (*manakir*), embracing indiscriminately legal corruption and alterations in dress, the unveiling of brides, the wearing of European trousers, patronal festivities, and the exploitation of popular credulity by the Brotherhoods.

Was he, in fact, attacking the Tijaniya order? It found a zealous defender at that time in Qadi Skiraj of Settat, a respected figure. In Algeria, until his death in 1934, Bin 'Aliwa organized a prosperous new brotherhood at Mostaganem. It counterbalanced the budding movement of the Association of the '*Ulama*'. And although maraboutism, as we have seen, had for some time past tended to lapse into lucrative hypocrisy, yet not all its devotees were suspect. As late as 1950, the list of personalities put forward by Shaikh Bashir Ibrahimi for the proposed Higher Islamic Council included several *zawiya* leaders. This shows the vitality of the doctrine, when it was not compromised by compliance with authority.

To return to Ibn al-Muwaqqit: he indicts almost the whole of contemporary life: the gramophone, records of women's voices, the habit of associating with 'Franks', the reading of newspapers and magazines, the disturbing influence on young men who made Europe their *Ka'ba*. There was nothing left for this despiser of history but the choice that confronted des Esseintes: conversion or suicide. His conversion had been only too thorough: he offered suicide to his contemporaries—following a vision, he prophesied the end of the world in 1370.[2] The date, fortunately, was already past. But this apocalypse is of interest as showing the end of an age.

[1] *Al-Zawiya* is the title given by Tuhami al-Wazzani to his strange book, published at Tetuan. *Zawiya*: monastery, or seminary of mystic devotion.
[2] Ibn al-Muwaqqit, al-Rihla al-marrakushiya, ed. 1351 vol. I, especially p. 45 (the new *Ka'ba*), p. 52 (the Press), p. 140 (congregations); vol. II, p. 96, (the gramophone); vol. III, p. 27 (women), etc. Cf. Faure, *Hesperis*, 1952, pp. 165 ff.

Algerian chroniclers in the twenties relate a curious adventure. Si Muhammad bin Rahal[1] was a great bilingual man of letters, a politician whose noble figure dominated Western Algeria for thirty years, and the darling of the French Republic. He withdrew from parliamentary life, donned traditional dress, and joined the rustic community of the Derqawa. He died in 1928, on his former estate of Nedroma, having become *muqaddim*[2] of that ascetic and violent brotherhood! 'Discarding his polished boots, our prince walked the highways barefoot . . . The people of Nedroma saw him prostrated in pious exercises at the foot of tombstones, and *zawiyas* became his favourite haunts.'[3] The most striking feature of this conversion is the choice of the way of myticism. Bin Rahal may indeed have despaired of a political system under which he had been a high official, moreover an upright and beneficent one.[4] But the fact that he joined one of those Brotherhoods which most thinkers in the Maghrib had already repudiated is typical of the period. For ten years later Islam had changed its attitude. Once a refuge for hopeless enthusiasms, it came to reject any sort of compromise, all superstition, all cult of the past, and to declare itself rational. From 1931 onwards, the influence of the '*Ulama*' movement made itself felt throughout Algeria.

Just as tribal resistance gave place to political opposition of the modern type, so Islam, from being the ultimate moral sanctuary, became enterprising and aggressive; in so doing it assumed a rationalism that appears almost revolutionary. Its desire for a return to its own sources and for purity of dogma concealed an acceptance of the modern world and a just aspiration towards some positive compromise. Admittedly its reformist doctrine echoed Panislamic themes and looked towards the East; it was derived none the less from a profound North-African authenticity. This new Islam, standing for rationality, moderate progress and the golden mean, unhesitatingly condemned the old-fashioned, time-serving Islam which, while upholding ritual, had taken to soliciting for stipends. For marabouts and leaders of religious orders, once champions of resistance, had come to be considered as political traitors and social reactionaries, allies of the Administration[5]

---

[1] I owe biographical details to M. F. Llabador. Cf. also E. Janier, 'Si Mohammed Ben Rahal, 1856–1928', *Bulletin de la société des amis du vieux Tlemcen.* 1954, p. 5.

[2] *Muqaddim*: local official.

[3] Ch. Geniaux, 'Nedroma', *Revue des Deux Mondes*, 1 Feb. 1922.

[4] He anticipated Viollette's project. 'Whoever is not represented is not protected,' he said. He was opposed by E. Sabatier; see Jean Mélia, *Le Centenaire de la Conquête* and *L'Algérie et les réformes indigènes*, 1930, pp. 40 ff.

[5] The organs of the movement, *al-Basa'ir* and *al-Shihab*, were involved in controversies, but these correspond to a widespread state of mind. Cf. for instance *Le Libéral* (Tunis), 17, 31 Oct. 7 Nov. 1925.

The conflict between Shaikh Bin 'Aliwa,[1] of Mostaganem, who may be called the last great marabout, and Shaikh Bin Badis, of Constantine, the first reformist, went beyond controversy, involving accusations of attempted murder.

In fact al-'Uqbi and Bin Badis, in spite of themselves, represent, at a level of richer human values and greater historical significance, a truer adaptation to the French presence in the Maghrib that that of the marabouts. Not so much because the latter included many hypocritical stipend-seekers, decadent exploiters and false friends of France, but–to consider only the social fact and not individual cases–because the old Islam they stood for, even in its decline, was more fundamentally opposed to a certain form of civilization than that of the '*Ulama*'. The Administration did not bother about such distinctions. It only recognized the compliancy of the marabouts and the independence of the '*Ulama*'. It made use of the former against the latter, banned freedom of oratory in the mosques, opposed efforts at education, encouraged rival associations, strangled the opposition press as far as possible and set the police machinery in motion. This struggle against a movement which was essentially religious and moral was in part responsible for the degradation of France's 'native policy'. Without attempting to tell the story of events, let us consider these deplorable results as springing from a faulty analysis of the situation.

Too often France confined herself to superficial levels, concerned with manoeuvres, proposals, incidents and circumstances, whereas tremendous upheavals were shaking North African society to its depths, especially from 1930 onwards. The opposition, often without realizing it, interpreted these movements better. It enjoyed the advantage of irresistible themes, such as that of liberty; it was connected, more by its symbols than by its programme, with the very heart of the problem; and thus it could afford to sustain an inconclusive quarrel against authority. Its strength came not from what it formulated but from what it heralded. And it heralded the imperative demands of reason.

A North African Philology

Was North Africa, at this period, an ally of the *logos*, of rational discourse? And if so, in what way, within what limits and with what consequences? In other words, what were the limits, the role and the effects of that involvement of which I have stressed the enormous importance, inherent in a conflict of this sort between opponents of such temperament and at a moment like this? This leads us to assess how far systems of government on the one hand, and the hypotheses put forward by the

[1] Augustin Berque, 'Un mystique moderniste, le sheikh Benalioua', in the *Actes du Congrès de Tlemcen des Sociétés Savantes d'Afrique du Nord*, 1935; also study of *Le Neo-wahhabisme nord-africain*.

opposition on the other, aim at consistency and attain efficiency, prove themselves equal to the realities of the situation.

Lyautey's experiment, in the immediate post-war period, was characterized by its readiness to accept various solutions. This open-mindedness is liable to prove misleading in the long run. At the time, it achieved great successes; indeed, it cast such lurid light on the future that the famous circular of 1920 remained censored for thirty years. Needless to say, the Marshal's policy was not entirely homogeneous. The great man's most personal contribution seems to have been the idea of an aristocratic, and incidentally capitalist, principality. Morocco was to combine D'Annunzio's Fiume and the Belgian Katanga. But Lyautey, *le patron*, also introduced the 'Ain Sefra method of psychological conquest and 'contacts' with a flavour of aestheticism (for instance Isabelle Eberhardt).[1] He surrounded himself with Arab Bureau officers of classic type such as Delman and Berriau. Yet he dared not, any more than others had done, challenge the *colon* symbol. There was a heroic strain in this complex, hybrid policy, and on the whole it succeeded. A State was organized. The entente with the Makhzen seemed likely to prove durable.[2] As well as economic equipment, a Franco-Muslim understanding was sought, whose architects felt that they had found 'far from the mechanized world, a spring of living water, rising from the bowels of the earth, and which intoxicated them'.[3] The method had its dark sides, of course: shady speculation and the power of the 'great caïds'. The rising of Abd el-Krim (1925) relegated it into anachronism. And this was universally realized, since the awe-inspiring soldier was replaced by a pacifistic parliamentarian.

The type of rule that followed was characteristic of the Third Republic. It eventually prevailed from the time of Jonnart to that of G. Le Beau. It started from a basic assumption: the permanence of French domination; from an observed fact: the impossibility of defying the influence of the men in power locally; and from a subsidiary and compensatory concern for the Muslim population. In this sense, any 'native policy' is a recipe for domination, and at the same time an alibi.

Sometimes brutal, sometimes kindly, but most often tortuous, the system expressed itself in judicial trivialities, without any sort of doctrine or foresight.[4] For a long time the French in Algeria backed the great

---

[1] Whom he had known, and made use of, in 'Ain Sefra, 1903–4.

[2] A fair assessment by J. Dresch, 'Lyautey', in *Les Techniciens de la Colonisation*, 1945, pp. 150 ff.

[3] Jean Gallotti, 'En marge de l'exposition Lyautey', *Le monde français*, 1948, p. 82. This short article by one of Lyautey's collaborators recreates with admirable sharpness the atmosphere of that period in which, 'thanks to the caprice of a paradoxical master, even the Administration assumed a smiling aspect'.

[4] This is much deplored by such specialized publications as *L'Afrique française*, in which essays on 'native policy' are frequent. To this category belong

families which were already being supplanted by Brotherhoods and marabouts. Then they backed the marabouts, when these were in full retreat before the reformist movement. Eventually they were to back the middle peasants, when the rift formed between the masses and the intelligentsia. Thus, at the best, they fought a rearguard action. But do we need to wonder at this failure to foresee or even to imagine things? It is a characteristic of the colonial phenomenon that, despite its 'total' character, it can no more master its own totality that it can discern its own effect on its surroundings. The strength and weakness of the nationalist movement are just the reverse. Very much a minority movement to start with, significant of the people yet scarcely representative of them, and displaying forces which, though undoubtedly growing, were still scanty, it prevailed by means of its greater powers of integration. And it was thus that it eventually won the day, in the reintegration of national unity, over the colossus which divided that unity and was itself divided.

I do not mean that one should rest content with explanations in terms of right and wrong, with one side all white, the other all black. Even when they subsequently prove correct, from the historical point of view they must be re-examined. True, in 1920 the Maghrib, considered as a whole, had got beyond the opening scene; the play had reached Act Two. But like any other drama, it allowed for a surprise in the dénouement. This was no simple conflict between clear-cut protagonists, but a constant succession of situations, all gradually tending in the same direction, but all implying a multitude of misleading possibilities. Nowhere is the contrast between life as lived and life as planned more strongly marked than between the infinite variety of existence here and the politicians who sought to govern it. The heroes of the period were for the most part hesitant and divided men.[1] Their biographies only assumed some unity in retrospect, if they succeeded. If they failed, reverted to that ambiguity in which reality consisted at the time.

In so far as the nationalist movement had leaders, and Heaven knows that the Maghrib produced plenty of active ones–Bourguiba, Bin Badis, Abbas, 'Allal al-Fasi for instance–they merely provided this nebula with the sign that polarized it. They instructed the mass of the people in the language of new life. But the complexity, or even the identity of the forces confronting one another often escaped them. Among all these forces the present-day historian, despite the negative privilege of looking backward, can scarcely distinguish between the factors that represent the dissatisfaction of youth, the frustration of rising classes or that of declining classes, national anger, or more subtle

the works of Rodd Balek and *Un africain*. Towards the end of our period, R. Montagne set up his C.H.E.A.M. to fulfil these requirements.

[1] As J. Lacouture has clearly brought out in *Cinq hommes et la France*, particularly and almost excessively with respect to Ferhat Abbas.

movements. Wounded piety joins hands with irreligion. Nostalgia for the past mingles with revolt against the past. In their attitude towards the European, many are torn between attraction and repulsion. Can one fix the proportion of these various factors among themselves? And indeed should one attempt to do so? For this intermingling reveals the ambiguity of things and men in the Maghrib at that time.

In fact, the leaders' instinct outclassed the cunning of specialists in 'native policy' and the sagacity of academics. But its own theory was not clearly formulated until later on. Torn between the ideal and the real, between intransigence and expediency, it underwent, like the administration, the alternate vicissitudes of crisis and lull, violence and compromise, but also the opportunities provided by initiative or luck. And its progress reflects the general tendency of things and symbols, and their mutual interaction, spreading far beyond individual action and the restricted field of politics.

On the French side, certain bodies were, or should have been, qualified to work out a course of action not subject to the fluctuations of contemporary events. For some time past a Commission for Muslim Affairs[1] had been sitting in Paris, which sometimes consulted such authorities as Doutté, Augustin Bernard and Louis Massignon. In 1921 the legislator brought in a few Algerian notabilities. This deceived nobody. Hence the significance of another fact. The three pro-consuls met for the first time on 6 February 1923, at Algiers. The Press[2] described their meeting with enthusiasm. The serious-minded *Journal des Débats* congratulated these 'eminent handlers of men, exchanging experiences'. Now if we look a little closer we realize that these exchanges consisted of bickering over practical trivialities: contact between health authorities, quarrels over coastal fishing rights, questions of tourism, export of fruit, fiscal frauds, locust control, etc. The prevailing tone was of smug condescension. The inaugural speech of the 1923 Conference proclaimed 'the friendly tutelage that France must assume', seeking 'the gradual raising of the intellectual, material and moral level of the natives'. Proposed methods: 'the respect for religion and customs', humanitarianism, and other such fine phrases; nothing concrete in any case. Were the other conferences any better? The second opened at Rabat in 1924. Already the Marshal's power was on the decline. He had to face 'seditious' propositions: fortunately they were only those of Lucien Saint, the Tunisian delegate, talking about customs union. This type of project created great disturbances in economic systems whose

---

[1] Some of its deliberations met with sharp criticism. Thus on 21 March 1935 Viollette criticized in the Senate the attitude it took on the right to preach in mosques.

[2] *Akhbar*, 23 Feb. 1923. *Journal des Débats*, 22 Feb. 1923. Cf. also *Afrique française*, 1923, pp. 55 ff. about this meeting; *Afrique française* 1924, p. 275 about the second; *Renseignements coloniaux*, 1926, p. 193, about the third; *Renseignements coloniaux*, 1927, p. 169, about the fourth.

prosperity had already begun to depend largely on obtaining quotas from the parent state. In 1924 the difficulties of the immediate post-war period had been tackled. Mutual congratulations were called for. This conference was particularly sterile. The only thing worth mentioning is a report by Commandant Marty, referring to the first year's graduation list of the College Maulay Idris at Fez, which included 'Abd al-Kabir al-Fasi and 'Umar bin 'Abd al-Jalil, two future statesmen. Thus the future creeps forward. But such barely perceptible signs were certainly not understood at these gatherings.[1]

In 1926 Rober-Raynaud, in that serious paper *Le Temps*, wrote: 'It may be said that for the first time definitely useful work has been accomplished; hitherto it had merely been a matter of internal squabbling.' But it is hard to see in what respect this conference was better than its predecessors. And the fifth was no improvement on the fourth!

Meanwhile however, here are concrete examples of the kind of events that administrators had to tackle, far from these serene sanctuaries of official self-congratulation.

News Items

In June 1924, at Tunisia, where the nationalist movement had already made considerable strides, the Arab papers[2] brought an embarrassing incident into the limelight. Tremich, a judiciary *wakil* (defence counsel), assistant to Maître Guellati, came into conflict with the military authorities. The opposition accused the Director of Judiciary Services of intervening unduly against him. The controlling magistrate had clearly begun to feel uneasy, now that justice was no longer 'retained' but 'delegated'. So long as justice had been 'retained', he had naïvely assumed that discreet pressure on the ruler or in official circles could influence its course. This was no longer the case, and indeed was to become increasingly less so. The institutions created by the French as their privilege and their mission seemed thus to be turning against them. In any case French actions as well as French laws provided countless opportunities for the Tunisian opposition which was adept at cavilling. This resistance movement knew how to assume courtesy and discretion; on the other hand, it could go a long way and it could aspire very high. Lucien Saint caused a considerable scandal when he made Nasir Bey take back his abdication.[3]

[1] Cf. p. 264 on the subject of the creation of the Haut-Comité Méditerranéen (decree of 23 Feb. 1935).

[2] *Sawab*, 16 May 1924; *Murshid al-Umma*, 10 June 1924; *Nahda*, 30 May 1924

[3] *L'Internationale*, a Communist evening paper, Paris, 16 April 1922: 'It is infinitely easier to prevail over a bey by means of a platoon of cavalry than to triumph . . . over the demands of the oppressed.' The injunction to the ruler was to be reproduced, characteristically in Morocco, by means of G. Puaux (Jan. 1944), Marshal Juin, and General Guillaume . . .

Let us skip a dozen years. At Fez, one summer's day in 1934, the acclamation of the young Sultan by a youthful multitude for the first time caused the Protector some anxiety. This was the first step along the road that led, at last, in 1947, to the Tangier speech. But consider the crowd that acclaimed the Sultan; it included bourgeois intellectuals, of course, but also working people. One of the most evident advantages of the opposition lay in reconstituting to its own profit the old canonic nation, the citizens of the vanished Muslim state, the *sha'b*. The whole balance of the *madina* rested on a threefold equilibrium between students, merchants and artisans. But times had changed. The *madina* was breaking down. Its forces hesitated, in quest of new forms: it is significant that nationalism offered them one, and proposed its own ends.

The chronicles of the time often show the lowly sharing in the ideals of the élite. Returning to Tunisia, let us picture a meeting of the Destour party at Mahdia in 1922. Scarcely, as yet, a 'cell', but a gathering of some twenty or thirty people, grocers, hairdressers, chauffeurs, mechanics from the harbour, a few students from the Zaituna, even a petty leader. A few years later, at Tunis in 1929, a blind baker held a meeting in his bakehouse: the cause of the excitement was the detention of Guefrash, one of the 1925 protesters, who was in prison for having demonstrated at Gabès in favour of Abd el-Krim. There was talk of imprisonments and protests and petitions. Wild hopes were raised. Another day, the dockers of Bizerta refused to unload a cargo of chalk under pretext that the dust raised would make them infringe their fast.[1] This was a political excuse rather than a religious scruple, for the dockers were never particularly pious, and Finidori's propaganda by no means incited them to respect ritual. The important point to note is that the protest movement had spread downward to ever deeper strata.

The Destour opened branches throughout Tunis. There was one in the Rue Ghernuta, in the Pasha District, to which I shall refer later. And another in the Impasse Riyad, near Halfawin. A grocer, Shaikh Mahmud Karkar, harangued his audience after asking for subscriptions, which were often slow to come in. Behind him stood an enormously enlarged photograph of Shaikh Tha'alibi[2] in all his exile's glory. We can imagine what these 'plotters' talked about: the League of Nations, events in Palestine – Tha'alibi had taken part in the Congress of Jerusalem. Note the sequel: poor Karkar, who had been forbidden to set foot in Matmata, died in 1935, and the transference of his remains to Monastir gave rise to a demonstration in which poets and dignitaries took part.

Condemnation, exile and sometimes death gave tragic sanction to these conflicts with established power. Two orders were competing with

---

[1] *Afrique française*, 1928, p. 148.
[2] Known, even in Iraq, as 'the Zaghlul of Tunisia', *Renseignements coloniaux*, 1929, p. 163.

one another. Each sought to catch and canalize the strength of the popular movement arising on the wreckage of a ruined, but partially remade, society. Hence a certain romanticism, among those who took part, the exaltation of self-sacrifice, in short a revolutionary feeling. The fury of frustrated faith may well be imagined. The privileges it had arrogated to itself had been outraged by historic disasters. These old believers were painfully torn by contradictory impulses. They opposed the material world, which persecuted them; at the same time they adhered to that material world, and hoped some day to benefit by worldly advantages. This was the moral nebula to which nationalism merely gave a direction, while the administration itself promoted such an interpretation by its repressive measures.

The movement invented its own liturgy. For instance, street demonstrations (a new word: *muzahara*). The mob proceeded to a kind of purification of the city: a *tatwif* (circumambulation) of an unfamiliar sort. Thus on 29 September 1925 a procession of protest gathered on the Place Halfawin. It caused some disturbance among those who sat smoking hashish there, or listening to the song of goldfinches. It moved along the outer street, through Bab Carthagena, crossed the *Petite Malte* into the Place de France, and proceeded through the suqs. It was now in the heart of the old *madina*, the city; and at last, by way of the rue de la Qasba, reached the seat of government. Who was leading it? An obscure bookseller, who had to some extent forced the Destour's hand. We must emphasize this almost physical spontaneity. The demonstration provided an outlet and flourished a banner. The authorities were outclassed, in so far as they failed to grasp the significance of what was happening. In the long run, the match was a most uneven one.

Mastery over the street, however, still belonged to the police. And at no point did the opposing force make use of its real physical strength, although it contained within itself potential clashes and uprisings. It invoked a symbol, no more. The symbolic factor prevailed over the actual. The opposition spoke of national emancipation, sworn faith, liberty, whereas the administration spoke of public order. Although such very different things were at stake, the battle chose to be a tournament, or even a game of chess. Only, here and there on the chessboard, those 'accidents' cropped up that cause men's death. And yet the rivals were not yet enemies, nor even adversaries. Each sought, it seemed, to provide the country's moral configuration with those 'sighting-slits' to be found in certain modern machines: that little luminous arrow that points a direction and gives a meaning to the sum of data. Now official initiative seldom takes into account this 'sighting-slit' of the future. The nationalist movement has too many imponderable elements at its disposal: mass enthusiasm, the incantation of Arabic words, the intoxicating effect of shouting, that collective hysteria which sometimes escapes all control, and yet that faith in its leaders, that exciting sense that someone has 'arisen'[1] who will govern these forces and give them point. Finally, the solemnity of suffering and sometimes of death. What can authority set against such admirably conductive feelings? Its mass no doubt, its still powerful prestige, coercion and interest, or, more subtly, the customary course of things. But whereas, in fully developed countries, the force of custom is effective, in a Colonial country the appeal to everyday 'realities' disqualifies those who invoke them against enthusiasm.

The situation thus conferred on the most trivial events–a street procession, a speech in the backroom of some shop–a phenomenal importance, which the actions of the authorities attained ever more rarely, and this difference in significance can be explained by the different relations existing, in the two cases, between things and symbols.

Sophisms of Liberty

To mobilize things, to cause a symbol to emerge, implies a difficult balance between the ideal and reality. Difficult for the French, for they more or less indentified the exercise of their responsibilities with security of administration. Difficult for the men of the Maghrib, since they lacked the material, as well as the cultural, context. A good cause can be lost through exaggeration as well as through timidity, as soon as action ignores its concrete limitations. Thus, for various reasons, the Amir Khalid and Shaikh Tha'alibi went into exile, Abd el-Krim was defeated in open battle, the first Communist rising collapsed, and as a constant rule, extremism failed, just as compromise had been discredited; for those in power, the result was the same.

And yet what strikes one throughout all this period is the rising force with which claims were made. In spite of controversies, transactions, failures and relapses, the tendency persisted and progressed. How can one wonder at it? The Maghrib was reconstructing itself, out of its own destruction. Tribal revolts, national anticipation (as in the case of the Rif), xenophobia, Panislamism, demands for equality, reformism and of course nationalism, these are all instances of the same fundamental drive.

To be sure, manifestations vary, or contradict one another. 'Ali Bash Hanba had already talked of independence. Ten years later, Salah Farhat denied any sort of separatism.[2] The word independence rang out in Algiers in 1936. But few had got beyond the point of petitioning for

[1] The *za'im*, a name which is much more powerful than 'leader'.
[2] He even declared 'We are not nationalists' (*Le Libéral*, 29 Nov. 1924), defending himself against the accusation of a 'scandalous alliance with the Communists' levelled at him by Duran-Angliviel (*Tunis-socialiste*, 7 Nov. 1924). It is true that the *Libéral*'s position hardened after the bombardment of Damascus (26 Sept. 1925).

a democracy in the style of 1848, or else religious personalism, or merely reformism. This diversity, which still strikes us at a distance, was even more striking to a citizen of those days. The leaders tore one another asunder about such words. And of course the Administration meant to take advantage of that. If we take a closer look, however, we see that the Maghribi movement of self-assertion cannot be confined within any formulae. To borrow Renan's phrase, it 'finds a rich jewel-case of synonyms' for liberty. When the Tunisian paper *Le Libéral* declared its loyalism in 1925, it remained notwithstanding more revolutionary than certain theoretical professions of hostility, such as were still frequent at the time. The demand for '*la citoyenneté dans le statut*' (French citizenship without loss of private rights under orthodox or customary Muslim law) was characteristic of an Algerian patriot in 1930, whereas in 1934 a Moroccan patriot could, without betraying his ideal, demand an exact application of the Protectorate. History, which in retrospect is not concerned with ideological quibbles and personal rivalries, may sometimes recognize a positive content in some modest request, and on the contrary a suspect negativism in exaggerated claims. In any case, whether the slogan be radical assimilation, eventual independence or respect for Islam, analysis sees in all these diversities only varying expressions of the Maghribi spirit.

True, the colonial relationship exaggerates this diversity to the point of caricature. Everything in these movements comes to be defined in terms of that relationship, has to provide an 'answer' to that. Whether that answer is adequate or hypothetical, whether it displays infantilism or opportunism or, on the contrary, a grasp of reality, it runs the further great risk of becoming absorbed in altercation. What matters is that the Maghrib should be more than merely the native counterpart to colonial policy. The true force of a movement lies in its understanding of, or rather its instinct for, a North African reality which exists *in itself*;[1] it lies in the movement's capacity not only for present competition but for long-term creation. If the men of the Neo-Destour group outclassed those of the old, it was not through adopting more flexible tactics; for at the congress of Ksar Hilal in 1934 their revolt was in the name of greater strictness, while in 1938 they upheld violent action, which Dr. Materi, no doubt wisely, deplored. It was because they represented a popular will more closely bound up with the country's structure, and more modernist. This is so true that in spite of quarrels over programmes and personalities, most Algerian movements did in fact come to an agreement, after 1936, to make the same democratic claims. And they derived their solidarity not from the ideologies they proclaimed but from the various versions they provided of the same fact: the

[1] In theoretical terms, this is connected with the relations between positiveness and negativeness in nationalism and in its conflict with the Colonial phenomenon, which is itself highly complex.

profound transformation of a nation, which can be interpreted either in terms of renovated Islam, or of social revolution, or of Parliamentary promotion. In Morocco, the rift between the *Wataniyin* and the *Qaumiyin* was of small account; what mattered was the revolt of the middle-class intelligentsia, which had already mobilized the cities and was striving to take over the leadership of the countryside in a changed Morocco.

Official policy was thus gravely mistaken when it speculated on the character of individuals, on statements or on events, set off one personality against another, tried to detach a 'reformist' group from the nationalist movement in Tunis, backed the marabouts against the '*Ulama*' in Algiers, rejoiced at the rivalry, in Morocco, between al-Fasi and al Wazzani, approved of the Congress of Ksar Hilal because it 'broke' the Old Destour movement, just as later it was to encourage the breakaway of unions within the C.G.T.[1] And the economists are just as badly mistaken when they attribute patriotic agitation to unemployment or poverty, despite the evident connection of all these facts amongst themselves and with many others. Nationalism consists of a whole body of historic meanings to which democratic leaders, more by instinct than by reason, find the key words. This is a semantic renewal of North African life. But the secrets of the renewal must be sought far below the level of expressions, events and men. I shall return to this crucial point.[2]

One might even characterize the milieu and the moment by this contrast between the weakness of the actual claims made—for the law retained its force, and coexistence was never repudiated—and the persistence of a moral attitude based on emancipation. Only for a moral attitude to take shape, and find expression in facts, it must integrate a wide variety of factors. Now the stream of life has many confluents, but it also has deltas, where its branches diverge.

The Interplay of Reason and the Arbitrary

The state of dependence came increasingly to be felt as an outrage to the unwritten laws of the mind and heart. The generations that matured after 1925 were all the more conscious of this outrage in that they were bilingual, enamoured of high principles expressed in peremptory terms. Now the progress of enlightenment made them ever more painfully aware of what was obscure, illogical and, worse still, nameless. For if the Arabic language had no words to describe the objects that confronted the younger generation of those days, the motor car in 1920, then the tractor, then the aeroplane, the same thing was true of concepts and feelings. In all these spheres the Maghrib did not make the same linguistic effort as the Middle East. It became full of things without names, but also of names without things—things authentically its own,

[1] Confédération Générale du Travail.   [2] Cf. p. 356.

that is to say. Even the vital power of describing its inner perturbations was usurped by the French language. Henceforward not only action, but feeling and revolution must speak and think in French. And so any movement aiming at recovery must seek to restore signs to things. Hence came the deep and close connection between nationalism and the spreading of information. When Arabic broadcasting stations were set up at Algiers, Tunis and Rabat, a decisive step had been taken.

This linguistic advance, of course, has its intrinsic importance. But it interests us now chiefly because of the developments it reveals. What had happened? New symbols had emerged. All mankind needs hypotheses to live by. We see these hypotheses succeed one another, conflict or combine, in the shape of administrative programmes or political and social ideologies. A hypothesis is strong in so far as it tallies with the facts and is positive, that is to say affects the widest possible zone of inert reality around it. Now these hypotheses, which contradict one another, which exist only in relation to one another, all have this in common, that they seek to replace disequilibrium by new forms of equilibrium, unreason by reason. They make much ado about it. There is loud rivalry and controversy between the government and its adversaries. What matters is not so much the content as the fact of contradiction, of presenting an alternative, the role assumed by one or the other party in the affair. So that all the factors still dominant in practical life: the unacknowledged prestige of the marabout, the authority of a power which could no longer explain anything, since it could not explain itself, the reactionary attitude of those in possession – all this was indicted as *arbitrary*. We may take the word in its linguistic sense: what exists on its own account, without logical connection with any meaning. Now in this practice of arbitrariness the two sides have changed roles.

Let us look back at 1920. We can represent the North African situation as a circle which French intervention sought to penetrate by action and knowledge: but it came up against an obstacle, a hidden core, that of an inert primitivism, of tribal resistance and religion on the defensive. What had happened twenty years later? The Maghrib had taken its own initiative, in rivalry with that of the West, to define and appropriate reality. Hence this conflict of hypotheses: official continuity, the challenge of socialism or nationalism. But the latter came up against the hard core of political continuity. The French authorities too often based their resistance on the state of fact, unexplainable and even unjustifiable.

Of course, the exchange of roles did not take place in so clear-cut a fashion. It was by no means so conclusive as this image might suggest. In actual fact, each of the rivals had its own dynamism which varied according to the period, the geographic milieu or the kind of problem in question. Hence the advantages were equally balanced, or at least still open to question: so many sudden changes of fortune in that drama of understanding, which underlies the concrete history of the period. From time to time, one of the adversaries puts forward the best explanation of the whole, which at the same time is the best conductor of feelings and actions. The facts agglomerate round this idea. It is no matter of chance that the boldest hypothesis or the most seductive idea also conceals the greatest creative force and fighting power, at the same time as it throws its light the furthest.

Looking closer, then, we must subdivide the period. In the immediate post-war years, Lyautey's thesis made a more dazzling impression than all the rest. It also seemed the most plausible; it constructed the greatest number of facts with the minimum of tension. It thus wore certain aspects of legitimacy, or at least its illegitimacy was not too dangerously obvious. But soon after, the régime of the Protectorate had to admit itself hamstrung. It had not yet reached the point—as in Tunisia—of petty *coups d'état*, intrigues and quibbles, but it was no longer in basic contact with things. In Algeria there reigned alternately 'good' and 'bad' régimes, acknowledged and confirmed as such by public opinion and by facts.

Within this see-sawing movement, which assigned true mastery now to one side now to the other, the divorce between signs and things grew gradually wider. With ever increasing power, the nationalist movement constructed its system. A certain vibrant quality, the power to thrill and arouse enthusiasm, the force of the claims it proposed to ever-growing crowds, should have made it clear by 1930, and still more after 1934, that here was more than the stirring up of a minority by agitators. Henceforward it would yield only to brute force—in other words, once again, to the 'arbitrary'. True, other influences contended with it for primacy, not so much in the political sphere as in that of manners and minds. Even in those who protested, the influence of France permeated down to those subtle limits that divide the *animus* from the *anima*. And above all, by its deprivation of material things, which were then almost all in the hands of the French, the nationalist movement was both exacerbated and disarmed.

The chances, then, were not equal but divided. The future belonged to the adversary who could gather together the greatest number of things under the most dazzling of signs.

CHAPTER III

Enduring Factors in Maghrib Life

I propose to consider the history of North Africa during the score
of years between the two world wars in terms of a conflict for the
creation or conquest of material things, of the establishment or
restoration of symbols, of the varying role played by the two parties in
the dispute, of the effect of their competition on events and on the classi-
fying of men, facts and moments as 'good' or 'bad', 'lawful' or 'unlawful'.
Seen from the present day, and compared with what has been seen since,
the period may appear peaceful, unimpressive or uneventful. It was
none the less pervaded by a rhythm which the men who lived through
it interpreted, at the time, in their own way. There were numerical
progressions, an imperceptible movement of bodies and forms, phases
of affluence or poverty, alternations of crisis and pause in ethnic and
social relations: several kinds of duration thus seem to concur in the
general rhythm which I shall endeavour to analyse.

Physical Implications

The ever worsening conflict between symbols and things implies, as I
showed in the preceding chapter, a growing self-awareness by the men
of the Maghrib and a corresponding wasting away of the French system.
Now this twofold evolution corresponds to the evolution of elements
some of which can be seen and even measured, while others are more
difficult to discern.

Reports of the time often refer to demography, since it appears to
furnish arguments for the official thesis. Nobody at that time recognized
in the sharp rise of the curve after 1930, and particularly after 1935, this
retaliation of Eastern fertility, so striking both in the Maghrib and in
Egypt. This was how conquered nations submerged the colonial power.
Muslim humanity was rejuvenated by its own growth. By this means, it
was physically enfranchised from its ancient framework. As its body was
renewed it cast off the respect formerly owed to the archaic authority

of tribe, family or bureau. This upsurge displays not only a forward movement, but a rhythm. Generations, *ajyal*,[1] succeeded one another. The younger rebelled against his elder. Even before the 1914 war the 'Young Turks' rose against the 'Old Turbans'. The 'Young Algerians' emerged between 1925 and 1930. Then we meet the Moroccan *shabiba*, the Tunisian Neo-Destour and other young groups, even younger in spirit through having more completely destroyed all the old bonds within themselves.

Thus during the whole of this period there were prodigious changes in the social and mental set-up. These reflect not only after-effects of world events such as demobilization, etc. but also more local and often slighter phenomena which should be examined in detail: for instance the visit of some educational mission to France, the fact that a certain number of scholars were studying in Paris at such and such a time or came back at some particular moment. One might distinguish, amidst the political personalities of the time, those on whom their stay in post-war Paris left its mark, those who had been there at the time of the Colonial Exhibition or the Popular Front. One might go further and recognize the influence of some particular teacher.[2] Names of soldiers and initiators spring to one's lips. There is a characteristic interaction between the broadest phenomena and the minutest facts. Thus a good high-school teacher may have been indirectly responsible for some State institution . . .

If one had the means to do it, this attempt to reconstitute the concrete continuity of the country would combine the most down-to-earth preoccupation with material things and the highest sensitivity to impressions. In many cases, indeed, figures tell us nothing. What speaks is the general trend and colour of life. For instance, success in sport is an essential feature of the vitality then prevalent in the Maghrib. An Algerian triumphs at the Olympic Games, and we must remember all those cross-country runners, those boxing champions, those impetuous football forwards, that North Africa produced and still produces today. Is such an aptitude connected with ethnic evolution, with its hereditary features, or does it rather represent a sort of compensation for political inferiority? A Moroccan athlete, recently questioned, attributed this special disposition to childhood games to a more varied because more precarious diet, and to a sort of alacrity in the quest for food and sex. And also to the lack of school education, which means that the native child spends long hours playing about in the streets and squares and thus becomes an adept, particularly at football. And this margin of superiority is bound to decrease as conditions of life become normal for the young . . .

[1] The term replaces the classical *tabaqat*.
[2] Pupils of Sallefranque or Rémy Beaurieux in Morocco, for instance.

89

Other aspects are less pleasant. I am thinking of those terrible endemic diseases of the Maghrib, of the flare-up of typhus, of the widespread occurrence of malaria and venereal disease. Now these afflictions have social, even political effects. Several of them have been considered as inherent in a community. Consider the pamphlet on the treatment of 'Moroccan scurvy' by Dr. Gabriel Lévy-Lebhar, who had successfully treated the disease in certain urban groups in Morocco. He distinguishes between a *favus* of Berber origin, and tricophylia resulting from migratory movements.[1] Here medical analysis combines with social analysis. Quite recently Dr. Delanoë defined what he called, in technical terms, 'asystolia due to organic deficiency' in Morocco.[2] He pointed out the existence of cirrhosis in a country where by definition the Muslim element in the population admits of no alcoholism; and calls such cirrhosis 'Algerian' or 'Moroccan'.

As for venereal diseases, they were commonly held to be the lot of a crushing majority of the Maghribi people. In 1920 a doctor of repute published a book on 'Arab syphilis'.[3] The fear of contagion, particularly at a time when prophylaxis was little known, created such a segregation between Europeans and Muslims that one wonders whether the political myth did not play some part in the unanimity of practitioners. The pox intervened very conveniently to keep the native in his place. It did not interfere, however, with military recruitment or the employment of labour. Actually, it retreated, or more precisely it 'withdrew inward'. Among the suqs of the *bled* one saw less and less of the old-time disfigurements: that ravaged flesh, noses eaten away, *vitiligos*, all so dreadful that they were known in dialect not as *nuwar*, the 'flowers' of common syphilis, but as *jdam*, leprosy, attributed to some saint's curse. Meanwhile the medical attention lavished during the past twenty years had reduced the extent of the disease, and particularly of its outward manifestation. Native syphilis assumed a 'new lesional orientation, visceral or nervous'. Such is the progress of institutions! In any case the number of venereal diseases at Rabat hospital dropped from 22 per cent in 1935 to 20 per cent in 1940. Subsequently, particularly since 1953, the incidence has declined dramatically, owing no doubt to the use of certain medicaments, but also to determined medical action and the psychological development of the people. Only 1 per cent are now hospitalized at Rabat.[4] These figures indicate an internal trend which has unfortunately been neglected by historians and sociologists.

What about malaria? In the history of North Africa it assumes a

[1] G. Lévy-Lebhar, *Maroc médical*, nos. 360, 379, 1956.
[2] Dr. Delanoë, ibid., no. 401, 1958.
[3] Cf. H. Gauthier, *Histoire de la syphilis nord-africaine*, 1931, with its copious bibliography, p. 111. Lépinay and Rollier, *Initiation à la pathologie humaine au Maroc*, 1955.
[4] Statistics kindly provided by Dr. Faraj.

peculiar aspect and importance, since it is essentially a scourge of the plains and thus afflicts the Bedouins, the speakers of Arabic, creating a balance of health in favour of those who live in the mountains. Now malaria itself is declining. On this point we must cite the admirable work of Charles Nicolle in Tunis, and that of the Pasteur Institute in Algiers. The story of the marshland of the Aulad Mandil and its gradual reabsorption, as told by Dr. Sergent, has an epic quality.

Now the fate of infectious disease in the Maghrib[1] is closely connected with that of its people. Typhus, scabies, syphilis and malaria darkened human existence with a sense of precariousness that was akin to a sense of guilt: connected, in any case, with the passive acceptance of fate, *maktub*. Disease jeopardized not only man's life but his historic and social dignity. Is there not a relation between the progress of society and the decline of these maladies? For the moment the question is unlikely to receive any clear answer. But I think it should be asked, in view of any future socio-biological study of the Maghrib.

Historic Nature of Forms

Going, perhaps, to the opposite extreme, one might study the variation in aesthetic attitudes. Modern anthropology attaches great importance to the life of forms. It is far from considering changes in fashion as a superficial triviality.

In Tunis today, young people of all origins mingle in the evening *paseo*. Muslim girls wear European dress with elegance, and their figures seem to adapt themselves to its changing fashions. Now at Fez, as late as 1939, earnest bourgeois petitioned the Pasha to forbid the wearing of that subversive garment, the *jellaba*. The vogue for this was spreading, and it had a pernicious reputation; it diminished the difference between men's and women's dress. This enfranchisement coincided with the first claims to political emancipation. Two kinds of history were thus inaugurated simultaneously. Today, now that some progress has been achieved in both spheres, woman once more asserts her difference from man, and moves even more rapidly in the direction of Westernization.

One might notice variations here too, and it would not, indeed, be fruitless to enquire into their secret. But one would have to forswear certain conceptions of North African ethnology, which has always considered these garments as being fixed once and for all, in conformity with the idea of a certain immutability. Now, on the contrary, I can see two categories of phenomena which reflect, during this period and even more during those that preceded it, an intimate and continuous movement of forms.

[1] To echo the title of a book by Dr. Ch. Nicolle.

The Moroccan slipper, the babouche, the classic *belgha*, as worn by women, was adorned with lavish embroidery on the uppers: this, the *sherbil*, sometimes became a work of art. Now the pattern, *taba'*, varied from one pair to another. It used to vary—as late as the thirties—from one fashion to another. The leading designers of Fez, at the beginning of each year, created, by means of cut-out cardboard, extremely elaborate patterns, all differing from one another,[1] like the models of our great couturiers. A well-dressed woman would never wear one of last year's patterns. New slippers were worn at canonical festivals; for the calendar of fashion coincided with the liturgical calendar. There might surely be some interesting conclusions to be drawn from an inventory of these designs. But who is going to prepare it?

The same remarks might be made about designs of lace, the open-work patterns on the body of the lute, and the cut and trimming of the *jellaba*. The form and colour of this tunic, in Morocco, were not left to chance; they varied from year to year. Observers have neglected this qualitative history, formerly for lack of sufficiently precise methods, and today for lack of material to investigate. It was, moreover, not confined to the towns. In the far south of Morocco, the Idaw Semlal tribe practised the goldsmith's craft.[2] Each *taqbilt* boasted its special type. This geographical distribution of forms is superimposed on that of language and other social facts. At Fez,[3] where gold ornaments were sold by weight at the auctions of the Suq al-Nuqra, we find other variations. No woman of fashion would wear the same jewel more than two years running: a biennial rhythm prevailed here. Every two years the goldsmiths put out new models; the well-to-do lady would collect her rings, her combs, her diadems and necklaces, and send them to be melted down and remodelled. It is certainly not by chance that the customs of the old city show these chronological sequences, whereas the Shleuh tribe displays topographical variety.[4]

The alternation between space and continuity provides the analyst with a key to the whole body of North African societies. We have not yet achieved these observations, unfortunately. For whoever succeeds in cataloguing these forms—fashions in dress and types of ornament[5]

[1] These models are directly cut out with a *shafra* or shoemaker's paring-knife. I had a large collection of them at Fez in 1937.

[2] I refer to the fine collection made in the South of Morocco, particularly among the Idaw Semlal, by Besancenot and Dj. Jacques-Meunié.

[3] Nietzsche, in the astonishing Excursus 215 of his *Traveller and his Shadow*, contrasts changing fashion and 'national' characteristics in dress and ornament.

[4] Two types of differentiation. Cf. my article in *Cahiers de l'Homme*, no. 1, 1961, 'Expression et signification dans la vie arabe'.

[5] We should study, in particular, the patterns of carpets, relatively more familiar thanks to G. Marçais, Aug. Berque, Golvin, Revault, etc. The multiplicity of ornament in the bedspreads of Gafsa might be an interesting field of research; also the strange embellishments of the *khnif* in the High Atlas.

among others—might discover illuminating correspondences with other spatial or temporal series, extending to customs and languages, ideas and even the chronicle of events.

Economic Fluctuations

This subtle duration, or continuity, too frequently escapes our clumsy grasp. We find it easier to distinguish more obvious forms. About economic continuity, for instance, everybody has something to say, because everybody either profits by or suffers from it. Some deplore it, others praise it. Thus René Lespès described Algeria as 'a country where they work very hard'.[1] He did not question the moral value or the perennial nature of such work; and yet he was no conformist, but a lucid and generous mind. The ports and industries of Morocco and its agriculture were being equipped in monumental fashion, to the admiration of foreign visitors. 'The face of Morocco,' people used to say at the time. It was indeed a façade, but behind it a deeper reality was taking shape. Tunisia was making similar progress. When Daladier visited the country in January 1939, every government department presented a statement of its activities. While allowing for official optimism, the work accomplished seems to have outweighed the failures, although these were considerable. High claims were made for this achievement, of which the French were at once the initiators, entrepreneurs, capitalists and technicians—and of course the principal beneficiaries; but one would like to see these claims substantiated by detailed accounts.

Even these, when they exist, neglect the relationship—which indeed is still obscure—between the natural setting and the economic initiative, on the one hand; between the traditional and modern sectors of production and consumption, on the other; and between the levels effectively attained and the levels aimed at, according to the antagonistic psychology of the groups involved. Now these three sets of relations, among others, and their variation in time, are what enable us to make a sound judgement. Unfortunately, on these points we have no critical synthesis on which to rely. No doubt, indictments were frequent at the time. But although bringing useful corrections to the official accounts, they are equally devoid of scientific foundation. One thing, however, seems well established, since it results from the definitions themselves. The colonial achievement, in the Maghrib, was not intended for, and only indirectly affected, the welfare of the country itself. Exploitation may have been frequently judicious and sometimes even benevolent, but it was always focused on unilateral advantage. It thus tended to disintegrate the body that it professed to serve. And simultaneously it was itself disintegrating. I have noted, in the preceding pages, deficiencies in the purely technical

[1] *Pour comprendre l'Algérie*, 1937, p. 209.

approach to problems. The imperfections of the economic administration are even more glaring. Serious observers, towards the end of the period we are studying here, were to indict not only the dangerous inequality of distribution, but the drop in the yield of certain agricultural products, the disastrous effects of protectionism and malthusianism, and the failure to organize any co-ordinated action.[1]

Having made these prejudicial observations, must we admit the thesis that the North African economy, taken as a whole, progressed between 1919 and 1940? Even on this point, it seems that some distinction should be made between products and between countries. In Algeria, for instance, the soil grew poorer.[2] During the thirty years from 1910 to 1940 the curve dropped sharply after 1919, recovered somewhat greater regularity after 1927, but remained below its pre-war level. In barley, the Muslim's staple crop, the individual quotient remained stationary (about a hundredweight). The curve of extractive industries followed the hazards of the world market. With regard to livestock, the production of sheep dropped from an average of 1·56 per head in 1920 to 0·89 per head for 1934; that of cattle from 0·973 to 0·828. The vine harvest, on the other hand, was doubled: a single source of wealth, yet one whose influence on the whole movement cannot be denied.[3]

Studies of consumption would lead one to make even more searching distinctions. Thus in Morocco, for the two periods 1931–5 and 1936–40, the individual quotient shows a rise, for cereals, from 2·8 to 3·3 quintals, and for meat (106 to 112, as against the index figure 100 in 1951), a slight drop for green tea (1·26 kg. to 1·19), sugar remaining stationary (23·5 kg).[4]

Elsewhere in this study will be found notes on some homogeneous series of data, for instance on energy production in the three countries (pp. 39 ff.) and on cereals in Morocco (pp. 232 ff.).

It is neither within the aims nor the scope of the present work to achieve a complete, or even a plausible, statement of the situation. The sociologist can obviously not embark on these difficult researches unless the economist has led the way. Does this mean that his project is irremediably compromised? In a study concerned with bringing to light relationships of function and significance, must the inadequacy of documentation on some particular element involved in these relationships mean the abandonment of the undertaking? I do not believe so. No doubt it would be more orthodox to await the elucidation of these particular

[1] Cf. pp. 292 ff.
[2] Cf. *Algérie*, 1938, no. 12, p. 23. Emile Miège, in Morocco, notes a decrease in yield, over thirty years, from 6,48 to 6,3 quintals for hard wheat; 8,2 to 6,4 for soft wheat; 7,7 to 6,9 for barley; maize, however, rises from 4,2 to 4,6.
[3] Unpublished notes by M. Hincker.
[4] Id., ibid.

points, and this attitude would follow if one considered social history as a mere step towards history as sum-total. But the recent progress, in France, of an inclusive, *global* sociology, the stress laid on the role of structures, justify a more precocious endeavour. Without going so far as to say of social facts what Meillet once said jokingly of words, that they have no meaning but only functions, and while on the contrary seeking for the concrete references which alone give life to historic forms, I shall quote a few economic facts of the period, which although inadequately studied and incompletely classified, have their significance in the movement of the whole.

Apart from the economic process in the strict sense of the term–the monetary flux, the production and displacement of goods–the relationships in which this involves individuals and groups amongst themselves, on the one hand, and towards nature on the other, have their own importance. The variation in the market price of characteristic articles –oil, wine, tea, mutton–has immediate repercussions on differentiated attitudes. During times of stability, a tacit correspondence seems to connect the price of grain per quintal with that of a sheep, and with that of a day's labour. At times of crisis, this is disturbed. Social concord or bitterness result from these shifts. Economic fluctuation thus connects the worldwide movements of quantity with cycles of emotion and behaviour of which concrete local instances can be found. The same interaction is noticeable in the workings of an institution which plays a more direct and obvious part under the colonial system than in the parent state, namely the capitalist firm. If one were to note the Stock Market quotation of North African shares from 1919 to 1940 one would probably have a useful quantitative index. If one could concurrently establish the variations in wages and living standards in areas of production and in areas of consumption, this three-term relationship would describe the colonial economy more precisely than has been done hitherto. My study cannot aspire to such precision. From the sparse data I have collected, nevertheless, a rhythm emerges; and that was all I sought from them here.

The general conclusion, in four cases chosen somewhat at random, is a noticeable drop in constant money in relation to the pre-war era. The system, although offering huge benefits to its adherents,[2] may have been growing poorer itself. But this indication is of too general a nature to concern us here. More striking is the fluctuation of market prices. The post-war recovery once established (1923), the evolution continues as described below (expressed in 1914 francs).

[1] Unpublished notes by M. Hincker.
[2] The Keroulis company distributed between 26 and 29,9 million francs profit (*Revue des valeurs de l'Afrique du Nord*, March 1931.)

Year	Mukta al Hadid	Wanza	Keroulis	Chapeau de Gendarme
1925	1,292	867		245
1926		926	143	83
1928	1,766		232	
1929				
1930				
1934	535	87		
1937	795	232	87	26
1938				

Although the cycles undergone by two mining companies and two agricultural companies respectively cannot be collated exactly, the alternation of expansion followed by recession, then by recovery, is clearly evident.

Let us check this first impression by examining more numerous cases borrowed from the annual reports of Administrative Councils.[1]

The Algerian Society of Chemical Products and Fertilizers, established in 1906, and concerned with providing articles closely connected with the development of vine-growing: artificial fertilizers, hydrochloric acid, tartaric products—underwent a severe crisis after two brilliant financial years (1919 and 1920).[2] The same is true of many other firms which, in 1919, proceeded to substantial increases in capital: Juan Bastos, the famous cigarette company, the Algerian Company, the Franco-Moroccan Omnium, etc. In 1921 the Algerian Agricultural Society, although it had concentrated on the exploitation of two great domains instead of the sixteen it had initially acquired, showed an overdraft.[3] The U.C.I.A. (Union Commerciale Indochinoise et Africaine), in Morocco, had to withdraw from large-scale undertakings, which then slowed down, and to concentrate in commercial activities.[4] But the competition of trading firms accentuated the stagnation: the Moroccan Company had to admit to a deficit for the financial year 1921–2.[5]

Things settled down after that. A subsidiary company of the Banque de Paris et des Pays-Bas, the Compagnie Générale du Maroc (founded in 1912), a firm remarkable for the multiplicity of its undertakings, registered a net profit of 1,414,000 francs for the year 1912.[6] A good harvest

---

[1] Most of the following figures are taken from the *Revue des valeurs de l'Afrique du Nord* published by the Crédit foncier d'Algérie et de Tunisie. The economic historian of North Africa, lacking ready-made materials, should take his soundings retrospectively, like W. L. Thorp, by examining newspapers, reviews and consular reports 'in order to obtain a sort of global diagnosis of the economic situation in any given year'. But we cannot reconstruct the Business Annals of the Colonial Maghrib with any degree of accuracy! Cf. A. Piatier, *Statistique et observation économique*, 1961, vol. II, p. 591.

[2] RVAN, July 1931.   [3] RVAN, April 1925.
[4] RVAN, Feb. 1925.   [5] RVAN, March 1926.
[6] RVAN, Jan. 1927. The net profit for 1925 was 1,271,610 f 50.

made 1925 a profitable year for the Bank of Algeria, which issued loans on mortgage.[1] Mukta al-Hadid decided, on 10 March 1925, to increase capital by dividing up its old shares. Shares were then worth 4,950 francs. The credit statement, moreover, underestimated prosperity. Real shares were redeemed at 95 per cent. Owing to the amount of shares held by industry (250 million) this Association ranked as a general trading company.[2]

The polyvalence of firms is of course a generic feature, but in the Maghrib and especially in Morocco it assumed exaggerated proportions.[3] We should distinguish, however, between mines, which as we have seen were subject to the hazards of the world market, concessionary societies which reflect the influence of their Board of Directors more directly in profits[4] and agricultural societies, which follow the fortunes of colonization.

In any case, the depression which started in 1925 was to last ten years. It did not, indeed, involve the same difficulties for everyone. The variation in its effects was due in many cases to the inequality[5] in colonial speculation referred to above. The Moroccan Company, which in 1924–5 made 813,000 francs, made 5,199,000 in 1930–1 and 3,000,000 in 1932–3.[6] But in 1930 the Algerian Society of Chemical Products registered a drop of 11 per cent compared with 1929. The Bank of Algeria expressed grave anxiety at its general meeting on 27 December 1930[7] and again at its meeting on 26 November 1931. Worse still at that on 24 November 1932. The State Bank of Morocco had urgently to refloat colonial enterprises, which were in debt for over 500 million (1930). Its twenty-fourth financial year was a poor one. The dividends were no less than 160 francs per share.[8]

Recovery, from 1934–5 onward, was due in part to State measures of organization (Cereals Office) and huge injections of credit.[9] These were of unequal benefit to the parties involved. Moroccan colonization,

[1] RVAN, Feb. 1926. In 1900, faced with the risk of insolvency due to the depreciation of securities, the Bank was forced to refuse to accept directly the bills of Agricultural Banks. But it erected an elaborate credit system by means of intermediaries.

[2] RVAN, March 1925.

[3] Denounced by the left-wing press. Cf. for instance *Libération*, Casablanca 1945, *Tunis-Socialiste*, etc.

[4] For example the C.T.M. in Morocco, the Énergie Électrique at Bizerta, etc. The C.T.M. was founded, and granted a monopoly, on 22 Nov. 1919. Its capital rose from 5 million at that date to 40 million in 1931 (RVAN, April 1932). In 1930 it distributed 9,146,000 francs' profit. The dividends of the Énergie électrique rose, in relation to its capital, to 10 per cent in 1931 (RVAN, Dec. 1931).

[5] Economic history will have to analyse this inequality.

[6] Between 1919 and 1925 the Compagnie Marocaine distributed almost 12 million francs, as against the initial capital of 20 (RVAN, Jan. 1927).

[7] RVAN, Jan. 1931.

[8] RVAN, August 1931.

[9] Board of Directors of the Crédit Foncier d'Algérie et de Tunisie, 20 May 1937.

literally inflated, owed 232,453,000 francs in 1936 (about 500 per cultivated hectare).[1] Meanwhile the price of wheat per hundredweight had collapsed. In August 1934, when the Maghrib's economy seems to have touched rock bottom, the price of cattle seems to have diminished by 50 per cent compared with 1931 and 20 per cent in gold value compared with 1913.[2]

Financial years after 1936 show a recovery, partly due to the revalorization of production. There was a normal rise in cereals. An improvement in early vegetables, olives, citrus fruits; measures were taken to reorganize finances thoroughly. In 1937, North Africa benefited by poor harvests in the parent state. The Crédit Foncier noted 'a liquidation of the consequences of the crisis'.[3] When war began, the Maghrib was in a state of economic euphoria.

The general trend of the curve would be further confirmed if, instead of collecting scattered indications, we confined ourselves to the successive estimates of the economic situation made by a single institution. Thus the Reports of the Algerian Company[4] show the same fluctuation; 1920–1, severe crisis; then growing improvement, up till 1925; ten years of worsening depression; then recovery from 1934–5 onwards.

The Significance and Shape of Colonial History

Continuity, which can be recognized in the slightest as in the weightiest of facts, is thus bound up, to an extent and through connections which often escape us, with more substantial, although secret, movements: such as the physiology of men's bodies; with others, measurable and largely material, such as economics and demography; and with others, finally, which though wholly abstract are self-conscious and even self-assertive, such as the rise of political awareness. This mutual involvement and this infinite diversity both belong to history, in the sense that they reflect a process of becoming and a succession in time. But they are also structural, in the sense that they conform to certain social and mental configurations. They require another sort of distinction, that which might be made between the collective patterns which their progress follows, and the overflowing life that surrounds them.

For life is redundant and profuse.[5] And particularly life in North Africa, where because of and in spite of colonization, behaviour tends

[1] Report of the Crédit foncier d'Algérie et de Tunisie, 28 May 1932.

[2] *Débats parlementaires*, p. 2511, 22 Nov. 1934.

[3] Report of 30 June 1938.

[4] The reports of the Bank of Algeria, the State Bank of Morocco, the Crédit Foncier d'Algérie et de Tunisie and the Banque de Paris et des Pays-Bas give the same impression.

[5] As is language itself, from which modern anthropology seeks many analogical indications.

to be arbitrary, evasive, exaggerated, risky, absurd or, in more general terms, irregular. Sexuality for instance, the aesthetic enjoyment of the moment, quiet introspection or loud-mouthed extravagance each, no doubt, reflect subtle compensations, but in other respects are pure play, autonomous self-indulgence.

It is difficult to distinguish clearly between what is affected and what is neglected by colonial history. One paradoxical result is that in their respective situations, each of the two opposing groups may refuse to admit the other's place in history. By his actions as well as through his knowledge, the European disputes the native's share in the evolution which is taking place under his eyes and which he has to a large extent provoked. He reacts with authoritarian conservatism to archaic, traditionalist Muslim attitudes; he explains them by an ethnography that is obsessed with the primitive, or by a pluralistic psychology. On the other hand, the European often appears to the native merely as a *deus ex machina*, a god or rather a devil brought forth by the machine, a tempter and a destroyer, incapable of human adaptability. Utilitarian requirements on the one side, metaphysical prescriptions on the other thus prevented the two opponents from understanding the history confronting them. Great progress would have to be made, great sufferings undergone before either side would consent to admit the other's participation . . . It is true that by then the depth of men's feelings, the violence of their acts was to confer on history an anthropological dimension. When that time came, generosity and cruelty, sexual ardour and revolutionary faith, critical awareness and tumultuous passion would be fused in the same violence . . .

That point had not yet been reached in the inter-war period, the apogee of the colonial order. Although subsequent situations existed there in embryo and although many of the feelings later displayed can be obscurely traced there, the period is remarkable chiefly for the way it mastered, repressed or evaded them. Life in the Maghrib from 1919 to 1939 cannot be seen entirely in terms of the colonial relationship. The latter did not influence everything that it affected, nor, on the other hand, can it be held responsible for everything. On the French side, and still more on the Muslim side, many human beings, things, situations and events remained unconnected, or apparently unconnected with the colonial system, despite its tendency to ubiquity. It is a characteristic of colonialism that, although its methods are grandiose and its consequences all-embracing, it has only partial mastery or understanding of itself. Its hypotheses, unlike those of nationalism, are too small for it. Thus one cannot interpret solely in relation to its vicissitudes an existence of far wider significance.

Any analysis aiming at completeness is therefore obliged to contradict itself. Impressed by a violence that extends political passion into the sphere of human relations and eventually involves everything—God and sex included—with it, the historian is tempted to apply the polemical simplifications of his own day to the past. Not only, at the time we are concerned with, was decolonization not under way or even in prospect, but colonization dominated everything. Only a few bold spirits at that time defied it, only a few pioneers realized its fragility. Is this to be wondered at? These difficult analyses, these distinctions are easy for us to make today, in retrospect! At the time, such tenuous, if decisive, things were not recognized. That is the paradox of human behaviour. The conflict between fundamental realities is not clearly apparent to those who are living through it. The characteristic of that moment, which the historian seeks to recreate from a distance, filling it with the greatest possible amount of reality, is that it comprises hesitation between various judgments and choices, combining determinism, voluntary commitment and gratuitous action in the same existential fervour.

Stages of Historic Enlightenment

And yet from this confusion there emerges a global continuity, a duration, which affects the conflict between these two nations for the construction of a country and the quality of its life.

The great mass of the people are immediately aware, in their hearts, of the phases through which this conflict is passing. For, thanks to the living experience which, in so many ways, misleads them, they feel things rightly although they may not see them clearly. This restores significance to events, which, considered from a distance, are concealed by long-term realities and the long cycles of history. Lacking analyses, which were too little practised at the time,[1] only the intuition of individuals and that of groups occasionally casts that flash of light that pierces the darkness and reveals for a brief instant the elusive future behind the ambiguous present; and this focuses our attention once more on leaders and parties. Finally, we must also reckon with the influence of methodologies and themes. These seem to be carried along by a vitality peculiar to themselves, which makes some of them irresistible. Those, such as Socialism, which attain a certain degree of systematization, find it hard, none the less, to make contact with a reality whose strength lies in its very unintelligibility.

For a long time everything happened in North Africa as if the national movement expected more from France than from itself. What it was seeking, actually, during that score of years, was to secure freedom of movement within the system. No doubt it could not do anything else. But that is why, too, it so often seems to be arguing a case in law. The

[1] On the earliest 'modernist' Muslim historians, whose replacement of the old type of chronicler is highly revealing, see S. Bencheneb, 'Quelques historiens arabes modernes de l'Algérie,' *R. africaine*, 1956, pp. 475 ff.

pamphlet inspired by Shaikh Tha'alibi, *Tunisia's Martyrdom* (1920) takes a historical and constitutional point of view. The author puts forward not those metaphysical claims for which the Neo-Destour was later to criticize him, but a Beylical constitution granted long before the Protectorate. For Tunisia, in short, can claim priority in the constitutional history of the Mediterranean South even over Egypt. The question was thus, at the start, a temporal and even a legal one. The author blames the Protectorate for having abolished the said charter, in short for rendering absolute a power which had not been so. His criticism of colonization is more naïve. It would no doubt be a fruitful undertaking to see in what measure the facts alleged were correct at that time. For the author blames colonization not only for its noxious symbolism, which can hardly be denied, but also for technical failure, or at least incapacity, in terms of total growth, and that remains to be checked. In any case, the importance allotted to these rural problems reveals the shaikh's correct estimate, indeed his foresight, of the effort made subsequently by the Protectorate in favour of official colonization.

A very different note is struck by Muhammed 'Ali,[1] a former chauffeur, who had lived long expatriate and returned to Tunisia in 1924, armed with a German degree in political economy. He had followed the campaign of the intellectuals from abroad; it had given him certain illusions about the country's degree of maturity. On his return, he admits to feeling disappointment[2] at the precedence taken by political issues. The masses must be built up, he declares. He uses a specific mixture of Marxist criticism, nationalism and Arab taste. His biographer Haddad depicts him walking by night through the Madina, shocked at the resigned attitude of those proletarians who have to sleep in the streets and who yet accept 'God's decree', but above all, sorry for them. He carries revolt so far as to repudiate traditional Eastern music, which he holds guilty of weakening the national movement.[3] The tyranny of mastercraftsmen horrifies him as much as that of modern employers. He even objects to the C.G.T's monopoly, on the subject of which he had a considerable controversy with Durel.

On 12 October 1924, a meeting of regional syndicates founded, at Bizerta, a Confédération Générale du Travail Tunisien. It opened battle with a joint strike of the industrial workers of Hammam-Lif and the agricultural workers of Pothinville. Arrests were made; dissension followed between the Socialists, who were against secession, and the Communists, who were in favour of it. 'A plot against the security of the State . . .'

For the first time, a Tunisian militant shows some concern about the concrete bases of a demand. The historian discovers to his surprise in

---

[1] I refer here particularly to Tahar al-Haddad's book *al-'Ummal al-tunisiyun*, 1927.

[2] Ibid., p. 32.   [3] Ibid., p. 131. But is he not responsive to this music?

Haddad's book, with reference to the Bizerta dockers' struggle, what we should describe today as a study of living standards.[1] A certain traditionalism debars Muhammad 'Ali from referring to the class struggle,[2] though this may be tactical prudence on his part. In any case, he failed to rally the Old Destour,[3] who dropped him in a rather shocking fashion. He could not avoid condemnation, nor further exile.[4] We know too little about his story, as indeed about the whole development of proletarian conditions in the Maghrib[5] before, during and after his time, to attribute to him other merits than that of being a pioneer. That, however, is considerable.

When Haddad published his book on the Tunisian woman,[6] which is so much in advance of his country and of his time, it incurred almost universal disapproval, even from those who were subsequently to assume the most liberal attitude in this matter. The tone of the book is emotional. In the first part the author defends the Islamic conception of the family and of woman. He confronts conservative prejudices with the concept of a purified Islam. In the second part, he contrasts this doctrine with the deplorable practices of the time. His description is often crude and doubtless truthful. But its statistical part needs to be checked; how much was survival, and how much the general rule? Ethnologists might have taken advantage of testimony of this kind to complete, from within, studies too often exclusively external. Haddad compares woman to 'a family treasure, covered with dust'. He protests indignantly against those practices to which 'we men of the Maghrib cling in despite of the beliefs and habits bequeathed us by our mysterious history, mistakenly quoting the authority of Islam.' These remarks provoked a storm. Womanhood is one of those sanctuaries that still harbour the personality of the Maghrib. This was made evident when Sulaiman al-Jadhi[7] protested indignantly about an address to Muslim ladies made by Mme Lucien Saint. He saw therein an attempt at moral domination. 'Nationhood is a secret guarded by woman' who remain 'the ultimate foundation of our social edifice.' Pious people solemnly discussed whether it was *haram*,[8] forbidden, to listen to women's voices, or whether women ought

[1] Ibid., p. 99.

[2] I note one passage to this effect, ibid., p. 124-5.

[3] Habib Bourguiba, *La Tunisie et la France*, p. 381. A second wave of Tunisian syndicalism, led by Bilgasim Guenaoui (Qanawi), ended in compromise (Feb. 1938)

[4] He died a few years later in Hijaz, in a car accident. More light needs to be shed on his singular life-story.

[5] Not only those of the urban worker, but also of the *Khamis*.

[6] *Imra'atuna al-tunisiya*, Tunis.

[7] *Al-Fawa'id al-jamma*, p. 221 (extract reproduced from the *Murshid al-Umma*).

[8] *Imra'atuna al-tunisiya*, *al-'Alam al-adabi*, 1936, p. 25 (with reference to the controversies of Shaikh al-Khidr). On the evolution of Moroccan woman, *Majallat al-Maghrib*, March 1936.

to learn to write.[1] That such questions should be debated during the whole of the inter-war period, sometimes in reputedly progressive publications, is characteristic of the period, in contrast to that which followed it. In any case, the public outcry that arose in Tunis at that time reveals, very clearly, the passage from one set of symbols to another: from the ritual to the historic, and correspondingly from introspective withdrawal to expansion.

Meanwhile, however, antagonistic passions and ideals were focused less on the working-class or on womanhood than on other symbols, pregnant with controversial values. Such, in Algeria in the thirties, was that 'status' which soon lost much of its objective content, but was all the more significant on that account, as a token. Indeed, those who clamoured for status had no intention of maintaining a polygamy which belonged to the past and was no longer practised, nor even a religious right of which the civil side had become obsolete, once French law had curtailed it. If Algerians fought ardently in support of their claims to the 'citizenship without loss of personal status', it was out of loyalty to themselves. They clung to a sign. And paradoxically, the *colons*' party, for the reverse reasons, exaggerated the significance of the same symbol, which it declared incompatible with French citizenship. No one was more respectful than the *colon* towards those Qur'anic traditions which might prevent the indigenous masses from flooding into the French electorate! A few years later (1931) Ferhat Abbas (Farhat 'Abbas) published a collection of articles under the title *Young Algerian*, which utter a fervent plea for justice and equality. 'Justice and loyalty first, politics afterwards' is the title of the last chapter, which might be taken merely as a reformist or 'meliorist' petition. But let us look closer. Sadly restricted though their numbers were, the Western-educated Algerian élite embodied that assimilation to which the system paid lip-service. But this only made their inequality more intolerable. Their statements, putting the problem in rational terms, *à la française*, acquire overwhelming force from stressing the discrepancy that lay between being alike and being equal. At that time, to identify oneself with France was revolutionary, since it meant demanding liberty to the exclusion of any pluralistic alibi. And this demand, which was both a preliminary to Algerian nationalism and a result of familiarity with the ideas of 1789, contains seeds which proved valid for Algeria's emancipation and for what was to come after.

Meanwhile another movement, that of the '*Ulama*', made claims that were spiritual and moral in character, rather than political. It sought, sometimes unconsciously, to preserve the anthropological significance of the problem. A study of the various movements of the period would thus lead to a study of the psychical and social levels to which each belongs. There was undoubtedly a political movement which hesitated,

[1] Mubarak al-Mili, 'Ta'lim al-mar'a al-kitaba', *Shihab*, April-Sept. 1936.

with uncertain force, between Viollette's reformism and the immobilism which was ultimately to prevail. But other movements affected wider and less clearly defined spheres. I have mentioned that of the '*Ulama*'; there was also the first Syndicalist movement of Tunisia, the feminism of H 'addâd, the plebeian action group of the Étoile Nord Africaine.

In the middle of the decade during which these problems were being faced, there occurred the Centenary of the Capture of Algiers. The celebrations held on this occasion, as I shall later show, contributed not a little to the hardening of attitudes. At the same time these Centenary demonstrations, the promulgation of the Berber *dahir* (edict) and the Eucharistic Congress of Carthage fostered euphoria in some, resentment in others, and in every case, the fear or hope of radical solutions. Almost immediately afterwards, the world crisis shook the Maghrib.

Enduring Factors in Maghrib Life

Here we have to recognize economic fluctuation once again. Is it by chance that these diverse political and social hypotheses were being put forward during the depressive phase that we have noted? On this analogy, 1934, when the cycle reversed itself, ought also to constitute a fresh political start. And in fact, it was in 1934 that the Youth of Morocco published a Plan of Reforms of which one Resident[1] declared that 'it would make an excellent Doctor's thesis.' Its courteous, insidious tone is that of young men of the bourgeoisie, many of them members of the city's greatest families. They owed their precocious maturity to hereditary leadership. The reforms they proposed in no wise criticized the international engagements undertaken by the Monarchy, but sought to ensure that these were faithfully carried out. This was to be their position for the next ten years, during which time the Protectorate let slip its opportunity, and the Moroccan nation grew to maturity.

The armed resistance of Moroccan tribes to French penetration ended in 1934. Now, other phenomena were taking place at the time. In Algeria, Muslim and European workers united in demonstrations, organized by the C.G.T., the Trade Union movement, on a scale hitherto unknown. At Constantine, for the first time in any town in the colonial Maghrib, the insurgents carried the day in street fighting. This tumultuous movement was to grow, not only in Algeria but in Morocco (1935, 1936, 1937) and in Tunis, where the most serious of these conflicts broke out in 1938. The masses took over political action from the tribes, whose day was past. They included all sorts of incongruous elements, with nothing in common, apparently, but the disruption of their social background: bourgeois who had lost caste, dispossessed and uprooted peasants, unemployed artisans. A few years earlier these indivi-

[1] H. Ponsot, it is said.

duals in revolt against tradition, these outsiders, would have found shelter in the silent fold of mysticism. Now they were welcomed by working-class movements and political parties. For parties were growing rapidly, with the development of the Neo-Destour in Tunis and the *Hizb al-Watani* in Morocco, even, in certain cases, of Socialism. The more advanced of the younger generation were aware of the terrible power of the mob; terrible for its opponent and also for itself. To what might not this violence lead? Late in 1937, to everyone's surprise, there was the El-Menzel (Al-Manzil) incident. An illiterate Berber group, hitherto thought to be completely impervious to urban disturbances, attacked its own caïd. Unheard-of audacity! For the mass of country dwellers, particularly those of Berber origin, had long provided, and was for long afterwards to provide, the Western power with its most profitable field of action, its easily-won plebiscite. But henceforward the 'Young men' (*shabiba*), as they called themselves, were to endeavour to arouse the emotions of this mass, thus explaining it to itself. The battle over the control of the rural masses was on between the *shabiba* and the administration. The Islam of the marabouts, long protected by a primitive form of resistance, was replaced, under the leadership of increasingly active crowds, by a reformist, modernist Islam. In other words, there was competition for the conquest of the irrational breakwaters of North Africa.

Then the economic curve began to rise again. Money reappeared. Much capital was invested in the country, became incorporated in it and increased its importance. But the price paid was an insistent, sometimes suspect quest for the means of prosperity, or rather the means of acquiring wealth. And in this ostensibly uninterrupted progress there occurred, at a point that is hard to specify, a qualitative change. I am not implying that the mass of the Maghribi people did not benefit by economic progress (leaving aside for the moment the theoretical argument about pauperization). But except for a handful of initiates, they were not truly affected by it; any advantage they gained thereby was only indirect and general. Farseeing or generous observers were rightly alarmed; but they were wrong to see no other remedy than an increase of material welfare, or even a juster distribution of goods. These would have been inadequate. Not only did the French achievement in the Maghrib, substantial as it was, fail to win the adherence of the Maghribi himself, but it suffered from a fundamental divorce between the physical and the mental, between the economic field in its narrowest sense and life in its fullest sense. Indeed in the most recent period, such progress as was made in administrative methods, far from serving the cause of France, provoked a keener challenge to it.

Henceforward a growing divergence was apparent between returning prosperity and worsening dissension. The former fostered the latter, owing to a truly revolutionary divorce between material realities and their meaning.

Simultaneously, concrete factors and the interpretation given to them, the actual forces involved and the feeling aroused by them, the successes and failures of the administration, the victories and defeats of the opposition, all concurred to bring a crisis to a head. The strangest phenomena combined, as it turned out, to give decisive significance to the coming struggle.

The French régime which, to a large extent, had justified itself by the acceleration it had imposed on local conditions, came to see itself principally as a brake, as *something opposing*. It had ceased to accelerate; to use a neologism. it had begun to 'decelerate'. Meanwhile the very improvements in its technique, which had multiplied during the second part of this period, seemed to be working the wrong way. The *bled*, the rural areas, came increasingly to look towards the towns. The emphasis in North African life had hitherto been chiefly on the countryside. The conflict between the Administrator and the tribe, and between the pioneer settler and the Berber-Arab workman or fellah, had formed its essential part. From the thirties onwards it was in the towns that things were to happen. And the towns began to sprawl disproportionately. The population figures, hitherto kept down by social disease and infantile mortality, soared up. The upheaval in ways of life, the sharpening of conflicts, correspond to this altered rhythm.

After a certain stage, we find on every side an intensification not of disorder, indeed, nor of ethnic of even political hatred–these terms were not yet applicable–but of a fundamental set of problems.[1] These were put in Algeria about 1930 by Ferhat Abbas, Maurice Viollette and the '*Ulama*', more or less simultaneously; in Tunisia, particularly after 1934, by Bourguiba; and in Morocco at about the same time by the intelligentsia. Now their appeal, though still respectfully made, was dismissed in all three countries in the early thirties. One can scarcely tax the proconsuls with inexperience–J. Carde at Algiers, M. Peyrouton at Tunis or H. Ponsot at Rabat. A specialist such as Augustin Bernard collaborated in drawing up the Regnier decree, which replied to native claims by a strengthening of the Government's repressive powers; whether we attribute this to the pressure of local *colon* groups, to that of conservatives in the parent state, which itself was alarmed by Hitler's rise to power, or the advice of 'colonization technicians', France's choice seems to have been a deliberate one.

As it happened, it was a very serious one. The events which followed, in 1936, 37 and 38, inaugurated the cycle of ever more violent repression, which provoked ever more radical demands. The consequences are not yet exhausted, even today. But the die was cast in 1935. History, at that

---

[1] The quarrel that broke out over Maurice Viollette's book *L'Algérie vivra-t-elle?* (1931) is highly revealing of these.

moment, crossed a threshold. In all North Africa there was no material or moral phenomenon, on either side of that threshold, which did not reveal some change in rhythm or in quality.

Here we must close this initial study of the Maghrib during the inter-war period. It has afforded us a preliminary catalogue of the people and forces involved, the issues at stake and the rhythm of the contest. It has shown us on what a wide variety of planes history operates, and the complex way it is involved with daily life. We must now study these first results in detail and in depth.[1] First by examining the local realities that illustrate this history:[2] an undertaking which, obviously, might be indefinitely extended. I shall then resume the story from the time of the Centenary, after which the issues are more clearly formulated and fate quickens its pace.[3] I shall conclude by attempting–but surely I should have begun by doing so?–to define the phenomenology of a world now obsolete,[4] that Maghrib which carried the burden of its unsolved problems right up till the second world war.

[1] This method, consisting in an analysis of the same reality from three different angles in succession will involve apparent repetitions, which I shall endeavour to limit as far as possible by gradually leading my account towards its logical and chronological end ('The Maghrib, from its past to its future').

[2] Cf. p. 118 ff.   [3] Cf. p. 215 ff.   [4] Cf. p. 297 ff.

Part 2

Fragments of Local History

CHAPTER IV

Tribes

H istorical knowledge, and their own actions, have brought the Berbers' name into such disrepute that today the mere mention of it calls for reservations. However, if we still have to protect ourselves against this sort of sea-monster, we need not reject such reality as is ascribed to it by serious oceanographers.[1] While many Berbers persist in geographical retreats where centuries-old survivals abound, others have invaded the cities: the Kabyles in Algiers or the suburbs of Paris, the Shleuhs in Casablanca. They thus offer extreme examples for any study of North African types. Extreme in both senses: archaism and progress, collective solidarity and individualism, the highest spontaneity and the utmost derivativeness, even artificiality. This wealth, or excess, of reactions can moreover not be dissociated from a twofold historical repression, imposed first by the Arabs, then by the French. But although complex—indeed for that very reason—the case offers valuable elements to the analyst. Earlier, speaking of the sedentary inhabitants of the High Atlas, I showed what precise relations governed their collective life, their organization of space and time. Another group of Berbers must now supply the most highly characteristic example of a fundamental type of group and of economy: the tribe.

A morphology of the traditional groups of North Africa can distinguish between them from the start, according to their greater or lesser degree of adherence to the land. On the one hand, the high mountain

---

[1] The first important studies by what we might call the School of Rabat (Henri Basset, Henri Terrasse, Emile Laoust), followed by the work of R. Montagne, have renewed our knowledge of North Africa, particularly through the discoveries made in Berber territory. J. Célérier has made a searching study of the Middle Atlas, especially of transhumance. These discoveries have given rise to strange 'psychological' deductions. For instance J. Ladreit de Lacharrière, 'La création marocaine', *Temps*, 27 Dec. 1929; P. Mille, 'Croquis marocains', ibid, 14 Aug. 1930; this is the atmosphere of the famous *dahir*.

cantors, the *taqbilt* of the Shleuhs or the *tufik* of the Kabyles,[1] dense and closely self-contained; on the other, the widely roaming Tuareg. In between these two types there are many intermediate varieties, speaking Berber or Arabic, all in process of becoming sedentary, and each with its particular position in this wide variety of human types. Whether he takes root in a few acres of mountainside, or wanders over the vast arid spaces, the traditional Maghribi can primarily be defined by this relation with space. The greater or lesser extension of these groups, even though most of them are nowadays fixed at a certain stage of development, within a certain type, and over a determined area, constitutes a decisive element in their aspect. Even the most recent developments, such as the growth of the urban population and the emigration of workers, form part of the same series of types because they imply the same kind of relation between the behaviour of the group and the extent of its base.

Except for the two last-named phenomena, whose connection with the earlier ones had not been stressed by Colonial ethnologists,[2] this homogeneity struck all observers to the point of seeming to call for a comprehensive explanation. The Bedouin accounted for their own society in genetic terms, asserting common ancestry and the diffusion of descendants; French commentators substitute the hypothesis of migration. The present state of North Africa would thus be the result of a series of conflicts between sects, of transferences of population, of ethnic intermixtures.[3] Finally a third explanation, which might be described as structural, made its timid appearance.[4] It stressed lexicographical alternations, or curious cases of constancy in anthroponymy from one end of the Maghrib to the other. From the same viewpoint, other series of facts needed to be considered in conjunction: the 'symphonic' partitioning of the High Atlas, the division into two leagues (*saffs* or *liffs*) of many of its settlements, and finally the interconnection of the names of 'races' that appear in Ibn Khaldun's history: Zanata, Masmuda, etc. As a result of considerations which I cannot discuss again here, I came to view the North African tribe as a compromise between social groupings and contemporary history, between a certain form of logic and the data of the *milieu*.[5] The same compromise can be seen there in detail between agnatic ancestrality and relationship by marriage, between consanguinity and topography, status and contract. One can understand the

[1] M. Larnaude, 'Le groupement de la population berbère dans la Kabylie de Djurdura', *Cinquantenaire de la Faculté des Lettres d'Alger*, 1932, p. 269.

[2] L. Massignon and Colonel Justinard, however, at an early date showed the connection between the grouping of Berber workers in the Parisian district and their traditional habitat.

[3] This is the thesis of A. Bernard and N. Lacroix: *L'Évolution du nomadisme en Algérie*, 1906.

[4] Suggested in W. Marçais's masterly review of E. F. Gautier's *Siècles obscurs du Maghreb*. I have further developed the hypothesis myself.

[5] 'Qu'est-ce qu'une tribu nord-africaine', *L'éventail de l'histoire*, 1953.

vitality of this type which the French administration, owing to unforeseen circumstances, was forced to accept. For the 'Arab bureau' adopted tribalism; therein lies the secret of its past successes and its irremediable obsolescence.

Enormous Berber-speaking populations cover the Middle Atlas: the Zayan, an avid and bellicose 'confederation'; the Ait Yusi, broken up into three sections, those of Enjil, Guigu and the Mekla; the Ait Seghrushen, intermingling with the Ait Yusi and spreading out beyond them to the south; the Ait Shokhman, the Ait Wirra of warlike memory, around Ksiba. The inland roads are difficult, though much travelled over. The road from Fez, the *madina* which is the cultural centre, southwards to the Tafilalt, with the Sahara and even black Africa in the far distance, crosses the heart of the mountain mass over heights that are frequently covered in snow. Another road, taken by those who pacified the country, approaches the mountain mass at an angle from Meknes to El-Hajeb. At Azru[1] it meets the great mountain road which nowadays connects Fez and Marrakesh. The population groups found in these regions in the early days of the Protectorate call to mind their previous dwellings in the south-east and even in the middle of the Sahara. The Zemmur, who today live in the Mamora region not far from Rabat, inhabited the High Ziz a thousand years ago.[2] The Gueruan, from the neighbourhood of Meknes, came from the Tafilalt. Ma'qil Arabs, poor relations of the Bani Hilal, succeeded in penetrating the massif. Today there are Bani Ahsin in the Gharb. The Ait Yusi had hounded them, to the south of Fez, throughout the seventeenth century. The life of the Berber scholar al-Yusi illustrates some episodes of this struggle, which gradually drove the Arab group towards the North-west.[3] The Za'ir, at the gates of Rabat, are also descended from the Ma'qil. Thus the geographical division that runs from the Tafilalt to Rabat is a line of historic movements, spread out over hundreds, indeed thousands of years.

But let us turn to a briefer, more breathless chronicle, that of the interwar period. Three principal events stand out. On 27 March 1921, the great chief Moha u Hammu fell in the battle of Azlaghen Tazemmurt, shot by a band of pro-French Zayan that included his own sons. About 1933–4 sharp conflicts broke out, due to the effort of the Marmusha to continue their traditional transhumance in the Meknes region. In 1937 official reports regretfully note the first blows struck by nationalism at what was then called the 'Berber bloc'. French penetration, which had been increasingly persistent since 1920, was at that time barely completed. It had reached its terminal point in 1933, beyond the Plateau of the

---

[1] Through the 'lunar landscape' of Itto.

[2] Lesne, thesis on *Les Zemmour*.

[3] J. Berque, *Al-Yousi, problèmes de la culture marocaine au XVIᵉ siècle*, 1957, ch. II.

Lakes, near Jebel Sargho. It had lasted over twenty years. Not without difficulty. If in 1913 the French had already begun to drive back the Berbers at Itto and taken Khenifra, the defeat suffered by Mangin in person at Ksiba and the disaster of El-Heri cruelly revealed the mountain-dwellers' will to resist. Two centuries before, the great 'Alawi Maulay Isma'il had had to fight them with the aid of another Berber tribe, the Zemmur. Later another great sultan, Maulay Hasan, at the end of the nineteenth century, had succeeded in crossing the massif several times, securing precarious submission. But although there had been conflict between mountaineers and dwellers in the plain, *Bab uzaghar*, long before the French appeared, it undoubtedly assumed a graver character after their coming. Resistance grew sharper. The effort of these republics to repel the invader assumed a 'religious' character. This was by no means always expressed in theological formulae—at any rate not in orthodox Islam. But it drew strength from association with sacred things. This religious element, administered and fostered by 'marabouts'[1] and *mahdis*[2], represents the sense of cosmic wholeness, given specific form and integrated in the group. Alas, for the Berbers as for so many others throughout the world, this wholeness was on the point of breaking up. The rupture of relations between the group and nature, the warriors' defeat, the ensuing compromise and dejection are so many signs of that human experience of modern times which was gradually spreading to all the nations of the earth.

Already in 1877 Moha u Hammu,[3] of the family of the Imhazen, ruled over the Zayan. After a dozen years of struggle against his brothers, his uncles, his cousins and his neighbours, he allied himself with Maulay Hasan and was able to extend his hegemony to the whole western face of the Middle Atlas, as far as the Ait Wirras on one side and the Ait Yusis on the other. This important chief showed little obedience to the Makhzen. He was a recalcitrant vassal. The sultan had much difficulty in making him carry out arbitration, let alone orders. In this connection, we hear of prisoners being taken, which was a startling innovation, since imprisonment was unknown to Berber custom; an adversary or a criminal might be deprived of anything, even his life, but never his liberty. Now the Berber authorities that took over power in the last quarter of the nineteenth century, somewhat as the Glawa, Mtugga and Gundafa did in Southern Morocco, brought in new practices, including imprisonment. The tribe complained of this, and the sultan had great difficulty in getting some of the unfortunate prisoners released. The power of

[1] Or *igurramen*, plural of the Berber word *agurram*, 'man of God', 'marabout'.
[2] The sociologists of the Maghrib, investigating its Berber past, have revealed archaeological traces of one of the greatest historic *mahdis*, Ibn Tumart, and survivals of this thousand-year-old legend in the Wadi Massat.
[3] Sa'id Guennoun, *La montagne berbère*, pp. 48 ff.

Moha lasted until the arrival of the French. It was so great that it acquired an aura of religious magic. Nobody had the right to set up a tent in a spot chosen by a member of the Imhazen. Nobody in the tribe had the right to wear a turban as voluminous as the members of the chief's clan; it was a huge bale of cotton stuff, bought at the Qaisariya at Fez,[1] lavishly swathed round twenty or twenty-five times. No woman would dare to wear jewellery of the same type as that of the family. If the chief's wives might be veiled, more out of patriarchal pride than out of canonical scrupulousness, other women of the tribe were debarred from this custom. The potentate enslaved all around him. The older and the more powerful he grew, the less he distinguished between what was under his protection or his rule, and what belonged to him and was eagerly 'devoured' by him. Nobody might plough without having performed the duties of *tiwizi*[2] on his apanages, which were indistinguishable from the collective patrimony. Nobody could marry without his permission; it was he who provided his warriors with wives. His lands were tilled by regular serfs.[3]

Ambiguous relations were set up between him and the French. One of his sons, Miami, called 'son of the Fasiya', killed an officer; treacherously, so it was alleged, although he declared he had been taken by surprise. The old man banished him. Soon afterwards, his two elder sons and his nephews joined the French troops. Amongst them were Bu 'Azza, a kind of tribal champion, an amazing rider and fighter, and Hasan, who was to become pasha of Khenifra. These waged a series of petty battles against the dissidents. During one of them, the old man, who no longer took part in warfare himself, was standing on a hillock, watching his children fight, and was fatally wounded by a bullet that may have been fired by one of them. There was great grief not only among the insurgent tribesmen but among those who had gone over to the French. Even Marshal Lyautey expressed his sympathy, and in such terms, we learn from a good authority, Commander Sa'id Guennoun, that 'it may well be wondered whether Moha u Hammu, while remaining unsubdued to his last breath, had not given us some firm pledge of friendship'.

From 1922 onwards, resistance changed its manner. As General Guillaume wrote in the patient study he devoted to the French penetration of Morocco[4] 'the insurgent forces opposing us were now led solely by religious figures, incapable of organizing military resistance or leading warriors into battle; on the other hand they were adept at exploiting the

[1] A revealing tie-up between rural chiefdom, urban trade, and imported goods!

[2] 'Collective mutual aid', here misused as forced labour.

[3] Called *shanaqita*, pl. of *shinqiti*, from the name of the Mauritanian tribe from which they were believed to originate.

[4] General Auguste Guillaume, *Les Berbères marocains et la pacification de l'Atlas central*, 1946.

Berbers' credulity so as to excite their fanaticism to unparalleled heights.'[1] The comment smacks of a somewhat over-naïve rationalism.

This rising of 'marabouts' deserves a closer study. Medicine-men, auspicious figures, bringing good luck to the first ploughing or the inauguration of pasturage, ensuring protection against agricultural pests or against women's sterility, they represented above all the alliance between man and his land. Thus they had to rise against the foreign advance which disturbed that relationship, in fact, many of them believed in their own mission as 'masters of the hour'.[2] But that hour was to be brief, and advancing modernity quelled the final protests of integrated man. It had done so at home, implacably. It pursued the same brutal course elsewhere, in the form of colonial expansion.

There were countless picturesque, disturbing or touching incidents. During the process of penetration towards the sources of the Muluya in 1922, powerful tribes such as the Bani Mguild, the Ait Ihand and the Ishkern retreated without joining battle. This was not their custom. The reason was that their marabout had recited to them an ancient prophecy of the Imhiwash family,[3] according to which the holy ancestor had set up cairns, *kerkurs*, heaps of stones, to measure the advance of the stranger; all such territories would be abandoned, and resistance only kept up from one last redoubt, but 'this would restore all the rest to them into the bargain'. In the summer of 1930, the marabout Sidi al-Wali charged an enemy post, unarmed, on a fiery horse; he died a hero's death. Among the Ait Shokhman, Sidi al-Makki was captured at last. There is a most moving photograph of him; his aquiline features recall the kinship between man and his flocks. An unwrinkled old face, a thick white beard on firm flesh, a fine type of fighter for liberty! One must not think harshly of these marabouts. Their chiefs were dead, or defeated, or else had compromised. Yet they 'rose up'. What matter if it was in the name of archaic beliefs? These interpretations of the divine, after all, express man's loyalty to his mother Nature.

Against this background of unchronicled warfare, at a level where individual actions scarcely count, one can guess at more enduring loyalties and deeper spontaneities. In a contrary direction to French penetration, which went from the north-west to the south-east, other movements had tended, from time immemorial, to come from the south-east towards the north-west, with the unwearying regularity of transhumance. These foothills, these lowlands, these hummocky zones in which the winter remained mild, are dear to the herdsman. Each region has its botanical individuality. The observer can perceive it on the very soil, provided he can recognize the immense variety of plant life with all its

---

[1] General Guillaume, op. cit. p. 28.   [2] Another name for the *mahdi*.
[3] A marabout family of the region lying between the High and the Middle Atlas, which played an important part during the period of pacification.

scents, colours and properties.[1] The plateau of Ment, a little below the cone of Aguelmus, in that still wild region between Khenifra and Ulmes, offers a great range of herbs and grasses: the *ajuga iva*, in Berber *shandaqura*, a medicinal herb; the *artemisia herba alba*, in Arabic *shih*, gleaming white over the steppes; or again that plant with miniature chandeliers from which an alkaloid can be extracted which affects the brain, the *harmal*, to be found everywhere from Morocco to Iraq; and the *merryut*, the white horehound, and the *bsal Far'un* or sea scilla, which recalls the glories of Pharaoh and the ruins of Volubilis,[2] and the origan, *fliyo*, which in old days Morocco used to export as far as China. These plant-populations obey laws of association no less complex than those of mankind. Thus the country of the Ait Wirra[3] is characterized by dense growths of mint, *timijja*, of origan and of pyrethrum. The country of the Ait Mazigh,[4] whose name is of such good augury, since *amazigh* means a free man, produces several varieties of thyme. A plateau like the Sggat, above Wawizert, near the present dam of Bin al-Widan, used to be thick with small varieties of centaury, artemisia and ephedra.

If we are struck by such details, how much more do they affect the herdsman, whose life depends on the interaction between the movements of his group and the stability of mountain flora! And this is why the phenomenon of transhumance, by its necessary and almost solemn character, overrides all others.[5]

In 1919, army posts already surrounded the Middle Atlas. But the officer in command at Maulay Bu 'Azza wrote that 'the situation of the Circle must serve as a lesson; the posts are so remote from one another that they can control nothing. At periods of transhumance, contingents of unsubjugated tribesmen infiltrate between them, overrun them, settle down and become masters of the country.'[6] Thus the herdsmen's effort prevailed over the soldiers', and in many respects cancelled it out. Sometimes, however, the flocks withdrew as the army advanced. This presented a crucial problem for the tribesmen, for they would have to go down into the plain before the coming of winter. Hence many attacks

[1] Unpublished study by G. Jassenetsky.

[2] Volubilis is locally called Qsar Far'un, with a possible pun between the pagan name of Pharaoh and that of the sea scilla.

[3] The home of Moha u Sa'id, another great Berber chief. The Ait Wirra captured relatives of the Resident, Th. Steeg, during a hunting-party. Sa'id Guennoun, 'Les rôdeurs du Moyen Atlas', *Afrique française*, 1927, p. 483). The ransom demanded was shared out equally throughout the tribe.

[4] The name Imazighen is sometimes given to the entire group of the peoples of the Middle Atlas, in contrast to the Scleuh and Rifan groups. Lieut. Schoenn published a important study on the Imazighen in *Renseignements coloniaux*, 1928, pp. 737 ff.

[5] It is not confined, of course, to the Berber world. See Captain Lehuraux, 'Le nomadisme et la colonisation dans les hauts plateaux de l'Algérie', *Renseignements coloniaux*, from Jan. 1931 onwards (with preface by M. Larnaude).

[6] Commandant Laforgue, quoted by Gen. Guillaume, op. cit., p. 184.

were made on army posts in October, when the flocks were hungry; their plaintive bleating aroused the herdsmen's courage, but it also excited the cupidity of their chiefs. Moha's power was based on his rights over an *azaghar*,[1] and the money he derived from it in dues. Under the new régime, these restrictions naturally grew harsher. In former days a state of armed equilibrium, a kind of Proudhonian liberty regulated things, or else organized their irregularity. The active force was not so much the aggressiveness of groups, as has too frequently been implied, but a contractual and legal streak inherent in Berber civilization. And now the French advance subdivided the mountain into 'bureaux', imposed rules and fixed limits; it broke up the pasture for the flocks and the sky for human beings.

An investigation[2] made in the region of Meknes (1926) reports (in a paragraph entitled 'exceptional transhumance'), on difficulties with the Marmusha. Every winter they would go down with their 120,000 sheep into territory belonging to the Ait Arfa of Timhadit, at a fee of one franc per head. This was no longer a free inter-tribal transaction; the thing was becoming institutionalized. And still further difficulties resulted from the shock between the old order and the new: during the winter of 1930–1 the Ait Morghad of Midelt were transferred among the Bani Mtir, as a political measure; during the same winter, the Ait Irhan moved their flocks down among the Ait Sgugu of Ulmes, owing to the refusal of the Zayan to allow them access to their *azaghar*. And this is characteristic of the Zayan warriors, who seem to have lost none of their arrogance under the Protectorate. But the authorities endeavoured to settle these conflicts. Between 1920 and 1930, in the Meknes region alone, I note no less than thirteen official transhumance agreements between tribes or bureaux. These agreements were concluded by deeds executed and authenticated by a notary, in front of the judiciary *jama'as*, or tribal councils. This was the name of the collegiate magistracy in which the exercise of common law was consolidated and made rigid. A new species of functionary, the '*jama'a* secretary', appeared beside those of the bureaux. All this new personnel had to adapt itself as best it could to the traditional realities. In the words of the C.O. in charge of the Meknes region: 'Transhumance results in movements which affect the tribes in turn and simultaneously, so that certain perimeters serve both as the route by which some of them travel in winter and the ground on which others spend the summer. The synchronism noticeable in North Africa in the movements of nomads does not occur in those of the transhumants. This is because the functioning of communities and the diversity in the conditions of local life have determined another sort of

[1] 'Plain', 'lowland', in contrast with *adrar*, 'high ground'.
[2] Throughout this paragraph I have made use of unpublished administrative records.

opportunism more noticeable in this region than in any other.' The officer describes as 'opportunism' what I should call the course of history.

Already in 1930 'the organization of transhumance in the Marmusha tribe and that of the Ait Yub, another tribe of the same region, had become precarious, because it was subject to annual authorization from Meknes and Fez.' 'Serious efforts still have to be made,' writes a *chef de cercle*, 'although it appears indisputable that this delicate problem of transhumance, for the Marmusha and the Ait Yub tribes, will only be satisfactorily regulated when these tribes have become more sedentary, or rather when, under pressure of necessity, they have fully exploited the resources of their valleys in collective lands, restricting the production of sheep to the capacity of these.' The Marmusha used to send 120,000 sheep down into the Fez region; this figure was reduced to 37,000 by the Fez conference of 1931.

At that moment, indeed, a serious conflict broke out. The Marmusha were accustomed to moving down to the less harsh regions of the North-west. Now this created almost insoluble complications for the foreign administrator. For the Marmusha, who were in the Taza region, wanted to graze their flocks near Fez, while the inhabitants of this region refused to admit them, since they had themselves been refused access to pastures included in the Meknes area. The whole of the military hierarchy was involved in conflicts, not only between tribes but between Directors of Bureaux. In the end the Fez region allowed a mere 22,000 sheep to be brought in. The Marmusha thus found themselves squeezed in by the progress of cultivation on the plain, which restricted the movements of the mountain tribes on one side, and on the other by the progress of the Service des Eaux et Forêts. The latter quite rightly considered that the life of the region depended in the last resort on a balance between forest and pasture. It tried to protect the fine woodlands of oaks and cedars. But it was under these very trees that Berber flocks had been wont to graze. If ever there had been 'collective lands', these were they! The herdsmen were thus caught between two forces: an administrative move from the Water and Forestry Commission, and a move towards agricul-tural development from the *colons*. They were expected to pay for everyone, and by and large to bear the cost of the Protectorate.

It is a characteristic of transhumance that the slightest happening on low-lying ground has repercussions that reach the highest mountain regions. And it was from this that the Marmusha suffered. Correlatively, the various divisions of the Affaires Indigènes and of the Civil Control carried their quarrels from the plain to the peaks. On 28 October 1933 the C.O. of the Taza region took up the cudgels for his people. Deriving his argument from the successive restrictions imposed on their trans-humance in the regions of Fez and Meknes, he denounced an agreement concluded in 1924 with the territory of Budenib, allowing the Ait Seghrushen of Talsint to pass into the Circle of Missur. In his turn, the

C.O. of the Circle of Budenib prepared to break the agreements concluded with his neighbours. The affair threatened to assume international proportions. In old days the tribes would have resorted to arms. Now, the wrath of Directors of Bureaux found expression in angry official letters. The truth was that the only solution lay in reducing the flocks, which also implied reducing the vitality, the prestige, indeed the human value of the pastoral people.

For transhumance reflects the effort of groups to adjust human interests to natural factors. It acts as a corrective to altitude and geography. Grass, rain, temperature, the aspect of the land on the one hand; man and his flocks on the other. Hence it brings into play certain mysterious powers of fertility, on which of course the herdsman has no direct influence as a modern stock-breeder would have, but which he hopes to affect by the invocation of saints and the connivance of men. Hence, too, a whole spatial strategy. Freedom of movement must be preserved, the privilege of the warlike mountaineer maintained as against the peace-loving man of the plains. On the other hand, the herdsman is abundantly exploited by the town-dweller. For the merchants of the Qaisariya at Fez, he constitutes a sort of colonial customer who will purchase cotton stuff for turbans, teapots, heavy slippers and rough woollen materials. In the autumn he makes copious offerings to the *mausim*, the fair, of the Kitanniyin, in the neighbourhood of Bab Sidi Bu Jida. But his visits to the city do not affect his love for his plateaux. There the air is bleak, the colours pale, the vegetation harsh and tough. The depths of Lake Azigza, or the Aguelmane Sidi 'Ali, reflect a mournful sky. Such ruggedness has its exalting side. Life is good under the goatskin tents; whoever has experienced it, if only as a guest, will never forget it. A former colleague of Lyautey's, who had studied at the École Polytechnique, settled down to raise sheep somewhere between Sefru and Boulmane.[1]

Here we come close to the hidden secret of North Africa.[2] This organization of shepherds and warriors has its cyclical alternations; it forms the link between the irrigator in the oases and the grain-cultivator in the plains, and fulfils a complementary function, that of the producer of wool, meat and hides. It completes the circuit of traditional economy, in which everything goes on as it has done for a thousand years. But these interactions do not take place along predetermined lines. Each tribe, each group tries to keep its way of life uncommitted. The movement of tribes and flocks is governed not only by immemorial custom, but also by human calculation. The very obstacles it encounters make it more deliberate. Group personalities represent the perpetual transaction,

[1] He was steeped in traditional lore and a follower of R. Guenon.

[2] As in Kabylia, or in the Aurès, of which Germaine Tillion made a profound and sympathetic study on the eve of the second world war. The present work must regretfully confine itself to the study of those types with which I am directly acquainted.

the shifting contours in which the interaction between human fertility and that of the land, between man's will and what opposes it, takes place. Hence all the vicissitudes of the story, the constant oscillation between deliberation and violence, anarchy and the rule of chiefs, a particularist and a universalist culture. The general picture is of extensive states of equilibrium, part natural and part cultural, which in old days may perhaps have spread over the whole of the Maghrib.

The secret of this morphological variation, if we were capable of perceiving and defining it, would undoubtedly help us to decipher the entire history of North Africa. E. F. Gautier has written perceptively of this ancient history, where groupings spread out endlessly and then collapsed, where gradual growth was followed by contraction and sudden soarings by falls. But it is around names and ideas that associations are formed and then broken. Between the theory of ancestral unity and the real diversity of origins there is a vital contrast. For instance, some call themselves Zemmur, while knowing that they come from forty or fifty different origins. Inversely, the diversity of names, which drives topographers to despair, contrasts with and counterbalances the homogeneity of ways of life, and the slight differences which, within each group, disrupt and yet confirm these similarities.[1]

Under the French régime, which at that period was making irresistible and apparently definitive progress, the Bureau des Affaires Indigènes took its place within the system I have sought to define. The *hakim*[2] aspired to the virtues of a mountain chieftain on his own account. Thus he led to war those who came under his administration. We all remember the part played by the Berber Goums, under their officers' leadership, in the Italian campaign. One must realize the appeal to brutality and sensuality which this represented in the earlier period under discussion. In one of his stories Le Glay describes an advancing column accompanied by its doctor and its topographer in a pass between mountains. Now one of these mountains, in shape and in colour, recalled the breast of the pretty girl who was travelling with one of the officers. The map was therefore duly inscribed, *bzûlat ar-Rabatiya*, the breast of the girl from Rabat. The anecdote, which is certainly based on fact, suggests powerful emotions.

The bureaucratic order unfortunately put an end to these. Henceforward a harsher truth underlay legend. The whole world of transhumance, owing to the administration's intervention, became static. Many officers' reports vehemently denounce the way settlers had occupied the low-lying lands. 'This colonization,' says a letter of 1921,

---

[1] This theme has been impressively, and painfully, developed by Paul Mus.

[2] The name (derived from the pre-islamic magistracy) given to the head of the *bureau arabe*, whether an official of the A.I., Civil Controller or Administrator.

'whether official or private, has grown so widespread that it has considerably reduced the land available to the tribes from the North.' A chain of reactions took place. The Ait Arfa were deprived of transhumance in 1930, since the plain was occupied, and consequently could not take in the flocks of the Ait Yusi during the winter. The Ait Yusi of the Guigu, having been unable to move their flocks, could not take in the Marmusha. And all these misfortunes were intensified in the case of the Marmusha, who were the furthest south-east of all these tribes.

This very lucid report also indicates how bureaucratic regularity detracts from the flexibility of the old system. It notes the abandonment of patriarchal values, and the way in which one tribe, when divided between different bureaux, loses its sense of fraternity. The collective spirit is weakened; the individual becomes more keenly self-aware. It is significant that certain stock-breeders were already signing contracts with owners of stubble fields. This shows more clearly than anything how the collective order was being supplanted by an individualist order. This individualism was the consequence and the instrument of modern times. We are thus faced with new conjunctures, new groupings. These include both country and town; they are led up to by the lengthy propagation of slogans, and give evidence of hitherto unknown forms of social life. The men of the Maghrib passed through a number of stages, from the resistance of tribal chiefs to the complaints of herdsmen, before their final assertion of political rights.

In the autumn of 1937, coincident with events at Meknes and Fez, certain *talaba*[1] harangued the crowd at Khemisset, the chief town of the Zemmur and seat of important civil authorities. They introduced the question of nationalism into the affairs of the tribe. The Berbers began to talk of Ait Watan, that strange tribe created from the name of the *wataniyin*, 'nationalists'. It is all too easy, today, to judge these events in the light of what happened in the summer of 1954. On this occasion, there was an uprising at Khenifra; the Marmusha, first and almost alone among Moroccan tribes, rebelled. They launched a surprise attack on the *burj* of the A.I. We should not seek for any too precise explanation. But the incident suggests the flare-up of old resentments. Who knows whether the restriction of transhumance had not contributed to this belated revolt by slow and secret ways? Such consequences would indeed be paradoxical, in that Berber land so highly prized, to preserve which the famous *dahir* had been passed . . .[2]

But possibly this was merely the effect of a reversal which can be observed, from a certain moment onward, throughout the colonial history of the Maghrib. Every 'success' turns back against itself. The man of the A.I., the well-respected *hakim*, who had correctly adapted himself to tribal ways, was becoming imperceptibly an administrative

---

[1] 'Persons seeking knowledge.'   [2] Cf. p. 218 ff.

Robinson Crusoe, ruling a set of Man Fridays. Underneath the new organizations, which at first were forcibly endured and even accepted for the sake of their impressive qualities, or else in exchange for immediate advantages, an indomitable reality was coming to light once more. The 'zone of insecurity' cut off a large part of the Berber-speaking tribes from their lowlands. This separation had had useful results: for instance, it had made purchases of land subject to official authorization. But it sanctioned the existence of a Berber reserve, a sort of national park which was to be sheltered from the ideologies of the plain, whether Arab or French. Now in this order of things, nothing can be sheltered indefinitely. Finally, the lucidity which must be recognized in the reports of 1930 and 1935 on transhumance proved impotent in the long run. It undoubtedly denounced the harmful effects of the occupation of the lowlands on the economy, the life and even the mentality of the tribes. But it could not seriously combat colonization.

It almost seems as if, seeking to maintain its purity against foreseeable difficulties and dangers in the Moroccan plains, this policy had taken a turn which was to be its ruin: the cult of exceptional successes. A Berber college was founded at Azru, which was to train a future élite in authority and administration; and at the École Militaire of Dar Baida, many sons of chiefs were trained as officers. But both these institutions, in fact, produced the future cadres of an independent Morocco. In this connection one might contrast three types of men who at that period were close to one another in space and in time: the marabout, that defender of his country against foreign intrusion, dying bravely in the name of the God who guarantees the relation between the group, its flocks and its land; the awe-inspiring *hakim* in his *burj*, trying, but in vain, to set up a protective barrier of purity within the colonial regime; and finally the man who at this period was only a child or a youth, either at the College of Azru or the École Militaire, who already repudiated both the first and the second type, whatever apparent respect he still paid them. It was to him that the future was to belong. And even more than to him, it belonged to the sons of the herdsmen, however far they still were from understanding themselves.

Here as elsewhere, history, like the poet's Eternal Feminine, swept all these people onward and upward. The French method strove vainly and breathlessly to follow this upward movement beyond a certain point. It intended to keep going within the limits of its own effects. It had reached the maturity of its type in this period and in this geographical setting, where it undoubtedly represented an advance over the old rule of the Makhzen, since it was in touch with the ecological foundations of this civilization. It sought to free these people from their ancestral bondage. But it could not cope with their demand for a national personality, nor with a social aspiration which it had itself provoked and should therefore have tried to satisfy. This was the mistake made, in particular, in the case of the Berber *dahir*. It speculated on what already existed; it banished that which was in process of becoming.

Is this perhaps an explanation after the event, inadequate by the mere fact of being political? Now political and even psychological truths conceal realities that are far more primitive. I have looked for these at ground level, in those very pastures where the mountain flocks graze. These are the realities from which chronicled events proceed, and which they reveal. The fiercely ambiguous attitude of the mountain dwellers takes the form now of secret transactions with the rising power, now of sudden acts of violence. On the one hand there is the docile acceptance of the *bureaux*, on the other the death of Moha u Hamma, or the attack made by the *hakim* who liked to call himself, and to be called, 'father'. And things were not going to stop at this point.

CHAPTER V

Villages

In a country like Morocco, if we divide the sum total of the rural population by the number of *suqs* (markets), we get a rough 'quotient of assemblage'; about 10,000 inhabitants at the present time, certainly less in the earlier period. We find here one of the primary forms of Maghribi economy and social life. This figure, which represents the number frequenting an average *suq*, is also that of the traditional township, Wazzan, for instance, or else Mahdia at the further end of North Africa. The latter is a regular small town, the former a large village, according to historic and cultural qualifications bound up with a system which derives at the same time from the Middle East and from the Mediterranean. Hierarchies existed formerly which culminated in those towns described as cities (*villes citadines*) in contrast with the rest. But let us confine ourselves to the humbler level of life in the *bled*. Here we find alternation between the scattered habitat of the tribe, and the township; for 10,000 is also the average size of the Moroccan tribe. Thus a sort of typological bifurcation takes place at the base, according to whether or not there is synoecism:[1] the same elementary relations between the group and the space it inhabits persist with the variations imposed on these by culture and history. Now one of these variations, corresponding to the colonial phase, has considerably strengthened one of these terms, the village, and seriously affected the other, the tribe.

From Tribe to Commune

Local life, in North Africa, implies the rule of chiefs. And primarily, that of the 'native chief'. In Algeria, and even more in Tunisia, this personage had become somewhat decadent after the first world war; but in Morocco he still displayed only too much vigour. The 'Lords of the Atlas' called forth the enthusiasm of tourists, visiting writers, and, less

[1] I have developed these ideas further in 'Medinas, villeneuves et bidonvilles', *Cahiers de Tunisie*, nos. 21–22, 1959, pp. 8 ff.

innocently, that of the Protectorate. A long way below these great caïds came all the rest of rural Morocco. For here the 'tribe' was still what we should call an operative notion. In the other two countries it had not wholly disappeared from ideas and customs. It covered a number of widely differing systems, from the still vigorous small tribes of the South to the artificial aggregates of Tunisian caïdates, by way of Berber cantons and Algerian communes (*duwar*). It was thus chiefly a question of government, but one whose origin went back a long way. Over a century ago, 'in the midst of the chaos we were faced with, the native chiefs appeared to us as a factor of order. Their principle was authority, and this principle was in conformity with our own. An alliance was soon concluded. This period was one of glory for the native chiefs. We learned from them to know the country, its resources, the administrative traditions, the mind of its population, even the conventions that must be observed with individuals and with masses.'[1] In short, a catalogue of prescriptions. But Enfantin had already indicted those whom he described as 'the most poetic brigands in the world.'[2] Almost from the first, in fact, criticisms were made. As early as the July monarchy, objections had been levelled at the anachronism of a function which, in name at any rate, lingered on in independent Morocco, which retained the title of Caïd and even instituted 'super-caïds'.

Although, in the Maghrib of the twenties, one cannot anywhere discount the march of history—that modernism to which everything was related, either for or against, even in those regions that remained most primitive—a territorial gamut of types, roughly corresponding to their chronological succession, extended from the remote and still romantic rule of warrior chiefs to the familiar ground of modern officialdom. A certain continuity linked haughty figures resembling those of old with commonplace bureaucrats, while a whole series of intermediaries and hybrids lay between the two types. Where are we to class such different personages as the caliph Jallul bin Lakhdar, of the Larbaʿ, Shaikh al-ʿArab Bu ʿAziz bin Gana, of Biskra, the 'frock-coated agha' of Algiers and the potentates of Dir, the Glawi and the Mtuggi? The same continuity, at all events, linked them to the Tunisian Caïd, who was merely a rural bureaucrat intermediary between the *duwar* and the administration.

Haughty or servile, all shared in the fortunes and the terrible risks of authority. All were reputed to 'make the burnous sweat'. But some of them were still able to eliminate their adversaries by means of imprisonment or murder,[3] while others could only set the police after them,

---

[1] Villot, *Moeurs, coûtumes et institution des indigènes de l'Algérie*, 1888, p. 306.

[2] Enfantin, *Colonisation de l'Algérie*, 1843, p. 390.

[3] The quarrel between the Glawi and his secretary, the *fqih* ʿUmar al-Miskini, brought appalling things to light; these were promptly concealed, and the indiscreet *fqih* was banished to his native tribe (1934).

unless they preferred to resort to the typical 'Arab intrigue'[1] that had acquired the dignity of a national custom. The Glawi, crippled with debts despite his connection with the mining trusts and his right to levy taxes on his own account, had every intention of getting himself refloated by the Resident. Others merely managed to get their intervention paid for, or to secure a free lunch. Some were honest, in the administrative sense of the word. But these, overburdened with heavy obligations, were ruining themselves financially and politically. An evolution which varied according to districts, and which the French régime never carried through, made the virtues of the warrior seem anachronistic, and increasingly postulated, or appeared to postulate, those of the bureaucrat. Mingling with the hereditary nomad, the happy brigand, the ex-guerrilla leader, we find, more and more, retired officers and even, at a later date, in Algeria and Tunisia, candidates chosen by competition. A violent contrast was thus apparent between the powerful brutes who still governed in too many places and the timid souls who were expected to achieve the impossible, to combine efficiency with law-abidingness, upright administration with inadequate emoluments, lavish hospitality with strict economy. Crafty accomplices of the system, or its dupes in so far as they were honourable, what could they do? Some of them sought to defend themselves through syndicalism. There was in Tunisia a Friendly Association of Caïds, Kahias and Caliphs, with an annual meeting and banquet. This was also the case in Algeria. In 1937 the Report of the President of this peculiar Trade Union combined a note of Popular Front propaganda with the barbed and wily flatteries characteristic of the old Chiefs' régime.[2]

The confusion prevalent in language and in life naturally dominated the administration, and consequently the local structures imposed by this. An immense part of the Maghrib, from Mogador to Gabès, was covered by the mixed communes of Algeria and by the regions of Tunisia and Morocco under civil control. Here there reigned an extraordinary mixture of patriarchal tradition, Colonial harshness and French-style public law. The genre could justify itself by arguments which were historic rather than moral, realistic rather than rational. But, to an even greater extent, it gave rise to suspicion. Thus it fostered controversy not only among those who were its subjects, but among its own agents. In any case it was incompatible with its own avowed aims. As we have seen, of the three systems practised in North Africa only that of Morocco remained openly loyal to the old *qabila*.[3] Elsewhere, systematic efforts were made to destroy it.

---

[1] *Ztawer*, in Moroccan dialect. The term soon passed into native folklore.

[2] Smati, *Rapport sur le recrutement des caïds algériens*, Algiers, Attali, 1937.

[3] 'Tribe' or 'canton' (amongst mountain-dwellers). In the east they use the term *'arsh*.

In Algeria the land laws of 1863 which broke up the tribal entity also founded the *duwar*, that half-hearted attempt at a commune. The Governor's circular creating the 'mixed commune' appeared at the very moment when France was preparing her own municipal laws. And so the special 'administrators' which it instituted, a sort of 'mounted sub-prefects', were to some extent municipal magistrates.[1] But there was a basic difference. The mixed commune had none of the characteristics of a municipality. At most it might be defined as an aggregate of potential communes.[2] Its municipal commission, dominated by the authorities and composed of local notabilities, owed nothing to democracy save electoral wiles. But as an organ of transition and transaction, it corresponded through its very equivocalness to the ambiguous evolution of the milieu.

I have already spoken of the reforms of 1919. Resuming the trend set by the *Senatus-consultus* of 1863, after a pause of half a century, they allotted limited municipal functions to the *jama'a* of the *duwar* and its president. The development of the latter's role caused some concern among the caïds.[3] Moreover the electorate was still confined to those natives who had been enfranchised: only about one-half. Some 431,000 electors thus took part, more or less spontaneously, in the election of a thousand *jama'a* of mixed communes, 234 *jama'a* of autonomous communes (*de plein exercice*) and 350 municipal councils.[4] But the people's way of life, and administrative practice even more, lagged behind the law. Let us seek a concrete illustration of the uncertainties and risks involved, at the level of the *duwar* commune.

In 1934 the *duwar* of Aghbal,[5] in the region of Guraya on the Dahra seaboard, to the west of Cherchel, comprised 2,000 inhabitants settled on 3,000 hectares, which implies a high density. The population lived mainly by cultivating meagre cereal crops, and also by collecting various products, such as acorns, which provided forty tons a year; also mallows, thistles and various greenstuffs. They used the branches of resinous pines as lighting. Their life was poverty-stricken, and almost completely bound up with the past. Like the Kabyles, they cultivated primitive pulses of a kind elsewhere discarded. Their total collective income was about 800,000 francs, which represents 400 francs per head per annum;

[1] Maxime Champ, *La Commune mixte*. Cf. also H. Brenot, *Le Douar*, Algiers, 1928.

[2] This was later realized, when the 'municipal centres' were set up, particularly in Kabylia.

[3] J. Menaut, 'De Caracalla à M. Clémenceau', *Afrique française*, May 1935, pp. 271 ff.

[4] Brochure entitled *Quelques aspects de la vie sociale et de l'évolution des indigènes*, 1923.

[5] Cf. Lapalud's thesis, *Le Douar Aghbal*. This served as basis for an extremely pessimistic study by G. H. Bousquet.

in other words, poverty. Even so, half the budget was provided by emigrants.

In 1930 the administrator Martial Rémond, a specialist in Kabyle matters, devoted a study to the canton of Sidi Rashid, north of Fort National.[1] Here the people lived in scattered hamlets, but their inheritance might be divided over different parts of the land. There was communal cultivation of the plain. Sheep from the south, and the oxen which would be hired for ploughing, were brought up to the suqs. Already some progress in the rotation of crops could be observed, and even a certain development of arboriculture. A tendency to resist division, inherent in the Kabyle mind, had formerly led to the indefinite preservation of their olive groves, *abendu*, among co-heirs. But now the number of olive-trees was diminishing, while that of fig-trees increased. Since its fruit could be dried for export the fig-tree had powerful patrons, such as the financial delegate Guastavino. Our Kabyles took increasing advantage of this. As the population grew, the production of cereals became more and more inadequate. But the inhabitants of the canton included twenty-three schoolteachers, ten civil servants of various sorts, eight clerks and 1,500 schoolchildren: an enormous proportion for the time. Half the administration's subjects worked overseas.

Sidi Rashid was 'evolving', while Aghbal remained poverty-stricken. But in both cases, traditional society was visibly breaking up and seeking new forms. Although incredibly remote from French officials, whose presence on the spot was increasingly rare,[2] this society had been profoundly affected by the French system.Both the people and their landscape underwent alteration, in the ambiguous pseudo-municipal status and under the legalistic cloak which concealed, and altered without destroying, primitive conflicts. Only historians, or native novelists, will some day be able to tell us what severances, adulterations, and new creations have taken place in the intimate life of these villages.[3]

In Algeria and in Tunisia, immediately after the end of the first world war and increasingly thereafter, the official system became detached from these tremendous realities. A form which was already obsolescent was torn in different directions by the exploitation of the country and by that country's awakening consciousness. In 1925, during the Rif war, the voluntary mobilization of a number of Algerian *harkas* led to the realization of certain disquieting facts. In 1930, the celebration of the Centenary revealed a glimpse of the machine's dilapidation under its

[1] Martial Rémond, *Un village kabyle*, 1930.

[2] Particularly since motorized transport became available to officials, and except in the remoter regions of Morocco they ceased doing their rounds on horseback. The scandalous state of 'under-administration' was belatedly noted, in Algeria, in enquiries made after 1954.

[3] For instance Feraoun, Mammeri, Malek Ouary. Marguerite Taos, in her *Rue des Tambourins*, 1961, gives a distressing picture of the Kabyle village and the breakup of family life.

festal trappings. French and Algerian agents of the mixed commune were involved in the same discredit. In 1932[1] the President of the Syndicate of Administrators rebelled, not against calumnies which he scornfully rejected, but against 'a tenacious legend'; it must obviously have existed. The whole local administration stood accused of jobbery, sexual misconduct and political intrigue. The legend illustrates the process by which an authority is gradually degraded from the plane of rights to that of privileges, and thence to the plane of abuses. The third stage had been reached in Algeria. By 1937, the function of the administrator had belatedly shifted towards economic and social action.[2] In fact, it retained an equivocal character. The initiative of the Bureau Arabe type of authority gradually collapsed under the weight of protests and suspicions, while no live sort of institution was created to replace it. For one does not replace the dead. Bureaucratic sluggishness thus alternated with individual impulses, sometimes meritorious but almost always unsuccessful. And the opinion of the Muslims oscillated between nostalgia for a patriarchal past and the hope of a juster future. Meanwhile they protected themselves from the régime as best they could, unless on the other hand they took advantage of it.

Thus the communal tradition of the Maghrib found no expression here, any more than in the so-called *communes de plein exercice*, where the elected native representatives, invariably in the minority, constituted only a make-weight personnel; neither did it find expression in Morocco, where the tribe was still respected, more as a convention of the Makhzen than as a sociological entity. Still less in Tunisia where nothing, from the artificial caïdate to the fractions into which the former tribes–Zlas or Swasis–were broken up, preserved the local character of public life or safeguarded ancient solidarities. Here the basic process of delimitation of ownership did not leave existing groups intact. In the south, estates were split up into such large sections, and sometimes so arbitrarily, that there was nothing to ensure the existence of local communities. Tunisia thus postponed, for a long time no doubt, the controversial question of communes.[3]

But if the commune did not come fast enough, the need for it was increasingly felt, enhanced by its very setbacks. The old appeal of the community spirit, stimulated by modern ideas, demanded a renewal all the more vehemently since the crowded conditions of modern life tended in the same direction. Physical and mental conditions were in advance of institutions.

---

[1] Gerbié, *Cinquantenaire de la création des communes mixtes*, Algiers, 1932, p. 24.

[2] Cf. p. 283.

[3] It can scarcely be said that independent Morocco or Tunisia have yet solved this vital problem (1962).

Andalusian Villages[1]

Masqueray constructed his great book on a three-term variation which he had discovered between the citadel-granaries of the Aurès, the Kabyle village or *thadderth*, and the Mozabite city. He undoubtedly exaggerated the comparison between forms found to the south and north of the Mediterranean. Too much influenced by Greek and Roman history, he laid excessive stress on Berber society; he thus neglected other forms of agglomeration, which might by contrast be described as Arab. For instance, the *medsher* (village) of the Jebala, between the Gharb and the Moroccan Rif, with its cottages thatched with *shqalliya* (sprouting straw). Or the large villages of Tunisian Sahil, about which I shall give further details. The zone of 'village dialect' that corresponds to this area reveals forms of language earlier than the expansion of the Bani Hilal. An old Maghrib, from pre-Bedouin days, thus contributed to those new developments of sedentarism which it was to acquire, during the modern period, first from the Andalusian immigration and, much later, from European implantation.

Let us trace the first of these two contributions by the marks it has left in the valley of the Mejerda. After the fall of Cordova, Spanish Muslims flowed back into North Africa. These refugees, equipped with their technique and their capital, spread from Rabat to Tunis and even further in successive waves. At the beginning of the seventeenth century the Moorish people colonized the seaboard in their turn. They introduced many innovations as regards dwellings, manufacture and the cultivation of trees. Their contribution to rural life is what concerns us here.

Let us take a walk through the streets of Ariana. On the terraces you see a barn of a sort unfamiliar in the Maghrib, the *mestareq*; it is peculiar to these Andalusian villages. A donkey driver passes, armed with a kind of double fork on which agricultural instruments are carried to the fields, and which bears a curious and evidently Romance name: 'shalamush'. When my guide and I leave Ariana and reach Qal'at el-Andles, we are taken in hand by the representative of the municipality, whose name is Shbila, clearly reminiscent of Seville. In the village we find other Spanish names: Batalius for instance, Beris (Perez), etc. A sort of Romance Middle East is disclosed to us as we pursue our enquiry. Many customs, in these villages, go back to that period of their history. For instance, the procession of bride and bridegroom at their wedding in front of the village saint, Sidi Hauwal al-Wadi, 'who makes the river change its course'. In fact, the village stays on its *qal'a*, its mountain peak, but the agricultural lands on the plain suffer considerably from the divagations of the river, and it is quite understandable that a saint should have concerned himself with this before the Mejerda Office did so. A whole series

[1] My guide here was the learned Mustafa Ka'ak, to whom I am most grateful.

of practices are known here as *nta' jeddu*, 'one's grandfather's way'; said with reference to an observance or a way of preparing food, it implies the persistence of Andalusian custom in spite of everything. Thus *banadesh* recalls the Spanish *empanadas*, while *basapan* corresponds to our marzipan, and so on.

These are only details of everyday life. The Romance element goes even deeper. It can be discovered in the very plan of dwellings. Instead of that radioconcentric plan, that introverted set of mazes characteristic of the Middle Eastern agglomeration, we find here the rectilinear inter-sections, the orthogonal order which had been that of Hellenistic towns and which, by a paradoxical if belated coincidence, the French colonial power had revived: 600 villages in Algeria alone are laid out at right angles. So are the Andalusian villages of the Mejerda, such as Sa'ida, Jdeida, Tebulba, Gerrish el-Oued (al-Wadi), Mejez el Bab, Slugiya, Testur. Everywhere you find traces of conscious planning, of a concern for art: those superposed arches, for instance, to be seen in the *zawiya* of the small town of Slugiya, which was deserted by its Andalusians and taken over by Bedouin once again, but which none the less retains the clear imprint of its origins. Its atmosphere is at once meditative and light-hearted, its attitude to life differs both from that of the surrounding Bedouinism and from most Sahil villages. On every side you behold monuments whose majesty is in strange contrast to their rustic setting. This fine Andalusian minaret in Baroque style is composed of three sections: a foundation of stones, often Roman stones used over again, for the different periods of the past dovetail into one another: the Andalu-sian fabric proper, a wall of red bricks whose delicate relief work makes them ornamental in their own right; finally, surfaces of majolica. True, the upper part from which the muezzin calls to prayer has probably been added recently. But the rest is Spanish enough. In many other buildings, some detail recalls ancient Romanic origins: a relief rising above the roof of the mosque, in the region of the *mihrab*;[1] or some almost Byzantine rose windows pierced in the wall. A village as humble as Testur contains an important *zawiya*, that of Sidi Nasir bin 'Alam, which seems to have been built by Moroccan Andalusians: an absolute marvel of carved plaster. Unfortunately it is little known and has hardly been studied, so that its full historic and human significance remains unexploited.

Algerian 'Colonized' Villages

The impression of successfully assimilated Western influence remains. This residual Spanishness, these vestiges of Europe that we find here, touchingly blended with Muslim and Maghribi inspiration, contrast with the triumphant Europeanism of those many other villages which

[1] *mihrab*: the direction of Mecca, indicated by a niche in the Mosque.

are known as 'colonised'. In any case they are contemporary with the colonization of the Maghrib, and colonial by function. Whether in Algeria, Morocco or Tunisia, it seems that in these the Maghrib has provided not one element of inspiration, not even the setting, but at most the material, the object, or occasionally some accessory motif. We can define European implantation, at least in its first phase, as a struggle to introduce villages of this type, new or renovated, into the rural landscape. It inserted them wherever there was a gap in the native system, between the tribe and the city, in that physical and moral zone where, by reason of historic circumstances, nomadic elements began to break away from the sedentary group. The latter underwent profound upheaval. Apart from the traditional large village, a new urban order introduced other units: the smaller village, or 'centre of colonization', the *chef-lieu* or provincial capital, and, crowning all, the *villeneuve*, which abolished or ousted the *madina*.

Thus the French order supplanted the *madina* at the summit. At the base, it scattered villages over the sublittoral plains. Finally, it instituted, between the base and the summit, a centralizing hierarchy comprising intermediary levels previously unknown. Thus it inaugurated an entirely new typology of dwellings, of economy, of groupings. This reacted on the old, just as the old reacted on the new. For these villages fulfilled not merely their modern function, but pre-established conditions also. Primarily, a geographical requirement: they had to dominate a hinterland, to enjoy a certain free space. And on the other hand, while they constituted, within the modern set-up, the lower rung of the new techniques of life and organization (*mairie*, mixed commune, or civil control; bank agency; branch of distributive firms) they also stimulated native concentrations of a new type. In the thirties these often formed a majority. The village, which provided a fulcrum for the process of penetration and an essentially European method of restocking and replacing the population, perforce became the most favourable field for contact between Muslims and Europeans, and even, increasingly, a native kind of structure.

Colomb-Béchar

About 1930, the people of the borderland region between Algeria and Morocco and the Sahara in general – not yet transfigured by any hope of mining discoveries, despite Eirik Labonne's prophecies – led a primitive and lethargic existence. The best of its inhabitants took part in 'useless service'[1] while others speculated, and the whole community just managed to keep body and soul together. The small township of Colomb Béchar,

---

[1] A term used by Montherlant, who visited the region between 1925 and 1930. He admirably conveys the atmosphere of Colomb-Béchar in *Les Auligny*, 1956, pp. 48 ff.

'with its varied crowd, its occasional well-cut suits, its bustle, its shops boasting their modern equipment', could not cancel out the sense of oppressive poverty conveyed by its ragged hordes, drowsing amid a swarm of flies. There was something degenerate about it, something tainted and unhealthy. Here, side by side, with an effect that was occasionally picturesque but more often absurd or disquieting, could be seen the relics of an unfriendly past–for dissidence persisted there, in the form of *jish-s* (armed bands)–and the compromises made by a shabby present. The mercantile aspects of the present were displayed in the main street and in the mixed districts. 'In spite of the absence of displays to tempt the purchaser, trade reigns here, with its patient and tenacious activity'; petty retailers, petty artisans, and a bustling crowd of passers-by exchanging low-toned comments, usually spiteful and slanderous, expressive of the bitterness of a society on the make or on the decline. 'Behind this first showy barrier . . . there appear austere figures, strong sullen faces, whose psychology is hard to decipher.' This is the romanticism of the South, or rather of the West, since these are from Tafilat. 'The street Muslim conceals under his rags' (proletarianization) 'which gleam crimson and gold in the sunlight' (an aesthetic refinement which scarcely compensates for their raggedness) 'a solemn attitude of defiance.' Finally, the natives everywhere are appallingly dirty, and this also applies to other sections of the community: 'it is indeed a shocking fact that in this civilized day and age, many Europeans and settlers, out of slackness or from contagion, incur the same accusation of uncleanliness.[1]

The style is of its period, so is the indictment; the Maghrib had not yet achieved its D.D.T. revolution. And our witness, a doctor, had improvements to suggest: the extension of horticulture, salvation through work, in short a well-intentioned paternalism, which on the whole was valid for its time. Finally, we should mention the gardens in which these ancient Saharan settlers cultivated apricot orchards under palm trees beneath which they grew vegetables. Here and there bloomed a dazzling flower, characteristic of Colomb-Béchar, yet scarcely redeeming all that misery: the hundred-petalled rose . . .

Frenda

From Tiaret to Mascara, on the high Algerian plateau, the road makes a sharp bend southward towards Shott el-Shergi (Shatt al-Sharqi). The first sign of Frenda is its belfry, rising at the summit of a slope from which can be seen the ridges of the Ga'da, in those days still wooded. Frenda was the seat of a mixed commune administering 25,000 inhabitants, including several thousand Europeans. It was an old settlement,

---

[1] The comments in brackets are my own. The quotations are from a study by Dr. Céard, *Renseignements coloniaux*, 1931.

and its name is presumably of Berber origin. Roman ruins lie nearby; there are tombs with tumuli, the Jdar, under which General Solomon may perhaps have been buried at the time of the Byzantine reconquest. And it was in the castle of Tawghzut[1] that Ibn Khaldun, in captivity, is said to have written his *Prolegomena*.

The mixed commune, the church, the small houses of the officials, the police station, and the Foreign Legion barracks surround a grassy square, opening on to a main street lined with Jewish shops. Thursday's market is held on a steep slope running down towards the Arab village with its tortuous, teeming streets, surrounded by the remains of ramparts. The whole place overlooks a plain patterned with ploughland, through which winds a tributary of the Shelif, the Oued (Wadi) el-'Abd.

The air is keen on the high plateaux, the horizon wide. In springtime the land is covered with tiny reddish daisies. The roads smell of dust and honey. Every winter the snow piles up there, but summer scorches the acacias with which the village is planted. Local headdresses still include ostrich feathers, and legends of lions still linger in people's memory. The old horseman of the mixed commune, Buswifa, had served under the Empire, and talked about 'Badinguet's wars'. The war that was just over had decimated the conscripted tribesmen, but whetted the appetite of the survivors. In the school playground three languages were spoken: chiefly Arabic, but also French and Spanish.[2] But through the influence of a Savoyard schoolmaster, M. Armand, the French attitude—anti-clerical, socialist and favouring assimilation—was taken as model by this noisy crowd of youngsters, and further sharpened their conflicting atavistic tendencies.

The last contingent of Larba's, moving north-east in transhumance, reached this region every spring. They invaded the southern boundary of cereal plantations, as a result of which stampedes were frequent over the Suq el-Khemis (Suq al-Khamis); subsequently, bludgeons would be confiscated and burnt in a great bonfire in the mixed commune. But chiefly there were numerous infringements of grazing rights, and conflicts with European farmers. These grew so acute in the neighbouring region of Sersu that the Government itself became alarmed, and took legal action. The root of the problem was that colonization, cereal growing and a sedentary way of life had encroached too far on the herdsman's domain.[3]

Rightly or wrongly, the nomads felt that like the old tribal order they had been dealt a death blow. The powerful tribes of old, Hashem or Flitta, those whom the words of Abd el-Kader had fired, had now split up into *duwars*, whoise caïds found it hard to counteract the growing

---

[1] Mubarak al-Mili, *Ta'rikh al-Jaza'ir*, vol. II, p. 374.
[2] There was still one Berber-speaking *duwar* at the time, the Bani Wingel.
[3] These phenomena, with which Lehuraux's important study has familiarized us, underlie the political expansion of the Farhat family in Laghwat.

influence of *jama'a* presidents. Frenda's noble family, the Bu Medin[1], although still exercising the function of caïds, had lost its wealth and its prestige. It had been partially dislodged from its authority by the rise of small upstart chiefs, the most energetic of whom, the bashagha Hammu, recently decorated, had just had an enormous Legion of Honour cross painted on his dining-room ceiling. Religious institutions had undergone the same vicissitudes. The marabout suffered the same decadence as the *jiyyid* (noble). The once terrifying Derqawas still had a *zawiya* in the district, standing at the foot of a stately cliff, but considerably weakened and grown bourgeois. The annual feast or *wa'da* of Sidi 'Amar had lost its meaning. In a series of 'accidents' in the immediate post-war period those notabilities who had most loyally served France, such as the merchant Bin Jallul and the agriculturist Bin 'Asla, appear to have been liquidated. New types had sprung up. Muhammad Swalah,[2] son of a poor family, had already passed his *agrégation* and was teaching at the Lycée of Algiers. He was one of the first 'advanced' Algerians. At one time he thought of taking up politics. Local administration was breaking up, owing to the creation of a *commune de plein exercice*: this meant the end of the Bureau Arabe or what was left of it.

In the twenties, the most powerful figure here was a wealthy *colon*, Raymond Porthe. He had acquired most of his property through his father-in-law, Duines, a pioneer of the heroic period. The chiefs of that time, the great bashagha of Frenda who repulsed the assault of Bu 'Amama, and the administrator Ximenes, a Kiplingesque figure, may have hindered or encouraged Duines' ambitions; the fact remains that they disappeared leaving no inheritance, while he left thousands of acres. The son-in-law, who was no pioneer but an energetic and ruthless employer of labour, exploited his vast patrimony in vineyards and cereals, flour milling and trading in foodstuffs. He withstood the crisis, while so many all round him went under. Meanwhile the Administration did not give up its attempt at official colonization. Immediately after the end of the war it prospected a new area in the region of Ternanesh. The agglomeration of Tagremaret was, a few years later, to be set up as a centre by Dominique Luciani. But all such endeavours languished or failed; the decadence of many of these centres disturbed official circles and even University professors.

Sidi 'Isa in the Hodna

If we consider life in another Algerian village in the thirties – Sidi 'Isa in the Hodna – the first thing we see, rising protectively above a Wednesday

---

[1] This family has recently become allied to the Amir Khalid.

[2] Author of the manuals in which two generations of students (among them the author of this book) have learnt the rudiments of written Arabic.

market, is the saint's cupola.[1] This saint was a great discoverer of springs and medicines, who still proved very helpful to those who invoked him to cure their flocks of mange. The local hierarchy for miles around claimed descent from him. Their extensive range included the marabout, custodian and exploiter of the tomb; a semi-wild *khauniya* with tragic eyes, who roamed the steppe under a huge tent, amid servants and disciples; finally a 'big native chief', Europeanized to a remarkable extent. Ahmad bin 'Abd al-Krim had had a secondary education and married a French wife, whom actually he kept in seclusion. He had fought in the 1914 war, and more recently led a *harka* on the Rif front.

A second feature of the scene was the mixed commune. This differed, even more widely than the Frenda commune of the twenties, from the old Affaires Indigènes type, without conforming to the French type of communal administration which current myths might imply. The period was one of hesitation and lassitude. The methods of government were out of date, and appeared so both to the agents who exercised them and to most of those who were their subjects. The 'horseman'[2] of the mixed commune deplored the growing insubordination of the tribes. On his travels, he was less often invited to partake of spiced coffee or delicious *rfis tunsi*.[3] Certain caïds, argumentative and prone to radical views, were 'bad' caïds, in the sense of a 'bad' priest–denying their own function. They were recruited moreover from elements collected here, there and everywhere, from the army or the *madrasa*.[4] For better or worse, they were becoming professionalized. The bashagha owed his prestige more to family tradition than to politics;[5] he was visibly becoming a figure of folklore. The administrator had lost his last juridical powers, since the concept of the 'native population' became increasingly incompatible with the evolution of its way of life. He could still arrest a thief taken *in flagrante delictu* in the suq, and shut him up in the sheds at the Bureau before handing him over to the police; but the matter was a delicate one, and he mostly confined himself to threats.[6] However, we may note innovations, directly or indirectly attributable to Governor-General Viollette, A visiting nurse called at the *duwars*. The administrator Destaing tried out some useful experiments in rural modernization. In the *wadis* of Leham and Jnan he set up little fences of brushwood around which market gardens were created. He encouraged co-operation. The whole of this region, inhabited by former nomads insecurely settled and

[1] Trumelet, *L'Algérie légendaire*, 1892. pp. 83 ff.
[2] *Le cavalier de commune mixte*. A kind of militiaman or janissary. Called in Morocco *mkhazeni*.
[3] A delicacy of southern Algeria; ground dates mixed with semolina.
[4] *madrasa*: school of law and theology.
[5] The Caïd of Sidi Hajeres, belonging to the *saff* of the Bin Tunis, is generally opposed to the *saff* of the Bin 'Abd al-Krim.
[6] He has lost his repressive powers. But a brutal tradition still persists.

more addicted to the pastoral than to the agricultural life, only needed
a little economic aid to become sedentary.

A third feature of the village was the *cantine*, a term derived from
African army slang. A great deal of alcohol, including anisette, was drank
there. But it was also a club, where people met in the evenings. The
notabilities of the village, both European and Muslim, forgathered there
in picturesque confusion. Here might be seen the officials of the mixed
commune, the investigating inspector whose duty was to demarcate the
plots of common land in process of private appropriation, the *bash'adil*
(a kind of secretary to the qadi), the rural policeman, the Italian mason.
And even, believe it or not, the marabout who had emerged from his
sanctuary and sat unashamedly sipping an aperitif of dubious red hue
labelled 'tomato juice'. The landlady was a stout Alsatian widow, who
dabbled in sheep-dealing. Her son, in his complexion, his accent and
his manners, betrayed a formidable and moreover lucrative degree of
arabization. Several of these worthy citizens, when market-day was over,
forgathered in patriarchal brothels, where each of them kept an attractive prostitute from the South.

In this atmosphere of commonplace mediocrity and collective self-
satisfaction, where all values, local or imported, had suffered equal
degradation, such news as that of Doumer's assassination, or the rising
of 6 February 1934, or the Popular Front elections, aroused much
passion if little idealism. In fact, the whole system was tottering. The
'great family' dominating the commune was sinking deeper into debt.
The subsidies it drew, rightly or wrongly, to defray the costs of the
Centenary celebrations, were inadequate to satisfy relentless creditors.
The observance of marabout rites became corrupt as it grew less strict.
It enabled the marabout to pay less wages to his stable boys; they would
not take their revenge on his barley, for, as he said, 'they are afraid of
Sidi 'Isa.' Bitter feelings spread, and suspicion of officials in Algiers and
even in Paris. Some deplored their weakness, while others resented their
spasmodic acts of authority. These were merely moral reflections of the
changes that grew more pronounced from 1935 onwards. During this
phase, Arab influence spread in the villages. Pioneer colonization had
vanished. It had been based on adventure, technique and contacts. This
implied a considerable penetration of the local milieu, an acquaintance
with native idioms. But this contact with the soil was becoming a thing
of the past. Precisely at this period, a great movement began in Algeria:
the *Mutualité*, or Mutual Aid society. It was an arrangement which had
various merits, but which tended to 'bureaucratize' credit in the hands
of a minority of big *colons*, and incidentally of Muslim dignitaries; yet
another stage, despite appearances, on the way to dehumanization'.
The fellah, more than anyone else, was to pay the price for it. The protection he might expect from an administration which had finally, under
Le Beau's governorship, attained a degree of paternalism representing

considerable progress in this country, was merely accessory to his own massive effort, from which others benefited.

The commune of Sidi 'Isa at this time witnessed the belated and somewhat paradoxical creation of a new centre of colonization, at Shellala in the Adaura.[1] It was known as Maginot, a name suggestive of frontiers . . . Agricultural colonization was allotted to Europeans and sheep-breeding to natives. This division, however, did not prevent the *colon* from speculating with flocks, nor the fellah from growing a few crops on the river bank, or wherever he came in contact with the European. A brochure published about the Maginot centre reveals characteristic optimism. The agronomist expects the fellah to make progress through imitation and continuity. 'Unfortunately it must also be noted that too often the native only achieves a poor copy of European accomplishment.' His livestock proves inadequate in number and in quality, his harvests are full of weeds. No doubt his intentions are good; but the *colon* will have the task of making this arid soil bear fruit.

Bu Sa'ada

This history has its witnesses, who have already pronounced judgment on it. The son of the Qadi of Sidi 'Isa, Mustafa Lasheraf (al-Ashraf), had pursued serious studies at Algiers. His youthful experiences undoubtedly affected his later attitudes. Here and there a school-teacher, or even some old 'pro-Arab' settler, or a student riding from *duwar* to *duwar* trying to understand this society, became aware, without complacency and sometimes with distress, of the transition from one period to another. In the region we are considering, the noblest of these witnesses, who attained a kind of symbolic power through his life and his death, was the painter Dinet.

Dinet[2] had long ago been absorbed into the Arab world. He had settled at Bu Sa'ada, 'where amid the dark green of fig trees and vines there gleam the vivid rose of the oleander and the burning crimson of pomegranate blossom.'[3] Dinet lived here with a Mozabite friend, Sulaiman bin Ibrahim, whose wife did the chores for the whole household. This peculiar *ménage*, though perfectly respectable, could not fail to arouse suspicion; particularly among the authorities. A character like Dinet surprised and alarmed them. Veiled hostility reigned between the painter and the Army officials.[4] In due course, in 1912, the old Bureau Arabe disappeared, and was replaced by a civilian régime. Dinet held himself,

---

[1] P. Boyer, *Esquisse du domaine agricole de Sidi Aissa*, 1940.

[2] See his biography by Jeanne Dinet-Rollince.

[3] Isabelle Eberhardt, *Notes de route*, 1914, pp. 285 ff. Marie-Anne de Bovet, *L'Algérie*, 1919, pp. 177 ff.

[4] There was at this time a sensational quarrel over property between the Ud Sidi Brahim and the Agha Si Nadir, which developed into armed aggression.

and was held by part of the population, responsible for a change which at the time seemed for the better. Nowadays his paintings may disappoint us, but their artistic weakness does not affect their documentary value. Dinet became a convert to Islam. He died in 1929, shortly after his journey to Mecca. *A Pilgrimage to the House of Allah* is the title of his last book, or rather of the book written by his disciple, with illustrations by himself.

Not all his experiences were on this lofty plane. Bu Sa'ada provides sensual satisfactions in plenty. One cannot forbear, in this connection, to mention the women of Aulad Nail, known to the African army as *alouettes naïves* although there was little naïvety about them, and who retained from time immemorial a ritual character that was not always illusory. With their perfection of figure and their glowing flesh they imparted an ageless beauty to the movements of the dance and the gestures of eroticism. Their response to man's lust, devoid of sensibility or individual feeling, attained a fusion and a completeness of immemorial quality. But these priestesses were also whores. They excelled at vociferation; 'suddenly we heard appalling shrieks: the ladies were fighting! And they were adept at it, scratching each other's faces with the spikes of their bracelets, *swar* (probably the plural of *sura*), those huge silver bracelets of Berber origin which here, as in the far Sous, made redoubtable weapons, sometimes weighing over two pounds. 'They strike one another terrible blows with these spikes. They scratch, they bite, they tear each other's hair out, and sometimes one or other of the combatants is armed with a bludgeon or a knife!' During one of these epic fights, Dinet lost his model, the woman who inspired him, the famous Jummana, who was maltreated by the police to the point of losing the use of her body, and that is saying something![1]

No unnecessary barriers are set up between love and prayer by the human heart or by village custom. Not far from Bu Sa'ada stands the *zawiya* of El-Hamel where, some thirty years ago, Isabelle Eberhardt visited the female marabout Lalla Zainab.[2] This was one of the great centres of brotherhood mysticism. Here Shaikh al-Qasimi, amid a crowd of disciples and followers, carried on the tradition of a famous family. I do not know what were his relations with the painter, who followed with keen interest every stirring of life in Islam, from East to West, who entertained the fallen Khedive of Egypt, 'Abbas Hilmi, and who militantly opposed the Rif war. Dinet, in any case, was not a failure, not one of those who give up the struggle. He sold a large number of pictures and was welcomed in the wealthiest society of Algiers and Paris. There

---

[1] J. Dinet-Rollince, op. cit., p. 122. Cf. E. Dermenghem, *Le pays d'Abel*, 1961, pp. 63 ff.

[2] According to a characteristic process, the numerous family of the marabout Sidi Bilqasim had split up into 'religious' and 'political' factions. It included two caïds in 1930.

is always something ambiguous about any conversion, and a journey to
Mecca is a rash gesture. Yet Dinet got away with it, thanks to the protection of the 'Ibadis. He died on his return, on Christmas Day. Bu
Sa'ada, which was the best part of him, preserved his body under a white
qubba.[1] The testimony borne by this man's life, more profound than that
of his paintings, has survived, and links up in our minds with that of
other critics of the destructive West: Isabelle Eberhardt, René Guenon,
F. Bonjean, Emile Dermenghem. And by a striking coincidence, these
names immediately suggest to our minds Cairo, Fez, the 'land of Abel'.

In the Moroccan Gharb: Suq al-Arba'

The sons of Abel, who are now victims of a relentless process of seden,
tarization, were the law-givers in the Maghrib for many centuries.
Constantly routed by Imperial adversaries, yet managing to infiltrate
into every cranny of the physical and moral landscape, they spread from
East to West as far as the ocean. At these extreme confines, in the
Moroccan Gharb,[2] around Suq al-Arba' and Petitjean, we find Bani
Hilal and Ma'qil, more or less organized into 'tribes'. Some of these are
artificial, such as the Sherarda. Others, like the Bani Ahsin, come from
the Sahara. Others again, like the Sefyan, the Khlot, the Bani Malik
were driven hither by the failure of great dynastic adventures. The
Gharb, nowadays fully cultivated, still wore a primitive look in 1920.
The Sebu river, which meanders slowly through it, has as tributaries the
Beht and the Wargha, which come from Berber lands. If we followed the
Wargha upstream we should reach the heart of the Rif. But if we left
the Rif to the north-east and the hills of Jebala to the north we should
come to that plain which forms a kind of triangle broadening out from
Fort Lyautey towards Suq al-Arba' in the north-east and Petitjean in
the south-east.[3]

Suq al-Arba' is historic soil. Here we find a Roman hillock, honoured
with a saint. Although the Arab tribes have settled there, they retain
their adventurous character. Everyone was a smuggler there in the good
old days, and everyone has remained so to some extent. The great local
families all sprang from such valorous stock: the Rmiqi, who dominate
al-Qsar, in the Spanish zone; the Caïd Sharqawi and his rival Shaikh
Bil-'Asri, of the Jebel Dahl, where a heretical *zawiya* still exists. The
younger generation assert themselves by stealing cattle, for which
receivers provide a 'port' (*marsa*) while subtle negotiation with the chiefs
ensures impunity. One chief, Si Taiyib Sharqawi, belonging to the holy

[1] *qubba*: a small funeral monument surmounted by a cupola.
[2] On which the *Archives marocaines* have published a masterly study by
Michaux-Bellaire.
[3] Cf. p. 49.

fraction of the Aulad Khalifa, started doing business, about 1910, with a French pioneer then settled at al-Qsar, 'Consul' Boisset.[1] He supplied provisions for Brémond's column, thus consolidating his family's position for roughly the duration of the Protectorate. The leadership of the region was taken over jointly by caïds and *colons*, while official administrators acted only as outsiders or complaisant connivers.

The landscape underwent visible alteration. A road cut through it towards the sea, running across the fertile Blad Hallufa. It started from a cross roads whose axis was formed by the road from Tangier to Rabat. Two avenues diverged, on either side of the Agency of the Compagnie Algérienne. Not far off was the office of the C.T.M. Here was the traditional small public square of the 'settlers' village'. It came to life on Thursdays, which was market-day. Every day, poor wretches stood around there, street porters, pickpockets, beggars, odd-job men, or that fakir from the *zawiya* of the Jebel Dahl who carried a huge wooden rosary and was suspected of being a procurer, to say the least: all fallen sons of the Bani Hilal, the flotsam and jetsam of modern life.

Big companies established themselves there. First prospectors, agents and brokers bought land on security. They acquired the rights of great families come down in the world, such as the Aulad Dawiya and the Aulad Bin'auda. Next, the need for registration involved the establishment of boundaries, in which many a third party's land was swallowed up. The advantage of the operation consisted, in fact, of transforming into a Roman *dominium* an old, casual and slack tenure made up of personal relations between an important person and the crowd of his clients. This tightening-up had the result of driving out the small fellah, whom one could then employ as agricultural labourer, since Providence thinks of everything. The title to the property sanctioned this operation by conferring retroactive legality on it. Henceforward the sprawling landscape of the Gharb was precisely partitioned into fractions, where a variety of agricultural methods were practised. Work was soon mechanized. Techniques developed at an increasingly uneven rate. The tractor with its plough, suitable for deep tilling, and fitted with discs instead of ploughshares, ensured an irreversible advance not only over native methods of cultivation but even over those of the first Algerian settlers. If the yield of traditional tillage was four to the hectare, and that of the *colons* of Bel Abbes eight, the cereal farmer of Northern Morocco considered himself unlucky if his harvest dropped below twelve. The Exchequer of the Protectorate sanctioned this in its way by reducing by 50 per cent the tax on lands sown by European methods.

And yet this favoured farmer was liable to run into debt. Too often he was no son of the soil, but a product of finance or bureaucracy, sometimes a skilled technician, more rarely just a yokel. And, of course, above all else, a man neither better nor worse than others, and thus subject to

[1] T. Garcia Figueras, *Marruecos*, Tetuan, 1955, p. 131.

the seasonal risks, the terrible Moroccan hazards of fog and drought. For lack of rain in January, his suckers might wilt; a downpour in April, and cryptogamic diseases would ravage his plants. Driven forward helplessly by the system, he might be seduced by the facile demagogic attraction of credit, of the hire-purchase system, and by the temptation to make excessive use of administrative backing. Some farmers–obviously not the best of them–relentlessly frequented the travelling law-courts held on Wednesdays at the Civil Control Office. They would bring suits against some neighbour for infringement of pasture rights, or some workman for breach of contract, or, worse still, some associate who could not pay his debts. They would also defend their own partners. Strange associations were formed through this 'protection' which, although no longer part of international law, was still an essential feature of the Administration and indeed of the economic system. But there could still be found, here and there, a *tajir*[1] of the good old type, reliable in business, Arabic-speaking, jovial in his ways, well thought of far and wide, and consulted by the fellahs as agricultural expert, even as arbiter in lawsuits over inheritance. Moïse Nahon, born at Tangier in 1870, had studied some agriculture and had some experience in Algeria. He settled down here as *colon*; whence his *Propos d'un vieux Marocain* and *Notes d'un colon du Gharb*, a collection of articles published in the *Vigie Marocaine*. To one of these studies the then Rector, G. Hardy, contributes an enthusiastic preface. He stresses the winning personality of this 'frail little man whose eyes glittered behind his spectacles, and whose courteous gestures did not conceal his inflexible will. He had a sort of contained warmth, a discreet radiance which seemed to be fed by mysterious fires.' The two books have lost none of their interest. They breathe optimism, a sort of idealism about the *modus vivendi*. Unlike many of his colleagues, Nahon believed in the perfectibility of local society, and therefore in what he called the 'social role of the *colon*.' These good Samaritans were to be found among pioneers like himself, *hadha dyaulna*,[2] or among still idealistic newcomers, *hadha uld familya*.[3] Their good intentions were frustrated by a latent conspiracy due not to human perversity nor to any sort of moral curse, but to the system whereby France's authority, the prestige of her administrators, the very merits of certain colonists were self-destroyed for the benefit of a minority. In those zones where colonization was on a large scale, such misappropriation was almost unmitigated. Its indirect advantages, from which the mass of the people benefited, could not outweigh its pernicious results. In the long run the system was doomed. But at the time few people knew this, and nobody, or hardly anybody, said so.

In September 1929 a humble school-teacher arrived from his native

[1] *tajir*: *colon*, literally trader. [2] 'He's one of ours.'
[3] 'He's a member of the family.'

Besançon, who has kindly allowed me to consult his unpublished recollections. He was immediately struck by the intense impression of mingled neglect and improvisation 'emanating from the broad, dusty streets. This small village, too new and still unfinished, seemed to have grown too fast, and was not even suggestive of a provincial market town.' The crudity of social relations in a community which was simultaneously being destroyed and remade shocked the young man: 'Nothing was done for nothing; everything had to be paid for, the struggle for life betrayed itself in all its harshness behind the façade of smiles.' He describes a picturesque figure, the former Vice-Consul of al-Qsar, who had created a regular trust (the actual word is used): 'The farm, the bakery, the flour mill, the ironmonger, shops selling building materials and motor fuel . . .' And a whole gallery of local types: besides *colons* big and small, there were the middlemen, the land-agent always ready to offer you a bargain, a well-placed plot of land, or to guarantee a rapid rise in value; the money-lender, who was adept at losing judiciously when he played cards. 'Yet another operated chiefly among Moroccans, and lent them money at high interest. Most of these deals were done in the leading café of the village, the Hôtel Martine. Not to know the Hôtel Martine was to show oneself to be an outsider.' The *cantine* provided one form of social life. 'And when you mentioned to Martine someone who did not frequent his inn, he would say with a scornful grimace: "I don't know such a person." ' There was in fact a hierarchy of social sets: that of the big *colons*, that of the Civil Control, and the less select but more active sets centred round the two inns. Here and there a picturesque figure emerges: for instance that of Ouilbou. This former N.C.O. of the *tabors* had escaped from the massacre at Fez (1912) and lain for three days hidden by his Moroccan wife in the closet of his house. Now he owned a small farm with a large kitchen opening on to a courtyard full of manure and free-ranging cattle. One day he undertook, for a bet, to exterminate his huge population of flies merely by blowing on them. He brought his colleagues, honest peasants gaping in anticipation of the miracle, into his house, closed doors and windows and blacked out everything. He was then heard to blow with extraordinary force. After a moment, when the light was switched on, the floor was seen to be covered with a thick layer of dead insects, which could be picked up by the bucket. How had he done it? He had simply made use of the first 'Flytox' squirts, still unknown at that time. In a miraculous fashion he had inaugurated the reign of insecticides, which were gradually to change a great many things in this country.

The school-teacher was at first bewildered by conditions so strange to him. Then he adapted himself to them. From 1935 onwards, when he became head of an educational sector, he inaugurated a method which introduced children to the care of plantations, spread agricultural techniques and tended to educate peasants in citizenship. M. Mathiot is still there today, long after the big *colon* and the Civil Controller have departed.[1]

And what about local history? In 1925, there was great agitation: the men of the Rif had reached the Vilmorin farm, twenty kilometres away to the north-east. They set fire to it. But then they stopped short, for the flat horizon of the plain scared these mountain-dwellers. A *harka* (armed band) was raised against them. Arab chiefs joined eagerly in a conflict which for them was traditional, against the *siba* (revolt) of the North. The caliph Jallul z-Zwaidi, of Had Kurt, won great glory in the fight; Caïd Mansuri fell in battle, while Caïd Hammu Tahra was wounded in the arm. Then the era of civilians returned.

After this the chronicle is concerned only with conflicts of interest, with cases of forgery such as inevitably occur in speculation on property. A qadi who had been dismissed returned to his home town, Fez, which welcomed him piously as Professor at the Great Mosque. We hear of the tragic suicide of an Italian girl. And of administrative scandals; in the summer of 1935 the Resident, Monsieur Ponsot, inaugurated with great ceremony the seaside resort of Maulay Buselham: an ancient hallowed site, henceforward doomed to be the playground of summer visitors. In these regions, still scarred by the struggle of the *mujahidin* against the Portuguese, not far from the battlefield where the Infante Don Sebastian fell, villas and bungalows sprang up in confusion. The Syndicat d'Initiative, which had proved unable to preserve a traditional style, also failed to repair the harbour bar, which was being deformed by the relentless current at the estuary of a *marja*.[2]

This seaside resort, however, brought back a summer liveliness to a region which had been severely affected by economic crisis and political dissension. Feelings were high for and against the 'sixth of February', Peyrouton, Noguès, or Franco. From 6 July 1936 onwards, the latter recruited for his regular troops a number of young fellahs whom poverty had driven from their land. The *interventor* of al-Qsar, disguised under a Moorish woman's veil, was enabled by his pasha al-Mallali[3] to take refuge at Suq al-Arba', and hide there for a certain time. Controversy grew sharper, both in the *cantines* and at the Maison du Colon, between the Croix de Feu under their president Monziès and the supporters of the Popular Front under Dr. Castan. These were France's dilemmas . . .

Morocco had her dilemmas, too. A building entrepreneur, a native of Fez, started preaching nationalism. The adepts of the Tijaniya order

---

[1] Mathiot, unpublished *Souvenirs*.

[2] *marja*: seaboard marshes, which the Office of Public Works attempted to reclaim.

[3] He belonged to the brotherhood of the Tijaniya, as did Caïd Sharqawi and the Rmiqi family.

were suspected of subversive views. They were too favourably inclined towards al-Qsar, the seat of Spanish[1] and German intrigues. On the other hand the Nasiriya, whose establishment in the neighbourhood was led by a respected shaikh, Sidi 'Allal al-Badwi, were avowed Francophiles. The educated people of the region followed with concealed excitement the events taking place in the cities. The new qadi was a Bannani from Fez, son of a famous ascetic and man of law.[2] He might well feel alarm at his isolation. His task was a hard one, what with injunctions from the Controller, the pursuit of his own career in the Makhzen, competition from great Muslim landowners, brokers and settlers, and the insipid innocuity expected from him. New conflicts had not banished the old; an intrigue on several levels went on constantly; everything served to promote it, the disgrace of Caïd Sharqawi, the succession of Caïd 'Abd al-Mula, changes in the administration and thereby in the system, a burst of speculation in land, disagreement between *colons*, cattle theft on a grand scale, tortuous criminal cases which might be faked . . .

And meanwhile the township was being beautified. On its southern side a working-class district known as Kallito, the eucalyptus grove, grew up. On the northern side, near the Mda bridge, where lovers strolled on summer evenings, stretched the orchard of Da'da'a, above which towered the Mound of the Saint, where Roman pottery had recently been found. The Civil Control had two stations: that of Had Kurt, towards the interior, and that of Meshra bil Ksiri, on the Sebu. In 1935 the latter was suppressed, and the administration of the Mukhtar was carried on from the provincial headquarters.

But this was merely an economic measure, implying no liberalization. There was, on the contrary, a sharp conflict of authority between the *chef de circonscription* and the caïd. The whole traditional hierarchy was falling into disrepute. The Civil Control grew more strenuous in its intervention. It held itself, and was held, responsible for a bureaucratic correctness which the system made impossible. Confronted with the task of direct administration, owing to the corruption of its local agents, it thereby contributed to the greater demoralization of the latter. A concern for efficiency drove it to usurp an ever greater share in Moroccan affairs. It thus lost any chance of educating others, and even, in the long run, of retaining its own efficiency. By the end of the period, its administration was undoubtedly more aggressive than at the beginning, and less willingly accepted. Economic inequality was intensified, and resentment grew bitter.

[1] The Spanish *intervenciones* had their representative in the Bureau Arabe, the famous Colonel Capaz, whose legend lingered among the frontier tribes long after his disappearance in the Civil War.

[2] Shaikh 'Abd al-'Aziz Bannani, who belonged to the Derqawiya, and had out of humility become a water-carrier in the suqs. The neighbouring chapel, Had Kurt, had as its qadi a great Islamic scholar, 'Abd al-Hafiz al-Fasi.

In the Tunisian Sahil: Ksur Essaf

The Sahil, in Tunisia, is one of the few genuinely peasant regions of North Africa.[1] Its capital, Sousse, numbered only some twenty thousand inhabitants between the two wars. But it had two other towns: Monastir and Mahdiya, and even more characteristically, a number of big townships with several thousand inhabitants, such as Msaken, Moknine, Ksar Hilal, Ksur Essaf, etc. In 1956 their joint population was 280,000–about three-quarters of the total rural population of 380,000. In the old part of Sahil, the entire population was divided between the townships of Monastir, Mahdiya and Ksur Essaf. Over the region as a whole, the big towns accounted for only 16 per cent of the inhabitants, the townships 36 per cent–over a third. Their vigour is undeniable, from a sociological point of view. We have evidence of it as early as the fourteenth century, when the Mediterranean countryside of North Africa first began to recover from Bedouin expansion. In the fifteenth century, along the coast, the famous corsair Dragut (Dharghuth) fought the Spaniards. Legends connect the name of a holy *mujahid*,[2] Sidi 'Ali Mahjub, with the struggle against the Infidel. He was said to have been killed at the *Sqifat al-Ka'hla*, a gate of the old town of Mahdiya. His body, torn into pieces and thrown into the sea, was miraculously recovered and, by its own order, carried to a place where it stopped of its own accord: Ksur Essaf. Several centuries passed; other powers dominated the region. In our own day the energies of the Sahil people, closely linked with the development of the Neo-Destour, have proved a dominant factor in Tunisia's newly-recovered independence. The harbour of Mahdiya has been equipped, a textile 'complex' created at Ksar Hilal, and a co-operative oil-refinery at Moknin; thus the whole province feels the benefit of its leadership. The 'supreme fighter' (Bourguiba) comes from Monastir.

This modern vitality merely reflects the strength of a society devoted to arboriculture and practically untouched by colonization.[3] Olive-trees dominate the rural landscape over a broad section from the sea to the Lower Steppe, but do not grow within some distance of El-Djem. The chequer-board layout of the plantations may still conform to a Roman plan.[4] Whenever possible use is made of the slightest flat surfaces; these provide *impulvia* (*mesqat*). The earth at the foot of the trees is shaped into a basin, *hud*, the properties divided by raised ridges of soil or *tabya* (pl. *twabi*), covered, ever since the sixteenth century, with

---

[1] For our special knowledge of which we are indebted to the powerful study by J. Despois, *Sahel et Basse Steppe*. But my chief thanks are due to the Tunisian friend who enabled me, on several brief visits, to take part in the life of Ksur Essaf: M. Habib Bin Slama.

[2] *mujahid*: warrior engaged in the holy war against the infidel.

[3] The territorial expansion of the village undoubtedly suffered, however, from that of the 'Habus 'Aziza 'Uthmana', cf. Poncet, *Cahiers de Tunisie*, 1960, no. 31, p. 144. [4] This is Ch. Saumagne's opinion.

cacti,[1] so that parts of the land look like copses. This agricultural economy can be illustrated by some recent figures. The area of the Sahil is 413,000 hectares, of which 354,000 are cultivated: a remarkable proportion for North Africa. And out of this almost half, 140,000 hectares, are planted with trees. These eight million olive trees are not really productive by modern standards. None the less they are characteristic of the system. For 38·3 per cent of the land is devoted to them, whereas ploughland occupies only 48·4 per cent, less than one-half;[2] more than one-third for trees and less than one-half for cereals!

But despite this homogeneity of characteristics, the various districts of the Sahil each have their own personality. Certain villages practise fishing, such as Sallacta, Tebulba or Saiyada. Ksar Hilal is concerned with cotton weaving. Elsewhere we find pottery, jewellery, quarrying, wool or the manufacture of belts and slippers of esparto grass. This diversity is enhanced by psychological vocations, which are confirmed by adages and lampoons; 'Better a thousand Jews than one man from Akuda,' the neighbours say; or again, 'Msaken, wretched by day, knives (*skaken*) drawn by night.' Certain regions predispose their sons to certain livelihoods: to be clerks or pedlars, tradesmen or seasonal labourers, etc. Indeed, purely agricultural resources do not play as important a part as the preceding figures might imply. Even in the olive groves, the agricultural income constitutes only 56 per cent to 66 per cent of the whole. The general average of the income from agriculture is only 52 per cent. If we group the 'other resources' together, we find 41 per cent for what can be described as 'casual'. This is a common fact in North Africa, but particularly paradoxical here, in this region of old-established regular peasantry. A whole section of the available assets remains concealed, or vanishes, since the wily inhabitants refuse to cling to strictly defined economic activities but find certain opportunities, if not actual profit, in other directions. This is a disquieting sign to the economist, but fascinating to the sociologist. The average income is not higher than 40 dinars per head per annum, or 47 dinars if we count it in units of consumption: considerably above the Tunisian average. Enough to allow some people to hoard, even to invest. But these stick to building, to extended olive-growing, or even to the purchase of jewellery. For jewellery appeals to women more than cash investment. Their capital thus becomes an integral part of their physical attraction, their conjugal

[1] According to a technique which the engineer Gosselin considers superior to that of the new plantations. Recent legislation has forbidden the uprooting of cactus, for reasons connected with the struggle against the tree's parasites. In fact, both instinctively and deliberately, an effort is being made to re-establish the Mediterranean character of the landscape. This was clearly seen by Gabriel Ardant, *La Tunisie d'aujourd'hui et de demain*, 1961, p. 64.

[2] Most of the figures quoted in this chapter are taken from an unpublished investigation by the SERESA (Société d'Études et de Recherche du Secteur Agricole).

dignity. This does not protect them from the usurer. Not long ago the total amount of jewellery deposited with the moneylenders of the Sahil was estimated at 180,000 dinars–about 2 million new francs.

This ancient Mediterranean land, with its plantations and its townships, recalls Andalusia or Sicily, and like them suffers from a disproportion between the growth of the human population and that of its resources. This was already noticeable, although less dramatically, before the last world war.

Ksur Essaf, twelve kilometres to the south of Mahdiya, was formerly the seat of a *kahyalik* or vice-caïdate. Today it is a *muʿtamdiya*, the principal township in a circumscription of nine districts (shaikhats). Two of the latter, for one reason or another, were associated with the two rival clans, or the two eponymous systems, of the village: the northeastern part towards the seaside by the Zrarʿa, and further inland, in the direction of El-Djem and Sidi 'Alwan, the part dominated by the supporters of Sidi Masʿud. Within this small circumscription, village names are intermingled with Bedouin names, in which we recognize the two great divisions of the Mthalith: Ud Nasir (with the Bradʿa) and Ud Zid (with the Tlalsa and the Zelba). Thus village forms and tribal forms coexist in confusion, which recalls, on a reduced scale, a problem common to the whole of North Africa.

By the middle of the nineteenth century, these ancient forms had already begun to enter a new phase, precipitated by the French occupation. In 1881 a Khalifa named 'Ali Baiyud was in command at Ksur Essaf, while the Mthalith owed obedience to a different Khalifa, in residence at Sfax. Traditionally, the administration was on a personal rather than a local basis. If Mahdiya yielded without any resistance, things were different in the village we are considering. Was it because this township, with its 8,000 inhabitants, boasted the tombs of two warriors of the holy wars: Sidi 'Ali and Sidi Tahar, or for other reasons? In any case, it displayed its energy through the iniative of 'Ali Bhar, from the district, who mobilized a group of young men and was acclaimed 'bey' and 'general'. Unfortunately the squadron of Admiral Garnault, informed apparently by one of the village women, landed a shell on his house. The Khalifa Baiyud imprisoned the rebel in a disused well (*majen*). Two youthful trouble-makers were interned, for a while, at Toulon.[1] Another shell fell at Bab al-Qsar, wounding and crippling one 'Ali Njim. The village was forced to pay a fine, along with others of the region, Tebulba, Mqalta, El-Djem. The same thing happened among the Mthalith, some of whom took refuge in Tripolitania. The old man, nephew of the 'general', who told me these stories, eighty years later, now serves as *imam* of Sidi 'Ali Mahjub; so persistent are village traditions and values, transposed from age to age under renewed forms.

A little way from the village, two saints, Sidi al-Shuwali on the Mahdiya

[1] G. Payre, *Monographie de contrôle civil de Mahdiya.*

side and Sidi Musaiyih on the El-Djem side, probably mark out a perimeter the area within which is divided between Sidi 'Ali Mahjub and Sidi Tahar. The other saints—some forty strong—seem to be spread out along an axis. Cemeteries distinguish clearly between villagers, *beldi*, and outsiders, *berrani*, even when these have become old inhabitants. Still other saints are scattered over the countryside, such as Sidi Bu Jeblin at Sallacta, and in the thick of the olive groves Sidi Bu Ghdir, who cures the whooping cough.

The day I visited the village I was taken round by a descendant of Sidi Tahar al-Mazughi, the second patron of Ksur Essaf. He had formerly been a mechanical draughtsman's clerk, and recalled the good old days with nostalgia. He showed me the site of the original village, about where the present road to el-Djem begins. It used to spread, according to him, from the cupola of Sidi Tahar to that of Sidi Mas'ud (thus he excluded the rival clan of the Zrar'a). The site is now inhabited by three families, those of Hattur Bin Slama and Baiyud.[1] But the township has naturally spread far beyond its original boundaries. Today it forms a quadrilateral, roughly oriented from east to west and lying on a slope. A rocky hill, known as Lallahum, rises above the huddle of dwellings. Its height is no more than fifty metres, whereas Sidi 'Ali Mahjub, although lower down, is a good twenty-five. There is a certain regularity about the layout of the buildings; each of them is planned to receive the rays of the rising sun in its yard. But the slope of the hill has to be considered, as well as a sort of traditional town-planning. Not by chance, the plan becomes more open, the yards grow more spacious and the roads spread wider apart, the further one goes from the centre. At Ksur Essaf, as at any other village in the plain, a number of roads meet: to Mahdiya (12 km); to Sallacta and the sea; to Sidi 'Alwan, and towards El-Djem. Starting from a central maze, new districts diverge in all directions. This star-shaped development is automatically continued along the roads. For instance, on the Sallacta road, a kind of administrative district has been organized, which even includes a bathing establishment.

The story is worth retailing. Two or three years ago, while boring was in progress for purposes of irrigation, an artesian well was discovered, whose waters were unfortunately warm and brackish. A Bedouin dipped his foot in it and was cured of a wound. Thenceforward the waters of Sidi 'Ali Mahjub became famous for miles around. The sick of all ages and both sexes flocked to an improvised pool, set up by the Municipality in conditions which disturbed the Minister of Hygiene. The curative properties of this water became so famous as to be mentioned in a speech by Bourguiba himself. Since then a more modern type of bath has been built. Many people spoke of *baraka*—grace or blessing.

[1] This theory of the village layout is doubtless influenced by exaggerated family traditions. There is evidence that the original village had a wider perimeter. The contradiction is characteristic.

The cult of saints persisted, despite the compromises it had had to make during the colonial epoch, despite the administrative campaigns which had not hesitated to demolish the *qubbas* nor to secularize the *zawiyas*, nor even to set up a Destour cell in one of the sanctuaries, Sidi bin Khruf. It persisted because, apart from the question of belief, it formed an integral part of the old village structure, serving as guarantee and illustration of its general unity, its internal divisions and its passions.

The families formed two groups. On one side the Mhajba, descendants of Sidi 'Ali. Amongst these the Zrar'a,[1] the richest, the Ud bin Maryam who had inherited the *habus*, and three other branches. Connected with Sidi Mesa'ud were the Bin Slama and the Baiyud,[2] the former having been joined by the Njima and the Hlawi from Sfax. The family dwellings retained their grouping. Each of these districts, if we can carry the investigation far enough, would appear as having its distinct personality, as different from the rest as are the villages of the Sahil amongst themselves. Thus, even today, the Bin Slama are reputed to have a cure for diseases of the eye, the Tliq to be able to set dislocated limbs, the Njima are renowned for their commercial aptitude, and so on. Two old men, *hajj* Salih Bin Slama and *hajj* 'Ali al-Hlawi, formerly filled the role of arbitrators. The *'arsh* (plural *'urush*) or tribes, have each, in fact, their own particular qualification, complimentary or derogatory; it is merely a matter of one's point of view. They maintain their identity by means of consanguinate marriage. This is carried to such a degree that recent investigations have noted, in the Sahil, a high proportion of strict endogamy (marriage with one's uncle's daughter). To marry one's uncle's daughter is somehow to be united with oneself. By this means the family type is maintained, to a sometimes incredible degree, while the ancestral patrimony is safeguarded. If we expand the circle to include more distant cousinships, this endogamic tendency affects almost half (43 per cent) of their marriages; and this was in 1959![3]

Thirty years ago, each family not only had its saint or saints, but also its own special position with regard to confraternal affiliations. Thus the Dar 'Amir 'served' the Sulaimiya, the Bin Slama and the Bkharsa the Qadiriya, and the Zgerni the 'Isawiya. The latter *zawiya*, today deconsecrated like the other two, now houses a carpet factory. The day I visited it, my guide carefully picked up and carried away the *bendir* (tabor) of Sidi bin 'Isa . . .

The old village with its tortuous lanes, its dead-ends and its complex, involuted character seemed turned inward, in systematic contrast with the organization of the rural landscape all around. The irregularity of its

---

[1] Their name seems to indicate the privilege of agricultural *initium*.

[2] The Bkharsa were connected with the Bin Slama; the Hattur with the Baiyud. (Their name seems to be derived from a dialectal *'attur*, 'tailless, stemless', cf. W. Marçais' comments on the Botr, 'acaulous'.)

[3] According to the unpublished investigation by the SERESA.

plan, growing more noticeable the further one penetrates into the heart of the village, contrasts with the regularity of the plantation. Indeed, the life of the community was both burdened and supported by the density of the population. But it could breathe freely in the olive groves, where there was always room, more or less, and even more freely in the cereal-growing tracts beyond. A third area, along the coast, at Sallacta, which was good for grazing and market-gardening, and over which were dotted country houses, *jnan l-bhar*, constituted the third term of this rural life, organized around the central village. Life alternated in two phases, one of social concentration within the inhabited area, the other of expansion in nature. Each of the two had its own rhythm, its own character, and the health of the community depended on the harmonious contrast between them. Even today, certain regular correspondences can be distinguished between the division of the village into families and that of the land into districts. In the olive groves, each family sought to keep or reconstitute its share, thus producing an intertwined structure favourable to mutual help, and at the same time ensuring equality of ecological chances. This explains the toponymic division of the lands around the village. To the north: al-'Aryana, z-Za'atriya z-Zughbi; to the west, sh-Shara, z-Zwam; to the south, sh-Sha'ba, l-Hriqa, l-Qlu'; to the east, r-Rumaniya, l-Qur'a, s-Sbakh, s-Sabuniya, l-Qarya. Observations of the same kind might no doubt be made about the cereal-growing areas, which consist of 'large lands', *'ard kabira*.

On a wider scale, outside the bounds of their village and, strictly speaking, outside those of Sahil society, the people of Ksur Essaf, turning to good account their spirit of enterprise and the relative security provided them by the sale of oil, went far afield to invest in crops or herds. Their dealings then were with the 'Arabs', *'Aruba*, of the Mthalith tribe, or with the Swasi. Thus an exchange took place whose basis is ecological. But the Bedouin, versatile and passionate, sometimes avenged their economic and cultural inferiority by aggressive encroachment. At such times they had to be appeased by offerings. On the site of the present market-place, the village women sometimes had to bring them great plates of *'asida*, gruel, carried on their heads. And the nomad, with his ancient glamour and his present destitution, with the contradictory vices and virtues inherent in him since pre-Islamic days, would then ride away with great dignity.

As we have seen, the village got some of its resources from the sea. It was thus highly susceptible to the direction of the wind, which also affected agriculture. The south-east wind, the *shluq*, made the olive blossoms drop; warm and damp, it sometimes brought rain, as did the *sherqi* from the east and the *smawi* from the north-east, the off-sea wind. The *bash* or *shili* from the south-west corresponds to our sirocco. The *dahrawi* blows from the north. The *jebli* from the north-west brings a lull, *bana*. Only in fine weather do these unadventurous sailors cast their nets. When the fisherman comes home, bearing his loaded basket, he is welcomed with great excitement; this means relief from the exclusive diet of cereals, such as *bsisa* or *kuskusi* seasoned only with oil. A little animal protein improves that day's fare. This is so important that custom, and, consequently, the Administration, have established a rota for fishing days, during the season for dace (*garrus*) or mullet (*buri*). The Baldiya (the most ancient group of families), the Mhajba, the Twahriya and the Barraniyin take their turn, scrupulously. Humbler families, having neither boat nor net, contribute provisions to the fishing expedition of their group. Another trait of solidarity. Even the luck of the sea is governed by the structure of the village . . .

During the first world war, conscription deprived the village of many of its sons. This is the theme of a lament: *Ya 'aini nuhi bi-demu'i hazina. L'ulad klathum Fransa wa mshina* 'O my eye' (traditional opening of a song), 'desolation, tears, mourning! France has devoured our sons. We are lost.' Those who came back from the war, however, were frequently invested with the enviable authority of the Old Soldier. They had seen many things. They criticized the old way of life, and they put up with it rather than fully readapting themselves to it. This type of man was on the increase. The village now produced a number of State employees, many of whom formed a new élite: a Beylical officer, school teachers, railwaymen, a postman, a male nurse, a chemist's assistant.

Money flowed in from other sources besides the old peasant economy, yet it was readily poured back into the latter. There was an increase in plantation: in 1884, the Sahil had only 602,000 olive trees, by 1930 it boasted 959,000. At the same time, there was an increase in taxation, which provided over a million and a half francs by 1947. This unprecedented mobilization of economic resources brought about a reorganization of property, which, however, maintained its old balance more or less. At Ksur Essaf, for instance, properties of over 100 hectares were rare, only 0·4 per cent among the owners of cultivated land; over 50 hectares, 0·5 per cent; over 10, 10 per cent; over 5, 30 per cent; and under 5 hectares, 50 per cent. For a variety of reasons this pyramidal ration remains unchanged, whether because social forces resist the concentration of land, or whether on the contrary because available funds were now being withdrawn from agriculture and invested, more profitably, in olive-growing. The ratio is entirely different for the tree-growing areas: 42 per cent of landowners grow more than 100 olive trees; 30 per cent more than 50; 21 per cent more than 10, 4·9 per cent more than 5, and none less than 5. This is convincing evidence of the phenomenon of concentration, so powerful in the modern world.

Agricultural progress goes side by side with economic concentration and also with demographic acceleration. Ksur Essaf today boasts of having 17,000 inhabitants; statistics show only 12,000 to 14,000; during the inter-war period, only 8,000 to 9,000. Whatever the exact truth may be, the village has grown enormously in a single generation. And this has important results on its social equilibrium. If we extend our study to cover the whole of the Sahil, we notice that available labour power is greatly in excess of opportunities for employment. Roughly, only one-third of the available man-power is consistently employed in agriculture. And even this depends on the season; at harvest time, and during ploughing and olive-picking, the proportion rises to one-half. But in the spring and late summer, not more than 15 to 20 per cent are thus employed. A visitor to the village at such times is aware of the preponderance of idlers. They lounge about in an impressive crowd at the Moorish café, drinking that harsh tea to which so many ill effects have been ascribed. Today we speak of under-employment or unemployment, and planners make efforts to provide jobs. This was not the case forty years ago. The course of things alarmed nobody until about 1935. In old days, traditional life included a considerable proportion of *far niente*, of basking in the sun, *iteshemmeshû*. If we can picture the customary attitude at the beginning of the inter-war period, traces of which are still clearly visible, we will understand what work meant for village people at that date. It was part of the rhythm by which man shared in the life of nature, and clearly decreed by Providence. And man's share was a slight one, for God is great. If there existed a wide margin of available time and energy, I believe that the community benefited rather than suffered thereby. In this vacant space it found room for its rites, its festivals, for strolling, for the easy-going collection of casual profits, which, together with stock breeding, provided a considerable share of its income. In short, the group found herein an opportunity for the exercise of its personality, and for play.

After 1930, however, things moved faster. Needs increased, money flowed; salaries and wages played a more important role; everything assumed a stricter legal aspect, formed part of a more exacting economic system. Contracts, both in agriculture and in stock-breeding, became marked with a prosaic harshness. The quality, the very flavour of life had altered. This phenomenon was common to the whole of North Africa. But in the village we are considering it was perhaps particularly striking, since it affected an old-established population of tree-cultivators. If a third of the labour force remained untapped, this now represented a considerable wastage both economic and human.[1] Moreover, we should relate this figure to another: only one-third of the villages' resources came directly from agricultural production. One-third of its

[1] This is why the nationalist press shows great concern about the 'death agony of the Sahil', cf. *Action tunisienne*, 7 Dec. 1932, 15 Dec. 1932, 17 Dec. 1932. A group of notabilities in Sousse, led by Muhammad Nasir al-Hidda, formed a league against the excess of the *Sadaq* (dowry) and the subsequent spread of celibacy, cf. *Tunisie française*, 5 Oct. 1936.

time spent at work, one-third of its income from agriculture. All the rest was in excess of, and in contradiction to, that 'causal' economic process which aims at adjusting the result to the effort. In relation to that process, now becoming widespread due to the nearby enterprises of Europeans at Sousse and Mahdiya, this community was beginning to lose not only its productivity but also its necessity, and consequently its moral code. Within the village itself, human relations already felt the effects of this. A carefree correspondence had reigned in the old days between the balance of family power and the distribution of land. Toponymy and anthroponymy were in agreement. On the one hand, plots to be cultivated; on the other, family names. Herein consisted the ancestral equilibrium. Henceforward, the system of ownership became increasingly confused, its cultural values and its relation to the structure of the village disappeared; ancient virtues, indeed, were being exchanged for new potentialities. The strong absorbed the weak. This is why the rural proletariat numbered 25 to 30 per cent. It had become a proletariat not only because of the poverty of its resources, but also because it had endured so many dispossessions in the ethical sphere.

These new proletarians did things which were 'not done'. They bought their bread instead of kneading it themselves. They ate out in the street, which would once have made them blush. They no longer built protective walls around their homes. Their women had cast off the veil. No doubt they still obeyed the neighbourhood's code of honour, and periodically joined other housewives in working parties for preparing *couscous*. But soon customs could not protect them from the disintegrating effects of poverty. They must often have been tempted to escape along the road to Tunis. And meanwhile the rich built higher walls, swathed their womenfolk, withdrawn in the seclusion of their homes, while, outside, their enterprises expanded and encroached on the privacy of others.

Formerly women had played an important part in provisioning: as 'processors', of course, but also as 'producers', since they took their part in harvesting, thus contributing substantially towards the family resources–if only by devoting several hours a day to hunting for edible plants, *khubbeyza* (mallow), *sefnariya* (wild carrot), *selq* (wild spinach), *tallghuda* (cardoon), *qorrisa* (a kind of bitter lettuce) and so forth. But this system, linked with the utilization of semi-wild plants, the patient wait for windfalls and long excursions through the countryside, had begun to collapse. The inequality of incomes increased. The growing stringency of domestic life was a partial result of that of the economic system.

The agnatic system, meanwhile, asserted its honour in protest against these political misfortunes. An institution becomes stricter, more extreme, more extravagant when it feels itself threatened or despised.

This was the case with the system which in the old days had brought together, although in mutual antagonism, the ten or so family groups that made up Ksur Essaf.

The most progressive man in the village–one of the earliest militant Socialists in Tunisia–had brought up his younger brother Hadi, and was surprised at the patriarchal respect the latter persisted in showing him, in spite of his liberal education. But this respect was merely a form of compensation for mercantile rapacity, old-fashioned traditionalism and a propensity towards exploitation. The stability of village society was being disturbed and disrupted in various ways. Hadi's kindliness within the family circle contrasted with his harshness as employer. And in general, the villagers, obliged and at the same time anxious to adapt themselves to European techniques, resorted to a way of life which was no longer traditional but conservative and even reactionary. North African society, involved in widespread depreciation, thus lost its special rhythms and its internal divisions. The peasant of the Sahil, exaggerating his acquisitive faculties, borrowed external habits from his tribal neighbour. The nomadic horseman, formerly despised for his lack of enterprise, now figured as a useful foil to modernism. He accepted this role, since his pride grew as his fortunes declined, and found therein some consolation for his economic decadence. Among the Zelba, in the nineteen-thirties, we hear of a family struggling to maintain a splendid tent which it took four camels to lift, but which could house four hundred guests on feast days! The Mthalith, exploited by the inheritors of the huge *habus* of 'Aziza 'Uthmana and by usurers who lent money on the security of future harvests, were fast ruining themselves in such ways. At least they enjoyed the slight compensation of seeing themselves imitated by the townsfolk of Mahdiya, where the consortium of the Bin Rumdan, with its oil refineries, its transport systems and its caïdate, was then expanding. The citizens would leave their shops and fishing-nets on any excuse to go prancing about on horseback like Arabs. A certain internal equilibrium was thus attained, no doubt, but at the cost of much extravagance, of paradoxical and aggressive attempts to reconcile the incompatible. Thus a Maghribi, hopelessly torn between two extremes, might try to confront the European with a combination of completely modern activities and a totally exotic mode of life.[1]

The impossibility of reconciling these extremes, which such practices inevitably drive further apart, is illustrated by the confusion that beset the rural bourgeoisie in the Sahil itself. Such confusion, in the political sphere, is familiar. But more intimate phenomena reveal it even more clearly. A passion for law-suits was one form of self-defence resorted to by men of the old school, feeling themselves threatened. In the Mahdiya region we hear of 600–800 labour disputes, 1,200 disputes over posses-

[1] This is one aspect of the cult of 'Arabism' in contemporary society of Mediterranean Islam. Cf. also p. 195.

sion, 400 or 500 property claims, and 1,500 or 2,000 infringements of grazing rights. Now in any rural society, infringement of grazing rights marks the point where that society is breaking down, where the stock-breeder no longer observes the unwritten law but breaks his tacit agreement with the tree-planter and the tiller of the soil. For the cultivation of trees is clearly impossible where such rules are not respected, and where the crop cannot be left hanging under the protection of Providence, in other words of the community.

There were many other disorders, some of a more 'confidential' nature, such as sexual deviations, which were so numerous as to shock judges, moralists and political militants. They were usually the result of the shortage of women, itself explained either by polygamy, which rounded up the available girls for the benefit of rich men, or more recently by the segregation of the sexes. They had passed into folklore. A popular sketch depicted a student from the Zaituna returning, white-capped, to visit his cousin the fellah. He feels thirsty: 'Pass me the water-jug.' But he uses Arabic words conducive to *double-entendres*: he calls the jug first *sh-sharbiya*, which sounds like *sharr bi-ya*, 'have pity on me!,' then *d-darjiya*, which sounds like *darr jiya*, 'come and milk me,' and finally *l-halbiya*, which sounds like *hall bi-ya*, 'take me!' This calls forth roars of coarse laughter, but the laughter conceals deep uneasiness.

In 1929 Ksur Essaf became a 'municipality'. Naturally, this merely implied 'municipal services', and not that communal construction which every régime in North Africa, whether pre-Colonial, Colonial or independent, has avoided so far. But the old community way of life was so strong that it dominated the artificial organization. All governing bodies, for the past thirty years, have been obliged, willy-nilly, to respect the balance between the two. But this patriarchal leadership was affected by the appearance of a new type of leader. I have already referred to Beylical officials and Socialistic functionaries; at this period they were still at school. A French school teacher, M. Lods, spent his whole teaching life at Ksur Essaf. He retired there in 1922–3, after working there since 1886, and was buried on the actual seashore, at Sallacta. He had planted a few vines there, and had even thought of making wine. Like all school teachers, he felt an aptitude for growing things. This no doubt remained unfulfilled, since nothing is left of his endeavours, although Sallacta has quite a few market gardens. It is a very ancient place, respected for that reason. It contains old tombs, in which from time to time some Moroccan sorcerer hunts for treasure. During Lod's lifetime, two of his workmen, digging the ground, found an old jar, *mukhfiya*, containing a small hoard of Byzantine or Arab gold pieces. These were sold for five francs apiece to a usurer in Mahdiya. Another time, a Moroccan appeared who persuaded some of the more credulous local inhabitants to search the tomb of Sidi Bu Jeblin. A jar was found here, but it proved empty. The end of the story is surprising: the saint was decanonized. Obviously he was not a very holy man if he could not keep his treasure. Such is the altered attitude towards their rites shown by these proud, ironical and tradition-loving peasants.

The village, meanwhile, was affected by the increasing restiveness being displayed everywhere from the time of the first world war onwards, throughout the Sahil, indeed throughout the whole of Tunisia. Petty local leaders arose, such as Muhammad Shtiwi, 'Ali al-Buzidi, 'Ali Bin Slama al-'Akkari, and, on the other hand, a Syndicalist from the Njima family, who is today station-master at Sousse. For all these people it was a time of activity and development and promise for the future. It was not at Ksur Essaf, however, that the most sensational events took place–the affray at Moknine and, above all, the congress of Ksar Hilal.[1]

Ksar Hilal stands about midway between Mahdiya and Monastir. This village, too, practises a variety of activities, more ingenious than those of Ksur Essaf, since they include the weaving of cotton and wool, the making of babouches and of those peasant women's kerchiefs called *tqarrita*. By the thirties a new mentality had grown up there, a conflict between the young and the old, between the adult generation and their elders, between the living and their ancestors. A native of the village, Hajj 'Ali Sawwa,[2] who had made his fortune in the city, paid for the building of a public school, and worked on it himself as builder's labourer: a serious sign of altered attitudes. More important, after the presentation of the Old Destour Manifesto, *al-matalib al-mu'akkada*, on 12–13 May 1933, conflicts broke out in the party's headquarters. One fine day, certain activists recently returned from studying in France (one of them named Habib Bourguiba, another Dr. Materi, a third Bahri Giga) broke openly with the Party and summoned a congress in this Sahil township, at no great distance from the one we have been studying: the village story thus plays its part in the great history of the Maghrib (March 1934).

At the same time, it retained its characteristic atmosphere. The principal leader and many of his companions were from the Sahil. The night before the Congress met, an incident occurred which caused consternation among its organizers: a poultry-thief had been caught and shot by the police. This preoccupied people's minds and cast a gloom over the proceedings. The police were likely to be on the alert. Moreover, it was a bad omen. Nevertheless, some sixty cells, notably that of Ksur Essaf,

[1] Which followed events related elsewhere in this book, cf. p. 250. In the following paragraph I have closely followed the commemorative brochure, *Mu'tamar Qasr al-Hilâl*, 1934.

[2] Cf. *Voix du Tunisien*, 15 March 1932. This benefactor now has a street named after him at Ksar Hilal, as have many other petty local leaders in these townships and in Ksur Essaf itself. A significant and touching example of civic pride and recourse to a new eponymic system.

responded to the appeal. The Congress opened under the chairmanship of a local activist. The brochure published for the occasion depicts characteristic local scenes: a crowd thronging between white-washed walls, and the chosen leaders walking in triumph between palm trees. All the vitality of rural, provincial and village life was bound up with the nation's hopes. This was no city bourgeoisie, more or less connected with the old mosque tradition, but on the contrary people sprung from the soil. Naturally, they tried to differ from the Old Destour by their intransigence. But it was through their realism that they won the day. We can well observe a trait of the Sahil mentality here. For the Sahil had known no colonization. From the beginning, this movement was free from that dependence on outside influences which so frequently characterizes other nationalist movements in Mediterranean Islam, particularly in the case of dispossessed or injured bourgeois classes, as at Damascus, Fez and Tunis. The Neo-Destour, in this resembling the first Egyptian Wafd, heralds for the first time the taking-over of national history by the peasantry.

Ksur Essaf, from a distance, took part in the movement. The township had its own petty leaders. Relations with the authorities became increasingly bitter. At the same time, the rift between the generations became deeper. Traditionalism became more and more a thing of the past. Figures emerged such as the present-day Mayor and deputy, Salah bin 'Ali. They joined forces with those I have already mentioned, to form a miniature General Staff which dominated the township for a long time. Also during this period, a native of this village who had joined the International Socialist Party played an active political role in Tunis and was a frequent contributor to *Tunis Socialiste*. This journal, on the eve of the Popular Front or during Blum's ministry, held frequent enquiries such as 'What is a caïd?', studied the role of the qadis, argued with the *Nahda*, which stoutly defended the tenants of the *habus*, whereas Tunis socialists held that this property ought to pass into the hands of local communities. 'A friend of Ksur Essaf' brought a fellah along to the editorial offices to describe his heart-rending situation. Then followed the disappointment of Popular Front hopes, the cruel incident of 9 April 1938, and the war. One day a dissatisfied ex-soldier, Adjutant 'Abd al-Salam Laqsaibi, rebelled openly. He captured the Kahya, and made the police look foolish. During the reprisals that followed, seven men were killed; during the last two years, streets in the village have been named after them.

These days are past.[1] A former rebel, now working as road-mender, greets me with a smile, recalling his resistance against the Vichy régime.

---

[1] I have abstained from altering these lines, which were written before the Bizerta affair.

An old Destourian welcomes me into his tobacconist's shop, with a somewhat bitter comment on the young people, who neglect him. I take tea in the office of the *mu'tamid*, the delegate, who is the maternal uncle of a minister from the Sahil.

And as we leave the Town Hall, evening falls on the village. The white-washed walls take on an ochre glow, recovering the solidity and depth of which the violent sunlight had deprived them. The smell of dairy produce, of grilled meat, of cummin bread pervades the air, and with it an atmosphere of peace and hope. The small courtyards are astir with the familiar noises of everyday life. The President of the Fishermen's Co-operative has come back from Sallacta, but without any fish, for according to him the sea was too rough. He is exaggerating; but it scarcely matters. Everybody has gone home; everybody is in his right place. And the enquirer, who is also the guest of Maghribi hospitality, feels himself rewarded, having sought—beneath the crude colours and the schematized developments—for some plenitude, his own or that of others. For a brief moment he enjoys his harmony, his affinity with an old way of life, more enduring and more complex than it appears to the scientific observer or the man of action, and richer with the values of the future.

Life in the Village

Thus whether it proceeds from its own native traditions or, on the contrary, from innovation, the village has become the most living force in the rural Maghrib, and tends to overrun all other forms of social life. To reconstruct it, I have tried to consider it between two symmetrical ways of approach. On the one hand, the search for fundamental relations between the group and nature, *its* nature. On the other, a phenomenology which takes into account the slightest incident, the most moving expressions. But for all its prodigious diversity of places, cases and situations, the picture is broadly characteristic of the Maghrib. It consists of an antagonism between two elements which, at the time, held conflict in suspense; each of the two through its opinions, its language, its very aspect, strove to repress the other into the past. Colonization rejected the old way of living, the native methods of agriculture. But other dynamic forces arose which tended to push colonization itself into the past.

This movement was not homogeneous. Uneven developments took place within it. Time, variously conceived of and lived by each individual, sought a common rhythm. It did not succeed: whence the intense and hazardous nature of the chronicle. No institution was able to make any forcible impression on the whole; neither the old, communal way of life, nor the modern system, which a few had taken over. These disagreements became even more pronounced in certain sectors. The new district of the town, the Frenchified *Place de la Mairie* with its bandstand and its plane trees, contrasts with the Arab district, sometimes called 'negro district'. Economic and social success or failure quickly underlined the disproportion between cultural techniques, the anachronistic nature of observances, the inequalities of education, all the contrasts involved in that propinquity and that mutual influence that were inescapable.

Algeria of the Tell, the valley of the Mejerda, the Moroccan sea-coast carry to extreme limits a composite life in which small-town intrigues intermingle with the violence of pioneering days. The native community breaks up and is recreated, against, and usually regardless of, law. Local big-wigs become busy mediators between their kindred and the stranger, between past and present. Thus they aim at a new hegemony. Marabouts, members of brotherhoods, in touch with the Divine, undertake mediations which are even more lucrative, since they bring the other world into play. The power of the French *cacique* combines the wiles of the petty administrator and the prestige of the great landowner. Added to which we have the *colon*, the settler, a capable administrator and a pernicious symbol: the man of the Arab bureau, divided between anachronistic efficiency and bureaucratic apathy. And the whole thing is badly integrated, or disintegrating, split into strata of wealth and social dignity, driven by lusts and ravaged by resentment, with its validity already called in question. It is criticized from many angles; that of the old soldier, the school teacher, the '*ulama*' and the nationalist. True, the various forces coexist, but the basic hypothesis is out of date. Broadly speaking, two cliques are in opposition to one another, which have taken over the old name of *saffs*.[1] The alliance between high administrative officials, the *Élus*,[2] the Lodge, the Church, the Caïd, and the big landowner divides the champions between those who take advantage of it and those who oppose it. The heterogeneity of races, the furious competition of interests, the violence of words and gestures are smoothed out by a hypocritical provincialism. Through its ways of life, as through its aspect, the village seeks to imitate Meridional France, whereas from all sides it is threatened by a Maghrib which seeks to belong to the Middle East.

[1] Isabelle Eberhardt suffered from this during her stay at Tenès at the beginning of this century, and it has been dealt with at length in her biographies; cf. particularly that of R. Randau and the recent one by Jean Noël.

[2] Shortly after the first world war, when political rights, including the right to sit in local assemblies, were given to certain categories of Muslims with high educational qualifications, distinguished military service, etc., although they were not French citizens, these Muslims formed themselves into a group called the Fédération des Élus Musulmans, led by Dr. Bendjelloul and Ferhat Abbas, whose main object was in fact to campaign for French citizenship for their members.

And this Maghrib is on the way up, whatever its opponents may do. Even in the colonized villages around Oran the native population maintains its preponderance, not, indeed, in institutions nor always in actual numbers, but in the outward aspect of the village and its way of life. At school, European children are in the minority. The village high-day is not Sunday, but market day. Many *petits blancs*, farm managers, mechanics, roadmenders, animal gelders, have crossed that demarcation line of which Kipling speaks, on the other side of which Islam reigns supreme. French children, whose fathers may be officers or doctors or administrators, are aware, with a keenness that maturity ought to convert into political liberalism, of the young Arab's superior adaptation to his native land.[1] 'Ali is adept at hunting lizards and gerboas; he can shoot with a catapult or a woollen sling plaited by his sister, or make many-coloured cords with a forked reed. 'Ali collects plants, offers me strings of mushrooms, *tifef* (a sort of sow-thistle), *gern jdi* (wild artichokes), *zidhum* (sweet onions), and all sorts of salads.' How deeply rooted he is in his native soil, what mysterious aptitudes my little friend displays!

'A nearby tribe is that of the Mharga, which means "burnt". Hence a play on words: they are consumed with love from adolescence to old age, they have proved themselves great seducers; many of their ancestors died victims of passion, some, like the Bani Udhra of the pre-Islamic era, pined away from unsatisfied love, perished at the age of twenty! But a more typical figure is the bold night-rover, a knife between his teeth, taking by force the woman he desires in her own tent, lying by her husband's side.' This, indeed, is a romantic anecdote that recurs frequently in the tales of old chroniclers. What struck the writer, as a child, was the stress on the theme of sex, which made the Maghribi world all round him a fiery, ardent world in which honour and shame, good and evil almost, were identified with the active or passive principles, with success or failure in erotic conquest. And the closer the contact between the two societies, the more marked grew their differences. Details of clothing assumed a mythical significance. 'Our dress is ample and flowing, yours tight; you bare your heads in church and keep on your shoes, we take off our shoes and keep our heads covered...We eat only of an animal that has been ritually slaughtered; you, on the contrary, feed on *jifa* (animals that have not been slaughtered according to the canon)...'

The religious theme, the magic of the East, recur constantly in their minds; the faith they defend is identified with their group solidarity. Thus the men of the Maghrib seek, and after a fashion find, compensa-

---

[1] I have borrowed here from the vivid recollections of Albert Lentin, 'Jours d'El-Hasi', published in the *Revue Africaine*, 1961, pp. 49 ff. Cf. also the lively sketches of another native of Constantine, Stephen Chasseray, author of the *Chroniques de l'Oued Melhouf*.

tions. These are dubious compounds, on more grounds than one, attitudes of 'bad faith' as Sartre might say; but what else can they do? And the French boy, as he listens to his companions' words, is intuitively aware of a mighty latent force. The pity is that, when he reaches man's estate, he will reject these admirable concepts. It is one of the paradoxical things about a 'new country' that youth quickly loses its spontaneous reactions and assumes the selfish wisdom of maturity.

The North African village of the inter-war period–that fertile field of contact between Europeans and the men of the Maghrib, even where statistics show one of these to be lacking; where the sedentary way of life has conquered the nomadic, and Cain has vanquished Abel–has stabilized discords without resolving them. This is why it led a mixed and hybrid life, where a sort of provincial charm disguised the urgency of conflicts. And that is why it went through phases of equilibrium and disequilibrium, which alternated more and more dramatically, and which we could retrace in its own inner history, if our sight were keen enough to discern them. It offers, in turn, forms of action and of expression for a history whose forces are drawn from below and whose ideas are derived from on high.[1]

[1] Distortions will only cease when the village has achieved self-integration, which presupposes the integration and stabilization of the country itself.

CHAPTER VI

Fez Between Two World Wars

B y the time the Protectorate was established, centuries of greatness had already made the *madina* of Fez one of the great places of the Maghrib and of Islam.[1] The Wadi, which an ingenious system of sluice-gates in the Bujelud garden divides between the three urban zones, brings drinking-water, freshness and ritual purity to every home. Then its waters, as though bearing away the sins of the city, flow into a channel, the Bu Khareb, which forms a hinge between the two slopes of Qarawiyin and the Andalus. The houses, each built round a central court, clustering in an immense honeycomb; the maze of narrow streets where the shade of greyish walls and bowers of Virginia creeper temper the burning heat of the day; the crowds of pedlars and idlers streaming endlessly past; all this, which might be anarchistic and ugly, is transformed into a harmonious urban whole. Tradesmen and artisans, for the most part grouped into their separate districts, celebrate their periodical forgatherings, daily or weekly in the suqs where the voice of the *dallal*[2] resounds. The transit of merchandise from the south towards the sea, and from overseas towards the interior, the processing of country produce, the provisioning of vast inland areas have maintained here, from time immemorial, a flourishing economic life. Fez, wily and rapacious, provides innumerable sanctuaries for its own purification. These are set out in some twenty sectors, each defined by a mosque where a weekly *khutba*[3] is delivered. Its piety, its pride, its vitality meet in the

[1] R. Le Tourneau, *Fès avant le Protectorat*, a study which in the main holds good for the interwar period, during which most of its documentation was collected.

[2] *Dallal*, the town crier; on whom I published a study, in collaboration with G. H. Bousquet, in the *Revue d'économie politique*, May 1940, showing the prominent part he played in the traditional economic structure of the city. The importance of this role has since been confirmed, *a contrario*, by the disappearance of the *dallal*–as well as that of the *amin*, 'Corporation receiver'–owing to the modernization of the *madina*'s economy.

[3] *Khutba*: weekly sermon. The municipal significance of this was shown by W. Marçais in a well-known article.

monumental Mosque of Qarawiyin, the heart of the city, where hundreds of students seek initiation into the higher branches of learning, under venerable teachers.[1] And the spiritual impulse that springs up from this unanimity, like a fountain from its basin, rains down exaltation and good works in the daily life of the inhabitants and in their collective history. It inspires their customs and their language, unifies their attitudes and transcends social conflicts. Charitable gifts and pious foundations are considered to provide amply for municipal services, and, accumulating over the years, have increased the city's monumental mass.

This wonderful bourgeois city had subsisted on, and been preserved by, the age-old conflict between its mercantile tradition and its symbolic plan;[2] how was it to meet the challenge of modern times? Since 1912 it had realized that popular risings were powerless against up-to-date troops. In the defeat of the Berber assailants, and the extension of subjugated areas, it quickly discerned fresh prospects of gain. Its problem was to reconcile a profitable surface adherence with the ineradicability of its profounder life. Its whole story, from 1912 to 1956, reflects this ingenious endeavour. And the fundamental ambiguity of its relations with the Protectorate was met with corresponding ambiguity by French attitudes. In these, aesthetic appreciation and political respect were mingled with the anxiety aroused by this refractory mass, with its tenacious culture and its equivocal allegiance.

A first measure, of great consequence, helped to preserve the site from any contamination. Already the old town had set the gardens of Bujelud, with their rushing streams, between itself and suburbs of lesser dignity, such as Fez Jdid, which was still half Bedouin, and the Jewish quarter of Mellah. Reciprocally, but in virtue of the same principle, the immense *mishwar*[3] of the Imperial Palace, at the junction of the two suburbs, stood apart from the city proper. The French therefore decided to build their own town, separate from these four unequal masses, on the plateau of Dar Debibagh.[4] Already in 1916 thay had laid out a commercial sector and an industrial sector. By 1918 the plots available for building homes and small shops had all been sold except six. Half of them had been acquired by Jews, for the older elements of the population reacted uncertainly to the dangerous criterion of adaptation. In 1917 Commandant Sciard, who had already exhausted on these develop-

---

[1] J. Berque, 'Dans le Maroc nouveau. Le rôle d'une Université islamique,' *Annales d'histoire économique et sociale*, 1937, no. 51, p. 193 ff. I apologize for having to quote in this chapter several of my own writings which deal with first-hand observation made at the time.

[2] Id. 'Medinas, Villeneuves et Bidonvilles', *Cahiers de Tunisie*, 9159, p. 12.

[3] *mishwar*: an inner esplanade in the Sultan's palace (Morocco).

[4] The following information comes from unpublished municipal records.

ments all the credit allowed him by the loan of 1914, sketched out a new plan, which gave the new town the aspect it wears today. Lyautey's architect, Prost, and Captain Mellier, one of the few men who understood Fez, met on 8 September 1917, to discuss the new town and the rearrangement of the market-place of Bab Semmarin. This stands almost at the centre of the urban configuration. From here, the boulevard of Bukhsisat leads to the new town, by way of the Mellah. The central artery of Fez Jdid opens, on the left, on to Maulay 'Abdallah, the prostitutes' district, which rings with the whine of huge irrigation wheels; on the right, on to Bujelud. Through Bab Jiyaf (the 'carrion gate') a steep path leads up to the *madina*. The need to connect these different units amongst themselves, and the whole group of them to the imperial Rabat-Ujda road, in a practical and, if possible, aesthetic fashion, created a ticklish problem for town-planners. Various projects were compared. The municipality wanted the connection to be made between Burj Shaikh Ahmad (the southern burj) and Bab Jiyaf. The Office of Public works proposed a transversal road between the Bab Jiyaf–Bab Hadid section and the Imperial road. The Regional Chief proposed a third plant. The Public Works' plant was adopted, since it was to the advantage of the Fez Electrical Company, already installed in its ravine. But certain arguments from military men are worth quoting, for they illustrate the method pursued.

'Are we going to acquire the land by means of expropriation? It consists of market gardens, wonderfully well watered. They could not be bought for less than six francs per metre, and even that is far below their value to the natives who own them; this amounts to about 30,000 francs for acquisition of the road. But if we pay for access to this road, the natives who previously gave up their lands for earlier roads will regret their past generosity and feel themselves cheated. Are we going to ask for this valuable land to be graciously given us? Hitherto the natives (apart from one protégé of the English) have allowed us to acquire those roads which we have shown them to be in the general interest. But they will find it hard to understand the general interest of the proposed road. The objection I can foresee is that this road is only being made to satisfy the needs of the electricity works. I therefore feel scarcely in a position to ask the owners of these market gardens to give up part of their land to us, and I consider it would be better not to take this step.[1]'

In any case, developments were carried on, more lavishly for the new town, it is true, but with some concern for the needs of the old. In the immediate post-war period the various bodies that had been set up were organized, notably that municipal council, the Majlis al-Baladi, of which Lyautey was so proud, and which was not completely under the

[1] Letter 446, R.V. 2, 30 June 1918 (in Lyautey's correspondence), highly revealing of the Bureau Arabe's attitude, and quoted *in extenso* for that reason.

thumb of Pasha al-Baghdadi. With the progress of pacification, commerce prospered. In the heart of the Madina, in the Rue Rahbat al-Kis, a daring French sugar-merchant, M. Ancey, and, close by, a branch of the State Bank, united to renovate economic methods.[1] Road-building progressed. It was constantly divided between the municipal ideal of speed and cheapness, and that of the Department of Fine Arts, which was to respect the site. Once again, the eternal conflict between the *qadim* and the *jadid*.

The adaptation envisaged was considerate of the city's hierarchies, the balance of its relations, its aims. Lyautey intended to preserve Fez, in its setting as in its customs, from any brutal impact. Fez, meanwhile, wishing to retain control over its own transformation, was ready to come to terms. Thus the dominant class of tradesmen, *tjjar*, borrowed – or thought it was borrowing – from the outside world only what suited it: the use of the telephone, of electric light, of the typewriter. Some citizens opened little offices at Qattanin, and at Sagha, where they huddled over specially constructed desks. They condescended to go to evening classes to learn French; they contributed to the Salon du Goût Français in Paris, in 1923; they sent their children to the Collège Maulay Idris, on which Lyautey kept a watchful eye, through the intermediary of Commandant Marty.[2] True, they remained faithful to their old trading habits! no joint-stock companies, and above all no contracts. They protested loudly against banking interest, although they made use of credit and were not averse to usurious financing. They spent on splendid trousseaux, extravagant dowries, the purchase of giant mules and the construction of indoor gardens, more than was approved of by the moral code of Islam or by modern economic principles. The younger generation was aware of this. The time was soon to come when it would boldly indict its elders for their sumptuary expenses and their ostentation, which, however, gave the city its crowning glory and restored its self-confidence.[3]

In a more realistic spirit, Fez proceeded to strengthen itself by buying up, from neighbouring tribes, the lands that lay around its ramparts. Relations between town and country were thus established, thanks to the first profits from the Protectorate and the new security of transactions, relations which would have been of great value to the nation had they not been one-sided. The townsman – stout, constricted in his elegant clothes, often breathless and even asthmatic – did not often visit his farm. Towards his Bedouins he behaved, at best, with condescension. Meanwhile, however, crowds of country folk thronged the

---

[1] See article by 'Abd al-Wahhab Lahlu, *Hesperis*, 1937, pp. 223 ff.

[2] Commandant Marty, *Le Maroc nouveau*. This expert finally left the town in disgrace, suspected of proselytism: *mazlum*, a victim of injustice, his many Moroccan friends declared.

[3] I have dealt with this at greater length in *Mélanges Lévi-Provençal*, 1962.

employment centres.[1] Apart from Fez Djid, which already belonged to them, they had begun to settle in the outskirts of the city. This caused considerable uneasiness. A good deal later, in 1938, some big-wig in the Majlis al-Baladi actually demanded that special buses be set aside for this scum. There was no question of any movement back to the land. The Administration, indeed, tried to instil better agricultural methods, through the mouth of a learned shaikh, 'Ali Zaki. This attempt became legendary through its complete failure. For the time being one single man of the new school, Muhammad al-Marnisi, opted for modern economic methods, cultivated profitable links with European business enterprise and embarked on a career in the Chamber of Agriculture which was to last as long as the system.

It is in this continuous tradition of limited adaptation and support that we should trace the internal history of the town, both before and after the Rif incident. The men who mattered were those who, whether on the French or on the Muslim side, played the part of mediators. I have already mentioned some of the Frenchmen and must add the name of the most revered of them all, Dr. Christiani.[2] On the Moroccan side, economic innovation provides a reliable criterion. In 1923, Sharif Mshish al-'Alami cancelled the selling of shad by auction and organized the trade industrially. At this period, the first generation of scholars graduated from the Collège Maulay Idris. And simultaneously the Majlis al-Baladi protested violently against the opening of a girls' school. Kemalism provoked shocked horror.

These circumspect changes, whether accepted or resisted, aroused men's feelings. The town knew this, took credit for it, even used it as a weapon against the Administration. It thus regained the role of a model, which long centuries had bequeathed it. It had always provided a pattern for Morocco. The men of the old school realized that they must needs do a profitable deal with the world. They endeavoured to do so, with all the concealed energy of which they were capable. Doubtless they had to endure renewed reproaches from the younger generation for a piety that thinly disguised their sensuality, for their hypocritical decorum, their envenomed politeness, and the verbal nature of their courage. Divided between dread and attraction, loyal to those labyrinths, their city, their culture and their state of mind, they felt that the time for their withdrawal was at hand. In their fifties they usually joined some mystic brotherhood. But that did not preserve them from awareness of a state of things when they would have to choose between saying no and going to extremes, between reaction and revolution.

Their sons were to adopt the second of these attitudes. And the men

---

[1] Known locally as *muquefs* (*mauqifs*), 'stations'.

[2] Director of the Cocard Hospital, in the former Qasba of the Sherarda. He is remembered with great respect. One should also mention such men as Oulibou and Odinot, and a very few others.

of the old school were delighted to be contradicted by these sons, whose future audacities they foresaw. But in the meantime, perhaps, someone else would have arisen? it might even be one of these rustics, crude of manner and careless of ritual purity, as coarse as any Frenchman, but capable of dying, according to all the rules, for values which he had not earned . . .

The Abd el-Krim affair, in 1925, reveals other forms of resistance which the French advance met with in unsubjugated Morocco in a harsher key. But besides their aspects of tribal honour, xenophobic energy and zeal in waging a 'holy war', it revealed others, some of them notably in advance of their time. The leader here was no local marabout, promising paradise to those who fought the infidel, but a political chief whose ambitions now included the idea of nationhood, and even a share in the international game.[1] The support given him by the Comintern and the French Communist Party, the allies he found within the Islamic world where, at that period, the second *thaura* of Damascus was in full swing, make of Abd el-Krim a type whose significance is enhanced by his final defeat by disproportionate forces. At this point, however, we need only note the repercussions of his brief epic in the bourgeois citadel.

From the beginning of the year, things happened fast. At Thursday's *suq*, people from the North brought surprising news. In the offices of the Regional Bureau, or at Dar Tazi, the headquarters of the Region, a visitor from Fez would be aware of unaccustomed activity. By January, the Rifan chief had got the better of his old enemy, Sharif Raisuli, who had once terrorized Europeans at the very gates of Tangier. This hero of old Morocco, now grown obese, his round face framed with a fringe of beard, ended up like a fallen ogre, in the harshest captivity. Abd el-Krim celebrated the occasion with great festivities at Ajdir. Soon, on the rainy hills of the Pre-Rif and the Jebala, winter paralysed everything. As soon as it ended, Abd el-Krim 'swallowed up' the Bani-Zerwal, who had hitherto resisted him, and burnt the *zawiya* of the Derqawa. By 18 April he appeared to have complete control of the tribe. From this position he harried the Jaiya and rallied to his side the Bani Uriaghel and the Sles of the Urtzagh. He announced that he would enter Fez during the octave of the 'Id. May, in fact, saw the beginning of his onslaught on Fez, defended after a fashion by Colombat and Freydenberg. Was the hero of the holy war, the tough Northern mountaineer, going to restore the city to an Islamic power? This would prove a severe test for its citizens, who had already accepted the French régime. Nevertheless some chord within them responded, and people of standing withdrew their children

[1] Bournazel commented with surprise: 'There are no more children.' Quoted by H. Bordeaux, *Capitaine de Bournazel*, 1957, p. 99.

from the French school. By the end of May, however, French troops, operating in two masses based on Tissa and Fez al-Bali, succeeded in protecting the town. After all, this *mahdi* might only be a *rogui*[1] doomed to jail like so many others . . .

Abd el-Krim, checked in the centre, struck out eastwards towards Taza, and westwards, where the defection of the Jebala enabled him to reach the threshold of the Gharb. However, he no longer enjoyed the advantage of a surprise attack. The official myth was already being built up against him. French statesmen such as Painlevé and Eynac visited Fez, where the 'Id al-Kabir was celebrated on 18 June. From July onwards reinforcements flowed in ceaselessly. The Third Republic decided to send its greatest military leader against Abd el-Krim. All this made Lyautey and his Morocco a thing of the past. In September, thanks to these absurdly powerful forces, the French zone was almost entirely reoccupied. On the Spanish side Sanjurjo, in liaison with the French General Staff, improved his positions. Abd el-Krim could only hope to negotiate for favourable terms. Confidential soundings, in which picturesque figures of old Morocco such as Pierre Parent and Auguste Montagne took part, raised expectations of the issues. It was no longer in doubt after the breaking-off of the Ujda talks. But the disproportion between the results and the large-scale means employed, the weakness of the French rear, the possibilities of psychological switchover that had been revealed, the inglorious conclusion of the Lyautey régime, made a deep impression on people's minds. On 3 October the old Marshal took his leave of Fez. The ceremony, on the Place Nejjarin, was impressive and moving, like so many other features of his proconsulate; yet everybody knew that a world had come to an end.

By 1925 depression was on the way. It was to last ten years. Fez suffered first from a sudden rise in the cost of living, which Commandant Le Gueval did not succeed in controlling. Wheat rose to 125 francs per quintal, mutton to 8 francs per kilo, whereas the municipal worker's wage was 7·50 francs a day. By August wheat had risen to 135 francs, mutton to 9·75. The influx of soldiers did indeed provide a considerable stimulus, but also caused inflation, from which bazaar-keepers, hoteliers and prostitutes reaped more benefit than did the consumer. The Place du Commerce, on the edge of Mellah, famous for its Maroc-Hôtel and its Cinéma d'Apollon, rang with cacophonous dance-music all night. The inauguration of an enormous brothel was celebrated with a public reception (26 September 1925); it was a municipal event! A policeman who had insulted an 'adil (the Qadi's clerk of the court) was duly dismissed. A legionary was found murdered; arms were stolen from the Dar Mahres camp. There was a revival of the sale of *kif* (hashish), not unconnected with political propaganda. Two Europeans were assaulted, seventy-five kilometres along the Taza road. Traffic offences increased.

[1] A religious agitator.

The soldiery and those who made money out of them filled the town. Not until November did it begin to get clear of them.

But the depreciation of the franc, the high cost of rents, the rise in the price of commodities (mutton rose to 10 francs per kilo) prolonged the economic and moral effects of this period of agitation, speculation and debauchery. Fortunately the rainy winter gave hopes of a good year for agriculture, and hence for profitable trading with the Bedouins in the Qaisariya. Was the military era done with? On 9 November the new Resident-General, Steeg, appeared in Fez, causing some astonishment by wearing a top hat and making pacifist speeches.[1]

The Majlis al-Baladi knew nothing about its municipal budget, except what the officials deigned to tell it. In the matter of public works, it was far less demanding than the European sector of the town, which held one-tenth of its population. Questions might have elicited, for instance, that the programme for 1927 included the construction of sewers for the 'Residential and Commercial Sector', a road leading to the Dar Mahrez hospital, and the equipment of offices of Public Works in the New Town; for the Madina, merely the erection of a poorhouse and a delousing centre at Bab Segma. The differences are significant. The Madina oscillated between privilege and indigence; one state was the counterpart of the other, but they represented different social elements.

Goodwill, rather than financial help, was needed by the worthies who, building on the periphery of the town, towards Bab el-Gisa or Bab Jdid, encroached on the profusion of gardens which they were bound by law to respect; in the new districts of Zenj Fur, for instance, or Derb el-Miter. But for them, too, the crisis was a severe one. It gave rise to a general slump, *ksad*. Artisans, shopkeepers, even tradesmen had recourse to the moneylender. Family belongings and furniture found their way to the public auction. In 1930, a commission to enquire into tax relief had to sit for a fortnight in the Majlis, examining three hundred and fifty-seven claims. The exemptions amounted to a mere 50,000 francs, but the political effect was considerable. On 18 December, the Majlis met under the presidency of General Ducla. The assembly was a patrician one; it included two members of the Moqri family, three of the Tazi, and other famous city names. All were friendly towards the régime. There was one matter, however, on which they remained intransigent: the water of the Wadi. Now, further upstream, settlers were moving in. The Majlis expressed keen anxiety. They were pacified by the promise that drinking water would be brought into the Madina.

A year later the first pipes were laid: the opening ceremony was performed by the Resident, Lucien Saint, and a triumphal arch, wreathed with bougainvillea, was set up at Bujellud. The town guilds flaunted their banners. Shouts of excitement rang out. The Resident's

[1] Details taken from the *Bulletin des renseignements municipaux* for 1925.

speech was translated, so the press tells us, 'into impeccable dialect'.
No doubt obstinate opponents saw something sinister about the affair.
But progress swept everything before it. This was a great date in the
history of the town.[1]

A great date, not only from the ecological but also from the social,
dare one say the sentimental point of view. For the town's water supply
was closely connected with the town's freedom. Hence the anxiety displayed by these highborn citizens. They were well aware of the singular
nature of their own genius, of which they made a weapon and sometimes
even a profession; so were the administrators, who strove by every
means to come to terms with it. They did not succeed, for their efforts
remained dispersed. They failed, and with good reason, to understand
how an event affecting one community could turn into a national
phenomenon. Sometimes they tried to grasp it through its aesthetic
aspect, sometimes, on the contrary, by offering economic help. The two
approaches were insufficient. Translated into action, they left a gap
through which flowed a vehement stream of claims and protests. How
could it have been otherwise? In their effort to control the city's development, the authorities could not fulfil all their ambitions nor even satisfy
their own interests. The colonial situation made this impossible. Reciprocally, in its response to this effort, the town could not achieve complete
adaptation. Self-interest, among other things, prevented it. True, it was
able to take advantage of its new security, of the possibilities of export
and transit, of the growing needs of the consumer and of more rapid
communications. But at the same time it felt itself cheated, or, more
exactly, disappointed in some of its hopes. Its ascendancy was dwindling
over the land that surrounded it.

In these prosaic days, Fez paid dearly for its past privileges, the town
plan laid down 'from above', in which it gloried, its imposing old-
fashioned prestige, all the features which made of it a Maghribi or indeed
an Islamic capital, rather than just the *chef-lieu* of a region. It strove
indeed, with all its ancient cunning, to take advantage of the new state
of things. It sent its qadis, its commercial agents to the remotest Moroccan townships, as far afield as Saint Louis or even Japan. The export of
babouches, the import of cotton goods were its links with the outside
world. But two dangerous competitors barred its way. The Bureau des
Affaires Indigènes severed its links with the tribes, while the *colons*
outdid it in land investment; and its business methods, hoarding and
speculation, could not compete with the capitalism of the banks. Meanwhile, geographically and logically, Casablanca was supplanting Fez.
It had all the advantages of a maritime emporium over an inland
marketplace. All roads now led to the ocean: the Tadla road for instance,
the shortest way through the fertile Chaouia. The hinterland of Casa-

[1] *Courrier du Maroc*, 24 Nov. 1931.

blanca was growing inordinately. Simply by using new commercial methods, wholesale dealings, settlement through bills of exchange and credit, it captured the trade of South Morocco and the Tafilalt, traditional tributaries of the merchants of Fez. Some of the latter saw this so clearly that from 1935 onward they moved over to the coast town. In 1938 the vice-president of the Association of former pupils of the Collège Maulay Idris shifted his business from Fez to Casablanca; desertion of his city, but foresight from a national point of view.

Thus, more and more, Fez found itself cut off, not in its existence but in its hopes—and hope is inseparable from existence; it was forced to make a difficult fresh start. It reacted in its own way. It countered French policy with a display of piety; it brought into play the prestige of its ancient University, which, though no longer productive, was still an active centre of protest and emotion. From the economic point of view it strove, also, to exalt its own capitalism and even to give it a revolutionary tinge. It was not by chance that the greatest fortunes, which, at that time, were consecrated to the import trade, were those of citizens who were to play an increasing political role: Ahmad Mikwar, for instance, who became treasurer of the Nationalist Party. Threatened from all sides, the city reacted by accusing the Protectorate of illegality. And at the same time it made use of it as far as possible. In both cases, it performed an act of piety.

Let us see, by comparison, how another capital, a purely regional one, reacted under similar circumstance. Marrakesh[1] held sway over the Atlas and Haouz regions and the world of the Shleuhs. From the further end of the plain, as soon as the arid chain of the Jebilet has been left behind, one can make out the minaret of the Kutubia and behind it, towering over the red walls and palm trees of Ibn Tumart, rises snow-capped Bu Iblan.

The city is afflicted by drought. If we skim through the records of its town council for 1930, we see the same complaint recurring: 'troubles due to drought,' 'slump in production.' Marrakesh suffers from under-development, as we should say today, to a more crippling extent than does the North. The price of essential commodities is only half those of Fez. Beef is worth 4·50 francs: camel meat, of which a great deal is eaten, between 3 and 5·50 francs. This speaks volumes about the remuneration of stock breeders and the standard of living. The market price-list carefully notes local products, whose cheapness is staggering. *Khbiza*, a sort of biscuit eaten by the poor, costs 1·10 francs for 650 grammes. This implies not so much cheapness as poverty. In fact, the city authorities deplore the dwindling of trade, for instance a drop in consignments of cattle. This affected the leather-workers, who traditionally made those handsome, gold-embroidered saddles on which the

[1] Details taken from the *Bulletin des renseignements municipaux* for 1930.

town's grandees sat during their processions; obviously such an industry was the first to suffer.

These difficulties were not offset by the magnificence of the official functions provided as an outlet. The solemn entry of the Sultan on 19 March, a visit from the President of the Republic and other ceremonies, did not save the town from an economic inertia that involved growing demoralization. A huge crowd of prostitutes, heraldic and shameless, were said to fatten the Pasha's treasury with their fees. The French authorities scarcely interfered with methods of primitive accumulation which sought to make profit out of such elementary motives as fear, appetite and lust. The rapacious taxation of the Glawi, over a vast area, completed the ravages due to locusts, which afflicted such tribes as the Ultana, the Ftwaka, the Tuggana and the Mesfiwa. Strategic and political interests covered everything. Only the initiates, such as Robert Montagne—who was then propounding his thesis in the Sorbonne—knew that the 'great caïd' would prove the inevitable destroyer of that Shleuh democracy on which the French sought to lean. They knew it, but they were often unwilling to say so. On the other hand, the Youth Party demonstrated on the occasion of the Berber *dahir*.[1] The *fqih* Mukhtar Susi was a victim of repression. Many more had to suffer from the sinister khalifa al-Biyaz. Moreover, of the three great caïds only one was still rising, Hajj Thami al-Glawi. His ambitions had now grown; he aimed at becoming Viceroy. His shady connections with the Epinat group of mines and his support from the French Radical Socialists, enabled him to sustain a splendid, if burdensome and rapacious, way of life. There is a striking example of the privileges he enjoyed, given in the *Bulletin Municipal*. The document estimates at 2 million francs per annum the loss to the budget caused by the Pasha's exemption from paying toll. But this privilege was bought in 1930 for the price of 45,000 francs. This speaks volumes about the place and the period, about administrative tolerance and the balance-sheet of a great caïd!

If the life of Marrakesh reflects, in a highly picturesque fashion and with archaic exactness, its profound connection with the surrounding region, yet the city remained, through good and evil fortune, a typical provincial Southern town. Fez on the contrary, though cut off from its hinterland, was the more jealously concerned on that account to represent its general movement. The whole municipal history of Fez was made up of a continual and subtle interplay between a material reality which was badly compromised and an ideal that was still ambitious.

[1] On the occasion of which Fez held a *latif* (special type of rogation in the mosques). Cf. *Afrique française*, 1913, p. 515. The Administration has to disown the activities of Father Ange Kohler in the parish of the Madina, rightly or wrongly accused of proselytizing.

The artisan,[1] the third force in the city's life, was, according to an adage, now *mandil* now *qandil*–dish-clout or lamp-post–according to whether he lay crushed in subjection or rose in revolt. His production at this time was relatively considerable, as a few figures will show.

The workers of Fez produced 300,000 pairs of babouches a year, of which about one-tenth were shipped to Senegal. This colonial sideline of Fez's craftsmanship is paralleled by the export of tarbushes from Tunis to Guinea and other countries of Negro Africa. The *drazat*, or weaving industries, employed 700 looms, each of which could produce three metres of stuff per day. The coppersmiths, *saffarin*, worked some fifty tons of metal per year into cauldrons and trays. The tanners used, for tannin, 2,000 cwt. of tamaris gum, *takaout*, and 3,000 cwt. of green oak bark, *fernan*. They processed 50,000 cattle hides, 75,000 goat hides and 250,000 sheep hides. Finally, we should mention an institution peculiar to the Madina, the auctions, which employed multitudes of town criers. Almost all dealing between various bodies and trades was done through the intermediary of the town crier, according to old customs representing collective solidarity, ostentation and joyous expansiveness. Now the business done under the auspices of the Fez town crier was reckoned, at the time, to amount to 200 million francs.

The bulk of the artisans were divided into corporations, which I have called guilds, because of a superficial analogy, since no Arabic word exists, in Fez, to describe them: they are simply known as *al-hiraf*, the crafts. Some of them comprised a very large number of workers.[2] The slipper-makers, *kherraza*, numbered some 7,100, consisting of 2,840 employers, plus workmen and apprentices. This craft alone accounted for two-thirds of the town's artisans; whence the importance of this huge guild, itself divided into two sections, the *blaighiya* who made men's slippers and the *msakhriya* who made slippers for women. Another very different type of guild was the *debbagha*, the tanners' guild, with which may be included that of the *lebbata*, the tawers; there were some 800 of these, including 280 employers. They had already undergone certain elementary forms of economic concentration. The tanners' boss was often an entrepreneur of sorts; he was then nicknamed 'the satchel man', *ma'allem shkayri*. The weavers numbered 1,700, of whom 520 were employers. They were divided into those who produced fine fabrics, *jlalbiya*, and those who made coarse fabrics and thick wools, *bundaf*, such as countrymen wore. The 1,100 *harrara* wove handkerchiefs and women's silk sashes. They were even more disastrously ruined than the rest. The coppersmiths, finally, worked almost

---

[1] J. Berque, 'Deux ans d'action artisanale à Fès,' *Questions nord-africaines*, 25 June 1939. Fez was ravaged by usury. During a sensational lawsuit in 1933–4, it was revealed that a loan of 300,000 francs would be repaid as 840,000 francs. The current rate was 40 per cent.
[2] Municipal statistics of 1938.

exclusively for the upper classes and the tourists. This was a small guild with only 170 employers, but a very active one.[1] In all, 11,000 workers were grouped into these large corporations, energetic centres of community life.

Now between 1930 and 1935 this primitive but highly organized way of life seemed fatally endangered. For instance, we note in the documents of 1932 some effects of the world drop in prices. It affected the export trade in leather, hides and wool, in a word the whole of the rural contribution to the urban market. The processing industries suffered both from the effects of this crisis and from the competition of manufactured goods imported from abroad! The artisan was further crippled by onerous taxation, by tolls and by those market rights which the Nationalist party criticized and which the Resident had the good sense to abolish. And meanwhile, native producers were forced to go on buying at prices in excess of the world tariff. For one thing, they had to satisfy consumer needs which were not yet obsolete; for another, production was based on a way of life which still put up resistance. In any case, we can understand how, when wool from Mazamet appeared in Morocco at a lower price than Moroccan wool, it provoked a crisis—particularly since the world market got its supplies by buying cheap, foreign fabrics poured into the Qaisariya. The fact is that these were all manufactured goods which, by virtue of the Act of Algeciras, competed freely with local products during the whole duration of the Protectorate. This 'colonial' aspect of things cannot be minimized.

There were complaints in plenty! Notice, for instance, the petition of the slipper-makers of Fez against Japanese competition in 1933. The townsfolk themselves, by some strange aberration, took a fancy to the Japanese-made shoes with vamps of glossy white leather, which could be polished. This was a fatal advantage over the traditional babouche, which tended to turn yellow and had to be replaced periodically. The workers' only hope was protectionism. They rioted whenever a new product appeared or a technical invention made them foresee unemployment. They demonstrated against the use of chemical tannin, or of an instrument for plaiting braid, or the extension of machinery in general. These are constant reactions of manual workers in all countries and all ages against mechanical progress. And yet Moroccan hides were already being processed in European-run tanneries, particularly at Mogador, the products of which were being sold on the market place in Fez. Ironically enough, the exquisite art of the book-binder, in which the Service of Native Arts and Crafts was rightly interested, only used hides tanned by European methods. Beside the ancient guilds new ones arose, resulting from the tourist trade, such as the makers of purses and cushions, recruited from among the immigrants from Bani Zerwal. The picturesque

[1] The guild had its own petty leaders and its poets. One of these, Mikwar, published in 1937 a highly classical volume of verse.

guild of *kurduniya* was composed largely of ex-soldiers; it produced clumsy sandals and boots in the new style, disdaining the work of local tanners. The weavers, like the slipper-makers, had no hope of revival. All round, they met with competition from Japanese cotton goods, Lyons silks and English cloth. Sales dropped everywhere and bitter resentment grew.

True, a few firms prospered: those known by the horrible name of 'bazaarists'. But artisans thus dependent on tourists' purchases, however generous, no longer formed part of a living circuit between urban production and rural consumption. They became denatured and depersonalized. The effects of this break were manifest in native crafts, which were now being ruined by bad workmanship, the invasion of chemical colours, the addition of metal feet to the traditional tray, the use of new, cheap materials. For instance, nickel silver, an alloy of brass, pushed by a Belgian consortium, invaded Morocco; with its silvery sheen, it tended to oust the warm glow of copper in the making of utensils.

To the depression of the working class, corresponding to that of the merchant class, was now added that of the University. The three traditional orders were thus declining, each for its own reasons, and all together in their mutal relations, on which the continued life of the city depended.

Out of the 800 to 900 students attending the Qarawiyin in 1935, only about 150 came from the town. The others, the vast majority, were from the *bled*, the countryside; they were known locally as the *afaqiyun*, people from the far horizon.[1] There was a wide difference of habits and appearance between these humble rustics and the Fasi youth, which was more concerned with universal problems but had at that time almost entirely forsworn the study of law for that of literature–an unprecedented development in Maghribi ideas and tastes. The Middle East being about half a century ahead of the Maghrib in this sphere, it was therefore in imitation of the Middle East, and of the regulations laid down by Cairo in 1930 for the Azhar, that an attempt was made to standardize the old University. But this provoked the quarrel of the *nizam*, the new curriculum.

The Qarawiyin, and its traditional studies, had hitherto been set apart, sheltered more or less from the interference of the Protectorate, whereas everywhere else direct administration made relentless progress. Of course, indirectly, the influence of the milieu and of the ruling power made itself felt within the precincts. Even here, the triumph of modernity was the more decisive, as the old figures faded out. By the thirties, in fact, the venerable *fuqaha*', the men of letters, had disappeared: Bil Qurshi, Ahmad bin Jilali, Bil Khiyat. They made way for *'ulama'* of a

---

[1] The word recurs with the same meaning in the Zaituna of Tunis, but not, so far as I know, in the Middle East.

more questioning turn of mind, infused with fresh blood, yet still on the whole averse to innovation. The organization of the *nizam* attempted a sort of deal between the old and the new, without in any way interfering with the mission of the Qarawiyin or the locus of studies, as was later to be done. Cycles were organized; primary, secondary and superior, the whole course lasting twelve years. Examinations, syllabuses and textbooks–things hitherto unknown–were decided on. There followed a complete change of protagonists, an upheaval in methods of study and a dwindling of audiences. The ancient preponderance of *fiqh*, the religious law, was threatened by this diversified education. Formerly any professor worthy of the name spent several years of his life commenting Sidi Khalil's *Mukhtasar*. Now, the syllabus included other matters, some of which, it was whispered, were conducive to unbelief. To tell the truth, none of these dry-as-dust texts seem likely to produce such effects! But the overthrow of a deep-rooted pedagogical system involved psychological disturbances. Formerly the personal decision, *tatauwu'*, of the teacher, had been held all-sufficient. At dawn or late at night, in the mosque or in the *zawiya*, the crowd that gathered to drink in his learned words had included artisans and tradesmen as well as students. Thus the city's unanimity was confirmed. The teacher played his part as social symbol. From now on, he became merely an instructor or, worse still, an official. For he received a monthly salary. This was secretly held against him. An old controversy about this issue lingers in all Muslim writings on the subject. The intellectual, in old days, was rewarded only by the gifts of his audience, or the generosity of his sovereign, the *sila*. Nowadays he has entered the ranks of those who receive a monthly pay check, the *manda* in local parlance. He had profaned his calling.

The fate of these ancient mosques was a bitter one. Their archaicism exposed them to criticism, and modernism altered their nature. Abused and mocked as teaching centres, they lost the leadership of the very movements which they sheltered.[1]

The nationalist movement, which inspired reform, benefited by the resentment this aroused. It attempted to take over the role of urban unification which the old University had lost. Already in 1934 it had proposed a Plan of Reforms, a mature and realistic document which did not receive due attention from the French. Backed by bourgeois wealth, rousing delirious excitement among the swashbucklers of certain conspiratorial groups, it preached the theme of a purified Islam, breaking with all practices that were supererogatory or merely sumptuary. When a division broke out in the party, the Qarawiyin, paradoxically, tended to

[1] My study, quoted above, which appeared in *Les Annales* under the pseudonym of F. Jabre, deals with developments at this precise moment (1937). Cf. article by 'Abdallah Guennoun on the evolution of the Qarawiyin, in *al-Maghrib*, June 1938.

support the leader who had studied at the École des Sciences Politiques and was inclined to Socialism. At the same time, the leader who had been trained at the Qarawiyin had on his staff an agronomic engineer and several of the first modern graduates. This interchange clearly reflects the give-and-take inherent in the city's balance. Indeed, whether openly or not, it was in the assertion of nationalist claims that the city sought for its own lost unity. But the quarrel between ancients and moderns remained open. The old teaching staff was not replaced by the new. For a long time, whenever a traditional jurist or preacher revived the old type of lecture, he still attracted the same crowds as of old, and competed to some extent with modern developments. The Fasi, like the Frenchman, champions lost causes and premature causes. Hence his anxiety; hence, too, his rebelliousness.

A more decisive centre of modernization was the actively functioning Collège Maulay Idris, where sympathetic masters such as Sallefranque and François Bonjean were teaching. These and some others, delving deep in search of a secret truth, pierced the dense strata of selfishness and conformism to reach the *foggara*[1] of mutual knowledge between North Africans and French. Indeed, from the thirties onward, Bonjean's vision was wonderfully penetrating. His *Filles de la Nuit*, based on the reality of life and, at the same time, springing from his heart, 'tributary of the like and the unlike at once' illustrates the miracle of this co-existence.

But, falling short of his wisdom or reaching beyond it, Fez was breaking into history. Everywhere, committees and coteries, small groups and parties displayed feverish activity. Festivities provided the opportunity for tentative and transient syntheses. Such tactics indeed were practised by the nationalist movement in its earlier years. All these movements obeyed a twofold rhythm: expansion followed by withdrawal, corresponding to another twofold rhythm followed by the administrators: concession, repression. Among the more sensational incidents of the time there was, for example, the circulation of a pamphlet, in 1935, denouncing the misdeeds of the Protectorate. It came from the Spanish zone, and was written by Makki Nasiri. One must also mention the demonstration of 8 May 1934, at Maulay Idris, where the young Sultan had the pleasure of being assured by an enthusiastic crowd that he was the only legitimate master. The Resident promptly removed him from the scene. Other demonstrations, subtler and more private, went just as far. Witness for instance an article by Ahmad Bahnini, a former pupil of the Collège Maulay Idris, on the decadence of Andalusian music, the invasion of Egyptian aesthetic taste.[2] Or these

---

[1] 'Underground canal', chiefly used in southern regions. Cf. the *Contes fasis* and *Nouveaux contes fasis* written by E. Dermenghem in collaboration with Muhammad al-Fasi.

[2] *Nabigha bi-Fas, M.al-Maghrib,* Nov. 1934.

anonymous lines of verse: 'Life assumes a changed aspect; a bird flies toward the horizon, roses speak of love to a flower.' *Ma dha ushahidu fi taiyma innahu sirr al-wujud*: 'What do I see in creation? the secret of being.' Thus the new generation questioned itself about the future. Its disturbed state of mind was revealed by scandals that nobody, at one time, could have imagined. The son of a very high personage was jailed for drunkenness; in 1936 a sharif of the House of Wazzan was seized by the police for drug-trafficking. And a scion of a great house, brother of a nationalist leader, was converted to Christianity.

The effect of a counter-irritant was produced by the nomination of Marcel Peyrouton as Resident-General, followed in the summer of 1936 by that of General Noguès, which was not welcomed by Peyrouton's supporters. The Popular Front was in full swing at the time. The Moroccan Committee of Action had high hopes. It had the support of the French Left wing. At Fez itself, in the Madina, Socialists like Maître Fernandez made a valiant effort to establish understanding. But nationalist demands grew more violent. The movement had by now, in spite of difficulties, obtained possession of several newspapers: *L'Action Populaire, Le Maghrib, L'Atlas, L'Action du Peuple, al-'Alam, al-Difa'*. It seized upon the economic and moral phenomena described above. It adjured the authorities to suppress the tax on animals slaughtered during religious feasts—here economic considerations combined with ritual ones; to make Friday a holiday—at the time, the Nationalist Party was trying to close shops on that day. There were polemics about University teachers' salaries, about Berber politics, about the decadence of Arabic studies; there were demands for reform of the University. And a great many other demands, of local interest and not going beyond democratic reformism, at any rate in words, but which already raised considerable problems for the future. The situation of the Madina had worsened by 1937; there was a deplorable contrast between the activity of the New Town and the depression of the Old, where people looked sad, averted their faces when a foreigner passed, and wore dilapidated clothes on their thin bodies. The town had become gloomy, secretive, decadent; its beauty was a mere nostalgic dream, its teeming life only the promise of death.

Over an area of 250 hectares, its population numbered 100,000; an average of 430 per hectare, but with strong variations between zones. In the old residential districts, such as Swiqa bin Safi, it rose to 1,145 per ha. or more. On the other hand it dropped, on the right bank of the Wadi, to 160 in the Fekhkharin. Add to this the 14,000 inhabitants of the modern town—Maulay Abdallah, Mellah, Fez Jdid; a total of 150,000. Who was in control of this mass of people? Where did the real power lie?

The municipal services were superimposed on the town rather than really rooted in it. They had not succeeded in integrating the progress of technique and local government with the life of Fez. They were still far from being in control of things, and did not even claim to be in control of people. Their powers, in the Madina, were of very limited scope: over water, electricity, road-mending, the night watch. Can it be said that the Majlis al-Baladi, the Municipal Council, made good their deficiencies? Scarcely, for it consisted merely of provisional co-operation between easy-going notabilities. And yet, in so far as these expressed a bourgeois mentality which itself was connected with the deeper strata, they brought considerable weight to bear on the conduct of the town and even that of the country. Only, between this bourgeois movement and the march of modern times, an uneasy balance reigned. Any action taken was chiefly negative. So much so that in 1935 the municipal services, which had hitherto kept some of their offices in the Madina, moved over into the New Town, to instal themselves in the huge building which they still occupy today (formerly a maternity hospital, founded by Madame Saint in 1931). The annexe in the Madina was simply suppressed. For a year or two its buildings in the Duh district remained unoccupied. No clearer admission could be made of the fact that the government was exclusively concerned with the new town, where it had to face grave riots.

In 1936 and 1937, the same nationalist movements broke out in Fez as in the rest of the Maghrib. The European militants of the C.G.T. were frequently followed by the Muslim masses. Thus in October 1936 there was a bakers' strike, which conservatives attributed to the recent spread of Syndicalism to Moroccan workers. In fact, it was a question not of rights but of tolerance. During the hard winter there was a building strike. Labourers were then earning 5 francs per day. Solidarity grew among the workers of the carriage-building industry; the head of the Municipal Services had to arbitrate. In the spring of 1937, the busmen had a disagreement with their Director, Audibert; the buses stopped.[1] The municipal workshops themselves called off work; so did the workers at the industrial flour mills, some of which—Perez et Coudert, Lévy, Baruk—envisaged having to close down. Social and political quarrels grew keener. The celebration of 14 July 1937, the elections which took place during this period, involved incidents to which the authorities paid excessive attention.

Between the colossal building of the Urbaine, where many officers' and civil servants' families lived, and the terrace of the Renaissance Café, where they forgathered in the late afternoon, the new town displayed plenty of life. It had its own paper, Le Courrier, which did not lag behind those of the coast, it had exhibitions, revues and concerts. In summer the smart set went swimming at the 'Ain Shkeff Dam, a few kilometres from

---

[1] But the carrier Laghzawi ensured transport. The wages of bus workers, which varied between 10 and 17 fr. per day, rose by 1 franc thanks to the strike. The Company's daily takings were on an average 7000 fr. per diem.

the town. On a more modest level, there were countless Bowling Clubs, Associations of ex-soldiers, of large families, of Corsicans or of Lorrainers. Some of these managed to get considerable help from the municipal budget. Clamorous public demands, which were sometimes devoid of idealism, led the authorities to launch out on sumptuary public works. The splendid swimming pool of the new town,[1] built in 1936, started an administrative conflict. The General Secretary of the Protectorate wrote, curtly, that 'projects should not be realized until they have been authorized,' a piece of pompous sagacity which goes directly against all that 'Lyautey's lesson' had stood for in this country: 'initiative is successful disobedience . . .'

Since 1932, the Pasha Muhammed Tazi exercised a more authentic power, which he confidently inherited from the tradition of the Makhzen. He would ride up to his tribunal on mule-back, surrounded by a dozen *mukhaznis* in red caps. He was a dictatorial figure, without physical or moral prestige; widely recognized as the representative of an arbitrary power devoid of feudal glamour and grown bureaucratic. His great enemy was the *muhtasib*,[2] an ambitious but unsuccessful man, protected by his brother the Grand Vizier al-Mukri. The third grandee was Sharif 'Abd al-Haiy al-Kittani, chief of a Brotherhood, an eminent scholar but a religious hypocrite with an enigmatic expression. The last two detested the former. All three, rivals in their allegiance to the French authorities, reviled one another ferociously.

The regional bureau, also known as 'information (*isti'lamat*) centre', almost always comprised officers whose career had been among the Berbers and who had little contact with the bourgeois citadel. Their ideal, ever since the disappearance of the pasha Baghdadi, had been the nomination of another Berber chief. Now, in October 1937, occurred the disastrous, or opportune, death of the Caïd of Ait 'Aiyash, who had been the anticipated leader of the townspeople.[3]

There were no profound links between the population and its official rulers. This was made clear during the crisis of 1937, whose effect on the town is all that need be considered here. At Meknes, the *colons'* utilization of the Wadi of Bufekran offended the Madina and provoked an affray. Fez achieved solidarity. In October the nationalist parties became masters of the town centre. Europeans were forbidden access to it.

[1] Used increasingly by the Moroccan section of the population.

[2] This old Andalusian magistracy survived in Fez, at that time, in an extra-administrative role, as trade auditor.

[3] Captain de la Tour, who came from Rabat for the funeral, brought a confidential order to General Blanc to occupy the Madina by force of arms. The Ait 'Aiyash tribe was encamped at the gates of the city. A schoolmaster from Géryville, Lakhdar, who later became professor at the Collège Maulay Idris, had taught the tribe ever since 1914.

Things reached such a point that towards the end of the month the Resident ordered the military occupation of the town, after having several leaders arrested during the night of 27–8 October; these included the man whose name, culture and appearance made him the most significant figure of the time: 'Allal al-Fasi. Two or three days later a crowd of demonstrators gathered for the Friday prayer–a classic occasion–in the Qarawiyin Mosque. They were forcibly ejected, and made to pass between two rows of *goumiers*, who had been brought from Boulmane and provided with pickaxe handles from the Municipal Works department. There was little bloodshed, in fact, but many blows were struck, many arrests made and some men sent into exile.

After this incident came a period of more or less superficial calm. This was the point at which General Noguès launched his policy of social improvement, with credit for the working class[1] and public assistance. Here was paternalism, indeed, but also a progress unprecedented at that time and in this country. The post of Municipal Deputy was re-established in the Madina. Considerable contact was achieved (witness the account in Shakib Arslan's *Nation arabe*).[2] It might be maintained that nationalism, at that moment, was chiefly the concern of the bourgeoisie, whereas a liberalization of the existing régime might hope to appeal to the workers on the one hand and the intellectuals on the other. This plausible idea was put to Ramadier and Viénot when they visited Fez. The former pupils of the Collège Maulay Idris, with Muhammad Zghari at their head, collaborated wholeheartedly with R. Le Tourneau. The Association des Amis de Fès brought together a number of Frenchmen and Moroccans, including men of great merit.[3] Three Artisans' Fairs attempted to set native economy on its feet again; they had at least the virtue of considering this for its own sake, and of giving the native worker his due. This indeed provided French reformism with one of its last chances in Morocco.[4]

To return to the city and its fate: let us make a brief synthetic survey of the whole inter-war period at Fez. The town's peculiar vitality, of which one is made forcibly aware, can find no parallel in North Africa, only much further east, in Damascus. For in Tunis, owing to the Neo-Destour, the influence of the people from the Sahil overruled that of the

[1] The Municipal Services published, on this occasion, two collections of poems by artisans. *Les Cahiers du Sud* published in translation a poem celebrating the renascence of the Guilds.

[2] 'Six mois de politique franco-marocaine,' May-Aug. 1938, pp. 1008–25. A complete statement of the Resident's achievement, preceded by a report which, while not eulogistic, is fairly favourable in tone compared with the usual style of this review.

[3] Mention should be made of Dr. Secret, the Bahnini brothers, and G. Ancey. The collection of these lectures would provide valuable documentation.

[4] Cf. pp. 283 ff.

middle class. But in Fez's vitality we recognize the spirit of a city exacerbated by its own difficulties. For the time being, the citizens of Fez had failed to assume leadership of their country. This they were only to attain several years later, through alliance with the 'Alawi dynasty.[1] And yet during this period, however fruitless their efforts in the political field, however disturbing their decadence on the economic plane, however cruel their moral conflict, they stubbornly pursued a mission of which the early French administrators, to their credit, had felt them to be capable. The crisis of 1937 was unfortunately not the last. Increasingly, the fate of the city community was to become the fate of Morocco, up till a quite recent period, almost until our own day. But the national problems whose pressure was felt all around affected, to some extent, the traditional character of the city. From 1935 onwards, the onslaught by new crowds from the furthest depths of Morocco, which collected in the poorer districts of Casablanca, threatened to bring an end, eventually, to bourgeois culture as well as to colonial domination.

[1] This took place on the occasion of the presentation of the Manifesto of 11 Jan. 1944.

CHAPTER VII

Quarters

I n North Africa, as elsewhere, during the period we are concerned
with, many great cities were turning into monsters. By the mid-
thirties they gave their inhabitants, and also the authorities, the
impression that they were defying the laws of normal growth. They
aroused pessimism, as well as enthusiasm;[1] their dizzy rate of growth was
fascinating and yet terrifying. Now one's neighbourhood is what protects
one from the monster. But whereas a neighbourhood is something one
can feel, one is hard put to define it. 'A restricted zone, whose indecisive
limits are not rigid boundaries but rather living and extensible fringes.'
It has 'a geographical and economic foundation,' yet 'man, with his
potentialities of knowledge, social relations and daily life, is primarily
the measure of its extent.' With the empirical neighbourhood we may
contrast the ideal neighbourhood, 'a clearly characterized locality, comprising a centre where lives may converge and whence they may radiate,
and comprising also a certain structure, with residential and commercial
streets. The geographical dimension should by rights be one with the
social dimension, the latter expressed by man's work and by his
leisure.'[2]

But why dissociate these two dimensions? Does not a purely residential district fail to define the real links that bind the new citizen to his
neighbourhood? The worker's familiar setting, which he can enjoy in
his rare leisure moments, is less the street or the block of flats than the
tavern, the sports ground or the club. This is the case in North Africa,
where every town was being invaded at this period by a population whose
homelessness was as characteristic as the irregularity of their resources.
There was a growing contrast between bourgeois and working-class

---

[1] It would be a useful, if wearisome, task to collect contemporary evidence
of this. It is particularly abundant in Morocco, because of the gigantic growth of
Casablanca.

[2] I have borrowed here and there from studies of urban sociology by Quoist,
Chombart de Lauwe, etc.

districts, both materially and morally.[1] The newcomers' dwellings were described in terms that reflect their tragic precariousness: *gourbi*, 'shed', 'shelter', 'shanty'. But these poor wretches cherished, perhaps for this very reason, a high ideal of family life. The paradoxical result was sometimes that the homeless man might insist on 'keeping his wife at home'. Hence our over-prudent town planners encountered many difficulties when they sought to rehouse this mob. They clung to a so-called 'vertical' conception, as against a 'horizontal' conception of building;[2] upper storeys were not approved of. Inner courtyards were maintained, but they were mere narrow channels of air. The poor wretch himself, building his hut out of petrol cans, stubbornly preserved his 'enclosure'. his *mrah*, sheltered from prying eyes. He thus retained a meaningless loyalty to the moral code of the wide open spaces, where privacy was a necessary compensation for a wandering life. In the traditional dwelling, indeed, the enclosed garden was man's answer to the sun-baked expanse outside. His flocks, his wealth and his activities alternately gathered together within the ring of tents, and scattered outside it, far afield. And the proletarian, alternately confined in his tin shack and wandering out endlessly in search of a livelihood, reproduced as in a painful caricature this alternation of retreat and expansion which was basic to the men of the Maghrib.[3]

But while these shanty towns, through the mobility and the diversity of origin of their inhabitants, enlarged the social bounds of the town to the same extent as the growth of its economic hinterland and the increase of its activities, the population that thus proliferated sought new forms of organization. Whereas the European colony, through its mayors, controllers and vice-presidents,[4] dominated the official administration, the Muslim bourgeoisie and working class, allies and rivals in turn, tended to express themselves through political and social demands, separately or together. Moreover these modes of expression reflect a fundamental competition between the native and the foreigner, not only against the latter as representing power, wealth or pressure, but against a rival proliferation. For the town was also the place where the poor whites tended to concentrate. Daily life, however, with its concrete needs did not always conform to these broad lines. Poverty had its compromises, as much as wealth. And here again we recognize the

---

[1] The term *bidonville*, shanty-town, became widespread at the time. I find it, for instance, in Félicien Challaye's book (1934), with reference to Tunisia. The term is frequently used in the *Bulletin économique* of Morocco in 1936.

[2] The fact that this abortive development was taken seriously by colonial town planners is not only typical of the time, but also has its psychological significance.

[3] Cf. pp. 353 ff.

[4] As at Casablanca and Tunis, where the Pasha in theory fills the post of President, but where the real leadership is contested between these busy personalities and the representative of the French Government.

'neighbourhood', with its variety of sites and characteristics. High or low neighbourhoods, European, or 'Arab', or mixed neighbourhoods; all these distinctions cross with economic and moral qualifications to enhance, or sometimes to modify, the contrast between types. In this respect North Africa provides an extraordinarily complex range.

From the 'negro village' of Oran to the Maarif of Casablanca, where Cerdan was to keep a café, from the Bab el Oued (al-Wadi) of Algiers where Spanish was no longer spoken, to the 'Little Sicily' in Tunis where nobody as yet spoke French, not forgetting the noble, silent regions where the old bourgeoisie of Fez furtively pursued their own interests—the inventory would be a rich one.[1]

A parallel list might be made of the wide variety of institutions. These were most frequently clandestine, but sometimes attained the level of overt organizations. 'The term District Committee is currently used to describe a group of those who belong to some particular district, forming a society or prefecture with an administrative council and a headquarters.' It pursued 'aims of administrative and social action in the city, and many functions and responsibilities resulting from urban cohabitation.' According to the officials of course, this role must consist not of 'inquisition or systematic criticism, but of notifying certain needs or lacunae.'[2] Paradoxically, it would seem, since the social life in question is by definition fragmentary and localized, these committees came together in a federation with a president, co-ordinating bodies, a common headquarters, etc. Thus we find active citizens giving up their leisure, after work or on Sunday mornings, to concern themselves, in the name of their neighbourhood, with a wide variety of questions: a mayoral reception, pedestrian crossings, the repair of stairways, the catching of stray cats and dogs, the supply of extra benches for public squares, against the removal of tramway stops or letter-boxes, the improvement of lighting or taxi services, and so forth; a whole jumble of petty problems, characterized by a meticulous but courteous pursuit of particular interests.

But this spontaneous movement, on which any future construction in the Maghrib would have to base itself, did not at that time go very far nor aspire very high. It stopped half-way to efficiency. Its leaders rarely reached the municipal council. On the other hand, a crowd of electoral agents, henchmen of the police or political parties, meddlers and parasites of every sort invaded the district on behalf of the authorities, the more intensively as the latter grew alarmed at what was happening underneath. For these interminglings, these resentments, these privations and rivalries—although their real existence and even their image

[1] Monographs only became general—to a modest extent—after the last world war.
[2] The municipal review of Algiers, *Alger-Revue*, frequently quotes their interventions.

was deliberately suppressed–aroused uneasy apprehension among the upper orders, municipal politicians, pashas and moneyed men.

The transmission of orders, rewards and penalties that is part of the relationship between the government of a city and its concrete life was enforced with increased rigour when the neighbourhood concerned was predominantly working-class, and thus specifically 'native'. Some day, when we have sufficient data at our disposal, we shall discover resemblances between the character of a district in its urban topography, and the type of social control used over it. Where one district is dominated by the *sbire* armed with his ox-hide whip, or even by the Senegalese soldier with his bayonet, another enjoys a free outlook over a handsome city landscape;[1] where one lives in apprehension of blows or 'trouble', the other is aware of its authority and the 'responsibilities'[2] that this involves, to counterweigh its advantages.

At these high levels of Maghribi city life, the Muslim notabilities, so confident and inspiring such confidence, the dignitary so stout that he is said to 'flow' rather than walk, the cumbersome 'vice-presidents' who are rife in Tunis or Casablanca, alternate with more active types: men from the *bled*, on the way up socially; ambitious young bourgeois, municipal officials of dedicated or opportunist character. Oran, afflicted with brackish water, turned for help to a skilful dowser, credited with almost magical powers: the Abbé Lambert, an astonishing figure in dusty cassock and tropical helmet, an unorthodox priest at odds with his bishop and an expert demagogue.[3] There were even some good mayors. But the demagogic movements[4] that stirred up working-class districts joined forces there with nascent nationalism, which also represented an attempt to build up and restore the oppressed and unorganized. The first activities of the Hizb at Fez, or the Destour in Tunis, were as inseparably connected with the resentment of the poorer districts, home of depressed artisans and ruined tradesmen, as was the P.P.A. (Parti Populaire Algérien) with that of the Algerian dockers, tramwaymen,

---

[1] For instance Ahfa (Casablanca), El Biar or the heights of Telemly (Algiers) and the 'residential' districts almost everywhere.

[2] In this connection two points must be made, in anticipation of future studies. The first a general one: town planning, in addition to its functional role, plays a standardizing role which in some cases may come to supplant the law. The other a particular one. The aesthetic factor plays a considerable part in this process, in traditional city life (cf. what is said here about Fez and Tunis). It is shown in artistic and intellectual initiatives, coming from certain French families, which dominate the Colonial order. In Algiers for instance, during the period under consideration: musical composition (de Galland, Simian), scientific experiment (G. Mercier). With which, of course, should be contrasted the *petit blanc* inspiration of Camus, Roblès, etc.

[3] Cf. Jean Marsillat, *L'Abbé Lambert et les Oranais*, 1936

[4] There arose thus a type of 'chief' whose expansion was cut short by the events after 1942, but which doubtless inspired the disturbing figure of Almaro in Emanuel Roblès' prophetic novel, *Les Hauteurs de la Ville*, (1946).

vegetable sellers, pedlars and hucksters. Thus the political future of the country depended to some extent[1] on the fate of back streets and the spread of suburbs.

In this way the North African neighbourhood, through the continual interaction between space, time, social rhythms and moral feelings, reflects broad historical laws together with the living warmth of a group in process of formation or re-formation.[2] Hence its potentiality for good or evil, for beauty or ugliness. These various factors may converge to produce harmony or discord, well-being or unhappiness. Hence it is necessary to illustrate not only material traits but also the role of collective feelings and of its bases. In Muslim life, these are often sought from religion. The minaret crowns the neighbourhood, gives it authenticity or salvation, sanctions or redeems it. But is this so peculiar to Islam? Town planners such as G. Bardet rightly stress the role of the 'urban lighthouse', namely the guiding idea that connects scattered phenomena and endows the agglomeration with individuality and optimism. And this is where we perceive how much the observation of North African cities can contribute to urban sociology in general, precisely because it stresses the role of the symbol, even of the conflict between rival symbols.

For conflict was rife everywhere, between past and present, between Islam and Europe, between revolt and submissive acceptance.

Tunis: the Nahj al-Basha[3]

The visitor to Tunis in 1961 is aware of a twofold revolution. Not only against external power: this no doubt is the most striking, and superficially 'political' aspect of things; but also against its own particular past. The very appearance of the town thus reminds us immediately of that key which serves to interpret the whole of contemporary Islam: a twofold questioning of The Other and of oneself.

The Place Lavigerie, indeed, has changed its name; the street once

[1] We should not however, exaggerate the role of the 'lumpen-proletariat'. The real basis of nationalism was not to be found here, but (even if we leave out of account the wealthy bourgeois) in the militant workers, the intellectuals and the discontented rural elements. The events subsequent to 1945 renewed these bases, and we are not at present in a position to embark on a precise historical picture.

[2] These relations are no secret for the modern town planner, cf. Le Corbusier, *Les Trois Établissements humains*, 1959.

[3] The documentation of this paragraph on the Nahj al-Basha owes much to the walks I took there with so learned a guide as M. Mustafa Ka'ak, Curator of the Bibliothèque Nationale; with my friend the late Farid Ghazi; with Muhammad Mamluk, former secretary of the Council of the Madina. M. Hammadi Lasram welcomed me to his family palace. I am deeply grateful to many other Tunisian friends, particularly to Henri de Montéty.

known as Rue de l'Église is now called Rue de la Mosquée; the plaque that bore the inscription Place de la Résidence has been changed to Place de *L'Istiqlal*, or Independence. Other phenomena, less obvious but more profound, reveal an even sharper struggle against the traditional mode of being. Everywhere in this bourgeois city with its conservative reputation, saints and cupolas, relics and cemeteries are disappearing. A building of the early eighteenth century, the *turba*[1] of Qara Mustafa, in the Qasba district, having been branded with dishonour, fell into ruins, to the despair of archaeologists but to the delight of innovators (1960). The Great Mosque had its façade cleaned, but at the same time lost its educational function, and one of the rites most closely connected with the Islamic personality, Ramadan, was openly challenged. No doubt the removal of the statues of Lavigerie and Jules Ferry marked the end of the colonial era. But simultaneously, or soon after, an impartial iconoclasm attacked the heroes of old tradition.

The Madina forms an oval, outlined by the outer boulevards. The traditional north-south axis is prolonged in both directions by two suburbs still called *ribat*.[2] The town seems also to have developed from west to east, flowing down from the heights of the Qasba through successive generations and finally reaching the present European town, built entirely on the grid system, its stiff geometry contrasting with the curves of the Madina. The latter, indeed, far from displaying around its principal sanctuary the radio-concentric plan dear to the Middle East, is pierced through with almost rectilinear thoroughfares that cross at right angles.[3] A second characteristic of the town is the obvious continuity between the contributions of rival civilizations. During three or four centuries waves of Andalusian emigrants were received into the old town, which was already maturely established. It also accepted Muradi Turks and numbers of Tunisian, Berber or Tripolitanian Bedouins. Meanwhile, by an inverse process, the true citizen, the *beldi* (*baladi*) emphasized his own characteristics as against the newcomers, and reasserted himself through hybridization. The personality of the community was made up, here as elsewhere, from a delicate balance between assimilation and dissimilation.

This dissimilation reaches its peak in the 'quarter' *par excellence*, the *Hara* or ghetto.[4] This extreme case of specialization and, up to a point, of segregation, expresses as a picturesque municipal entity a difference of origin and religion. Unless paradoxically, but in a more illuminating fashion, the religious and even the racial argument merely serves to explain a particularism which is both excluded and exclusive. Certain

[1] *turba*: dome-shaped funeral monument.
[2] The *rabad* of Muslim Spain.
[3] According to Pellegrin, this recalls the Roman plan.
[4] Studied in detail by P. Sebag.

dialect characteristics, at all events, incline one to believe this.[1] However this may be, during the whole inter-war period which concerns us particularly, the role and the presence of the Jews in the Madina had dwindled. By now they have almost completely evacuated the Suq al-Grana and the Suq al-Uzar, having gradually moved over into the modern town to take up trade with the French. This has been going on for twenty or thirty years, a whole generation before another emigration, which is in full force today–that of the Tunisians themselves, bourgeois included, gradually overflowing into the European town.

It is fascinating to study those wavering fringes–spatial, linguistic and moral–that exist around various groups and at various epochs. You may find, for instance, a grocer from Jerba, settled just on the edge of the Jewish district, a thing which would once have been unimaginable. In the Suq al-Grana men from the south have today taken over types of trade which were formerly Jewish. These transitions and exchanges are echoes in a variety of dialogues, gestures and anecdotes springing from the corresponding variety in the types of merchandise. Naturally the most decisive variety is that contributed by Europe. Today one can see in these old streets objects as unexpected as golf shoes, brassières, American gadgets and old numbers of *La Vie Parisienne*. But the flood of Europeanism has not yet submerged everything. And we can still rediscover, behind these pictures of 1960, those of 1930 and even earlier. They help us to imagine the life of Tunis of those days in all its unity and plurality. A multiplicity of types were contrasted less by their origins or even their religious creed than by their appearance, their way of acting and speaking. In any case they were opposed to one another by their competitive impulses. For this is one form of emulation, which is itself a form of alliance. Each group influenced the rest, not only automatically, through its particular ideas, but by far subtler inductive effects.

It is in these floating frontiers and according to these variable qualifications that one should attempt to study a neighbourhood. One might describe this as a unit that can be distinguished from its neighbours when it combines a sufficient number of distinctive features: a certain architectural tradition, a common origin, or else an empirical homogeneity, such as physical appearance, economic vocation or community of folklore or dialect: the whole thing liable to evolution, variable in its content, influencing those around it and influenced by them, but displaying an individuality within the body of the city, and aware of it. Nowadays it is all visibly fading into the past, appearing increasingly only as one stratum among many in a history which is marked as much by the continuity of its epochs as by their innovations. For this history flows down, as I have said, from the Qasba towards the lake, from the rule of the Almohad dynasty to the international traffic of today. The French period, which had dominated all the rest, is now itself thrust into the

[1] Unpublished study by David Cohen.

background, confounded with the rest by the town planning of tomorrow.

We have seen how, in the Madina of Tunis, the urban whole is divided into a variety of districts; we must also follow the inverse order, going outward from the family dwelling to the neighbourhood, and from this to the city. Several houses are arranged to form a cul-de-sac or narrow lane. A palace of any importance is preceded by a vestibule, the *driba*. At the entrace stands a small lodge, the *bit d-driba*, with often a sort of usher, an old man who performs various responsible functions: he will escort a small girl to school, which her parents may not do; if an importunate visitor persists, in spite of the abuse or even the volleys of pebbles hurled at him by the children, acting as protective scouts,[1] the old man will have the task of politely getting rid of him. He will even do so on his own initiative if the visitor is a foreigner, or too young, with a 'green' or roving eye, *'ainuh l-khadra*,[2] liable to cause offence. At this entrance guests are received in an upper chamber called *'ali d-driba*. Usually the casual stroller, who is not received into the privacy of the home, and the beggar or needy student who picks up the alms laid out for him, the *sadaqat al-mastura*, stop there. A group of such houses form a unit which acquires its own name, apart from those of the various families, and thus its local identity and its role within the Madina. This miniature neighbourhood has its own social equipment: a sanctuary, a Moorish bath, a baker's oven, sometimes a Qur'anic school. The last often occupies the room built above a vaulted passage, *sabat*, of a sort frequently found in Tunis and dating back to Aramaic antiquity.

The 'quarter' is called *hara* only in the case of the ghetto; it usually bears the very Maghribi name of *huma*. At this level, the social symbol is no longer attached to the personality of some particular family, set forth in monumental gateways or ambitious architecture. It consists of public buildings, *madrasas* (colleges) or mosques, Government offices or commercial buildings, or tradesmen's *suqs*. Each district of the town was formerly under the administration of a *muharrik* (literally 'mover'), a sort of city major-domo, responsible for setting his *harika* in motion to supply the needs of the beylik. The whole body was ruled by an authoritative figure, the *Shaikh al-madina*, heir to old Andalusian magistracies.

The quarter is thus the meeting point between the vitality that springs from the base and the government of the city, or even that of the state. Marked with a special stamp by its monuments, thus bearing its own date as well as its own nationality, its individual atmosphere is the more clearly manifest as it stabilizes the two-way movement that links the

---

[1] They are brought up as such; it forms part of the code of honour of their *gens* and of their masculine prestige.

[2] Betraying the libertine.

city to the family. This identity, this spell are perceptible to the inhabitant, who is its agent as well as its product, and to the Bedouin visitor; even to the tourist. On the other hand, it fades away when the harmony between function and setting is weakened. The artisan who has lost the greater part of his economic importance, the tradesman in the *suqs* reduced to selling only imported articles, or lying in wait for tourists behind the windows of the bazaar, the Zaituna mosque itself, deprived of its teaching role, these lose both their urban function and their visual message. We note then a development in which, as the vital movement of the city disintegrates, quarters are abolished, colours grow neutral, and other differentiations take their place, based on economic classes or on inequality of participation in the new order. Concurrently, the aspect of urban topography alters, and urban history takes on a new meaning.

The visitor who walks up the Rue de la Qasba finds, where the Nahj Sidi bin 'Arus cuts that street at right angles, crossroads of history and of styles. On his left the style is Muradi; on his right it is Hafsid. These contrasts of period are characteristic of the townscape in which they linger and are harmonized. Sidi bin 'Arus was a saint who came, like so many others, from Morocco towards the end of the fifteenth century. Turning back, one can see the Minaret of the Zaituna. It is square, quite Western in style with its valance-like ornamentation, locally called *drej u-ktef*. Behind one is the octagonal minaret of Hammuda Pasha, highly Ottoman in style; it combines the most delicate contradictions of period and style. From the alternate black and white characteristic of Arab classicism, and the more complex contrasts of brown and light ochre of the Turkish period we pass without gradation to Corinthian capitals. Something, nevertheless, redeems this heterogeneous diversity: the indefinable style characteristic of the city gives harmony to the whole.

Entering the street from this end, we follow the path taken by the bourgeois on his return from the mosque after the Friday prayer, or his son returning from a meeting at the Khalduniya. But we might also proceed in the opposite direction, following the countryman on his way to the town.

From the northern suburb, Bab Swiqa, into which men of Moorish origin and lesser dignity introduced the tortuous *zenqa*, we should first cross the immediate periphery of the Madina. There is a whole circle of hostelries (*funduqs*) with inner courts once surrounding it, each opening on to a different point of the horizon. This was how the town welcomed those that came in from the countryside and at the same time radiated its own influence. The *funduq* was the meeting-point for these two movements. A family might perhaps take two generations to get past this stage in its bourgeois rise.

A type is thus established in the human sphere which corresponds to that of dwellings in the material sphere. The patrician homes strike one immediately when one enters the Nahj al-Basha. They greet one on either side with their monumental gates, their square or semi-circular arched doors, with studded panels. The lane that runs off to the right, Anq al-Jamal, has an attractive surface of alternate bricks and small pebbles set in mortar; the road runs under groined arches, frequent in Andalusian districts. The shady *sabats* (vaulted passages) provide the townsman with some of that privacy he enjoys in the cool courtyard of his own home. From the social as well as from the architectural point of view these courtyards play a major role. Seen from above, the Madina seems an immense agglomeration of hollow squares. The house[1] is built around its patio. It is sometimes crowned by a *kshuk*, or kiosk, a sort of top deck from which the head of the family can peacefully survey the neighbourhood. Below, it is completed by a well which may be six metres deep, as at the Dar Husain. Often, too, the patio is raised and transformed into a first-floor room, like the *qa'a* and *mu'allaqa* of the Middle East. This empty space, with or without a ceiling, is the heart of the dwelling; indeed the heart of the family and of the whole social group. Sometimes one notices arcades, known by an Andalusian name, *baratel*, surmounted by verandahs with latticed blinds, *moucharabiehs*; or a garden in bloom, next to some shed. Opposite the entrance gate a room called a *qbu* seems hollowed out in the wall by some centrifugal thrust. It is often highly ornamented, with *maqsuras* (small closets) at either end; it may have a coffered ceiling, alcoves and painted wood-work. The style is a mixture: Andalusian beds and divans, generally painted red to match the ceiling; Eastern carpets, copperwork and marquetry; Italian mirrors, chandeliers, gilded canopies, crystals and clocks; all symbolic of the time and reflecting the various influences.

All this delights the eye, while the observer can discern the components of an ancient history and an infinitely complex way of life. For one of these bourgeois, it is a cruel ordeal to be deprived, even temporarily, of his setting. One of them, a member of the X . . . family, told me that during the inter-war period his people, suddenly ruined, had to emigrate from their district to the Bab Swiqa suburb. It took years of effort for the children to regain their dignity as city-dwellers. At the same time they regained the city-dweller's attitudes and tastes. As we were passing by the sanctuary of Sidi Mahriz, my guide was recognized by a tradesman, who offered us a delicacy: a late-autumn *gnawiya*,[2] which would please his wife and cheer up his home. The townsman shows his awareness

---

[1] The meticulous description given by Muhammad Bairam, II, *Safwat al-I'tibar bi-mastaudat al-Ansar*, 1330, vol. II, pp. 130–2 has recently been translated by Father Magnin in *Ibla* (review of Institut des Belles-Lettres Arabes, Tunis). An impressive study of the palaces and houses of Tunis is being completed by P. Revault.

[2] Or *bamiya*, a sort of mallow beloved of the Egyptians.

of the seasons and his wish to maintain his links with the country-side.

This is the touching, even bucolic side of his life. But it has less attractive features, which the townsman does not hesitate to caricature in himself. The following adage, for instance, mocks the patriarchal egotism of great families: *Awwel hana, elli ibni guddam ed-dar wa'd-dukkan; thani hana, elli yaqullek astenna hatta nijik ana; thaleth hana, elli ibni guddam ej-jebbana.* 'The first humiliation is to see the big house and its *dukkana* built in front of you' (your rival blocks your view and overlooks the comings and goings of womenfolk in your courtyard), 'the second, to be told–wait, I shall come to see you presently' (you are thus put under an obligation), 'the third, to live in front of a graveyard' (a bad omen, and a bad economic sign, for the graveyard represents a peripheric zone over which the town is constantly spreading, unless, as happens nowadays, it transforms the graveyard into a public square . . .)

The Nahj al-Basha, a continuation of the Rue Sidi Bin 'Arus, is the home of many famous city families, each having its moral characteristics and its economic vocation. For instance, the Darghut family, which produced corsairs, farmers and men of learning; the Nifer and Bin 'Ashur families, who have provided a constant stream of learned men; the clans of Lakhwa, Shahid, Ja'it, Bil Qadi, 'Abbas; landed proprietors such as the Bilhawan, from whom a revolutionary leader sprang; families of saints, such as the descendants of Sidi bin 'Arus; others who formerly specialized in public functions, such as the Qassar, the Kahya, and the oldest of all, the Lasram. Finally, families of artisan origin, connected with the most famous guilds, notably the *shwayshiya*, who make *shishiyas* and are of old Andulasian stock. Others, given to commerce, have more recently embarked on government careers, for instance the Shnik, the Darmani, the Chelebi, the Mahrazi, who once combined study with silk-making.

How can such family differentiation persist today? through the prac-tice of a kind of endogamy. Not indeed for ritual or religious reasons, nor even out of respect for custom, but simply because the thing is fashion-able. For this subtly nuanced way of life is governed by good taste. And in the city, as among the Bedouins, 'the uncle's son' has a prior claim to his cousin's hand. This is not the only trait of tribal honour, and thus of Bedouin affinity; we had noted others in connection with a village of the Sahil. Such affinities may perhaps be found throughout the Islamo-Mediterranean world. The more these men are forced by history to evolve and compromise, the more they seek for an archetype of them-selves in the true or supposed values of the Bedouin, arbitrarily identi-fied with those of Arabism. And this is why, even in the most sedentary organizations, among Mesopotamian farmers and the townsfolk of Fez or Damascus, the ideal of the nomad remains paradoxically potent.[1] Curious comments are made in the remarkable description of his city written towards the end of the last century by Muhammad Bairam, a high dignitary addicted to travel and to concrete and curious observations. He mentions the 'fantasias', or equestrian galas, held by the city folk, and gives this explanation of an ideal of horsemanship which it is surprising to find among these bourgeois: *wa huwa'l-haqq li-annaha min sifat al-rajuliya wa'd-din*[2] 'and rightly, for it is associated with manliness, courage, nobility and also religion'.

It is precisely the integration of taste with morals which, drawing together all the elements of this way of life and asserting their meaning in this world and for the next, constitutes the Islam of the city-dweller, contrasting with the Islam of the countryman by its greater clearsightedness and circumspection, *tabassur*. Many conventions thus take on the colour of piety: the respect shown to one's father, bodily cleanliness, the 'sense of decency' forbidding a well-bred citizen to wear rings, whistle or dance as a Bedouin would do. Towards the end of the century we glimpse the figure of that *dhu muru'a*, as Bairam calls him, that man of honour in the old sense, and behind him that of the *grazioso*, the elegant gentleman, perhaps connected with the Spanish code of good breeding. Whence, notably, the importance of outward appearance and of dress. Beards are cut according to strict principles: one style for the Hanafis, another for the Malikis; the former, of Turkish origin, wear their beards clipped at the temples, while the Malikis wear theirs trimmed to a fine point. So that when religious men were grouped together in a *majlis*, they could be distinguished by two different kinds of beard as well as by their rites and by their behaviour.

This respect for the outward sign implies a high degree of respectability. A man of this older generation,[3] many examples of which still exist, prides himself on the antiquity and authenticity of his class. He distinguishes sharply between the older body of citizens and what he disdainfully calls the 'houses of the crust', *dar qshur*. His own house has deeper foundations. He speaks a slightly different language from that of other districts. As he has a smattering of legal knowledge and visits the Mosque morning and evening, he likes to use a kind of legal jargon known as *fiqhi, itkellem bel-fiqhi*. His conversation consists largely of circumlocutions. He displays great timidity in the face of events. Like the snail, which carefully puts out its horns, he gropes around him and quickly withdraws his hand if it comes up against anything unexpected.

[1] F. Bonjean has made a profound study of this persistence of Bedouin values in Muslin towns: 'A propos de romans arabes écrits en français par un occidental', *Revue de la Méditerranée*, 1961, pp. 127 ff. This is also the theme of the Iraqi sociologist as-Wardi.

[2] Bairam, ibid., p. 119. *Din* has here almost the sense of the Latin *religio*.

[3] Described, with great subtlety, by Father Demeerseman, *Ibla*, no. 3, 1937 v 4, 1938.

A critical observer might describe his life as negative; but it reflects solid values. He starts the day early with prayer and then goes off to market, for he allows nobody else to do his shopping, particularly the buying of the meat, which he brings back in a basket or parcel and hands over to the mistress of the house. For a while, he sits, or squats, in his shop; then another visit to the Mosque to pray, then back to the shop. The evening is devoted to pious meditation, to lectures on the Qur'an, to common prayer in some sanctuary, although Brotherhoods are no longer in favour.

Religious communities had begun to decline by this period. The older generation itself had grown suspicious of them, and its attitude was: *la ta'taqed wa la tantaqed*, 'don't believe, but don't criticize.' And it applied this wise principle to many other things. Its faith formed part of its practice of citizenship, so that almost every great family had its own oratory. In the Nahj al-Basha, we find sixteen of these sanctuaries. Only one of them has a *khutba*, or weekly sermon. This, moreover, is a Maliki principle. In the Maghrib, a neighbourhood is measured by the radius within which the muezzin can be heard calling to prayer. But the Nahj has other, more popular characteristics. You will still be shown, by the older folk, the *khelwa* or cell of Sidi 'Amir bin 'Isa. This was a slightly crazy saint, a follower of Sidi bil Lahsin, patron of Tunis. The belief has died away today, but the *khelwa* still exists, so long as it does not fall beneath the axe of the townplanner. We can imagine the way of life of the earlier generation, made up of contemplation and prayer and religious celebrations, taking place within a liturgical year whose rhythms are intermingled with those of family festivities. And also with those of the Beylik; on great religious feast days the Bey's procession would pass through the Madina with great pomp, accompanied by popular merry-making and the consumption of *uffada*, an amber-scented syrup, of starch-cakes and of pine-seed flavoured-gruel, *zququ*.[1]

Another characteristic of these townsfolk was their love of music. This was related to their piety. In former days, here and there in every district might be found a 'wake room', *hanut s-sahhara*, where young people of the best families forgathered for unpretentious musical parties. It was not uncommon to meet some adept of Sidi bil Lahsin (particularly of the 'Azzuziya branch) carrying a cage of goldfinches. This bird's song, and its variegated plumage, delighted the delicate taste of the connoisseur, particularly with the accompaniment of *kif*. One of the best informed musicians of the period between the wars, Rashid bin Ja'far, lived in this district. Earlier, another of its sons, Muhammad bin Lasram, had followed an exiled amir to Constantine end there collected *nuba*, melodic sequences. After a long eclipse, during which the musical tradition in Tunis was kept up by the Jews, the bourgeois took the initiative once more. In 1934, the Rashidiya was set up in the district to

[1] Marty, *Revue des Études islamiques*, 1935.

protect local taste against the invasion of Egyptianism. And the Rashidiya remained the instrument of Tunisian authenticity.

We must not, however, dwell longer on this Tunisian bourgeois whose constant features, seen against their impressive setting, might perhaps make us underestimate his mutations during the course of history.

By the end of the first world war a decisive transformation had begun to take place in this city community, whose life was planned for the enjoyment of the moment and the service of eternity. Its economic foundations were collapsing.[1] Its main resources had been craftsmanship, now threatened by competition from the import trade; service in the Beylik, where French functionaries were now its rivals; the renting of buildings to Jews, and above all landed estates, *henshirs*. Now it was here, between 1880 and 1920, that this bourgeois class suffered most violently the first shock of colonization. The Protectorate's initial drive was chiefly in the countryside. A sort of condensation of property was taking place. The new exploitation of the country was achieved partly at the expense of its extensive agriculture which, particularly in the *waqfs*, was in the hands of the city bourgeois. This unequal competition demoralized them. They lost confidence in themselves as producers, indeed in their power to 'keep up' their landed property, and some twenty years ago they began to neglect their estates. Those to whom the private *habus* had been transmitted went in for transactions which were immediately profitable, without concern for the future. Colonists and administrators took advantage of rivalries between claimants. But bourgeois solidarity asserted itself, negatively, to oppose the law passed in 1926, under Commandant Valentini, which effected a sort of dismemberment of these foundations to the advantage of the lessees.[2] However, when the opposition succeeded in getting this measure rescinded (1934), the *habus* owners had already lost almost everything.

From 1925 onwards certain bourgeois gave up their family homes and settled on the outskirts.[3] While the French took a fancy to the city palaces, the native townsfolk preferred living in villas: the exchange of tastes reflects the exchange of functions. The first citizen to leave was Hajj Ahmad Lasram, who settled in La Marsa. Other families escaped in their turn. In the D . . . family, comprising one brother and seven sisters, not one of these lives in the family home today. The sisters forgather there every year to preside over the washing of wool or the making of preserves, for this still forms part of the aristocratic way of life. But it will clearly not bind them indefinitely. Among the families of the Nahj al-Basha, some of the oldest have vanished from the district:

[1] Frequent references in the Press. E.g. *Dépêche tunisienne*, 27 Aug. 1934, with reference to the many houses falling into ruins in the Madina; *Tunis socialiste*, 1 March 1937, about discontent among artisans.

[2] Cf. p. 370.   [3] *Libéral*, 26 Sept. 1925.

the Bil Mami, the Ja'it, the Mahrazi, the Chelebi. By the thirties the incompatibility between the old and the new ways of life was more marked. The middle-aged bourgeois now wanted not only a secluded villa, but also a flat in the modern town. The narrow, carefully guarded streets of the old Madina had ensured safety for women and children and respect for tradition. These had gone; the blind-alleys had been torn open, violently exposed to the outside world. Children who had led a sheltered life now went a long way to school. The young people detested the cloistered seclusion of the old neighbourhood. A high functionary of the Protectorate settled in the house of one of these great families at this period. They gladly let it to him, because the parents wished to remove their daughters from such an atmosphere. The girls themselves wanted to go unveiled, which they would never have dared to do in the ancestral atmosphere. All sides, in short, adapted themselves to the rape of the Madina, but received very varied benefits from it.

This centrifugal movement developed just when the Loucheur law in France favoured the spread of cheaper dwellings.[1] Surprisingly enough, the members of this ancient bourgeoisie were the first to put this demo-cratic move into practice. Bashir Dingizli, of the Nahj al-Basha, was chairman of an Association for cheaper housing (the H.B.M. *Habitations Bon Marché*) which built an entirely Tunisian suburb, Al-'Umran, in 1921. It was later followed by another, Al-Taufiq. This type of dwelling became increasingly fashionable; it offered correct monotony instead of the lavish splendour of the palaces: communal and public interests, instead of the isolationism of family life: access to French ways of living, and the abandonment of ancestral customs; a decisive revolution!

Let us descend to the level of trivial and familiar details. There once reigned a subtle distinction between the vendors of various foodstuffs. There was the *'attar*, often a native of Jerba, who sold sugar, coffee, condiments, minor household goods, as well as, nowadays, notebooks and pens for schoolchildren. There was the *suqi*, also frequently from Jerba, who would have considered himself disgraced if he had sold anything other than salt, fats, cheese and oil. There was the *temmar* who sold oranges, mandarines and fruits in season; the *khaddar* for veget-ables; the *fehham*, often a Mozabite, for coal. After the first world war, however, all these branches of trade became confused, so much so that the administration appointed three *amins*, or syndics, with local powers, for the whole corporation. It could neglect these varieties, representative of the old trading system, without great inconvenience. And other professions appeared presently, such as the chemist's, called *sbisriya*. Stalls strove to be modern, displaying huge erections of tinned goods,

[1] See pamphlet, *Les Habitations à bon marché en Tunisie*, 1931. For the in-auguration of al-Taufiq, see *Dépêche tunisienne*, 1 Sept. 1934, and *Zahra*, 4 Sept. 1934.

which according to malicious people contained a number of illicit substances. Now people bought preserves, in order to acquire spirits
surreptitiously, somewhat as in the old days they used to visit the shops
of the *Grigi*, the sites of a few of which can still be seen in the Madina.[1]
The more tinned food is bought, the less is prepared at home, and the
housewife's life becomes easier. And yet in spite of everything the
cuisine in these districts has so far remained Arab. It has of course
undergone certain changes. The tastes, the ingredients, the preparation
remain the same, but the system has altered. Through the introduction
of new substances and recipes it has become disorganized and lost class,
as it were. The foreigner raves about it, the citizen still enjoys it as a leg-
acy from the old days, but it is becoming obsolete, like native dress and
speech.

During the years 1920–5 something hitherto unheard of took place:
namely, a number of love-matches. These threatened the tradition of
correct marriage with 'the uncle's daughter'. About 1935 this custom
seems to have begun to die out, together with the curious clauses that
families inserted in marriage contracts. For instance, a wife's insistence
that she shall not leave her own district: such a preoccupation vanishes
naturally. Then comes the scandal of marriages between young bourgeois and European women. The first of this sort, apparently, was that
of Bashir Dingizli, founder, as we have seen, of the H.B.M. and an
innovator in his own home. Lawyers and doctors followed suit. On the
whole, everybody was becoming Europeanized after a fashion, or rather
'Syrianized', *itasauwer*. For in Tunis the European is known as 'Syrian'.
This minor lexicographical puzzle may be explained as follows:
Tunisians following the pilgrims' way from 1900 onwards may have
been struck, as they passed through Cairo, by the appearance of the
Syrio-Lebanese who were then transporting the Beirut *nahda* (Renaissance) into Egypt; the influence of Europe was identified with that of the
Levant; one became 'Syrian' because one stood in relation to the tradi-
tional milieu as these Cairo Syrians stood in relation to the fellah of old,
or the old Cairo bourgeoisie.

Europeanization involves a general upheaval of habits. A sociological
study of cooking habits should be followed by one of dress: for all these
factors are connected. And it is not by chance that the old aspect of
things wears off and is supplanted by a new look, while the economic
foundations and the city's role are in process of disintegration, and while
language, tastes and desires are in process of change. These various
categories vary in the strength of their resistance to the movement. Thus
Europeanization has not yet affected all parts of the body. Head and
loins resist longest: floating tunics, wide trousers and turbans persist,
providing shelter for genitals and *'ura*, whereas everything else has been
betrayed. The feet, that despised portion of the anatomy, assert them-

[1] For instance at the corner of the Rue de la Qasba and the Rue al-Qassab.

selves first; there was never any quarrel about shoes, whereas the traditionalist long continued to consider narrow trousers obscene and hats or caps an outrage against religion.

But the decisive change comes from the spread of European culture to the entire younger generation. As a matter of fact, this district had already witnessed efforts at modernization. Almost a century ago Muhammad Qabadu, one of its residents, had tried to start classes for mathematics and science in the 'Asfuriya *madrasa*, which is still there and is now a students' hostel. In this district the first free school, that of Khair Allah bin Mustafa, was set up, which educated such men as Bashir Sfar, the initiator of the Khalduniya.[1] In 1900, in the place which gave the Nahj al-Basha its name, was founded the Renée Millet girls' school; this was for a long time under the direction of Mme Eigenschenck, and by 1929 it had 550 pupils, almost all from the bourgeoisie. However, during the inter-war period, the major phenomenon on a national scale was the return, in successive waves, of students from France.[2] The first wave, even before the 1914 war, included Muhammad Nu'man, Shadli Bakkush, 'Abd al-Jalil Za'ush, Mustafa Ka'ak. The second was dominated by Dr. Mahmud Materi; the third by Habib Bourguiba; the fourth by 'Ali Bilhawan. Each generation returned home with its own set of experiences and its individual style. To determine these styles would be to tell the history of Tunisian nationalism and, going deeper, of the growth of Tunisian consciousness. These young men had acquired new means of expression and a high degree of awareness. The growth of this awareness, and the new modes of expression, were revealed, in the field of letters, in the lectures given at the College Sadiqi or at the Khalduniya.[3] Almost all these touched on such subjects as mixed marriage, the role of youth, the difficulties of adolescence, the share of the younger generation in concrete achievements, the quarrel between the ancient and the modern. These adolescents were only incidentally interested in the past, or in the Middle Eastern world; they were chiefly interested in themselves—in themselves in relation to the omnipresent and omnipotent West. In 1936 several of them took part, directly or indirectly, in the transactions then taking place between the Popular Front movement, led by the newspaper *Tunis-Socialiste*, and the nationalist movement.

From this moment onwards a great many things happened in the internal history of Tunisia. Broadly speaking, the substitution of those who had been adolescents in 1925–30 for their elders in the leadership of the city and, gradually, of the country. True, the hierarchies of the Beylik still functioned, and the Protectorate, during this period, had the

---

[1] Fadil bin 'Ashur, *al-Haraka al-adabiya wal-fikriya fi Tunus*, 1956.
[2] Cf. the novel *Au soleil du beylik*, an unflattering portrait of these repatriates.
[3] Bin 'Ashur, op. cit, pp. 41 ff.

upper hand in open conflicts.[1] But it would be a grave mistake to attribute the real mastery of the town to the authority of the Shaikh al-Madina, or that *majlis al-'Urf*, that special council functioning under his presidency with such remarkable tact, and which included notabilities from the Nahj al-Basha–in 1928, for instance, we find among its members 'Abd al-'Aziz Nifar and 'Abd al-Wahid al-Mahrazi, while the secretary was Muhammad Mamluk and the Shaikh Shadli al-'Uqbi.

The Shaikh al-Madina was directly dependent upon the *Section d'État*. In May 1934, when Tahir Khair al-Din, Minister of Justice, retired, a large-scale movement of dignitaries swept 'Abd al-Jalil Za'ush, a former caïd of Sousse, to the leadership of the Madina.[2] At the same period, the head of the Section d'État[3] was a Frenchman of an old Tunisian family, a liberal humanist: Charles Saumagne. This African Latin loved to roam through the old streets. He often lingered in the *suqs*, for pleasure as well as from professional interest. To such a connoisseur, the aspect of the street revealed the political climate better than any police report. In normal times, the Madina retains its keen savour, where awareness of the essential is paradoxically mingled with a response to the transient moment. But sometimes it grows gloomy and withdraws into itself. At the end of September 1934, for instance, the closure of all shops filled it with a silence in which the visitor could hear the sinister echo of his own footsteps. This was a crucial year. A political threshold was being crossed. This took place in the midst of an economic and moral crisis: trade was at a standstill, craftsmanship was ruined, but the modernization of culture dared to attack religious teaching. Thus the pressure of nationalism made itself felt within the intimate life of the city.

As by rights, the Nahj al-Basha had played an essential role in the first Tunisian nationalist movement. The Destour had met in a house in the Rue Gharnuta; in the house of Ali Kahya, Tha'alibi, newly released from jail, received his friends (1921). Here were held the constitutional meetings of the Destour. Here was pronounced the condemnation of the Tunisian C.G.T. (1925). Shadli Darguth was an ally of 'Ali Bash Hanba;[4] while Muhyi al-Din al-Qlibi and Hammuda Mestiri lived close by. These were important figures in the first Destour, with which the Neo-Destour was to deal harshly. The latter drew its

---

[1] And even an 'election' where, in Nov. 1934, for instance, the Destour candidate Mukhtar Sa'ada was defeated when seeking to represent the artisans of the third category (food industry) to the Chamber of Commerce.

[2] *Dépêche tunisienne*, 19 May 1934.

[3] Section d'État, the name collectively given to the only three purely Tunisian State Services of the central government under the French Protectorate. It comprised: (1) the Ministry of State, (2) the Ministry of the Interior, (3) the Ministry of Tunisian Justice.

[4] Who was himself born in a house close to the opening of the Rue Gharnuta.

following from more democratic, peasant strata; and this was the direct contribution of Habib Bourguiba. However, it was in the very heart of the district, in the Rue du Tribunal close to Dar Lasram, that the Neo-Destour set up its headquarters (1936–8). The hero of the demonstrations of April 1938, Ali Bilhawan, also came from the Najh al-Basha.[1] When independence was won, he became head of the municipality of Tunis. Does this imply that the neighbourhood had acquired mastery over the city?[2] No, for the times were changed. Bilhawan himself, with his French education and the typically 'Arab' speech and attitudes he had acquired through his exile in the Middle East, was a revolutionary of a new type. His accession reflects not that of his district, but that of his class. He was a champion of the intelligentsia, of that class which throughout the Islamo-Mediterranean world now represented the hopes of the nation and of mankind.

As for the district, its role in the city had dwindled. Most of its sons, once they had attained modern culture and entered the liberal professions, moved into the new town, or the former suburban villas, to fill the gaps left by the departure of the French. The old palaces, although furnished anew, fell into sleepy obsolescence. More and more, people from the South, from Dwirat and Djerba, active, disrespectful and full of zest for life were moving in. Those from the Sahil, grown powerful, retained their peasant stubbornness. New Tunisia recognized its image in the man from the olive groves. Important figures of the inter-war period faded out, due to age or disgrace. Fadil bin 'Ashur maintained the intellectual prestige of his house.[3] But the aged Shaik Tahir shared the fate of the Great Mosque, whose intellectual leadership passed to the modern university, Muhammad Shauik, a belated supporter of nationalism, disappeared after his brief ministry. Moreover, there were no more big bourgeois in the Government: none, at any rate, from the Nahj al-Basha.

The bourgeoisie of Fez retained the leadership of their town and of their country only too well. This period of history was more disappointing for the bourgeoisie of Tunis. When one walks along its streets, through which the cars drive proudly but with prudent slowness, when one meets these representatives of a period that has been repudiated–

[1] After his return from Italy, in April 1943, Bourguiba received many visitors here in the house of Hadi Lakhwa.

[2] Among other buildings in this street, we may mention the one at the opening of the Rue Hafsiya, where, ever since 1929, an Association of Muslim Youth has had its headquarters; the one near the Rue Sidi Brahim, where theatrical and Boy Scout organizations met; and close to the opening of the Rue Sidi bu Sa 'id the permanent office of the Tunisian Communist Party (1945).

[3] During the whole inter-war period Zaituna reformism was front page news. Apart from the sense of 'corporate' feeling reflected in this movement, and its importance as a national symbol, it also reflects the city's uneasiness about its own significance.

and the Frenchman feels a certain responsibility for this repudiation—one cannot but be moved to see their slowly dying culture, quietly refusing to submit.

Algiers: The Laferrière District

Algiers,[1] after the French conquest, might have deserted its Turkish town and spread out ribbon-wise along the sea coast. It chose rather to climb upward. This created many problems of demolition and rebuilding. The new residential districts encroached widely on the base of the triangle of buildings whose whiteness had amazed Mediterranean navigators. This whiteness was broken up. The Turkish ramparts that had enclosed it were replaced, under the July monarchy, by others more widely open on to the sea. The vertical conquest went on. Along a long and practically level road, the present Rue d'Isly, tortuously winding stairways and slopes ran downwards. The town was extending irresistibly towards the south and the south-east. Beyond the Bab Azzun, where the southern end of the rampart sloped down to the sea, there grew up such districts as the Agha, Belcourt, Hussein Dey. The Second Empire put up its Front de Mer, a boulevard built on arcades, which gave Algiers the appearance of being perched on piles. A project was once again put forward to plan the town round a road cutting across vertically from the Casbah to the Place du Gouvernement. However, the alternative plan for development won the day by the end of the century.

The ring of fortifications broke up, near Mustapha in the south and Bab el Oued (al-Wadi) in the north. The slump of 1886–8 was followed by a phase of expansion, which was maintained by the activity of the port, now largely directed towards the Mediterranean. In conformity with the general movement, the port expanded southward from 1892 onwards. The Agha basin was opened, shortly before the municipality of Mustapha (pop. 34,000) attracted to itself the main body of the town (pop. 92,000). Algiers, a port for colliers and the exporting of wine, and a resort for English visitors after the turn of the century, became also the capital of an ever-growing economic hinterland. This marked the end of the old conception of town planning, always more or less dominated by fear of attack from land or sea. At the same time Algiers had been beautified, provided with hotels, public squares and casinos. Its winter resort committee became a Syndicat d'Initiative (1897). The tourist trade was catered for. This was, in fact, the period when the reputedly mild climate attracted wealthy consumptives, travellers enamoured of exoticism, and eventually artists and writers, some of them important.[2]

[1] Besides the classic study by René Lespès we now have that of R. Descloîtres, *L'Algérie des bidonvilles*, 1961, to which I have contributed a preface. This inaugurates a more modern type of methodology.

[2] This was André Gide's Algiers.

In the early years of the century Algiers received a statute which was to govern it until after the second world war. This was in the time of Governor General Laferrière; his name has been given to that large vertical breach which now replaces the southern rampart, symmetrical with another breach at the northern end of the rampart, the famous Esplanade of Bab el Oued, or Boulevard Général Farre. These are characteristic of the town-planning of Algiers in 1900.

The Southern development, which I shall consider next, played an important role in the history and aspect of the town, since it became what I might call the axis of the Centenary in 1930 and leads, at its top end, to the too-celebrated Forum.

From the sea, it is seen for a long time as a zone of yellowish ground, dotted with meagre clumps of trees or plantations of aloes, and rising gently at first, then sharply from the sea front (at the level of the dry dock) to the eucalyptus trees which, beyond the Rue Berthezène, surround what remains of the casemates. And then we see huge buildings rising to right and left of it, including the Post Office and the building of the *Dépêche Algérienne*, with their dazzling façades and their neo-Moorish mouldings: the apogee of the *style Jonnart*. By 1921 Algiers boasted 2,000 more buildings than in 1906, a third as much again. This was when the housing problem first arose, owing to the invasion of a crowd of workers, employees and petty bourgeois: a vast problem, for which a newly-formed H.B.M. Office professed to find a solution. The neediest of these newcomers settled in Bab el Oued, in Belcourt or near the disused Champ de Manoeuvres. The sector we are concerned with here, however, owed a fashionable urban atmosphere that was scarcely affected by the neighbourhood of more modest districts to the presence of the Grande Poste and the proximity of the University, to its splendid views over the sea and to the almost exclusively European crowd which frequented it. In less than a dozen years the character of this residential area had completely changed, especially on the borders of Mustapha. Before the 1914 war, the Rue Michelet, although lined with five-storey houses, still recalled its old existence as the Blida road. With its dusty roadway, its smell of rancid butter, its humble shops, there was still something rustic about it.[1] By 1920 it had become smart. The picturesque element now took refuge in outlying districts towards the right, such as the steep Rue de Mulhouse leading up to the Telemly.

This peripheral road, clinging to the side of the Sahil hills, lay only a very short way from the axis of the town. Algiers at that time was a long narrow strip, made up of steep slopes, steps and jutting projections. The eucalyptus and olive trees on the hillsides were less than ten minutes' walk from the Front de Mer. The upper cliff (the Rues Dupuch-Saint-Augustin and Berthezène) was separated from the axis (Rues d'Isly and

[1] R. Randau, *Les Algérianistes*, 1911, p. 36.

Michelet) and these from the Front de Mer by only a few dozen yards, measured vertically, indeed, as much as horizontally. The Laferrière district is one of those where the Sahil landscape and the sea-port are most directly united. A direct vista joins the sea to the mountain. Elsewhere the prospect is broken up. One has to climb precipitous steps to go from one level to another. Yet a good walker will soon cover the rising ground between the quays and the Orléans Barracks, close to the Sahil Gate. This zone, with its eucalyptus trees, casemates and waste ground, is frequented by soldiers using it as a short cut, and by shady characters. It combines the characteristics of the Mediterranean countryside with barbaric charm and with the squalor of a Parisian slum. Past a certain time of day it is unwise to wander through the woodlands known as Tagarins,[1] through which run 'Roman roads' and esplanades; these lead up to the Fort l'Empereur at the top, while the lazy tramway of the Messageries Sahéliennes, the TMS, climbs laboriously towards El Biar, pausing at picturesquely-named stops such as *La Scala* and *Les Deux Entêtés*.

Coming down from these heights to more frequented spots, we find the streets from early morning onwards alive with the cries of small tradesmen: pedlars, vendors of eggs, vegetables or fish. Each of them keeps up a clamorous din on a particular note to advertise his wares. Dishevelled housewives shout to one another from high Second Empire balconies. They do their shopping by letting down baskets at the end of a rope. This gives rise to violent altercations in various forms of Mediterranean lingua franca. Minor purchases are made in the street, major ones at La Lyre or Clausel's. Meanwhile the menfolk leave for their shops or offices. The blocks of flats gradually become empty.

Take one for instance, the last block in the Rue Lacépède, next to the eucalyptus grove. This building was put up by two Italian entrepreneurs. It housed a collection of types characteristic of the time and place: a great-nephew of Eugène de Redon, that municipal bigwig who was known as 'the duke of invective', postmen, clerks, retired couples, civil servants of lower and middle grades, all suffering to a greater or lesser extent from the inflation which, at that time, was making money so scarce that the Chamber of Commerce was obliged to put horrible little notes into circulation. One family, the X . . . s, was ruined by the depreciation of the franc. The father had been a rich dairyman from El Biar, one of those whose carriages used to come rattling proudly down the winding streets, causing the same accidents through excessive speed as cars do today. He had invested his fortune in market gardens at Belfort, close to Maison-Carrée. But the farm having been leased out, the rent lost all its purchase value after 1919. The children found themselves in straitened circumstances, and were to remain so until the expiry of the contract. From the balcony over the way an electrician, who had made his fortune,

[1] Andalusian immigrants of the seventeenth century.

looked across at the family who had lost theirs. He had acquired wealth by tendering for the electrical apparatus for the Exhibition and Fair of 1921; soon afterwards he lost it all and went bankrupt. Not far off there lived a hairdresser, a *colon* from Serson, the widow of the administrator of a mixed commune, a garage-owner and a lady of easy virtue. Each of these households lived in three rooms without washing facilities, sent its children to the Négrier school nearby, and laughed or bawled, quarrelled or caroused. The luckiest of them went to France in the summer; the rest made do with huts on the small neighbouring beaches, Jean-Bart or 'Ain Taya. There were no Muslims among them, except perhaps the *fatma* who did the chores (one of these still remembered the visit of the 'Emberour') and the hawkers on the sidewalks.

The *Echo d'Alger*, owned by the flour miller and senator Duroux, gives us a glimpse of Algiers in 1920. The first page is devoted to news from Metropolitan France. Local affairs, although plentiful and detailed, are relegated to the second page. This is in great contrast with the Press before 1900, which took a closer interest in Algerian affairs.[1] By conceding financial autonomy, the parent state—particularly as a result of the war—had concentrated attention on itself. This intellectual and moral allegiance affected Europeans as much as Muslims. It seems as if, instinctively or consciously, the small group of officials in whose hands local administration was concentrated were careful to keep the colony from any sort of ideological controversy, the credit or the blame for which was always given to the parent state. Other matters seemed more important. On the first page of the *Echo* we find—as we might do in any provincial newspaper—a conflict, indirectly expressed, between the two main tendencies of the day, the *tendance bleu horizon* resulting from the 1914 war and the timid red of dawning social and political awareness. Among the important articles of this year there are those signed by Gustave Mercier, son of the former Mayor of Constantine, on 'Algeria's Financial and Economic Autonomy'; these deal naturally with the Délégations Financières, that agrarian assembly which since the reforms of Laferrière had dominated the country.

Apart from this, the 1st of May provided ample copy. We read of a meeting on the Champ de Manoeuvres, attended by crowds which, for the first time, included Muslims, and at which the Red Flag was flown. One of the banners carried by the demonstrators proclaimed that *les gazeurs ont la gazouse*, which means, in local slang, that 'the gas workers are hungry'. This demonstration was neither approved by the Municipal Council, which had a fierce debate about it, nor by Louis Bertrand

---

[1] The *Souvenirs* of the old journalist Mallebay (Algiers, 1937) make one aware how much the 'Algerianness' of the Press in its early days had a dynamic quality which, although 'colonial', was better than the hypocritical stabilization of the years after 1919. The transition was, significantly, brought about by French-language Muslim journalism, of which Ferhat Abbas was the initiator.

who, from the sheltered groves of the Jardin Marengo, watched the procession go down the Rue Bab el Oued, and raved against it in pseudo-Nietzschean terms. On the terrace of the Brasserie Laferrière, in the hall of the Post Office, and at the barber's shop, the citizens discussed all these matters, which are frequently referred to in the newspaper and at the Municipal Council. Day-to-day life is reflected at this time in protests against Galoufa, 'cynical philosopher'[1] and catcher of stray dogs, in comments on insecurity–a whole younger generation having grown up while their fathers were away in the army, there was much talk of juvenile delinquency. Notably at Bab el Oued, a gang of youngsters calling themselves *les oxygénés* who wore their bleached hair fashionably sleeked back. Thieves with the picturesque nicknames of 'Typhus' or 'Wild Boar' were captured, after long efforts, by the police. Authoritative voices related these facts to similar examples of rural insecurity, all providing arguments against the Government. This was reflected in the elections to the Délégations Financières. A member of the Redon family stood as champion of what he called the 'party of administrative and financial autonomy'. He indicted the 'awakening of Muslim fanaticism' and demanded a harsher policy. But these fine feelings won him no favour; out of an electorate of 14,000 he won only 540 votes. On the other hand certain men were elected who later made their mark in Algerian history: Luciani, the Arabic scholar, who had just left the Government, and the industrialist Morard who remained for a long time Chairman of the Chamber of Commerce. On the Muslim side Bin Siam, representative of an old Moorish family. And many more, who were to dominate the town for a whole generation.

To turn to a more peaceful realm, that of culture: Algiers in 1920 already wore the air of a capital. The University Faculties, particularly that of Letters, situated not far from our district, contributed largely to this. Carcopino was still teaching there. As regards Muslim studies, there were several important names: those of E. F. Gautier, whose public lectures drew huge crowds; of the sociologist Henri Basset, who was about to leave for Morocco; of the historian Yver, the jurists Peltier and Morand, honest expounders of Muslim law; and of the great philologist Mohammed Ben Cheneb. Despite the zeal with which these learned men studied the country and its culture, increasing emphasis was to be laid on the diffusion of the aesthetic and intellectual values of the parent state. It seemed as if the country sought to atone for its excesses during the late nineteenth century by increasing 'francisation'. The problem posed in *Le Sang des Races* and *Pépète le Bien-Aimé*[2] was being solved by an assimilation of these 'Neos', of which France was justly proud. And it was towards such an assimilation that the

---

[1] Victor Trenga, *Berberopolis*, 1922, curious 'scenes of future life' and a highly perspicacious pamphlet.
[2] Powerful descriptions in support of a false thesis.

University,[1] like all the other institutions, directed its efforts. But did not this result in too thorough a liquidation, not indeed of particularism, which was to develop under a more dangerous form than that of Max Régis, but of the *nature* of the country? and the principal element in that nature, which was not neo-Latin but rather neo-Maghribi. Here, the authorities were guilty not only of neglect but of preterition. For the average Algerian–of European origin, that is–'Cagayous' was only a stock character from farce, without a living prototype; while the native appeared in the same farces as a supernumerary with traditional characteristics. And everybody roared with laughter at the caricatures in *La Dame de chez Makhlouf*.

The European population reacted excitedly against the tensions of the war period, moved by a rage to live, the turbulence of youth and the thrill of discovering a new world. There was much heavy gambling,[2] and crowds frequented the dance halls at the Exhibition Fair in the Champ de Manoeuvres. The first Chaplin films were shown at the Athénée; a grand hotel, the Excelsior, opened at the corner of Boulevard Laferrière and the Rue Michelet. The first jazz concert to be played on these African shores was heard. Amid this dizzy whirl, the affair of the Amir Khalid and what lay behind it was of concern only to specialists.

Algiers went on growing.[3] In 1926 the town had increased by 43 per cent over its 1906 population; it now had 112,000 inhabitants, of whom 45,000 were Muslims. This refers to Algiers proper; of its two great wings, Bab el Oued had increased by 103 per cent–74,000 inhabitants, of whom only 10,000 were Muslims, and Mustapha by 141 per cent– 28,000 inhabitants, including only 800 Muslims. The contrast was thus sharpened between the purely European suburbs and the old town–the lower and the upper–now being re-peopled with Muslims and Jews.[4] Already these filled the major part of the Bab Azzun arcades, and the neighbourhood of the Chartres and La Lyre markets. Only a European 'lumpen-proletariat' mingled in the Lower Casbah with a population which was no longer 'Moorish', but Kabyle. Meanwhile, however, the Laferrière district was unaffected by these changes. It remained somewhat aloof from the alterations wrought by human hands. The Excelsior Hotel vanished, making way for a bank, the Compagnie Algérienne. The

[1] With such productions as S. Faci, *L'Algérie sous l'égide de la France, contre la féodalité algérienne*, 1936.
[2] Mallebay assesses at 2 million francs (of the period) the profits realized by the three gaming-houses of Algiers during the 1920 season, *Annales africaines*, 10 April 1920.
[3] G. Audisio, 'Alger qui bâtit', *Jeunesse de la Méditerranée*, 1935, pp. 94 ff. has subtle observations on this subject. Algiers has also inspired Montherlant, *Il y a encore des paradis*, 1935; a paradise threatened by the sword, indeed . . .
[4] Cf. the diagrams in R. Descloîtres' *L'Algérie des bidonvilles*, p. 89.

Students' Association[1] had its headquarters in the same building. But what did affect the district was the radical alteration undergone in 1925, when the Administrative Centre was transferred to it. Slowly at first, the gaps were filled. The 'little mountain' disappeared from above the hotel of the XIXth division. Within a few years, the whole of this zone of fortifications and trenches, eucalyptus groves and vegetable gardens and wild nature was covered with building yards. A lift hollowed out of the rock joined the Rue d'Isly directly to the Rue Berthezène. In a leisurely fashion which provoked impatience or criticism, work proceeded on the war memorial, which involved a recasting of the Square Guynemer, and on the gigantic building which was to be the seat of the Governor-General. Neither Landowski's signature on the one nor Le Corbusier's backing for the other reassured local opinion, startled out of its provincial torpor by these developments. People could not resign themselves to losing all that empty space around the casemates, where children could play, and couples stroll in the evening.

Significantly enough, the town thus acquired an axis stretching vertically from the lower basin of the Agha, where the hydroplanes of the Postal Service[2] now alight, up towards Fort l'Empereur; and this is characteristic of Algiers at the time of its centenary. Now the tall white war memorial could be seen from far out to sea, and the honeycomb of the Government building from even farther. The latter, of course, was not finished in time. However, the Government moved in a few years after the centenary (1933).[3] The Square Bresson, with its famous Café Tantonville and its Opera House, was now the furthest point reached by bourgeois life in its advance toward the old town. The Forum of the city, people began to say, was no longer the Place du Gouvernement, but the grey concrete esplanade leading from the war memorial, under the windows of the Government building, towards the last remaining eucalyptus trees. The broadcasting studio became a focus from which the human voice reached into every home.[4] And the Salle Pierre Borde provided the town, at long last, with a decent setting for exhibitions and concerts. Chamber music was beginning to attract audiences; and not far off, in the Place Bugeaud and the Rue Charras, two avant-garde bookshops showed how much Algiers was coming into line with Paris.[5]

In fact a truly Parisian atmosphere now prevailed over the whole lower part of the Rue Michaud, from the Boulevard Laferrière to the

[1] Which has a very active sports association, the RUA.

[2] On the historic aspect, and the development of the port of Algiers, see a volume published by the Chamber of Commerce, *Documents statistiques*, 1929, pp. 3 ff.

[3] In 1934 Professor L. Milliot replaced J. Mirante as head of the Affaires Indigènes.

[4] Cf. pp. 375, 378.

[5] That of Charlot, the publisher, had a considerable influence.

Parc de Galland, with its elaborate displays, luxury goods, fastidious customers and crowds of elegant strollers. In the late afternoon, particularly, Africa seemed very remote. Algerian life was fulfilling its destiny through self-repudiation. This irresistible impulsion indicated the direction in which history was deliberately moving. The new patriciate of the wine trade now had its apartments, or rather its villas, in the upper part of the town. It asserted its preponderance, and satisfied its tastes, by an almost integral adoption of the ways of the parent state. True, there was in this tendency a certain element of self-deception or make-believe, and the prosaic reality lay not far off. But the importance of the sign cannot be neglected.

No doubt the district we are concerned with, whose inhabitants were of a humbler social stratum, remained untouched by these ambitious aims. But officials, artists and visitors, by their manners and speech, were fast altering the human element within this setting, now promoted to the dignity of a *city*. The disharmony arising out of this was slow to disappear. A kind of French provincialism, ridiculous and touching, combined with traditional Algerianism to offer the greatest contrast in tastes, ways and speech with the citified manners that seemed to follow inevitably from this urban revolution. The Laferrière district and Algiers in general felt ill at ease in their new dignity, and assumed its functions with an air of deprecating mockery. Thus another incongruity was added to those already existing in the town, and visitors from France sensed it immediately.[1] Algiers was trying to discover itself, through its attitudes as well as through its types. This was only natural. Characteristically, indeed, no synthesis was envisaged, either in the lower or the upper strata. But was such a synthesis really wanted?

Life, of course, submerged this stylistic discord. Within a radius of half a mile round the colossal edifice, buildings went up to house the organs of upper-class life, authority or culture. The old-fashioned barracks of the University[2] sacrificed its last remaining open space to erect worthier buildings in the Rue Michelet, with a sumptuous public hall, the Salle Stéphane Gsell (1931), surrounded by smart shops. These were boldly carved out of the abutments of the Faculty buildings. Not far off, on the sea front, the Palaces of Agriculture and of the Délégations Financières, the Préfecture, the Mairie, and an international Grand Hotel, the Aletti, stood at a short distance from one another. In the bar of the latter, political and business big-wigs from Europe, to whom air travel was no novelty, met French-Algerian big-wigs. The members of the ruling class who forgathered there, particularly the younger generation, represented a very different type from those of the twenties.

---

[1] Long afterwards, Jean Noël described the impression felt each time he returned to Algiers ('Couleur d'Alger'), *Algeria*, Spring 1961.

[2] Where a brilliant team of French intellectuals was teaching (P. Martino, L. Gernet and others).

In those days there had been no aeroplanes or even cars; they had driven from their farms in wagonettes, then taken the train to town, once or twice a year, on business. And they had got together democratically in some Jewish restaurant in the Rue de la Lyre, or round the greasy tables of harbour cafés.[1]

The change, in fact, was a dangerous one. The young *colon* who frequented the Aletti bar[2] was as different from those pioneers, his parents or grandparents, as was the Old Palace in the Rue Bruce, with its vestiges of the Barbaresque period, from the Kafkaesque new Government building. For the past half-century human mutation had closely corresponded to that of the urban landscape. When, in the early years of this century, the esplanade of the Boulevard Laferrière replaced the last remains of Louis-Philippe's fortifications, when the iron railing that protected the city from its suburb Mustapha, reputedly its frontier with the South, fell at last, a new era had begun. All historians were to emphasize its importance. Then, it has been said, Algeria's golden age began:[3] an era of stabilization, one-sided enrichment, and equipment. But then, in my view, Algeria ceased to be a 'natural' country. By this I do not mean a moral or a fortunate country–far from it–but on the contrary a land of clashes: a 'project' of uncertain tenor and dubious legitimacy, a prey to rival dynamic forces, where the crude avidity of Mediterranean immigrants had to confront the energies of a native revival. This pattern might have been that of nineteenth-century Mexico; but the reforms of the early twentieth century had averted it in Algeria, apparently for good. Since then, the reign of France and the rule of the *colon* went on apparently unquestioned. In exchange for a patriotic allegiance that also implied subservience in manners and ideas, the parent state offered the prize of wealth from vineyards.

Urban development at the time of the centenary embodied an apogee whose monumental aspect cannot conceal its grimmer sides. By what seems a symbolic coincidence, it was in 1930 that the birth-rate in the Casbah first exceeded the death-rate. The vitality of the native population, springing up from within, threatened the established system. From 1930, and particularly from 1935 onwards, the influx of crowds from the distant *bled* swelled the suburbs, and the masses, in their newly-acquired citizenship, became the arbiters of political destiny. Meanwhile on the Forum, empty of Muslims save for the crossing-sweepers, the taxi-drivers and a few caïds, there beat the heart of a proud and paradoxical system.

[1] For the picturesque side of the town, see R. Randau, *Sur le pavé d'Alger*.
[2] Certain small bars welcomed the *jeunesse dorée* and excluded the Jews.
[3] J.-N. Lambert, *Manuel de Législation algérienne*, Algiers, 1952, p. 50.

Part 3

The Reckoning

CHAPTER VIII

The False Apogee

In 1930, era of empires, certain men concerned with education were pondering over the partitioning of the earth. They sympathized with the feelings of Brother Wolf[1] – by which they meant the native – and this showed rare clearsightedness for the time. From Morocco to the Indian Archipelago, through an uninterrupted chain of 'possession', the European powers – France, Britain, Italy and Holland – dominated an Islam which, broadly speaking, had become colonial or semi-colonial. Europe derived profits and pride from it, but incurred grave responsibilities at the same time. Its power, while apparently triumphant, suffered threats and setbacks. In 1925 it was significantly defied by the men of the Rif on the one hand and the Druses on the other. Their uprisings, as well as the unrest in Egypt and Iraq, hint at the realities within the world partitioned by nineteenth-century conquerors and the victors of 1918 – realities which, though still powerless, were striving towards a better state of things. The inner truth, the truth of the future, was bursting through the cracks in an edifice whose falseness was already apparent.

The ubiquity of the French element at the time was none the less astonishing. In Syria, France had 'caught up' the descendants of Algerian exiles.[2] She was shortly to hunt down the last remaining 'Blue Men', on the confines of Mauretania. Nobody, in practice, called in question the superiority of Western education and of the French type of intellect, manners and literature. Islam strove towards modernization to satisfy requirements for which the old loyalties were increasingly inadequate. The rise of the Egyptian University during the previous years, the quite recent reform of the Azhar, and the activity of the three Arab Academies concurred, in different or rival ways, towards the same evolution. Needless to say this process, which everyone considered irreversible, entailed nuances or contrasts, according to the different countries,

---

[1] *Mon frère le loup*, by G. Hardy.
[2] Among whom certain groups still spoke Kabyle.

215

social strata and mental affinities. Between one nation and another, one group and another, almost between one individual and another, we find every sort of variety. A sample survey of all these types and reactions would note, here a return to the archaic, and there, opportunist acceptance of the new: here, fundamental alteration, and there, a superficial imitation; here, a vital compromise and there, a fatal one. Everywhere a composite and bastard reality prevailed. And nowhere was that state of joint-ownership, of intermixture and disparity more flagrant than in the Maghrib.

The Maghrib towards 1930

The previous chapters have brought out the complexity of a situation in which the *durée grave* and the *durée subtile*, the weighty and the intangible phenomena through whose evolution we measure time, were so intermingled that, from the almost infinite interplay of material and moral forces, a general rhythm was born.

True, this process varied according to geographical zones. This diversity was intensified by the traditional parcelling-out of the country, and by French policy which, whenever possible, encouraged local and particular characteristics. But it can be reduced, broadly speaking, to a few clearly marked types, within which, as I have already noted, we find alternation between the old and the new.[1] Formerly, three types existed: (1) the bourgeois town, be it Fez, Tunis or Tlemsen; (2) Bedouinism, with its extreme case, the Berbers; (3) sedentary village life, or what was left of it. Working on these foundations, France gained control of the towns by means of settlement, technical equipment, and the example of a way of life; of the Bedouins, by circumscribing them politically; and of rural sedentarism, which she encouraged to an exorbitant extent, by agriculture. The new economic system brought together a mass of workers and peasants who became both the agents and the object of these transformations. Fairly soon national groups were formed in the cities. In Tunis, where they were already active, they came up against the conservatism of the authorities and that of the capitalists, whereas the Bureau Arabe was still a potent force in the countryside. Three sorts of men, three sorts of attitude correspond to these three zones.

The further we move, in space or time, from pacification properly so called (a euphemism, in Morocco, for conquest), total resistance gives place to the action of the intelligentsia, itself bound up with apprenticeship to the West. But the nationalist movement, whose initiators were French-educated townsmen of a high intellectual level, had in its turn to win over the rural hinterland of the country and the deeper levels of its psyche. It had, too, to reconquer the village zone and

[1] The *qadim-jadid* alternation of the Arab East.

the 'moderate slopes' of opinion and behaviour, controlled by the colonial powers. Reciprocally, the French pursuit of total mastery, elucidation and appropriation was increasingly obstructed by its own contradictions. For the time being, the régime profited by, and at the same time suffered from, that state of things it had imposed. The Bureau Arabe mentality offered resistance, with a success that varied with the degree of isolation of the area, to the *colon* mentality; the latter's sway, almost absolute in Algeria, had to come to terms with native realities which were more mature in Tunis, more alarmingly primitive in Morocco. The true character of this period must be sought less in theories of assimilation or association, or in régimes of colonization or protectorate, than in the clash between these forces and these types. But the truth is not a simple one. The life of this society, as of any other, and more than that of any other, is complex. It is compact of vast themes intertwined, of unforeseen correspondences, and in any case it defies facile explanation. The whole of this North African world, from the newly subjugated Berber chief to the opposition-minded lawyer, from the intellectual in his tarbush to the *'alīm* in his turban, from the *colon* to the entrepreneur, and from the banker to the officer and the engineer–to mention only leading types–was in a state of confused excitement. And so, to an even greater extent, was the crowd around them.

We are only just beginning to perceive the distinctive features and the mutual implications of the different contexts in which all this was taking place. But history, carrying the whole thing towards a controversial future, simplifies and to some extent resolves this complexity by means of that very controversy. Its polemics, even when excessive, contribute to the progress of self-awareness, and thus, by an unexpected repercussion, facilitate our analysis. Thus the year 1930 witnessed three roughly contemporary and seemingly symmetrical events in the three North African countries. The celebration of the centenary in Algiers, the promulgation of the Berber *dahir* (the Sultan's edict) in Rabat, and the meeting of the Eucharistic Congress in Tunis reveal a fundamental concurrence between French action and the future of Mediterranean Islam.

The Berber Reservation

Many Berber-speaking tribes in the Maghrib had hitherto remained independent of canonic jurisdiction. Resolutely Muslim, they nevertheless rejected certain aspects of the religious institution. The Qadi's magistrature had affected them to an unequal extent, at the cost of subtle and hazardous agreements. Glosses in the Berber tongue were appended to the sacred texts, together with particularist legal comments. Hasty and tendencious study led to confusion between (1) an ecological system of laws, closely adapted to a certain way of life, (2) a system of organization, comparable to that which grew up within tribal 'customs', from Mesopotamia to the River Sus; and (3) an original culture, blending in various ways with Islamic and Arab culture. In any case, it is impossible to deny, as certain propagandists have done, the presence of Berbers in North Africa. Their existence is so far from being an invention of French policy that a rapid survey of the history of Western Islam is enough to reveal their vitality, which was in fact often fatal to the established order. Their role corresponds to that of the Kurds in Eastern Islam, presenting Arab culture with the same problems of assimilation, indeed of preponderance. It is not so much due to the somewhat hypothetical character of their origins. But their economic system, their speech, their touchy pride present, as we have seen,[1] an extreme case of rural individualism. They display in absolute form some of the characteristics they share with many Arabic-speaking Bedouins, a direct counter-type to the city-dweller, according to the subtlest social, economic and psychological relations. Finally, several of their groupings provide a vigorous safeguard for one of the Maghrib's most hopeful features, its communal solidarity. Doubtless their capacity for organization and legislation, and their historic character–contrasting moreover with their anarchism–must at all times (including the colonial period) have been repressed by the central power. This repression caused an explosive force to burst forth like a geyser whenever the opportunity arose; springing from very deep down, it was liable to shake the whole, or part, of the order imposed from above.

Obviously it was not these revolutionary possibilities which inspired the *dahir* of 1930, which Lucien Saint wrested from the young Sultan Sidi Muhammad bin Yusuf. A whole team of enthusiasts, led by a talented observer with somewhat reactionary leanings, Le Glay, had worked for this. The initiative also came from a long-standing pro-Berber tradition in neighbouring Algeria. On pretext of assimilation, which moreover was indefinitely postponed, it sought to violate, quite innocently, the pact concluded with the dynasty, by withdrawing these groups of mountain-dwellers as far as possible from the general development of the Islamic and Arab peoples. Thus, although starting from correct premises, it stopped half-way, inasmuch as it sought to deny their historical development to people who were eminently suited to make history, and even to plan it. Moreover, it confused the primitive and warlike transhumants of the Middle Atlas with the men of the High Atlas, who practised hydraulics, or those of the Anti-Atlas and the Sus, who were a kind of Mozabites without towns. Now these Berbers, particularly the more autonomous among them–those whose individual civilization cannot be questioned, the Shleuhs of Southern Morocco–were passionate Muslims. They would have been greatly surprised to hear their faith dissociated from their way of life and their civilization.

[1] Cf. p. III.

In any case their particularism, authentic though it was, was inevitably limited. It could not serve as a basis for separatism. On the contrary, the ideas that had inspired them at the time of the *siba* (dissidence) were incompatible with the Colonial situation. They had opposed the Muslim Makhzen by means of heterodox observances. They could only oppose the French Makhzen by assuming the ways of Islam. The very progress of communications led them to follow the pattern of Arab countries. Division is always mistaken; it gives rise to the accusation of cynicism, and obstructs those tendencies to unity and solidarity that inspire dismembered societies at such a moment of their history.

French policy failed to recognize this inner dynamism, and further, sought to isolate the Berbers from those French concepts and models which alone could have enabled them to skip certain stages. One might have imagined that the Shleuhs, for instance, would have missed out the stage of Middle Eastern culture and gone direct to a secular culture of Western type. In a way this was what the first teachers in Kabylia had aimed at. But the Protectorate had other views. In fact–we may say so today with the serenity of hindsight–its policy was derived purely and simply from a 'National Park outlook'. These tribes would be France's sequoias; her Berbers would remain good savages, worthy of love and respect, but whose ultimate promotion would consist in a N.C.O's stripes. Such a prospect, of course, was opposed by every instinct of these men, as well as by the general trend of things. In any case, since the French contribution in the Maghrib justified itself by the speeding-up of history, it became a constant and deliberate tendency among the left wing to try and transcend the stages not only of colonialism but also of nationalism, to construct Utopias that would elude contradictions. From this point of view, let us imagine what a man of the Seksawa or the Idaw Semal would have done in the place of the Tatar Sultan Galiev. But have we the right to formulate such a hypothesis? The aim of those who promoted the *dahir* was not to found a Berberistan, but to consolidate a reservation. They did not see that the inequality thus maintained on either side of the 'zone of insecurity' would lead those within to try and catch up with the swifter development of those without. And that is why the Berber College of Azru became a centre of Arabization, and why Berber originality was destroyed by the great caïds, particularly the Glawi, as well as by the officers of the Affaires Indigènes and even the judges of the Judiciary Jama'a. The *anflus*,[1] provided he could write, aimed at being a qadi!

By thus petrifying a *de facto* situation the *dahir* not only jeopardized the spiritual authority of the dynasty which had established French power in Morocco, it was also guilty of faulty analysis and a reactionary aim. It even brought into disrepute that element of reality which it put forward. It thus contributed to the wastefulness of the Colonial system,

[1] *anflus*: notability with collective, formerly ritual, functions.

as fatal to its authors as to its victims. And above all, it let loose a formidable conflict in the realm of feelings and ideas.[1]

The Defeat of St. Augustine[2]

'France's policy consists in de-Islamizing, secularizing and Christianizing a considerable fraction of the Moroccan population which France is bound by statute and in practice to protect.'[3] Such protests spread continuously as far as the distant Indian Archipelago, including Egypt, where they exercised the new-found vitality of the Arab press and provided an alibi for Anglophil rulers. There was no lack of pretexts. In 1932 there took place at Khemisset the inauguration of the Church of St. Theresa of the Infant Jesus. The Moroccan Socialist Party deplored the official sanction given to this ceremony. There were protests from the League of the Rights of Man, of Free Thought, etc. *La Volonté du Peuple*, a nationalist organ, bitterly pointed out that Christian worship was heavily subsidized and that churches were being built on Moroccan territory.[4] Freemasons also protested. The laying of a tablet to celebrate the fiftieth anniversary of the École Laïque was the occasion for a whole concert of political protests against what was going on. And what was going on was so serious than an important North African leader, speaking of the Eucharistic Congress at Carthage, could not repress his tears.

The Archbishop of Carthage at that time was a soldier-priest, Mgr. Lemaître, a former chaplain to native troops, General of a Brigade of Reserves, 'a stalwart fellow from the Morvan with a racy roughness of accent.'[5] He often took unfortunate action. Such was the erection of a statue of Cardinal Lavigerie, defiantly facing the Madina of Tunis at the Porte de France. Even more unfortunate was the Eucharistic Congress, celebrated in May 1930 with incredible solemnity. The crusades had begun again; posters declared as much, so did the dress worn by thousands of European children.[6] But the pupils of the Zaituna and Sadiqi deserted their classrooms to demonstrate. A number of them were arrested by the police and brought before the courts. A proclamation with 125 signatures appeared in the press, asserting that 'the true aim of the Congress was a violent crusade against Islam in North Africa.'

---

[1] Directed, on the Arab side, by Shakib Arslan, president of the Syro-Palestinian Committee. In August 1930 he gave a virulent lecture at Tetouan, reported by J. Cazenave in *La Dépêche algérienne of* 12 July 1931. In *La Nation arabe* he gives a favourable review of the pamphlet *Tempête sur le Maroc* and frequently refers to the Berber *dahir* (15 and 18 Aug. 1931; Sept.-Oct. 1931). This campaign is echoed in *L'Afrique française*, 1930, pp. 345, 442, 500.

[2] Title of an article in *Afrique-Action* (June 1961).

[3] *Voix du Tunisien*, 6 June 1931.

[4] 12 Jan. 1934, cf. *Renseignements coloniaux*, 1930, p. 391.

[5] Unpublished *Souvenirs* of Dr. Cohen-Hadria.

[6] *Afrique française*, June 1930. See pp. 350 ff.

Maghribi students in Paris wired their protests. A Tunisian newspaper also saw in this Congress a reminder of the Crusades, which 'had spilt so much blood, had flung so many human beings back into barbarism'.[1] Official orators had rashly congratulated themselves on the progress achieved among Muslim girls; there had been public ceremonies with loud-speakers and noisy music; this offended people's feelings, as did the levy of two millions imposed on the Tunisian budget.

While the political consequences of all this were as grave as anything resulting from French mistakes in North Africa, the Archbishop's excesses, by a stroke of irony, recoiled on his own head. The unfortunate effects of his administration, enhanced by economic crisis, incurred such criticism from the Vatican that he gave up all hope of a Cardinal's hat and was forced to accept a coadjutor.

Thus Muslims seriously came to believe that France, at her apogee, could remember the crusades and seek, by persuasion and by force, irrevocably to destroy their moral being. Such fears are all the more significant in that few objective facts justified them. Lavigerie's conversions, over the whole of Algeria, came to less than one thousand.[2] But how many rash acts were committed, what verbal outrages uttered![3]

All round the periphery of the Mediterranean Louis Bertrand ceaselessly went on extolling the Roman tradition as against that of Islam. For him, the priest represented merely the soul-saving aspect of colonialism.[4] And it is here that we must seek the key to the conflict. What later came to be called the French 'presence' tended to self-awareness, hence to self-justification. While the English were content with the *fact* of Colonialism, the French sought to vindicate it by far-fetched arguments. It became something more than the seizure of a state and its wealth. The exalting aspects of the work achieved, an ardent physical solidarity uniting these men of the Mediterranean, among whom, ethnically, the French were a minority, made this avid social group seek

[1] *Sawab*, 16 May 1930.

[2] *L'Humanité*, 19 Aug. 1931.

[3] Questionable statements had been made at the Social Week held in Marseilles in 1929. In Morocco, New Testaments in Berber had been distributed among the mountain-dwellers. Protestant as well as Catholic missions tended to boast of their achievements and even to exaggerate them, thereby arousing fears. Thus the International Review of Missions, published in Edinburgh, the *Mission d'Afrique*, the monthly organ of the Pères Blancs, and even the review *Terre d'Afrique* which appeared at that time at Rivet, in Algeria, inspired from a distance by Father Lammens, a great Orientalist who had become a dangerous adversary of Islam. In the same vein cf. particularly Canon Repeticci, *L'Algérie chrétienne*, 1930. *La Jeunesse catholique* no. 197, 1930, published in 'open forum' discussions on the evangelizing of the Maghribi people. Cf. on the other hand, the Egyptian papers *Wadi Nil*, 14 Oct. 1931; *Balagh*, 28 Feb. 1932; *Ahram*, 3 Feb. 1932, etc.

[4] L. Bertrand, article on Lavigerie in *La Revue des Deux Mondes*, 1 Dec. 1925. Cf. Ladreit de Lacharrière, *Afrique française*, 1926, p. 29.

for itself roots in the past. Rivalling the Arabs in its quest for *usul*, origins, it surpassed them by reason of its ampler history. Going further back than the spread of Islamic influence in the 'dark ages', it revived the concept of Christian Africa. The theme was more than a literary one. In this competition, at all levels, between the man of the Maghrib and the neo-Latin, Augustine and Cyprian were summoned to Foucauld's aid against the horsemen of 'Uqba. Whence the special significance assumed, in this country, by the restoration of ruins and even by archaeology. The worthy achievements of P. Monceaux, Stéphane Gsell and Albertini played a part, without their knowledge, in this communal attempt to take root. This was the real threat to the North African personality. It went far beyond the effort of the evangelists; this was imprudent and sporadic in its aims, but its actual weakness did not palliate the disturbing suggestions it aroused.[1]

The Celebration of the Centenary[2]

In 1930 Algiers had already begun to spread over the hillsides, and the sprinkling of little villas and bungalows along the sea-coast from Deux-Moulins to Hussein Dey had begun to spoil the pure line of the road-stead. The town planners took fright. Where the casemates, those last vestiges of the Louis-Philippe ramparts, had stood, the future Government building was slowly rising. There had been some difficulties and some scandals, about which nobody worried unduly. The Palace of the Délégations Financières had acquired frescoes and mosaics and a long hall. This little agrarian parliament had dominated the country for some thirty years. There was a great display of black frock-coats and red burnouses when it received the President of the Republic.

The combined resources of France and its colony were called on to defray the cost of the celebrations, which amounted to not less than a hundred million francs. Only five million francs, by express injunction from the French Government, were put aside for native relief work. The proportion speaks for itself. None the less ninety-three million francs had been spent when the High Commissioner for the Centenary, Gustave Mercier, who deliberately imitated Lyautey, came to read his report.[3] All kinds of congresses took place in Algiers, as though to make a triumphal statement of its achievements: Congresses of research on malaria, on water-power, congresses of Reserve Officers, of Rural

---

[1] There was another Eucharistic Congress held at Algiers in 1939. Unfortunately we have no record of the conversations that took place on this occasion between Cardinal Verdier and Mgr. Leynaud, nor the impressions made by his visit on this progressive and generous-minded prelate.

[2] G. Mercier, *Le Centenaire de l'Algérie*, 2 vols, 1931.

[3] Report of session of the Délégations Financières, 13 Jan. 1931; cf. *Renseignements coloniaux*, 1930, p. 391. According to the *Presse libre*, 9 June 1930, 7 million francs were allotted to the Governor General for entertainment expenses.

Settlers, of Firemen, of Youth Guilds; international music competitions, and so forth. Two or three thousand people took part altogether. A yacht race was watched from the Front de Mer boulevard, formerly dedicated to the Empress. There was an endless stream of official visits. These were not confined to the coast. There were festivities further inland: such as that fête in Kabylia where 8,000 young schoolchildren, duly instructed in La Fontaine's fables, greeted the President of the Republic. The crowning glory was a demonstration at Sidi Ferruch on 14 June 1930, to celebrate the centenary of the Department. The report expresses great satisfaction; some people had dreaded the possible repercussions of such a demonstration on the native population, but 'how little they understood the feelings that animated our friends, our brothers; order and perfect calm prevailed.'[1] Outwardly, no doubt, although it seems there was some muttering among the crowd when the Muslim delegation came forward to greet the visitors. What was going on in people's hearts?

Not all these demonstrations were on the same plane. Some of them provoke a smile; for instance, that evening of poetry at the Algiers Casino, when Cécile Sorel recited verse by the Comtesse de Noailles: *Azur, blancheur, dattiers, salut, terre africaine* . . . On the other hand, we must honour the names of those to whom the Congress on Malaria paid tribute: men such as Maillot and Laveran. The latter discovered a treatment for malaria, at Constantine, about 1880, and thus helped the recovery of many sufferers. Through and despite colonization, medical men, some of them outstanding such as Dr. Roux and Dr. Charles Nicolle, or those of the Pasteur Institute at Algiers, have done honour to France and to Africa. Nobody questions this. On the other hand, it will take a very long time and an almost inconceivable return to historic objectivity for the Muslim people to tolerate the monument to the glory of the *colon* inaugurated at Bufarik by the mayor, A. Froger.[2] The *colon*, in so far as he transformed the countryside and created a proletariat, did in fact make a concrete, if unwilling, contribution to later revolutions. But that was not what the officials were applauding when they listened to the Mayor's speech in front of the enormous bas-relief. And it was from Bufarik that Gaston Doumergue set off to inaugurate the column of Sidi Ferruch; the *colon*, significantly, took precedence! At Sidi 'Uqba, the bashagha Bu 'Aziz bin Gana exclaimed that if the Arabs had known the French in 1830 they would have loaded their guns with flowers! These Thousand and One Nights cannot make us forget certain outbreaks, quickly stifled, such as the heartbreaking words of one local president of the 'Rights of Man' when receiving Guernut: 'We implore your pity and your piety to ensure the application of those principles which are those of the Declaration of the Rights of Man and which can

[1] *Afrique du Nord illustrée*, 20 June, 1930; *Afrique française*, 1930, p. 415.
[2] *Afrique française*, 1930, p. 288.

be recognized in the essence of Islam.' Concurrently, there were spectacular displays of a somewhat tarnished and tattered majesty. Moreover, the opposition press denounced a superfluity of *bashaghas*; twenty-seven new ones had just been created. There were a score of supernumerary *aghas*, some of whom ill deserved the title, an attribute of warriors and administrators. The opposition press caricatured one of them, a former vendor of eggs . . .[1]

This brings us back to the financial side of things. Everyone was concerned with material success, in this country governed by the Knights Templar of the vineyard. At the Congress of Colonization, the Belgian delegate, who was surely an expert, asked his French colleagues: 'How do you manage to get your natives to work so well? 'An embarrassed silence followed. The gentleman from Brabant was tactless, and Katanga had not improved him. André Servier[2] kindly explained that the native's inherent defects–the parasitical character of the upper classes, the inertia of the lower–sprang not from racial infirmity but from economic and social factors which could be remedied. It was a consoling point of view.

Rulers in Conclave

Once the fireworks had died down the masters of the country deliberated once more. This is what we find in the reports of the Délégations financières[3] immediately after the end of the celebrations:

A proposal to institute a sealing tax on the export of cattle; another connected with the establishment of income tax–the Treasury maintained its demands. Revision of the estimates serving as a basis for land development? Raising of the rights of inspection of weights and measures; raising of the tax on petrol. A further glance reveals nothing more vital. The only thing taken seriously in these deliberations is hard cash, and thus, indirectly, production. Legislation on water supplies was discussed. Already in the time of Th. Steeg there had been a tendency to study basic things in agriculture. Fertility must be looked for where it lay. This attitude was a beneficial one; and fortunately the upright jurist Marcel Morand was a member of the commission. The exploitation of natural resources, and what goes with it, was the good side of the régime.

For the rest, we find the opening speech of the president, Galle, who was a leading figure locally during the whole period. He praised 'the development of general wealth in consequence of the extension of our economic equipment, and therefore of the rateable substances which increase every year.' Considerable efforts had indeed been made since

[1] *Presse libre*, 31 May 1930.
[2] 'La co-operation et les musulmans nord-africains', *Presse libre*, 30 May 1930.
[3] Report of Ordinary Session, 1931, no. 1, pp. 427, 437, 461, etc.

1920 to improve equipment, and these were to be carried still further. Large-scale projects were envisaged, while attention was to be paid to 'the restocking of herds, which have suffered considerably in the High Plateaux and the Southern Territories'; a sober reference to the decay of pastoral Algeria. Finally, consideration on the actual functioning of the institution. Let us examine this point for a moment.

The president showed himself very anxious not merely to maintain but to increase the prerogatives of his company.[1] (Certain frictions had already become apparent between Algeria and the Metropolitan Control on the occasion of the 1930 budget.) The parliamentary reporter had criticized the Algerian tendency to make money directly. He prescribed a more sustained respect for governmental privilege. In a word, as Galle ironically put it, he accused the Assembly of usurpation, of lèse-Parliament, and of exceeding the rights conceded by the charter of 1900. In fact, one is conscious of a certain critical resentment among these delegates against the measures imposed by France. Thus, steps were taken in 1930 to abolish the repressive tribunals which, for a long while, had dealt with offences committed by natives. Only this involved budgetary expenses, and the reporter complains of the repercussions of 'a "reform" the expediency and value of which only the future will tell us.' There is much of interest in this speech, pervaded by what we should today call a spirit of 'internal autonomy'.

A new Governor General, J. Carde, a colonial, succeeded M. Borde, the man of the centenary. The proconsul has to go very carefully with his local Parliament. No doubt he asserts the rights of Metropolitan Frenchmen: 'I shall sometimes have to ask for slight sacrifices from sectional interests, which are quite legitimate but which must give way before solutions satisfying the majority'; in other words, while allowing for the wishes of the so-called 'native' delegation, reasserting the governmental majority with the help of its faithful adherents. Thus everyone is satisfied: the colonial subject, who gets help in exchange for more verbal loyalty, and the colonizer, who increases and rewards his cadres by this means. The system, which is well-intentioned, pursues a policy of crude growth, of which the French *colon* and his native collaborators are, at different levels and with unequal rewards, the agents. Towards this aim, all the other services combine: advanced education, which is chiefly vocational, and school education which avoids intellectualism; and so forth.

Did the native delegation put the question any differently? Let us study the reports once more. One hopes to glimpse, in this official framework, something of the aspirations of the masses. Now what we find in these long-drawn-out deliberations are such questions as these:

[1] In the background, the whole question of the legislative power in Algeria is involved. Cf. Eugène Gross, *Echo d'Oran*, a series of articles in 1932; Sabatier, *Le Nord-Africain*, Jan.–March 1936.

Rights of entry into fig tree plantations, which closely concerned the Kabyle people; visiting nurses; lodging allowances; the transmission of the qadi's acts; complaints against the activities of the forestry department, which were ruining certain tribes; and as usual the competition between grazing and tilling, and the administrative and juridical forms deriving therefrom; complaints against the inefficient functioning of native insurance societies, which form a cruel contrast to the fine achievements of the *colons'* mutual aid societies, to which Muslim cultivators sought to affiliate; and muffled complaints against the Direction des Affaires Indigènes. It does not figure largely in these weighty volumes, but its presence is felt everywhere.

The Director, a Government commissioner, J. Mirante, is sometimes implicated, but always with due caution. For this old campaigner, familiar with every sort of wile, manipulates the strings. One cannot help smiling on hearing him accused by a European of having withheld a settler's share of land and given it to a Muslim. This Muslim, indeed, came under the category known as 'former servants'. But exactly what services had he performed? Elsewhere, a delegate from Mostaganem accuses the Director of having appointed a former chauffeur, who presumably had to be rewarded as Imam to the mosque. Under veiled criticisms, which no doubt had some provocation, envenomed references emerge here and there.

We need not pause over personal indictments, although they play an important role in a policy conceived after this fashion. In Tunisia, the disappearance of 'Père Roy' had more or less marked the end of a method. This lingered on in Algeria. The question is whether a more efficient or even a more moral system was to succeed it. All that interests us is the historic lesson of the sequence, namely that there was less and less room for a 'native policy' of whatever sort, and whoever directed it. Must one wonder at the lacunae, the hesitations and the ambiguity of the administrative discussion, which are surely in the nature of such things? In every country of the world this method of dismissing problems by breaking them up acts in the interests of the established power.

But where is the real power hidden here? Not in the debating delegations, granted. But not in the intrigues about native policy, nor among the Prefects. In fact, in nothing official or institutional.

The Opposition

The insincerity of these debates, their failure to express anything of importance, was offset to some extent by external controversies.

The people of Constantine–traditionally a centre of electoral strife, not completely crushed by Morinaud's authority–were of diverse origins and hot-headed, while the conflict between *caciques* (local leaders) had always had its picturesque aspect. In Algiers, Bailac (whose daughter Geneviève was the author of the satirical *Famille Hernandez*) inspired *La Presse libre*, which denounced the scandals of the centenary, the squandering of subsidies, the bribes, the swindles; in a word, the centenary, acclaimed by Mercier as a triumph, was made out to be 'the most deplorable fiasco . . . the most incredible muddle the human mind can conceive'.[1] Such violent terms no doubt exaggerated the situation, but they did draw attention to it. Meanwhile politicians bickered fiercely in the press, under vividly topical headlines: 'The swimmers of Constantine pay homage to M. Morinaud.' 'The torch is burning between the Mozabites and M. Morinaud.' Discussions over cereals and wine, the two most important things in that country at that time, went on endlessly. These day-to-day arguments bring out two orders of things significantly: personal antagonisms and the constancy of important interests. The French opposition papers expressed the resentment of the small against the great, the wrath of the needy *colon* and the humble official rather than any political demands or ideological issues. This petty-bourgeois bitterness flared up in connection with a slump in wheat, with rivalry with the South of France over viticulture, with attacks against retiring governors or struggles for local power. For instance, at the Congress of Agriculturists at Constantine, Saulnier and Bonnefoy flew at one another's throats. In all these discussions, Muslims were conspicuously absent. One of the controversialists loudly denounced the evil effects of the latifundia; he quite rightly deplored the inhuman process of land concentration, by which an aristocracy of landowners was constituted. 'All they need is serfs,' he cried ironically. 'But they've already got the *colons*.'[2] His indignant protest was made, in fact, in the name of the small settlers.

None the less, certain farsighted observers were distressed. Jean Mélia[3] pleaded on behalf of that 'native intelligentsia' which, he said, had been despised and kept out of all the celebrations, since the centenary could claim no spiritual conquest. It rejected these 'advanced' Muslims in favour of native chiefs, who seemed to belong to another epoch. The speeches made by Hajj Hammu and Bil Hajj on the beach at Sidi Ferruch did not symbolize the truth, any more than those distributions of red coats and Legion of Honour rosettes, or the horse solemnly presented to the President of the Republic.

But where could an authentic symbol be found?

Undoubtedly, for the majority of the population, in Islam. For 'the

---

[1] Jean Servac, *Presse libre*, 24 May 1930.

[2] Jules Paoli, *Presse libre*, 31 May 1930. At the same date, in the *Annales africaines* for 1 June 1930 and 1 July 1930, Mallebay waged a polemic against the pro-Arab Jean Mélia.

[3] *Presse libre*, 30 May 1930.

dominant way of thinking, among the Algerian people, is that of Islam, even if the most widespread trends in speech, learning and culture are a mingling of Arab and French. The marked unevenness between that way of thinking and these trends constitutes an undeniable, indeed a glaring fact.'[1]

I quote this comment from *Shihab*, the little review edited by Shaikh 'Abd al-Hamid bin Badis. What strikes one about it, retrospectively, is its correct sense of reality. It admirably combines an intransigence about ideals with tactical flexibility. In its portrayal of the country's rulers[2] it shows moderation and a due awareness of relative strengths. Deeply inspired by the Qur'an, as is shown by the prevailing tone, which is one of homily, it yet combines with this an extreme interest in contemporary movements and facts. If we skim through a copy of this review for 1930, we find echoes of Shabbi's lecture at the Tunis Khalduniya on the poetic imagination of the Arabs; a controversy on retention in the sexual act; a regretful reference to the 'malady of the young', their anarchical restlessness, their boredom, their paralysis in the face of history; the study of a commercial budget; references to the literary revival at Algiers, Constantine and Bougie. Its interest is not confined to the cities, but extends also to 'Ain Beida, Mila, Laghwat. With these new preoccupations, a new morphology of the country emerges. I have already stressed this point. The change in social life is closely connected with the change in behaviour. Bin Badis, a severe theologian, devoid of indulgence for the present, bravely throws out a bridge between the past and the future. But how does that present appear to him? This passage is an important one.[3]

Algerian society, he says, is sick, in mortal danger, as regards its faith and its language. It calls savagery courage, and weakness long-suffering. In spite of the efforts of the Progressive Club and the recent rise of Arabic printing, its culture is collapsing, like its economy. Its learning remains pedantic and ossified. 'But Algeria is not dead and will not die. It has not been, and will not be, absorbed. The proof of this lies in its earlier and in its recent history. Optimism must prevail over pessimism.'

Bin Badis belonged to that category of learned men who, applying the ideas of 'Abduh to the Maghrib, waged relentless war against the cult of the past under many of its forms. Hence the controversies between Taiyib al-'Uqbi, another great herald of this trend, and Bin 'Aliwa, of Mostaganem, the founder of a belated sect. Another reformer, Taufiq al-Madani, published a History of Algeria as an answer to the themes of

---

[1] *Shihab*, Feb. 1930, pp. 33 ff.

[2] E.g. of M. Borde, the Centenary governor, in the number for April 1930. Meanwhile *L'Afrique du Nord* of 9 July 1933, gives a sympathetic account of a meeting of the *'ulama'* at the Cercle du Progrès on 26 June 1932. The situation was far more ambiguous than it seems at a distance.

[3] 'Bain al-maut wal-haya', *Shibab*, April 1930, p. 157.

the centenary. The whole of the Maghrib, from Fez, where Bin 'Larbi al-'Alawi resumed the teaching of Busha'ib al-Dukkali, to Tunis, where the Zaituna was being modernized, was astir with the conflict between the *qadim* and the *jadid*, the old and the new, as was the Middle East of the same generation. But *Shihab* did not simply echo these arguments. Without perhaps explicitly realizing it, since it lacked the instruments of analysis, it envisaged the re-emergence of a personality. It was not unaware of the profound changes which French influences must imprint on that personality. It did not take a purely negative attitude. Maintaining the indefeasible right of faith, and thereby inter-preting in its own way the authentic tradition of the Maghrib, it courage-ously defended its dignity, but yet did not give way to an extremist attitude which would have been merely political in the narrowest sense.

Meanwhile a young chemist from Setif, Ferhat Abbas,[1] was working to the same end. I do not intend to dwell here on the divergences of method, of character and even of aims; that will be the task of the politi-cal historian, when he has at his disposal an adequate and objective documentation. There is a difference between the young chemist and the shaikh in his mosque, as there is between idealism *à la* Gambetta and religious personalism. But in fact all these expressions have a bearing on the same Algerian reality, though considered from widely different angles. At Constantine, *La Voix Indigène*, which combined a show of loyalism with the radicalism characteristic of a village schoolmaster, lamented the fate of 'unfortunate Muslim Algeria'. Its editor's main theme was inequality, but its acceptance of assimilation was the counter-part to the moral irredentism of *Shihab*. We find scores of examples of this inequality,[2] often picturesque, sometimes painful, but always dis-turbing, in small items entitled: 'May we ask . . .' 'Is it true that . . .' Here are incidents and scenes picked up here and there amid the vast proliferation of communes, villages and *duwars* which at that time, and at all times, made up Algeria. A native lieutenant with a brilliant war record was refused admission to a barber's shop; a graduate in philo-sophy was roughly turned out of his cab by a corporal in the Legion, who then took possession of his seat. Professor Mohammed Ben Cheneb, of the Faculty of Algiers, was forbidden to take part in a Congress in Poland to which he had been invited. His son, a candidate for the Agrégation in Literature, had to fight a whole year to get himself enrolled for the Préparation Militaire Supérieure. There was no question, here, of political suspicion: merely a call to order, the established order.

[1] Whose *Jeune Algérien*, a collection of earlier articles, appeared in 1931.
[2] Cf. for instance the number for 2 Jan. 1930.

229

A Shock

The excessive character of the centenary celebrations–the paeans of praise, the banquets, the processions–disturbed many people, Frenchmen as well as Muslims. For some it proved a real shock. Many of the national leaders of the Maghrib today are men of 'the 1930 generation'. And although such men as Viollette, Ferhat Abbas and Bourguiba were already experienced at the time, the three great events of that year provoked them to a reassessment that doubtless proved decisive. It was even more so in the case of many younger men, who at that time were studying in Paris. The Berber *dahir* sparked off the sequence of demonstrations in Morocco. Those in Tunis reached an unforeseen peak of violence and unanimity. In Algeria itself, Tamzali's motion before the Municipal Council of Algiers, and that of Bashterzi before the Council of Oran, inaugurated the movement known as *les Élus*.[1] It can today be taxed with over-moderation, or even accused of time-serving. But it did have the merit of taking Colonial history at its word, as it were. Finally, it was at this moment that, as we have seen, the *'ulama'* took action. A broad section of public opinion took upon itself to indict obscurantism and dishonourable behaviour. The praise which those in power lavished on themselves did not entirely stifle criticism. A loyalist journal, under the heading *Cahier du Centenaire*,[2] denounced the poverty of public education (30,000 children out of 500,000 attending school[3]), and the inhibitions and humiliations suffered by natives, whether as soldiers, officials or tax-payers, or before the law.

The fact that this did not unduly disturb those in authority[4] must give the historian food for thought, even if he refuses to take advantage of hindsight. Today we criticize this period for its selfishness and injustice, not without reason. But what it should chiefly be criticized for is the failure of its analysis of the problems.

[1] The name given, in the thirties, to a class of personalities who had been elected to colonial Assemblies in circumstance that were not always above suspicion.

[2] *Voix indigène*, 1 May 1930.

[3] Augustin Bernard, *L'Algérie*, p. 382, quoting official documents, speaks of 60,000 native children attending school in 1920. The number of school age was, estimated at 400,000 in 1928. Report of Délégations Financières, ordinary session, p. 147: 'Urgent requests are received on all sides. The native population demands schools, everywhere. They demand boys' schools immediately; and in a great many places they also ask for girls' schools' (ibid.).

[4] A curious passage of Montherlant's, written about 1930, shows how far literary aestheticism, even when sympathetic, can misunderstand the movement of history. Auligny, an A.I. officer, is conscious of 'the misery of Islam, its lack of valour, its lack of talent, its frustrated and rootless spirit.' It is indeed a 'poor defeated race'. Islam seems to him to be slumbering, and moaning in its dreams. 'A moribund race, to which contact with ourselves has dealt the death-blow, is lamenting—faintly and feebly, touching no one's feelings but its own, and playing on a reed that none can hear—the misfortunes of its homeland.'

Systems die not because they are mortal, but because they fail to correspond to reality. This is a cruel lesson in modesty, which, apart from all political questions, affects our researches. For how can the historian–secure, somewhat disingenuously, in his *a posteriori* judgments–be sure that he is seeing his own time accurately? What acute sensitivity he will need to understand his own epoch, not so much its outward manifestations as its inner meaning . . .

The second lesson to be learnt from the centenary conflicts is basically one of ethics. The triumph so proudly displayed in 1930 took too little account of the people and things to which it referred. Even if this triumph had been an authentic one–although in a very different sense from what was commonly supposed–it should have been realized that a victor is always responsible for his adversary. That victory is only won at the cost of exchanges, takings-over, liquidations. And that finally, in the Maghrib as elsewhere, yesterday as much as tomorrow, victory for any system involves the right to have lost.

CHAPTER IX

The Situation Worsens

The world crisis reached North Africa even later than Metropolitan France: in about 1932.[1] But since 1925 there had been local signs of a depression which was to last for ten years. The significance of this fact in relation to the general rhythm of North African life has already been noted; we must now pursue our investigation of the period following the centenary. The most important question we can ask in this connection is how far economic fluctuation affected the various elements of North African life both in themselves and in their relation to one another.

Evolution of Moroccan Agriculture[2]

Despite a lack of technical knowledge, I propose to refer to the easily interpretable statistics of the Moroccan *tertib*. This was a tax on agricultural products, which already existed prior to the Protectorate. A specialist agent, in two annual visits, made a census of crops and herds with the collaboration of the *jama'a*. The data resulting from this are as reliable as can be expected in that country and at that time.

Between 1920 and 1940, the area under indigenous cultivation roughly doubled. The increase chiefly affected soft wheat, which was grown in

[1] Report of the Council of Administration of the Crédit foncier of Algeria and Tunisia for 1933. The crisis had been felt earlier in Morocco (Act of Algeciras?): the first signs appeared in 1930. Cf. J. Dresch, 'Les courbes d'apparition, etc.', *Bulletin économique du Maroc*, Jan. 1936. In the *Revue des valeurs de l'Afrique du Nord*, the first mention occurs with reference to a weakening in the profits of the firm of Vinson (Algiers) as against the 1929 balance sheet. The same weakening affected the Phosphates Company of Gafsa. The financial year 1930 was considered 'disconcerting' (ibid., April 1931). On the other hand, the report of 21 May 1937 of the Crédit foncier of Algeria and Tunisia speaks of the 'liquidation of the consequences of the slump'.

[2] I owe thanks for information to the Moroccan Service concerned and to my friend J. Couleau.

imitation of the *colon*. It also affected barley, which remained the peasants' staple food. Leguminous plants underwent a similar evolution. No doubt these apparent increases were not unconnected with the tightening of fiscal control, which became ever more adept at unmasking evasions of the *tertib*. But they seem to correspond roughly to the actual state of affairs. Now these same statistics are less encouraging as regards the products themselves. Here we find irregularities amounting to fourfold. The production of cereals rose from ten million cwt. in the catastrophic year of 1922 to twenty million in 1924, dropped to thirteen million cwt. in 1935 and leapt up to 34 million cwt. in 1939. The production of vegetables seems on the whole to have remained stationary, and to have regressed in the case of such a basic foodstuff as the bean.[1]

The growth of agricultural production was accompanied by a decrease in stock-breeding, which was more dangerous. The number of cattle, from a total of about a million in 1920, rose to a million and a half in 1925 and then remained stationary until 1940. There was no appreciable increase, between the two latter dates, in the number of sheep, which stood at about ten million. The only marked increase was in the number of goats. But this reflects the overcrowding of mountain and forest pastures, and the consequent confinement of the fellah within the plain.

The latter fact is connected with the evident expansion of European methods of agriculture. The amount of cereal-growing land cultivated by these methods increased from 100,000 hectares in 1926 to nearly 250,000 in 1926 and to over 300,000 by 1939, a sixfold expansion between 1920 and 1940. In the same period of time, the area devoted to the production of vegetables by these methods increased tenfold. But, according to the *tertib* statistics, this expansion of the areas under European cultivation was accompanied by a slower yield. Comparison with traditionally cultivated areas gives surprising results. The fellah's productivity runs the *colon*'s close as regards hard wheat, surpasses it frequently as regards barley and maize, is openly inferior only in respect of soft wheat. Short of assuming that the *colon*'s yield was systematically under-estimated, one can now understand by what process of argument, based on facts of this sort, tax relief of 50 per cent was claimed for European creditors. But this is a double-edged argument . . .

For at the same time these figures reveal that during the period under consideration the gross increase in settlers' production was not on a level with the protection extended to them and the damage inflicted on native agriculture. There is, however, so much facile speculation on data of this type that I shall claim no more than to have set forth the results of a rapid but disturbing probe.

The inequality between traditional and modern techniques was not,

---

[1] A bad sign for domestic economy.

for this period at least, as decisive as has often been implied.[1] It is true that agriculture may increase its yield twofold, then threefold, by advancing successively to the stage of improved animal draught, then to that of mechanization and fertilization. But this truth, which is both theoretical and experimental, varies in relation to the context of the facts. It is hard for a farm to get going, even if it enjoys the benefit of long-accumulated stocks of humus. Only advanced agronomic science, when suitably adapted, could prevail decisively over the traditional methods, the inferiority–indeed, the continual latent failure–of which was then shown up by its successes. But during the intermediary period, chances were more evenly balanced, and the modern cultivator won the day more through his system than through his technique. It is true that the discrepancy between the two systems increased with the spread of colonization over the lands under tribal ownership.

Usury

Whereas for the farmer of modern type agriculture is a productive profession, it was neither a profession nor even a means of production for the traditional husbandman, but simply a way of life. He did not practise farming; he *was* a farmer. Thus when money was lent to him, the loan which another would use to buy machinery or to repay debts simply enabled him to perpetuate his way of life, to remain himself. He had illustrious precedents for this attitude. The middle-class citizen of Fez, who was ready enough to play Shylock to the detriment of other people, was himself forced to incur debts in order to keep up his rank. The native chiefs at the Algerian Centenary celebrations, in spite of substantial subsidies, spent more than they received in display. Their system was a splendid bottomless pit; it subsisted only through collaboration from the masses, which they squeezed, and the public funds which they misappropriated. Even so, they had to make use of the business ties which, paradoxically, connected the Glawi of Marrakesh with the Corcos, the Farhats of Laghwat with the Lalus. Each great caïd had his money-lender, just as each medieval duke had his Lombard. . . . The fellah, on the other hand, borrowed not in order to cut a fine figure, but, in most cases, in order to live or, more accurately, not to die. . . .

According to a monograph on the subject,[2] the total amount of debts owed to usurers within a single commune, that of Fort-National in Kabylia, in 1936, came to twenty-five millions, and affected practically the whole of the population (70,000): three-fifths to Europeans; the

[1] According to P. Rouveroux, *L'Agriculture algérienne en diagrammes*, 1930 the area and yield of cereal crops of Europeans and Muslims in Algeria rose respectively to 803,389 ha. 6,997,527 quintals and 2,327,306 ha., 12,222,351 quintals. Here again, the difference in yield is not that commonly assumed.

[2] Maissiat, *L'Usure*.

rest to lending societies, which as usual showed themselves evasive and prudent, thus leaving the usurers to take the risks and enjoy the profits of the basic operation.

If usury thus ravaged regions inhabited by small peasants and assiduous husbandmen, how much worse it was in the South, where famine was rife! In January 1926, the shaikh of one of the richest oases in Tuggurt borrowed the sum of 35,000 francs from a Biskra moneylender. He signed a bond for 53,000 francs, falling due in November 1928, without interest until that date, and then at a rate of 15 per cent until repayment. In November, of course, he defaulted. Besides, his brother needed 18,000 francs more. The two brothers together signed fresh bonds. In 1931 the creditor referred the matter to the courts. He demanded the repayment of some 200,000 francs. But he had paid out 35,000 in January 1928, 18,000 in November 1928, a total of 51,000; and since then he had collected over 35,000 francs' worth of harvest. Now he claimed repayment of 200,000 francs! He merely had to attach and dispossess this wealthy notable, owner of many palm trees, or else to make use of his claim as political pressure.

The authorities were helpless. Every time they enacted measures, for instance insisting on the load being counted out in cash before a Government official, or increasing the difficulty of borrowing, the rate of interest soared. This encouraged recourse to clandestine practices to such an extent that the intellectuals themselves took alarm. As the situation was becoming tragic, the Federation of Learned Societies expressed the wish that the administration should stop trying to put down usury, since 'the decrees of July 18 and of 7 January 1936 brought about a reform which injured everyone without really helping anyone'. The scepticism of these academics about official action would be hard to match.

It was a terrible phenomenon, and one which nobody could control. Should it be explained, as was commonly done in the thirties, by a psychological characteristic of the *milieu*? Usury in North Africa has been defined, somewhat contradictorily but in a vivid image, as 'a leech turned vampire', creeping in insidiously and then devouring the hapless peasant. The number of studies devoted to the subject is as considerable as their conclusions are ineffective. Let us see how Maissiat, who published his thesis in 1937, puts the problem. First of all, he attributes the evil to psychological causes. Of course, he blames the native husbandman; while 'in the matter of agricultural credit, the native is far from being given favoured treatment, he can provide no sure personal guarantee'. In terms characteristic of the period, the author denounces the 'innate and proverbial untrustworthiness' of the fellah 'despite the religious vow he utters as moral pledge to fulfil his obligations. Sometimes he meets his creditor empty-handed.' Such dubious ethnography need detain us no longer.

The true reason lies in the uncertainty of natural conditions and in the position of inferiority relative to the modern cultivator from which the fellah had to tackle them. The traditional system was characterized by its indefiniteness. It suffered from its precariousness, but took refuge in evanescence, like an unscrupulous tradesman resorting to bankruptcy. The fellah behaved like a hunted game-bird. He suffered from insecurity, but he made use of it. Hence the immorality of all these transactions, which derived furthermore from the fact that the Maghribi debtor was seldom one individual. Or rather, while one man might sign a bond, he merged with a broad group consisting of his family or tribe or even the whole community. Usury was only the negative and harmful aspect of a positive and profitable phenomenon of solidarity. Agricultural associations proliferated in North Africa as a safeguard against risks. Exactly for the same reasons, this weak and insecure society sought refuge in forms of association or credit outside any orthodox legal code, either Qur'anic or Napoleonic, the more so since moneylending with interest is forbidden by Muslim ethics. We should also take into account a kind of division of labour between elements of the population. Brokers and holders of capital stood apart from the rest of society; they were usually town-dwellers, members of some minority, Jews for instance but also Kabyles or Mozabites; in Morocco, the bourgeois of Fez, in Tunisia, the people of Jerba. Thus within a single social group minorities were set apart from the majority. The sinister events at Constantine in 1934 may be connected with such divisions. And in many respects the general status of Europeans in North Africa comes under the same heading.

Concentration

The most diverse factors: a retrograde division of labour in society, worsening relations with respect to land-ownership, the disparity of techniques and yields, financial restrictions, difficulties of commercialization, protectionism and favouritism, concurred to widen the gap between *colons* and fellahs on the one hand, large and small landowners on the other. Although such a conclusion seems inescapable, detailed studies which might confirm it are lacking. Here again the historian suffers from the deficiencies of the economist. Nevertheless he has some scattered observations at his disposal, most of them due to a competent observer, P. Berthault.[1] The most striking of these, in chronological order, are as follows:[2]

[1] I have at present no means of checking these on the spot.

[2] Augustin Bernard, *L'Algérie*, 1930, p. 436, had already pointed out 'a regrettable but unmistakable tendency, among both natives and Europeans, for small holdings to give place to vast domains.' On 10 June 1929, Raoux pointed out to the Délégations Financières, p. 827, that of Algerian vine-growers, 8,347 produced a total of 6,974,000 hectolitres, of which 6,600,000 were produced by only 525 vine-growers.

In 1914, the native agricultural population of Algeria was estimated at 3,650,000 and the European population at 225,954.[1] Fifteen years later, very different figures are reached, whether through changes in actual conditions or in methods of assessment. In 1930[2] the active agricultural population in Algeria is reckoned at 2,570,230 natives as against 86,413 Europeans. The two systems can by analysed as follows:

	Natives	Europeans
Number of landowners	1,338,770	34,281
	(in 1914:	(in 1914:
	1,775,613)	88,982)
Area owned	7,562,977 ha.	2,333,007 ha.
Average per landowner	5·50 ha.	67 ha.
Number of *métayers*	713,387	5,788
Number of farmers	55,606	8,170
Number of labourers	462,467	37,634

In Morocco,[3] at the same period, out of three million hectares of 'good' land, 800,000 belonged to the Moroccans and 722,000 to the *colons*, 242,000 of these being divided into 1,522 official shares. It was estimated that some 1,700,000 ha. of good land still remained to be tilled. Unfortunately this belonged to the Makhzen, to native landowners or to 'that wretched invention, collective ownership . . .'

The figures for 1934 are more trustworthy.[4] Berthault's assessment is as follows:

Out of twenty-one million ha. in Algeria, 9·5 ha. were private property, divided thus:

	Natives	Europeans
Area	7,300,000 ha.[5]	2,334,000 ha.
Number of landowners	417,000	25,795
Average area	17·5 ha.	90 ha.

European smallholdings were confined to the Sahil, to the coastal region. Here, according to this observer, 'the *colon* does not drive out the native', but rather attracted native labour. Examples are drawn from the territories of Sheragas, Saula, Ménerville, Saint-Arnaud and Littré. The *colon* functioned less as a cultivator than as a manager. He had to turn entrepreneur, or disappear. He needed considerable technical equipment and capital funds.

[1] V. Demontès, *L'Algérie agricole*, 1930, p. 65
[2] *Feuille des Renseignements et statistiques agricoles de la Direction de l'Agriculture algérienne*. Cf. *Afrique française*, Sept. 1930, p. 505; *Revue des valeurs de l'Afrique du Nord*, Nov. 1930.   [3] *Afrique du Nord illustrée*, 25 Oct. 1931.
[4] *Comptes rendus de l'Académie d'Agriculture*, 1934, pp. 946 ff.
[5] To which we must add 2,600,000 ha. of '*arsh*' land, a total of 9,678,000 hectares.

Berthault returns frequently to this theory, which discredits the myth about populating the country through colonization. He actually declares that the French peasantry no longer existed in Algeria. Here the 'small' vine-grower was the one who produced 400 hectolitres of wine, the 'large' vine-grower, more than 4,000.[1]

In 1936 the same author published a study in which he returned to the difficulties attributed to the land tenure system.[2] 'Francisation' or registration were meant to facilitate delimitation of ownership. There were in Algeria 4,600,000 hectares of 'francised' land (of which 1,600,000 belonged to Muslims) as against 7,400,000 ha. of Qur'anic status (of which 4·6 millions were of *milk* and 2·7 of *'arsh* land). In Tunisia, registration was applied to 1,427,131 ha. Official settlement, at first neglected, was more strongly developed from 1900 and particularly from 1919 onwards, to combat the growth of the Italian population. From 1910 to 1929, 270,982 ha. were allotted to 1,397 settlers. In Morocco, registration covered a million ha. of which half belonged to Europeans – 3,700 *colons* owning 835,000 ha. (the share of 'official' land-owners being respectively 1,735 and 270,000). Berthault deplores the terrible inequality endured by these 25,700 European cultivators, who owned only 2,300,000 ha. as against the 9 million (including, of course, the *'arsh* land) belonging to the 547,000 fellahs. He reiterates the 'social role' of the *colon*.

But let us look somewhat closer at the distribution of these 547,000 fellahs, already far less numerous than in 1930. 60 per cent of them, about 359,000, owned less than 10 ha.[3] that is to say an area less than the capacity of the *zuja* (the ploughing team). On the other hand, the Europeans included 25 per cent of large landowners. Their estates were almost big domains, which would be advantageous; in spite of the dema-gogic campaign against the vinegrowers and competition from the South of France, the *latifundia* would ensure an increase in the popula-tion! Interesting details follow about land capital and indebtedness. The comments made on these figures in the left-wing press expressed a very different attitude as, may well be imagined.[4]

---

[1] A clear indication of the growth of capitalist concentration: *Annales Africaines*, 1 Feb. 1935.

[2] 'La propriété rurale en Afrique du Nord' in *La propriété rurale*, Lectures of the National Agronomical Institute, 1936, pp. 132 ff.

[3] Or 60 per cent as against 0·2 per cent of big landowners (*Pour le paysan et l'artisan indigènes*, published by the Governor General, 1939).

[4] *Lutte sociale*, 1–15 Feb. 1936. According to this article 547,000 fellahs owned an average of 14 ha; 10,136 *colons* owned an average of almost 50 ha. Native property dropped from 9,224, 979 ha. in 1917 to 8,333,000 in 1927 and 7,563,000 in 1936. In the same vein, in 1936, N. d'Orient and M. Loew published a partisan yet prophetic account in *La Question algérienne*. Academic scholarship, thus faced with official publications on the one hand and their antidotes on the other, will have to make copious and careful researches, distinguishing between the various chronological phases and geographical milieux.

Thus, almost every year, this eminent agronomist, whose statements are more reliable than his conclusions, gave to the Academy of Agriculture or to the Press facts and figures which, for lack of cross-checking, I cannot set forth in a coherent synthesis. It is, however, clear that especially after 1935 dispossession was intensified, together with the uprooting of many small cultivators. 'Their situation', Charles Lévy had already admitted, 'is a wretched one; bad harvests are frequent; the fellah's expenses have increased; his share in the cost of the lorry that collects him and brings him back after market in the evening makes a considerable hole in his budget. And yet, after having used such convenient and comfortable means of locomotion, how can he bring himself to walk long distances barefoot under the hot sun?'[1] The traditional and the modern way of life are here interconnected. The fellah was at the painful and critical point of transition from one system to the other, and abuses crept in abundantly during the process.

European agriculture, though using other weapons and methods, suffered the effect of the same laws.[2] By acquiring great domains, the *colon* moved away from farming, which was his justification, to apanage, by which he stood condemned: a striking illustration of those traditional realities which his economic mission should have been to improve. In so doing he asserted his solidarity with that breed of rural landlords who, from the Atlantic to Iran, were running Mediterranean Islam. He had become the largest landowner of modern times.

If Tunisia suffered from its meagre yields, if Morocco kept looking to the future to reclaim its land, Algeria, more stable than the one and more worn out than the other, took up a paradoxical position. Berthault boldly proposes the idea that North African agriculture, by which he means that of the *colon*, must abandon cereals, which have served their time, or at any rate concern himself only with high quality baking flours; it should concentrate on rich cultures such as citrus fruits; and should give up the idea of a 'populating' mission, aiming rather at providing personnel for what we now call 'the traditional sector'. This process, akin to 'technical assistance',[3] might, if developed, require a reconsideration of the whole North African region. Cereal cultivation, even—indeed especially—when mechanized, should be left to the Maghribi masses, who have been unfairly and unfortunately supplanted in that

[1] Ch. Lévy was one of the first to argue in favour of what was not yet known as the *plan du Paysanat*. Cf. Congress of Rural Colonization of Algiers (26–29 May 1930), Part I, *Les problèmes économiques et sociaux*, 'L'amélioration de la condition des indigènes et de leurs rendements culturaux', p. 129 ff. Cf. also 'L'amélioration de la condition des indigenès et de leurs rendements culturaux', *Congrès de la colonisation rurale*, Algiers, 1931.

[2] P. Berthault, 'L'Algérie agricole dans la crise', *Comptes rendus de l'Académie d'Agriculture*, 1936, pp. 531 ff.; also in 1939, pp. 695 ff. (with reference to the High Plateaux of Constantine) and again in 1941, pp. 631 ff.

[3] The mistake was to connect it with capitalistic profit.

sphere. More specialized crops would be the particular concern of the European agronomist. Berthault naturally does not develop such ideas fully, but they can be found in embryo in his analyses. Note the shrewdness of such comments as this (1931): 'Colonization, conceived of as a policy of small-scale settlement, did not remain bound by the formula assigned to it for more than one generation. Already in the second generation of settlers we find three or four shares of an estate joining together to be cultivated as one. Smallholdings were being replaced by middle-sized or large estates and settlers' villages becoming depopulated.' A hundred years' support for colonization had not succeeded in creating a European peasantry in North Africa. 'If France has become increasingly a land of small peasant-holdings, Algerian colonization has tended on the contrary, despite the efforts of the administration, to become chiefly colonization by cadres, business chiefs and managing directors.'[1] This observation, made in 1931, is noteworthy. Berthault's perspicacity, however motivated, is undeniable.

The characteristic result of this evolution is a widening of the rift between the two economies. In the Securities List[2] published for 1934–5 by the Crédit Foncier of Algeria and Tunisia we find a catalogue, aiming at completeness, not only of all companies but of their directors. 955 such companies are listed, almost a thousand; over a tenth of these, 103, are concerned with speculation on property–over a fifth, if we add to these agriculturists' and settlers' associations; to which one might add companies not specifically mentioned, such as associations for research and enterprise. At least one-fifth of these activities are thus devoted, directly or not, to the land. This rural aspect, fundamental in North Africa, became more marked at a period when industrialization was weak. Barely nine collieries; but ninety-two companies concerned with phosphates, fertilizers, chemical products and mines, and eighteen metallurgical companies. Such a system is ill balanced. But worse still, if we examine the list of directors, we scarcely find one Maghribi name– I note only that of M. Demnati Husain, a humble Berber who started as a factory worker in France, became the right-hand man of Epinat and the business associate of the Glawi, and prospered in mining ventures. He went on being one of the capitalists of Southern Morocco. Apart from this 'assimilated' Maghribi and a few others such as Marnisi, at Fez, that shrewd collaborator of high financiers, we find no Muslim name. On the other hand, we note a number of personalities who have since acquired controversial notoriety, some of them members of twelve

[1] P. Berthault, Report to the Congress of Agricultural Engineers at the Colonial Exhibition of 1931, reproduced in the *Dépêche Algérienne* of 1 Dec. 1931.

[2] The last, if I am right, which this Bank published in the inter-war period for North Africa. The publication of the useful *Revue des Valeurs nord-africaines* was also interrupted.

or fifteen Boards of Directors. This can be explained by financial concentration[1] and it is against this that certain parties have protested constantly, but without success, during and after the Colonial era.

La kriz kain ya khu-ya[2]

For various reasons which have nothing to do with morality, colonization went through a difficult period. We have already seen that there was a slump in 1920. It endured another far more serious one in 1932. Already in 1931 the North African Congress at Tunis had noted that the cereal production of the *colons* had suffered severely.[3] Morocco recommended revision of debts, expansion and redistribution of estates. Tunisia showed the same distressing situation, worsened in her case by technical and administrative fiascos. In March 1935 Berthault, at the Commission of Protectorates, estimated the liabilities of Moroccan colonists at over 500 million francs,[4] and the Algerian mortgage debt at 2,000 million together, with 700 million long-dated bills.

Let us look closer at Algeria.[5] The centenary boom solved nothing. In bitter self-examination, the country realized that 'the squandering of public funds went hand in hand with the excess of private enterprise'. The large estates, overequipped and, as it were, inflated, expected their profit only from the distance which the régime managed to maintain between the meagreness of wages and the advantage gained from custom-free exports; whence the profound repercussion of Malthusian measures such as the restriction of vine growing.

Countless bills were protested; the number of legal distraints grew alarmingly. And observers proclaimed that Algeria was sick. She was being treated only by palliative measures. The Délégations Financières had seen things on too large a scale; so had everybody else. In the very midst of the centenary celebrations, in June 1930, the crisis in hard

---

[1] A more specialized study will have to examine the effects on North African life of this concentration, which was also applied to big banking organizations. The slump involved the disappearance, in France, of scores of small banks, and even difficulties for the Banque de Paris et des Pays-Bas, whose predominant role in Morocco is well known.

[2] Algerian dialect: 'It's the crisis, brother!' a semi-ironical expression frequently heard at the time.

[3] On this, too, Berthault is the best 'expert'. Cf. his report to the Commission of Protectorates in Mar. 1936, his lecture of '34, and his article 'La céréaliculture et les dettes', *Comptes rendus de l'Académie d'Agriculture*, 1937, pp. 39 ff.

[4] In 1934, the Director of Moroccan Agriculture wrote that out of 3,500 *colons*, 400 were completely unable to redeem their debts, and 500 others could only do so with great difficulty. On 31 Dec. 1935 the *colons*' debit balance to the Federal Treasury was 146 million francs.

[5] The setbacks of colonization had already provoked a scare, cf. J. Rouanet, *Dépêche algérienne*, 7 Feb. 1932.

wheat was so intense that the Assemblies had to be urgently convoked. These indulged in copious controversies about the percentage of wheat in the manufacture of cereal products; this is connected both with the agrarian bases of power and with the interventionist policy from which various pressure groups sought to gain advantage.

President Morard[1] gave a general definition of the crisis already threatening Algeria. It was at once political, social, economic and financial. For a long time it seemed likely to spare North Africa, but it had begun to affect that part of the continent. A few weeks before this meeting, a Congress of Mining Interests showed that the most favoured mines had suffered a loss of 30 to 40 per cent, and that for some this meant a slowing down of effort, for others complete stoppage. It meant stagnation for the export trade in cork, alfa and oil, whose prices dropped catastrophically. True, in respect of a key product, wine, the harvest was a good one. But the market prices seemed insufficient, and there were complaints about the new legislation which jeopardized the situation of the vine-growing industry. As regards cereals, the harvest had been good and market prices were reasonable. But there were fears of selling at a loss. The fruit and vegetable harvest was abundant, but inadequately protected against foreign competition. Railway traffic suffered a drop of 25 per cent. The remedies proposed consisted of protectionist measures imposed from above, in cruel contradiction to the liberal attitude professed on all sides. A single delegate protested against the authoritarian approach. This was a picturesque figure, Dromigny, the *cacique* of a village in the Sahil with the resounding name of Tefeschoun.[2] 'Our country,' he claimed, 'is the child of individual effort.' He denounced the demagogy that was rising on all sides: by which he meant the resort to inflation and *étatisme*, the multiplication of departmental offices, in a word all that was, for a while, to protect the Colonial system in North Africa. Meanwhile his observations may appear absurdly trivial: 'Having lately travelled by tram in Algiers, I shall illustrate the weakness and demagogic character of our rulers, who sometimes lack the will-power and energy to make themselves obeyed and to apply the regulations. I saw tramway employees whose persons and dress were lacking in cleanliness and who showed a want of elementary politeness and courtesy towards passengers.'

If such were the issues that preoccupied *colons* and 'non-*colons*', to use the local term, what has the Section Indigène of the Délégations Financières to say? Once again, the report of its sessions is profoundly disappointing. Not a word is said about the slump in the statement on the budget of native affairs. The only note that stands out from the anonymity of this report is not encouraging. It points out that the use of the Arabic tongue among officials is seriously declining. The French-

---

[1] Délégations Financières, 19 Dec. 1931.
[2] In the immediate post-war period he had countless battles with Mallebay.

men in this country reveal an increasing failure to understand the very elements of the Muslim's language, of their mentality and their aspirations.'[1] This is echoed by Gustave Mercier, who was once an Army interpreter. But not a word is said by the Section Indigène about the depression. The silence is characteristic. For Muslim economy was suffering even more than the settlers' economy from the economic stagnation. It did not benefit from the export of wine, which still maintained the level of foreign trade. All that part of Muslim economy which was dependent in one way or another, by employment, through trade channels or through borrowing, on European economy, felt more and more serious repercussions. And in those fields where it was sheltered from modern life, its rustic character did not always preserve it from destruction.[2]

Let us now consider the Tunisian documents. The economic sub-committee worked from 1929 to 1931. It, too, saw overproduction as the main danger. True, it demanded an intensification of work, but, the report says, 'the increase in yields must go hand in hand with the extension of land under cultivation, so as to diminish the unit-price of agricultural products'. This was well meant no doubt, but it scarcely conceals an ever more compelling quest for profits. Here, cumulative production, by which the régime sought to justify itself, clashed with the imperative demands of Finance. Production became dissociated from exchange, and exchange from consumption. Everybody at that time hoped to profit by, and everybody eventually suffered from, this dissociation, which demoralized the whole set-up.

'For the farmer today and tomorrow,' one report says, 'profit seems unlikely to result from a rise in prices: it represents rather the fruit of stubborn labour, of methods of cultivation suitably adapted to the conditions of the soil and the climate of each region, and of a full understanding of the economic system. To produce more and more was yesterday's formula. To produce in the best possible economic conditions has become a necessity today. As regards Tunisia, an essentially agricultural country, it is important to ensure adequate outlets.' Hence a new extension of colonization appeared vital. It should involve chiefly owners of considerable wealth; the official report does not recommend the establishment of settlers with only moderate means. 'The success of such *colons* is precarious in the unstable period we are now passing through. And the departments responsible should not engage in a policy of buying except with prudence and circumspection . . . Colonization will have to be applied to the lands of the *habus*, to forest regions, to the districts that are still unreclaimed, in any case to those vast areas whose

[1] A euphemism indeed.
[2] N. d'Orient and M. Loew, *La question algérienne*, provide substantial details on this point, pp. 155 ff.

sterility is patent to any informed observer, and which must definitely be freed from legal bonds which are more apparent than real.'[1]

We can appreciate the euphemism of the closing phrase. The result meant bitter suffering for the fellah. He would have to pay the price for all vicissitudes. His own misfortunes were increased through those of others. This shameless resort to state action is in such strong contrast with a policy based on production that the Tunisian report does not even realize that between 1920 and 1925 the *colon* had saved himself by means of mechanization, in other words by deeper technical knowledge. The problem was visibly growing more serious, and taking a turn for the worse. The colonial authorities were not concerned with the human realities of the country, or with laying valid foundations for its prosperity. They saw no remedy save in a superficial expansion, upheld by excessive protectionism.

It was the same in Morocco. In 1932 E. Biarnay, President of the Caisse de Crédit Agricole Mutuel of Rabat, analysed the causes of the depression: over-production, sale at a loss, under-consumption. I quote a movingly sincere extract from his report:

'Meanwhile, imagine for a moment that our outlets are closed, so that the *colon* is left stranded amidst the sacks and the cattle that he cannot sell. He must stay there, inactive on his own farm, unable to get any money to pay his debts or even the interest on them, or to remunerate his workers adequately. Would he not then hear his former workman Kaddur, now unemployed, calling out "I'm hungry"? And after that hoarse cry, would he not hear a murmur – Kaddur telling him, "And it was I who let you come into this land! My father told me that before then, all our people lived well here." Let us quickly forget this hypothesis, and say no more about it.'[2]

Hierarchies of Precariousness

The report sees no palliatives save in organizational and protective measures. And quite apart from the grievances of the North African *colon*, this results inevitably from the increasing division of the world into economic zones, from isolationism and customs barriers. Already the 7th North African Conference, concerned with the commercialization of wheat, particularly wheat grown by *colons*, was tending towards a development of credit on warrants, and such measures as the obligatory inclusion of local flours in bread-making. The tendencies of the three

[1] *Rapports des Commissions d'études économiques*, Tunis, 1932, vol. I, p. 181.
[2] *Bulletin de la Chambre d'Agriculture de Rabat, du Gharb et d'Ouezzan*, 1932, p. 60.

countries were once more revealed in the discussion: mutualism in Algeria, disguised assistance in Tunisia, and regalian munificence in Morocco.[1] By December 1934 the Imperial Economic Conference had tried to remedy the situation by granting customs privileges; and as a matter of fact the economy of the Maghrib improved after 1935. But in so far as this revival proceeded from governmental measures, it merely intensified the advantages enjoyed by the modern sector over the traditional sector.

Doubtless the export of hard wheat, barley, mutton and oil concerned the fellah directly. It would be an arduous task to analyse how far the new regulations helped him. We should have to follow the product, in each of the three countries, on its journey from pasture or ploughland to the embarkation quay. Taking into account local conditions, the role of intermediaries was naturally more considerable here than elsewhere. From brokerage to short-term loans provided by the Banks, the whole business was chiefly to the Europeans' advantage. The direct benefits of export economy and the local transactions arising from it were thus to a large extent of Colonial type. It should be ascertained how far this was so, and with what degree of Maghribi participation; again this varied according to the regions in question, the social strata, etc; more subjects for future research.

In any case, the *colon* risked only bankruptcy. And besides, he could hope to be refloated. He ran no risk of dying of hunger. True, his situation was scarcely comfortable. He had not been wise. Moreover, as E. F. Gautier admits, 'he cannot be wise: he is a peasant, but an adventurous peasant. In this country where large fortunes are not scarce, you will not find a *colon* who has not been distrained, who is not in the hands of the bank.' Gautier wrote this about 1930, and the situation grew worse after that. As a result of the drop in the market price of wine, a sharp conflict arose between Algerian vine-growers and those of the South of France. Wheat was the next controversial issue. Soft wheat dropped from 180 francs per quintal in 1926 to 110 francs in 1930, and to 85 in 1934; it was bought at 53 fr. per quintal by some unscrupulous merchants. It became steady in 1935 at under 60 fr. Hence, in some producing regions, particularly in the Shelif plain, so carefully described by X. Yacono,[2] a real revolt broke out: local papers such as the *Indépendant de Rélizane* preached what they called 'direct action'. And it was to take tremendous efforts by the Administration, the creation of a *Caisse de consolidation* for the funding of the floating debt, the granting of credits and the launching of various kinds of institution, to settle things again, notably through the creation of the Wheat Office in 1936.

[1] Cf. 'Comparaison des mesures d'allègement des dettes agricoles en Afrique du Nord', *Bulletin économique du Maroc*, July 1936, pp. 204 ff.

[2] X. Yacono, *La colonisation dans la plaine du Chelif*, vol. II, 1956, pp. 176 ff.

Now these measures, which display a laudable effort to study economic techniques more deeply, and even a certain firmness on the part of the State, since the opinion of the interested parties remained for a long time hostile to the authority of the offices, also reveals an increased appropriation of administrative initiative by Europeans. Let us retrace a few stages in this development.

After the war, a first wave of loans. Bank loans were used to create agricultural capital or to provide funds of which the agricultural authorities sometimes, as in Algeria, kept entire control. In 1925, a second stage: a sort of Credit Charter appeared in Algeria, with the law of 31 December 1925. Then followed the crisis of 1932. Not until 1936 was a *Caisse Centrale de Crédit agricole* set up in Algeria, with similiar institutions in Tunisia and Morocco, sometimes accompanied by *Caisses de Crédit artisanal* for the benefit of the impoverished working class. At this period we find a considerable difference in the methods of allocation and the amounts of credit. Algeria boasted an expansion of mutualism, which has been the subject of many studies; Messerschmidt's thesis shows the originality of the movement. At this period a large number of Co-operatives were formed in Algeria–in 1936, 355 were listed. The example of the wine, tobacco and distilling industries was widely followed. At Blida and Bone and in Kabylia a considerable number of Muslim cultivators joined such institutions. The development of these co-operatives, and the practice of the 'agricultural warrant', that is, loan on securities (e.g. grain) which remain in the hands of the borrower, ensured adequate funds for cultivators, particularly influential ones.

Now such measures consisted essentially of credits and of customs exemption on the quota system, and thus in an increased appropriation of the State by certain parties, to the indirect prejudice of the masses and of the consumer in France. Let us develop the latter point somewhat further. In 1933 the reports of the Crédit Foncier explain that Algeria remained relatively untouched by the world crisis, because its economy was evolving 'on the edge, rather than in the midst, of world difficulties.' This was beneficial for the time being, but deleterious in the long run. North African economy remained within an almost exclusively French circuit, which raised increasingly serious problems. For this involved an exchange of privileges and of weaknesses. The Imperial Conference, which began, in December 1934, to study the difficulties of overseas trade, saw a solution in exemption from customs duties. Overseas products would be allowed on the French market free of duty, by the quota system.

At this very period, in the three North African countries, useful research was going on in the technical field, particularly as regards the culture of trees. But the export trade in citrus fruits to Metropolitan France met with competition from Spain. This gave rise to difficulties, not only between the Maghrib and foreign countries on the one hand, the Maghrib and Metropolitan France on the other, but also among the three countries of the Maghrib. Interminable and unproductive palavers ensued. In vain did a decree of 5 July 1938 constitute a Citrus Fruits Committee: this held two sessions and listened to a documented report by M. Serda, but did not succeed in conciliating either the claims of France with those of Algeria, nor the respective claims of the three North African countries. Let us consider more closely the statistics relating to citrus fruits. In Algeria the area devoted to these increased from 8,300 ha. in 1927 to over 11,500 ha. in 1938, of which about one-tenth belonged to Muslims. In Morocco they owned a quarter; in Tunisia more, if olive groves are also included. None the less the question is one which chiefly concerned Europeans, both in respect to the area under cultivation and on account of highly restrictive practices.

The failure of an organization which affected them so closely was the more significant in that this question of duty-free quotas introduces an element of great theoretical interest into the analysis of colonialism. Colonization is often defined as the conquest of external markets. The relative decline of the French system in the world, and the seizure by certain groups of what profits it still promised, tightened the links between Metropolitan France and North Africa. But this was not a healthful solidarity. By favouring the *colon*'s production through the quota system, Metropolitan France became a kind of colonial market in reverse for him! This new characteristic combined with those previously noted—economic concentration, rival appetites, legislative incoherence—to confirm the deterioration of the system. In North Africa itself, European agriculture, wealthier than it admitted but more precarious than it knew, was growing exhausted. It lacked space; it lacked new ideas. Neither the expansion of areas under cultivation, nor technical progress, had succeeded in triumphing over the risks inherent in the historical conditions of the country. The reason for the failure consisted partly in 'natural difficulties', which these countries would of course have to face after they had won emancipation. But more fundamentally, it lay in the illogicality of the human relations involved.

A true reforming spirit would have tackled the reconstruction of these relations. On the contrary, the colonial system sought merely expedient solutions, and at a very superficial level. This involved it in a fresh contradiction. Whereas colonization was the primary activity in North Africa, seeking to conquer the very foundations of the country, and whereas it derived its prestige and its argument from its direct intrusion into the land itself, it made its own destiny increasingly dependent on indirect, even speculative processes, on artificial privileges wrested with ever-increasing harshness. This ominous symptom should, at the time, have preoccupied both the economist and the citizen.

CHAPTER X

The Knot Tightens

I magine a Left wing intellectual visiting North Africa in 1934–5, which was not easy for a man of his sort. He would have been fore-armed with countless confidential hints and warnings, precautions and protective measures. But if he knew how to use his eyes and ears, if he was lucky enough to be present in the right place when something was happening, he would have noted phenomena of a sort never before experienced in that country. A kind of psychological saturation caused incidents to break out, the consequences of which produced further and, in the long run, more serious incidents. Tribal resistance had recently ceased in Southern Morocco. But discontent was growing in Tunisia and in Algeria. In August 1934, the pogrom at Constantine revealed that antagonism might break out in violence. If our observer looked more deeply at the triumphant Colonial system he would recognize, as Ch.-A. Julien has shrewdly done,[1] a failure to extend the European population in the countryside, whereby the real state of affairs contradicted the régime's most conspicuous hypothesis. He would in any case note many utterances that betrayed secret or overt anger, often a sense of injustice or inequality and almost always of expected change. The whole country was in a state of expectancy; that much he would grasp, and would communicate to his friends or readers, provided he had avoided being seduced by the official propaganda, the discreet bribes, and the lavish banquets, and indeed by the effect of the incontestable achievements he had been shown. This was the case with Professor Félicien Challaye.[2] Although revealing naïvety in other respects, he never allowed himself to be taken in by the official version or even by the facts, if these happened to agree with the official version. His pacifism, which was to lead him to extreme positions, made him discern violence wherever it was concealed. And at the time of his visit to Tunisia violence was on the increase.

[1] *Histoire de l'Afrique du Nord*, 1931, p. 684. Such an observation, at that time, seemed outrageous and paradoxical.

[2] *Souvenirs de la colonisation*, 1935. He perceived the sudden deterioration of the system, pp. 174 ff.

Marcel Peyrouton took office in August 1933, and was immediately confronted with trouble in Monastir. This was the home town of a young leader, of whom nobody foresaw that twenty years later he was to govern an independent Tunisia. Repression now made use of unprecedented methods. Nevertheless, during the first part of his proconsulate the Resident played an artful hand. He made friendly advances to the Destour, and then took advantage of certain collective acts of imprudence and certain individual frailties on their part. He showed great flexibility in defending naturalized citizens, and thus, not unprofitably, incurred the wrath of the extreme Right wing[1] for being indifferent to French interests. He made war on usury, on administrative inefficiency, on some abuses of the colonial system. Thus winning favourable opinions even from certain nationalists and certain men of the Left, he embarked on a cunningly devious policy. At the elections to the Grand Conseil, which were doubtless influenced by the incidents of 6 February 1934, democracy met with a crushing defeat. Led by Colonna, the Fédération des Fonctionnaires inaugurated a course of action which the Socialists of 1920 had never foreseen. The defence of colonial interests seemed likely to prevail permanently, within the Federation, over Left wing idealism. The Resident encouraged this split by depriving the trade union movement of its leaders, the Syndicalists Durel and Bouzanquet. Next Peyrouton attacked the Destour.[2] Beside his harshness the moderate repressive measures, typically 'Third Republic', of previous Residents seemed mild indeed.[3]

The Men of the Olive Groves

In January 1934,[4] late one afternoon during Ramadan, Habib Bourguiba, accompanied by Tahar Sfar, arrived at his sister's home in Monastir.

[1] It is amusing to see the attacks of Charles Collomb against this 'anti-French liberal', *Évolution nord-africaine*, 8 Jan. 1935, give place to a more favourable estimate (ibid. 26 Jan. 1936). Peyrouton had decidedly become the 'tough customer' (*rajul*, the 'man') acclaimed in *La Vie tunisienne*, 17 Oct. 1935. It is curious to note the same shift of interpretation in the case of another North African leader, the Abbé Lambert, at precisely the same period. He was at first opposed by the Right wing, and this division resulted in the Socialist Dubois becoming Deputy for Oran. Then the Right wing recognized its own: cf. J. Marsillat, *L'abbé Lambert et les Oranais*, p. 130. A similar switch was shown by the municipality of Algiers, cf. *Évolution nord-africaine*, 17 June 1935. The whole thing, of course, was connected with events in France.

[2] On this point I refer to the remarkable unpublished memoirs of Dr. Cohen-Hadria, *Souvenirs d'un témoin socialiste*.

[3] A rising at Moknine (*Zahra*, 7 Sept. 1934), a village close to Ksar Hilal, and a demonstration were followed by repression and the banishment of the leader and his companions: cf. the texts collected by Habib Bourguiba. *La Tunisie et la France*, pp. 7 ff.

[4] Unpublished recollections of President Bourguiba, given to the author during an interview on 19 June 1961.

In vain she pressed him to stay for dinner; he was anxious, above all, to carry on his tour of Destour cells, starting with Ksar Hilal.

The two friends reached this large village an hour before sunset, and asked the first patriot they met to take them to the headquarters of the cell. They met with an evasive answer. A second and third attempt convinced them that members of the Brotherhood, formerly enthusiastic, were embarrassed at speaking to them, and turned away from them as if they had the plague. Evening drew on; after the long day's fast the two militants were exhausted and almost mad with hunger, thirst and nervous tension. A quarter of a century later, as the leader described the scene to me, he wept at remembering the insult to which he had been subjected. Nobody welcomed them, nobody listened to them. Only a somewhat eccentric old man, Ahmad bin 'Aiyad, consented to receive them in private after their supper, for which they had to return to Monastir.

The slanderous broadsheet distributed some time previously by the leaders of the Destour to ruin Bourguiba and his partisans had strongly influenced the men of the Sahil, always prone to suspicion. These quarrels can only be understood by going back several months. Bourguiba had first made an impression on the masses as lawyer and journalist. His articles in the *Voix du Tunisien* (from February 1931) and then in the *Action Tunisienne* (from 1 November 1931) disclosed a strongly individual attitude[1] which won him the mistrust and the resentment of the old guard. He knew instinctively that a nationalist movement[2] must break free of the pernicious alternation between intransigence and opportunism, and offer instead a different combination: radicalism and loyalty to history. He was therefore misunderstood when, on the one hand, he published articles by the highly conformist business man Muhammad Shnik, and on the other fomented the masses' sense of religious unity, in connection with the burial of naturalized citizens. He followed a tortuous logic, making alternate and simultaneous use of the forces of Islam and those of the West, cultivating Félicien Challaye and the League of the Rights of Man partly out of intellectual conviction but still more in order to show the populace that there was another France besides the Colonial power,[3] and he constantly took actions that disconcerted his Committee. On this plane he gained advantages whose

---

[1] From 'Voice' to 'Action'; a whole programme is implied. Bourguiba's first article in *L'Action* deals an analysis of the budget.

[2] Tahar Sfar, in the *Journal d'un exilé*, relating his thoughts at Zarzis, where he had been banished, gives an excellent historic account of the national movement, seen from the inside. Published in Tunis, 1960, pp. 15 ff. We also owe to this penetrating thinker a series of studies published subsequently under the title of *al-Iqtisad al-Siyasi*, 'Political Economy'. Father Demeerseman is preparing a book about this spiritual journey.

[3] Hence favourable to certain aspirations: but this ambiguity itself is 'colonial'.

positive value, despite setbacks and persecutions, was obvious to him. In the decrees of Manceron (1 May 1933) the first of which dissolved the Destour, the second suppressed its papers, while the third allotted a special place in burial grounds to the naturalized, he saw his opportunity.

It was in fact a macabre question of burial that brought about the Monastir incident in the summer of 1933. Peyrouton's proconsulate thus opened with scenes of brutality unheard of at that time, when mass arrests, grilling and torturing were unknown. The shock to people's feelings was profound. A party of petitioners, led by Bourguiba, visited the Beylical palace. They won the support of an influential courtier, Salim Jaza'iri. As a result of further intrigues, the Caïd of Monastir was removed from his post. For this fresh advantage gained, the committee of the Destour showed no gratitude to the *za'im*, the popular leader. Incurring their censure, he resigned from the executive (9 September 1933).

At this point there occurred the so-called 'secrets' incident. Peyrouton had had a long interview with the Destour committee. He took advantage of his physical authority, enhanced by his Rabelaisian speech and his insinuating, jovial or brutal manner, and worked on his visitors by means both of threats and promises until they agreed to dissociate themselves from the *Action Tunisienne*. Afterwards, horrified by their own weakness, they vowed to one another to hush the matter up. But one of them, Bahri Giga, withdrew, and warned Bourguiba. The committee expelled him; Tahar Sfar and Dr. Materi followed him. The intellectual and moral prestige of these dissidents was considerable. The Destour committee therefore resorted to strong measures.

It issued a circular, the effects of which confronted Bourguiba at Ksar Hilal on that January evening in 1934. He spoke, with growing excitement; his colloquial language, the sudden variations in his tone, his quick glances, his arguments, his indignation and his tears had their effect. While the old guard remained cautious, the younger generation acclaimed him with enthusiasm. Victory was in his hands. The secretary of the cell, Bu Zwita,[1] was finally won over, carried away by the force of this youthful movement which was henceforward to provide unfailing support for Bourguiba – not yet the 'supreme fighter', but a democratic leader whose powerful gifts threatened both his opponents and his rivals. And the Sahil, which had been so hard to convince, where he had even been ill-treated, became his most loyal fief.

I have already mentioned that Congress of Ksar Hilal (March 1934), of outstanding significance. Its originality did not lie in the emergence of a militant peasantry. Fifteen years previously, Zaghlul had roused the

---

[1] Whose name happens to suggest 'an olive tree'.

Egyptian fellahs. Nor did it lie in the use of eloquence; verbal persuasion and emotional appeals have always been powerful instruments in Mediterranean Islam, while broadcasting has intensified that power, and official propaganda itself has systematically made use of it. The originality of the Ksar Hilal episode consists in its recourse to history.[1] Rejecting half a century of national impotence, the Neo-Destour, partly by instinct, partly by calculation, interpreted both the natural development of the people and its deliberate aspiration towards a broader fulfilment. Based on nature, it sought to rise above itself in a world in process of becoming. And one cannot but recall the image of that Sahil olive tree which, rooted in the most individual soil, lends its branches to the international symbol.

The Shorn Colons

The settlers, affected by the world crisis, endeavoured to overcome the depression by intensifying their power over the State. They naturally blamed the latter for all their difficulties. Thus in Morocco at the end of 1933 they produced a sort of agrarian charter which they tried to force upon the Resident, at this time a prudent diplomat already famous in Damascus for his habit of temporizing. This document, published in full in the Bulletin of the Agricultural Chamber of the Gharb and Wazzan[2] has one prevailing theme: protectionism. It argues as follows:

The failure to finance colonization adequately would have social, economic, financial and political results such that the Government cannot even temporarily envisage this negative solution.

The problem is indeed of such importance as to affect not only Moroccan interests but, directly, those of France.

From the social point of view, France cannot allow her nationals to be brought down to the material level of the natives.

From the economic point of view, it would mean an immediate decrease in French imports to Morocco.

From the financial point of view, it would mean that France, having guaranteed Moroccan loans, would have to bear the burden of the defaulting Moroccan budget.

From the political point of view, which is particularly serious, it would mean the encouragement of native unrest.

The Resident could not entirely accept these reasons, nor the demand

[1] In Bourguiba's letter to Guernut, published by the *Action tunisienne* on 5 Mar. 1933, we find this phrase, which might stand as heading to this chapter: 'The Colonial fact has reached a dangerous turning in its history.' But Bourguiba, carried away by his feelings, anticipates things by one year.

[2] My information throughout this paragraph is taken from this Bulletin, completed by the recollections of one of the participants.

for 'a three years' truce in the recovery of taxes' presented by the Federation of Chambers of Agriculture. Meeting on 23 January 1934 under the chairmanship of Chavent, the Federation protested indignantly at this frustration of its claims. Morlot, the delegate from Ujda, proposed a hitherto unfamiliar method of forcing the authorities to take the requisite decision. He sought to foment a movement which should be both agrarian and para-military: 'We envisage the creation in each centre of a military formation, obeying a voluntarily accepted discipline. We are in an age of emblems: ours shall be the *shorn colon.*'

In fact, a large number of the participants had their heads shaved to illustrate their destitution. On 5 February 1934–an ominous date–they forgathered in plenary session at the Salle des Fêtes of the Municipal Services of Rabat. They elected a new Committee and drew up a series of complaints. They demanded: 'immediate cessation of judicial restraints' (the economic crisis was at its height; the *colons* were apprehensive of being forcibly distrained upon). 'The settlement of debts regulating liabilities over a period varying from thirty to fifty years' (admittedly a demagogic proposition). 'Lowered rate of interest on loans. Allocation of the French quota exclusively to *colons*. Control of imports of foreign wines. Prohibition of import of foreign cattle and meat. Reform of the Act of Algeciras. Reorganization of agricultural services . . .' Morlot, the Chairman, finally got the following resolution passed: 'The General Assembly of the Association . . . protests against the French Government's use of Morocco to satisfy political groups. It cannot tolerate the lack of concern for Moroccan interests shown by the authorities.' The violence of these comments is in striking contrast with the courteous tone of the Plan for Moroccan Reform, also dated 1934! The settlers furthermore remind the Government that 'patience has its limits, and Morocco cannot be held in fief for the benefit of speculators, backed by torpid officials; the settlers' representatives will continue to take part in public affairs only if a real effort . . . proves that the Administration is aware of the distress amid which Morocco is struggling.'

Towards noon the demonstrators assembled at the end of the long avenue leading towards the Residence from the Tuarga Mosque. The gathering became increasingly tumultuous. At one point, apparently, after a telephone message received from Paris,[1] the 'shorn colons' marched in fours towards the Residence along the Rue de la Marne. Barriers were set up to block their way; there was considerable violence from police and Senegalese troops, and some casualties in the ensuing clash. The demonstrators nonetheless made their way to the Government offices. A delegation led by Morlot was received by H. Ponsot, who once more temporized: a method he had successfully used in dealing with the Governments of the Syrian and Lebanese Republics. He postponed his

[1] Recollections of one of the participants, giving a glimpse of secret history.

meeting with the delegation until the afternoon. After this second interview, the delegation returned to their constituents; Morlot explained that in his opinion nothing had come of it but promises. The *colons*, exasperated, moved that all the elected representatives of the Chamber of Agriculture and other Chambers should resign without delay. Two virulent telegrams were sent off to the President of the Republic and the President of the two Chambers. Daladier, at that time President of the Council, merely got a copy, this being 6 February 1934!

In the other two African countries, we could find similar situations, although less violent in character. On 7 August 1934 an important meeting of *colons* at Gambetta Park in Tunis[1] inveighed against the impotence of the authorities. The over-valuation of lands, the lack of forethought in the distribution of shares, the harshness of judiciary distraints, the misdeeds of the banks, the inadequacy of credit: all these are familiar themes.[2] And yet, they declared, 'we love this land, we love its atmosphere, harsh though it is, and even its natives, with whom we wish to live in amity, undisturbed by foreign influences.'[3] Faced with widespread panic, M. Peyrouton had to cut short his stay in France. He sought to bring about recovery by firm measures. But sometimes the complaints retained a threatening note. French *colons* in Tunisia handed in their military cards to the Embassy. Similar incidents occurred in Algeria, where a whole succession of mayors resigned.[4] The most characteristic demonstration, however, was that held in Morocco, as we have seen.[5] It was moreover not unrelated to the one taking place at the same time in the Place de la Concorde. Certain information leads one to believe that direct contact existed that day between Rabat and Paris.

How is one to explain the failure to punish this rising, this Bastille Day in reverse? In a system so deeply concerned with decorum, with the prestige of the authorities, the Residence, that holy of holies, had been invaded by a horde of ungrateful stipendiaries. Of course one should not dismiss lightly the efforts and merits of individuals among them, nor the productivity of the whole group. But the price to be paid for this productivity was a high one! What impression could it make on the rural caïds who, at that very moment, may have been cooling their heels

[1] *Dépêche tunisienne*, 8 Aug. 1934.
[2] Cf. for instance *Vie tunisienne*, 24 Oct. 1933 (inflation of land prices); 19 Dec. 1933 (against the Banks); 20 April 1934 (plunder of the Treasury); 21 Aug. 1934 (poverty of the *colons*).
[3] *Vie tunisienne*, 29 Aug. 1933.
[4] Jean Bigorre, 'L'agitation agraire en Algérie', *Afrique française*, 1935, pp. 530 ff.
[5] According to *La Tunisie française*, 2 July 1935, Le Beau, president of the Chamber of Agriculture of Casablanca, threatened, if Peyrouton should leave Morocco, to march on Rabat and occupy the Residence! There was at this time in the countryside a mixed movement of self-defence groups.

in the waiting-room of the Direction des Affaires Indigènes, or the 'andalou' bourgeois of Rabat and Salé? Although some of these may have already assessed the strength of men capable of braving the *hakim,* they were surely far from imagining for what reasons the authorities, which they still respected, dealt so mildly with the demonstrators. And we ourselves, aware of the impoverished condition of the settler class, who were forced to beg from the Banks, the central administration and the Bureau Arabe, in a word essentially dependent on the Protectorate, can find no explanation for its audacity save the significance ascribed to it by the authorities. The revolt of the 'shorn *colons*' was the revolt of a symbol against its devotees . . .[1]

Street Scenes[2]

Until August 1934, the all-powerful *Dépêche de Constantine*[3] admitted the existence of the native population only under the headings 'News items' and 'Through the law-courts', in connection with brawls, petty larceny and attempted rape. And yet natives formed the majority of the town's population and were largely predominant in the department. Suddenly on 8 August their existence hit the headlines, so to speak, with the funeral of twenty-four Jewish victims of a riot. 'An abominable crime', proclaimed Morinaud, while Rabbi Lellouche hymned the martyr-dom of these 'French citizens, guilty only of their Jewish blood and their deep love for France.' Governor Carde visited the scene of the crime. In the Rue Abdallah Bey, a whole family had been massacred; in the Rue Fonantilles, the premises of a Jewish firm had been destroyed by fire, the owners, incidentally, being saved by a Muslim. As often happens in such cases, the noblest devotion appears side by side with the most sordid violence.

The sequence of causes and effects will probably never be made clear. It appears that during the night of 3–4 August a drunken Jewish soldier desecrated the mosque of Sidi Mabruk. A slight scuffle ensued, which nobody seems to have taken seriously. Meanwhile the Gallia-Sport Club was holding a festival at Sidi Mabruk. The Saturday night passed calmly; then agitation broke out afresh, with looting, incendiarism and slaughter. The Mayor, Morinaud, belatedly returning from his seaside holiday, summoned the Muslim members of the Conseil General. The leader of the Opposition, Dr. Bendjelloul (Bin Jalul), issued an appeal for calm. A curfew was declared, traffic was forbidden and Muslim cafés were closed. The police, then the army, intervened and regained control of the streets.

---

[1] Devotees through conviction or constraint, but that is not the point . . .

[2] Hitherto unprecedented, in my opinion. Neither the Jellaz affair (1911) nor the incidents at Fez in 1912 had been of this character.

[3] From which I have taken the chronological details of these events.

Gradually the tension lessened, although false rumours were rife. An ox escaping from the slaughterhouse almost started a panic. 144 arrests were made, including thirty on suspicion of murder. Incidents broke out at Hammam-Plaisance, at Khrub, at 'Ain Smara, Chateaudun-du-Rhummel, 'Ain Beida, Bizot. The investigators, seeking a link between these facts, noted an unusual crowd at the markets of El-Gerra and Hamma. At the market of Jemmapes, a gendarme wounded three natives in self-defence. Had there been a plot? Such evidently was the theory behind the Government's repressive measures.

On the contrary, the Muslim delegates in their appeal, addressed to the Governor General on 10 August, insisted that these deplorable events in no way affected their devotion to France. Were they seeking to deflect the harshness of reprisals, which might use this pogrom as a weapon against the nationalist movement? or were they seeing further, and insinuating that the responsibility lay, directly or indirectly, elsewhere than with a mob overwrought by its distress? The fact remains that the signatories of the document–including the lawyer Mukhtar Hajj Sa'id, who saved two Jewish families in the Rue Flatters, Dr. Bendjelloul, the Mufti, the municipal councillors, the journalist Mami Smail of the *Najah*, Bin Badis junior the schoolmaster, and many more–represented an élite whose suggestions should have been given serious consideration. Whether this was done by the Administrative Commission come from Algiers to investigate the matter, we have no means of telling; their conclusions were hushed up, and we are left with conjectures. An organized plot or an act of provocation, a spontaneous outburst or a deliberately created diversion: only the history of events, when its secret aspects are revealed, may perhaps shed light on the direct cause of these incidents some day.

'Reasons for a Decree'[1]

The agitation of the three North African countries, its effect on the action of financial groups and, in one case, on parliamentary life, the interest taken in Maurice Viollette's ideas by French public opinion, 'sensitized' to Algeria ever since the centenary celebrations and the Colonial exhibition, these were doubtless the factors which in March 1935 decided the Minister, Régnier, to study the problem on the spot. On his arrival, which aroused both hopes and apprehensions, he received a delegation of *colons* led by A. Froger.[2] 'Consider them well. These are

---

[1] Title of an article by J. Menaut, *Afrique française*, 1934, pp. 649 ff. about the decree of 23 Oct. 1934, which strengthened the authority of the Governor General. But this was as yet only a measure of administrative centralization. In the following paragraph we are dealing with a more serious measure.

[2] *Echo d'Alger*, 6 Mar. 1935.

noble-hearted Frenchmen. The great mass of the natives are on our side. Only a handful of scoundrels are against us. Everything can be summed up in one word: authority.' Meanwhile, however, at the January elections Dr. Bendjelloul had triumphed with a majority of over five thousand.[1] M. Chekiken set forth the demands of those who grouped themselves under the title (too often euphemistic) of *Les Élus* (the elected representatives). Amidst all these contradictory claims, to whom could the Minister turn? To his political friends in local sections, and to specialists like the Director of the Affaires Indigènes, L. Milliot, himself Algerian-born, an Arabic scholar and jurist of repute and a former companion of Lyautey.

Specialists, however, had a professional interest in minimizing the significance of complaints and in proposing individual solutions. As for the radicals, their interpretation reflects an edulcorated form of economism.[2] While they correctly stressed the evil effects of usury, they tended to dismiss those movements whose collective significance escaped them as mere agitation. Like Morocco and Tunisia at about the same time, Algeria witnessed the ominous apostasy of certain Left wing elements – Socialists and Syndicalists, middle and lower strata of the European population – who embraced the views of the Colonial authorities, combining them with a somewhat blatant social reformism. In 1935 there was as yet no sign of the distressing rifts or the suspect alliances which, after 1945, were to be the bane of the Left wing movement. For the time being French power was nowhere seriously called in question. This gave every encouragement to conservative elements, who now assumed a threatening tone. 'Monsieur le Ministre, you know nothing. Beware, for the Algerians are quick to anger,' wrote R. Laquière, in ominous anticipation of 1956.[3]

And so on 7 March, in a speech at Constantine, Régnier,[4] inaugurating a path along which many distinguished men were to follow him, stressed above all the need for restoring authority. 'Afterwards we shall resume our forward march at a speedier rhythm.' Such was the answer proposed by the Third Republic to that town whose wounds were still raw and where deep distrust divided the two, indeed the three, elements of the population. Was this an adequate reply to that 'North African

---

[1] To the horror of Charles Collomb, *Évolution nord-africaine*, 8 Jan. 1935: 'The Islamic crescent conceals the Bolshevik sickle!' On the other hand *Le Peuple algérien*, 6 Feb. 1935, denounces the electoral traffic of the *féodaux* Gratien Faure (Mila) and Maurin (Khenshela) *à l'ombre du gaudinisme en fleurs* (alluding to the influence of the Gaudin family).

[2] One might search in vain through the reports of the Tenth Congress of the Union of Confederated Syndicates of Constantine for a reference to native problems which was precise and concrete, not merely inspired by extremist assimilationism.

[3] 'Un siècle d'efforts et dix jours de voyage', *Presse libre*, 4 Mar. 1935.

[4] 'A conscientious and painstaking, but limited old man.' R. Randau, *Annales africaines*, 1 April 1935.

uneasiness' which now preoccupied even Father Jalabert?[1] In any case, the authorities' relief was overt when Professor Augustin Bernard, in an interview,[2] denounced 'the agitators from the parent state, the insults and denigrations of the Press' as the real cause of the trouble. The sly and over-facile confusion between the symptom and the disease betrays a certain analytical weakness, to say the least. In retrospect, we might view more harshly the incompetence of the Professor of Geography than the selfishness of the *colon*, the apprehensions of the *petit blanc*, and even the so-called prudence of administrative specialists. The latter were concerned solely with technical problems,[3] the former with their class interests. But what justification had the Professor?

Régnier, on his return, got the Senate to reject Viollette's proposal. This debate, in which French members of parliament for Algeria took part—Cuttoli, Roux-Freissineng, Duroux among others[4]—was an unusually grave one. It passed almost unnoticed. The press at that time was concerned with a variety of major events, such as the German denunciation of the military clauses of the Treaty of Versailles, and with individual happenings such as the capture of the bandit Spada, the air crash involving Governor Renard and the interrogation of the parricide Violette Nozière. It dismissed as an unimportant escapade the Minister's investigatory visit, which resulted not in the hoped for-regulations but in a recrudescence of repression. The decree of 30 March 1935 dealt with political offences in Algeria. Similar measures were to follow in Morocco and Tunisia.

When, during the autumn of 1935, Governor General Carde left Algeria, the funeral oration pronounced on him by Robert Randau[5] condemned 'the mistakes of an exhausted official,' guilty of having brought about 'disorder with the Administration, antisemitic riots, and the destitution of fellahs and *colons*.' In Tunisia and Morocco, the picture was equally gloomy. Viollette's project was shelved; so was the *Plan de reformes marocaines;* the Neo-Destour was repressed. A whole team of technical experts, with Peyrouton, Carde and Ponsot at its head, disastrously imposed its policy of prudent half-measures instead of the

---

[1] *Etudes*, 1935

[2] 'Ce que dit le professeur Aug. Bernard et ce qu'il ne dit pas', *Dépêche algérienne*, 28 Mar. 1935. Cf. a somewhat depressing article by Bernard, 'Le dénouement de la crise algérienne', *Renseignements coloniaux*, 1935, pp. 1 ff. Bernard describes as a *dénouement* what I have called a 'tightening of the knot!' So much the worse for us . . .

[3] R. Randau, *Annales africaines*, 15 Feb. 1935, describes the Service des Affaires Indigènes thus: 'It remains limited to peculiar intrigues; it knows only individuals; it concerns itself only with the heads of families, with the crowd of flatterers of every sort who surround it, soliciting favours.'

[4] *Journal officiel, Débats parlementaires*, pp. 341 ff., 364 ff., 371 ff.

[5] *Annales africaines*, 15 Oct. 1935.

basic reassessment demanded more or less openly by the native population, and the necessity of which was appreciated by clear-sighted critics.
The cause of the Maghrib, through its roots in popular life and
through its connections with world events, was now beyond the scope
of specialists. But it needed only a generous approach, in other words a
realistic one: the close analysis of a real situation. And this analysis
was never made. The death of Lyautey, which happened at this time,
marks, through the very ambiguity of the Marshal's figure, the end of a
period and the need for the right gift.

A Pattern

This moment, therefore, is one of considerable dramatic importance.
Today we see it as heralding a terribly uncertain future. But the fact
that many ulterior developments and therefore many anterior 'prepara-
tions' can be related to it does not imply that all these relations can be
defined in terms of cause and effect. The character of the whole country
was being refashioned with reference to the problem.

North Africa was no longer either the traditional aggregate, under
religious law, of cities plus Bedouinism, nor the pyramid of prefectures,
sub-prefectures, communes and *duwars* set up, under French rule,
according to hierarchies of political and administrative control. It had
become a *simultaneous* country.[1] Advances in communication,[2] notably
broadcasting,[3] ensured constant contact between the country's centre
and its extremities, disturbing traditional ways and even, to some extent,
geographical relations. The various opposition movements evolved in
the same fashion. 'Cells' sprang up throughout rural Tunisia. A nationalist network spread from Fez to the remotest *jama'a*. Small centres of
renascent communal life were inspired by the '*Ulama*' movement and
that of the Algerian 'Elected ones', much against the intentions of the
legislator. The whole face of the country was changing. Tlemsen and
Constantine became politically more important than Oran and even than
Algiers, which until quite recently had represented European supremacy.
Associations proliferated everywhere. At the time, nobody appreciated

[1] The Fifth Congress of the Association of North African Students (Tlemsen,
1935) proclaimed the necessity for unifying measures in the Maghrib.

[2] The railway connecting Marrakesh to Gabès by a single line (3,000 km) was
inaugurated in 1934; cf. *Dépêche tunisienne*, 12 May, 1934. Also in that year—an
equally important fact—an aircraft flew from Algiers to the border of French
West Africa, ignoring the ground-lighted route; the Sahara had been mastered
for the first time; we note with interest that among the crew was an assistant
photographer of Algerian nationality, Sa'id Mahmud, one of the first North
African muslims to enter this service. A friend of the '*Ulama*', a native of
Constantine, Bentchico, took part in an aerial cruise that took him into French
West Africa. Cf. *Shihab*, May 1936.

[3] On the progress of Algerian broadcasting, *Annales africaines*, 15 Oct. 1935.

this symptom at its true value. 'Plots' and 'agitation' were held responsible for what was really a morphological substitution. The relative
importance of tribes and towns, of mountain and plain, the affinity of
territories, the rhythm of exchanges, the spread of ideas and of action,
all this was altering visibly. Political zeal and cunning were soon to count
for more than *barud*, open conflict. Indeed, it was through failing to
understand this visible process of unification that the Colonial authorities
lost touch with reality. They still thought and acted in terms of the tribe
and the canton, whereas the Opposition worked through committees,
and spoke for the whole country; they obeyed the dictates of selfish
common-sense, whereas the Opposition represented history.

North Africa between the two wars, isolated from the rest of the
world by French rule as much as by its sea and desert frontiers, agitated
by a movement that gave it growing unity, must thus be seen as a
multi-dimensional object which has to be analysed from the most
diverse angles: time, space, coherence. It is a collective entity, unique
and inimitable, like any other specific historic object, and it has its own
logic as well as its physical substance and its duration. Significantly
enough, almost everything about it centres round a nucleus, the years
1934-5.

If this hypothesis is correct, the task of the analyst will be to define
the relationship which, within this whole, connects the various movements with the central theme. Now this relationship is somewhat loose.
During this twenty-year period the country was being equipped and
exploited, and, so to speak, charged with energy, a process marked by
the oscillations characteristic of economic phenomena and by the sometimes violent reactions of the milieu. The spread of Western culture
developed even more continuously, because it met with less and less
serious opposition. However, during the two last years of the period,
a certain renascence of classical Arabic, and the advent of a younger
generation which had made French culture its own, affected this continuity and radically altered its direction. Under countless alternative
banners, but stubbornly, although still divided between violent outbreaks and clandestine activity, the opposition made headway. The growing discord between political intentions and economic power was the
factor really responsible for the crises, followed by pauses, which
succeeded one another in an ever sharper rhythm and on an ever more
serious scale. Developments that were continuous, if fluctuating, thus
seem to contrast with others, whose rhythm was chaotic and broken. But
their combined results produce the total effect we had, at a first glance,
foreseen: disturbances, and then recovery, in the immediate post-war
period; a political lull, and the quest for economic creation; the false
apogee of the colonial system about 1930, coinciding with the raising of
the fundamental problem; then the economic crisis and France's refusal
to consider this problem; then the worsening of the situation.

For the human beings concerned, this meant the alternate heightening and lowering of tension. From time to time, feelings broke out irrepressibly, and then gloom and silence would reign in the madina,[1] with closed shops and lowering faces; sometimes excited crowds would swarm into the streets, and then the army might be called in, with its tanks and barbed wire and even, on occasion, its machine guns. The people of the Maghrib, particularly in the towns, were instinctively aware that something had broken down. And although no irreparable harm had yet been done, the emotional foundations of co-existence had been sapped–to an extent varying with different milieux and different social and psychological strata.

Increasingly stringent regulations failed to close the widening gap between the existing situation, in which France dominated, and the hopes of the greatest number–between the ideas and symbols that inspired the nation's youth, and the facts, which reflected the continued ascendancy of the foreigner. The divorce was taking place within a state of coexistence that did not preclude friendly human relations, and this made it all the more distressing.

Thus the continuity of certain developments and the gaps in others, the varying scope of efforts creating, or disrupting, unity, concur to make one's picture of this period one of increased harmony and yet of growing discord. Such a viewpoint may perhaps enable one to link up two approaches that are usually kept separate: objective analysis and moral judgment. A study of this sort also seeks to combine the historic with the structural; and it is in this fashion that we must interpret what happened in the Maghrib in 1934–5 as a watershed, a logical crux, and the centre of a pattern.

[1] After the repression of September, the Tunisian journal *Zahra* (6 Sept. 1934) gave a dramatic description of a silent town in which the passer-by hears nothing but the sound of his own footsteps in the empty streets.

CHAPTER XI

The Final Summons

The alteration taking place within a pattern provides the analyst with an objective means of assessing, not according to any absolute moral standard but relatively, that which the subjects of his study experience as good or evil: 'good' or 'bad' periods or leaders, the 'success' or 'failure' of certain actions. In fact the evolution of the whole North African set-up seems increasingly to consist of the divergence of two lines of development, the one corresponding to ideas and symbols, the other to facts and things. The Colonial era must be defined as a failure to interpret meanings. But this pessimistic definition–and its pessimism is justified in the long run–does not preclude certain qualifications.

From time to time a generous measure, a broadminded hypothesis, the sudden sense of companionship in suffering or (less frequently) in hope, might seem to bring together the two divergent branches. What ensued was not unanimity–there were too many discords in colonial society for that–but a sort of counterpoint. This found political expression in the promise of 'solutions'. The year 1936 witnessed several of these all-too-rare agreements between Maghribi aspirations, the views of certain Frenchmen and the nature of things. The measures proposed by Viénot, the Blum-Viollette project, for instance, dismissed by many people as Utopian, are seen in retrospect to have had great realistic potentialities. We can assert this, not on the evidence of our feelings, but by examining the context in which these proposals were made. Research, noting the convergence or divergence, the continuity or discontinuity of developments, can assess the aptitude of certain ideas to create, or to break up, unified wholes.

The Stagnation of the System

If a policy consists of systematizing in collective practice the significance extracted from a historic whole, there was no French policy in North

Africa between the two world wars.[1] No effort was made to organize constructive interplay between governmental action and the total relationship of Frenchmen and the people of the Maghrib. Parliamentary transactions, the influence of lobbies, the resistance of local authorities paralysed the initiative of the central power. An unstable legal system reflected the balance of forces. Only on rare occasions did it yield to the influence of some liberal inspiration, some accurate study of the facts, some successful improvisation.

These various factors were not consciously integrated. Those in charge of administration at the basic level were seeking to establish French power at a minimum cost, by liquidating the maximum of elementary tensions. They succeeded in varying degrees, the measure of their success being silence or anonymity. A good departmental chief never gets himself talked about, even favourably. By a painful paradox, this system, which had been forcibly introduced in the name of history and which could only be justified objectively by the acceleration it imparted to things, sought only to stifle the Maghrib's vitality. This was becoming increasingly impossible. Things went from bad to worse when the system came into conflict with centres and periods of activity: large towns, nascent industrial concentrations, surges of popular feeling. Local administration, however, was able to elude some of the fundamental problems; these became the responsibility of a superior authority, that of the proconsuls. Here were integrated, at a level of efficiency hitherto conclusive–since there had been no hostile uprisings and no prospect of insurrection, but merely political difficulties–governmental technique and the action of powerful interests. Naturally, the Colonial régime, on the whole and in the long run, united the two. But occasionally they conflicted. Economy of means compelled the Government official only to yield to the pressure of business interests within the psychological or material limits which the subject could endure.

This instrumental liberalism, so to speak, was emphasized in Morocco by the Lyautey tradition, the still redoubtable power of the tribes, and the threat of the 'Alawi monarchy,[2] which had already made itself felt. Elsewhere, the progress of institutional assimilation, the not inconsiderable influence of the 'elected' natives, the dreaded repercussions on opinion in Metropolitan France, restricted or disturbed Colonial concord. Individuals at various levels–administrators, even Parliamentarians–exerted their utmost skill trying to find a just balance between all these factors, in relation to particular situations, events and chances. They made a specialist study of influences, of resistances, of contingencies. And this was what was known as 'native policy', or simply 'policy',

[1] Whence the abundance of political literature, indefatigably concerned to 'defend' positions with formulae.

[2] In Tunisia, too, one should not minimize the role of certain beys, nor that of a tradition interpreted more or less respectfully by the Section d'État.

in North Africa: a stubborn and incoherent system, just occasionally guided by men of honesty, experience and even talent. Many wise thinkers, as difficulties increased and problems became clearer (as they did from 1930 onwards) realized the faultiness of the system.

Charléty, Rector of the Academy of Paris, organized a group of Islamic studies at the Centre de Politique Etrangère.[1] R. Montagne, its leading spirit, had lived both in Damascus and among the Berbers. He strove to make rulers and administrators aware of the evolution of the Middle Eastern world, the threat to the European establishment which this implies and the right way to avert it. The efforts made by this group were not all on the same level. We find the most commonplace preoccupations side by side with much more advanced ideas. Pierre Viénot became the spokesman for the latter. At a luncheon held on 9 July 1936, for the members of the association, he ventured to quote Lyautey's famous remark that 'we must be the artisans of an emancipation to be achieved under our guidance, but to our advantage'[2] (1920). Viénot combined, in a synthesis which is not as paradoxical as it may seem, Lyautey's teachings with those of Léon Blum. This was not the first time that Socialist views were to coincide with the anticipatory ideals of certain Africans; it was not to be the last. One can understand the force of such a combination, enhanced by the personal charm of the speaker. The ideas discussed at the Centre de Politique Etrangère were often far-sighted, and Viénot's interest suggests that these theoretical efforts might have a practical result.

The decree of 23 February 1935 instituted the Mediterranean High Committee.[3] Its main themes were traditional: it was concerned about a Muslim revival which might threaten France's position in the Maghrib and the Levant. It was also concerned about rivalries between the three Territories in the matter of protectionism. It prescribed a large-scale investigation, by a Commission of which Ch.-A. Julien, in 1936, was appointed secretary. This seemed a guarantee of democratic opportunities for the future. The Government seemed to be taking over the concept of broad movements and wide spaces, and to be turning its back on the excessively particularist policies hitherto in vogue, while on the other hand paying great attention to economic and social problems.

But the High Committee came up against internal and external difficulties. The rise of Fascism abroad gave increasing weight to conservative forces within France. The passions aroused by the success, then the gradual decline of the Popular Front, had distressing repercussions

[1] Cf. P.-E. Viard, *Les centres municipaux dans la Commune mixte d'Algérie*, Sirey, 1939.
[2] *La Tunisie française* greeted this, on 8 Aug. 1936, as might be expected.
[3] I should like to express my gratitude to Ch.-A. Julien for the extremely interesting information he has given me on this subject.

on the problems of Mediterranean Islam. Finally the High Committee had to bear the brunt of events which it had not deserved, and which put it in the paradoxical position of having to endorse repression at Fez (October 1937), at Tunis (April 1938), and in connection with the Parti Populaire Algérien (August 1937). It was forced to leave things to the initiative of local proconsuls, who themselves found events too much for them. For all these reasons, France's reaction to the whole network of problems confronting her, from Fez to Damascus, remained a negative one, in spite of this praiseworthy attempt at a synthesis.

Local Activity

It is not without interest that one of the most striking incidents in this history occurred, as we have seen, in March 1934 at Ksar Hilal, a small township in the Sahil. When in 1937 the old leader Shaikh Tha'alibi returned from the Middle East he was faced with organizations which had grown up without him and practically against him. When he tried to unite, or rather to reconcile, the Old and the New Destour, the latter appealed to its local cells. This would have been inconceivable ten years earlier. Tha'alibi had no doubt not moved beyond the concept of the theological *madina*. The Middle East had left its mark on him. When he appeared in some of these townships, at Beja or Mater for instance, he was greeted–like a certain French Minister later on—with tomatoes. Hence he got the ironical nickname of Shaikh *tematem*, 'the tomato Shaikh'. Bourguiba, on the other hand, held forty-two meetings in one year, from January 1937 to January 1938, attended by over ten thousand people! This appeal to a large, heterogeneous and mainly rural audience is typical of the movement at that period and of the leader who was henceforward to interpret it.

If in Morocco the disturbances that followed from changes in the economic system and in the way of life had not yet banished traditional groupings, in Tunisia and in Algeria new forms emerged as the old decayed. The village and the cell supplanted the vanishing tribe and the artificial 'fraction'. This revival of local vitality was accompanied by a re-organization of the whole area, with a change in its moral hierarchy as the leadership shifted from Tunis to the Sahil. Fez itself, that proud metropolis, was drained of its active elements, as the more energetic young bourgeois settled in the Rue de Strasbourg in Casablanca, preparing for the action they were to take some ten or fifteen years later.

This transformation was understood and used only by the nationalist forces; the Government, and even its official scientists, were unaware of it. A new political cadastration was taking place in the country. The nationalist parties now attacked, within the *bled* itself, what had been the vital factor of French power and its greatest achievement hitherto:

the loyalty of the rural masses. In Algeria, the country of a thousand cantons (*qaba'il*, 'tribes' = *Kabyles*), traditionally less centralized than Morocco or Tunisia, the individual chiefs who dominated the mixed commune, in association with the *bureau* and the local European *cacique*, now met with competition from an agitator, himself of local origin. At Biskra, three chiefs thus contended for influence, men of the old school and men of the new: the *Shaikh al-'Arab* Bin Gana (the hierarchy is traditional), one elected official, Dr. Sa'dan, and one militant Communist. From Tizi Ouzou came Sharif Benhabyles, at that period one of the enterprising élite. We had already encountered the young chemist Ferhat Abbas, at Sétif; Zahiri, connected with the '*Ulama*' at Oran; and Shaikh Ibrahimi, another of the '*Ulama*', at Tlemsen. And the leading personalities of Constantine, such as Dr. Bendjelloul or Shaikh Bin Badis, have been mentioned frequently enough.

The administration reacted to this local vitality, in which it saw merely a threat, by intensifying its repressive powers. Repeated statements stressed 'the security of the state' and 'anti-French propaganda'. But it also made some positive efforts. In Tunisia, under the impetus of Charles Saumagne, a broad programme for the peasantry was launched, including plans for rural communes. In Algeria—and this touches our theme more closely—a reform was inaugurated, though over-timidly. A degree of 1937 created Municipal Centres as the conclusion of a communal plan envisaged under the Second Empire and reinforced by the law of 1919.[1] But many jurists, hidebound by the laws of Metropolitan France and even more by colonial prejudice, contested these proposals, which were never to pass beyond the experimental stage. Basically, everyone was afraid of stirring up the mischief-making elements in the peasantry. It was neither the first nor the last time that these had proved a bugbear to the governing class.

In retrospect one is tempted to describe the whole life of this period in terms of the tragedy of our own time. We seek to read in it the factors that herald that tragedy, prepare it or delay it, excuse or emphasize it. But its own density, its texture, are not due only to this anticipation of history. The vigour of local life reveals something specific to North Africa, characteristic of its relations between town and country. And its authenticity is confirmed by the very fact that it was always challenged by the central power, at any period, whether of French sovereignty or Qur'anic investiture, whether dependent or independent. However little we understand it, we cannot fail to recognize in it, at the period under consideration here, a kind of effervescence. It suggests an image familiar in the Maghrib of those days: those acetylene lamps in use throughout the *bled*, which when lit produced extraordinary motions in carbide, when water was added to it. And sometimes there was an explosion . . .

[1] Cf. P. Ageron, 'Une politique algérienne libérale sous la IIIe République', *Revue d'histoire moderne et contemporaine*, 1960, pp. 121 ff.

A New Social Life

Not only new personalities but also new social units arose. Associations sprang up everywhere. Many of them, indeed, were directed towards deliberate action or tactical methods. In 1937 Mubarak al-Mili preached the restoration of the Arabic nation, for which the essential instrument was the foundation of societies, aimed at forming a community of spirit and of custom. He proposed moreover that attention be paid to the education of youth, to ensure the spread of certain practices.[1] These new forms frequently competed with the older ones. When in 1936 the pilgrims returned from Mecca, one of these new societies, Bin Badis's Association for Education and Instruction, offered to entertain them, so as to prevent the customary extravagance of private celebrations.[2] The Shaikh actively opposed these sumptuary excesses, unconsciously combining Islamic strictness with the economic protection of the bourgeoisie. He unhesitatingly combated a practice as deep-rooted as the entertainment of returning pilgrims. This detail is known to us only through the comment in the review *al-Shihab*, which points out that the Association's reception was frustrated by the manoeuvres of the official clergy of the Great Mosque. But it is a significant illustration of the rivalry of attitudes.

A remarkable unpublished thesis of the time[3] attempts a census of these societies, which proliferated so widely in the cities and in the countryside. It lists over 110 openly acknowledged, to which no doubt many more could be added. A glance at the places named as centres shows the intimate connection of these societies with the life of the townships: we read at random: Mostaganem, Biskra, Jijelli, Tebessa, Constantine, Suk-Ahras, Beni Ughlis, Summan (mixed), Chateaudun du Rhummel, Sedrata (a Sedrata remote from its 'Ibadi origins), Mila, Collo, Algiers of course, Tlemsen, Blida, Sidi bel-Abbes, Bu Sa'ada, Hussein Dey, Ghardaia, Medea, 'Ain-Temushent, Saint-Denis-du-Sig, 'Ain Beida. These new groups existed everywhere. Their tendencies often conflicted. Some of them, as at Oran, Tiaret and Sétif, protected the interests of naturalized French citizens. Others sprang from that Francophil and duly safeguarded reformism professed by the Federation of the 'elected ones', under Dr. Bendjelloul. Others gave battle in the name of those champions of assimilationism, the former schoolteachers. Ten were more or less openly Communist, six adhered to the Popular

---

[1] *al-Rabita al-'arabiya*, Dec. 1936, quoted by Vrolyk. Cf. *Shihab*, July 1935, for the characteristic inauguration of the Muslim Club of Mila. Al-Mili, apart from his *History* already quoted, is the author of an essay on deviations from religious observance in Algeria.

[2] *Shihab*, May 1935.

[3] F. Vrolyk, unpublished dissertation on *L'Évolution de la jeunesse musulmane d'Algérie* (Mar. 1937).

Front. But about fifty, almost half of the total, were derived from the 'Ulama' movement.[1]

The latter, to which frequent reference has been made, dates from May 1931 in its existing form. Its educational and cultural aims derived enormous popular appeal from Islamic symbolism, used both for defence and for attack. In direct opposition to the archaic and particularist forms of religion, such as that practised by Marabouts and brotherhoods, it had acquired a political character through force of circumstances, the ambition of its leaders and the effect of persecution. Conflicting both with the conformist bourgeoisie, that ally of clerical officialdom, and with rural traditionalism, it had the advantage of holding more convincing ideals and modern views. The rights of the individual, the purifying of religion, the revival of Arabism were strongly championed in towns and villages, where their dynamic power supplanted forces hitherto deep-rooted but decadent, authentic but outworn.[2]

In this connection we must also mention the Associations of Maghribi students,[3] which had been very active since the thirties,[4] and their annual congress. In 1935[5] this passed a resolution in favour of the unification of the Maghrib. This breadth of view was not confined to the Maghrib; al-Shihab, for instance, took a close interest in whatever happened in the Middle East.[6] Meanwhile some people pinned great hopes, possibly all their hopes, on Metropolitan France and its Popular Front.

Thus a new relationship between the local and the universal corresponds to the evolution of the economic system and of men's minds, to the basic morphological change. Naturally, it was not consciously formulated either by those directly concerned or by observers. The progress of the nationalist press, both in quantity and in quality, the interest taken in Egyptian publications on the one hand and the political press of the parent state on the other, are merely one indication of this. No one at the time appreciated it at its true significance. And if the awareness of the

---

[1] Id., ibid., p. 129–33.

[2] An incident betokening a rising force: the stevedores of Algiers, on the instigation of the 'Ulama', undertook the cleaning of the New Mosque; cf. *Action tunisienne*, 22 Nov. 1931.

[3] In 1935, 142 Maghribi students were duly registered in the University of Paris (Ministerial reply to a question of 31 Jan. 1935, quoted by the *Presse libre* of 24 Mar. 1935).

[4] Cf. *Nashra sanawiya talaba shimal Ifriqiya al-muslimin bi-Fransa* (1929–30). The president at that time was Muhammad Sakka, the vice-presidents Muhammad al-Fasi and 'Abd al-Rahman Muwaffaq. The publication was printed at Tetouan. The second Congress was held at Algiers, at the Cercle du Progrès, on 25 Aug. 1932.

[5] Tlemsen, Sept. 1935.

[6] Cf. a curious article on Arabism, signed *al- fata al-Zawawi*, in short, 'the young Berber' (May 1936).

nationalist movement had deepened, drawing strength from repression, it had by no means gained the mastery over ideas and things, or outclassed the official power in the treatment of realities, except through the intuition of some particular leader or his response to the instinct of the masses. The justice of its cause, the authenticity of its symbols were what counted then, rather than any deliberate action. Nevertheless the advent of the Popular Front caused both opponents, the Frenchmen as well as the Maghribi, to reassess their position.

Social Struggles[1]

The new factor about this period is that analysis and feeling combine, in France as well as in the Maghrib, to lay bare the faults of the system and to propose certain solutions.

Algeria had followed Metropolitan France in the rift between the C.G.T. and the C.G.T.U. On one side stood the entire body of schoolteachers, about one third of the railwaymen, half the P.T.T.[2], the customs officers; their resolutely reformist tendencies were shared by certain Muslim militants, champions of total assimilationism. On the other side the railwaymen formed the most active element. With them certain unions representing private enterprise, among them the wet coopers, a most important body in a wine-growing country; we must also mention the pipe-makers of the Constantine region, sea-fishermen, dockers, and even some agricultural labourers.

The fluctuations of French policy are reflected to an exaggerated extent in these two organizations and within the syndicalist movement. The strikes which made most impression, the builders' strike and that of the dockers of Oran and Algiers (1927–9) were not specially aimed at the Colonial situation. However, the C.G.T.U. (*Confédération générale de travail unifiée*) was the more concerned of the two to integrate its interests with those of the country. It employed themes of local importance: for instance it pressed the claim for equal pay for equal work, it denounced the scandal of 'special' wages for Muslim workers. Finally, many of its militants, members of the Communist Party, had been active at the time of the Rif war. Already certain groups displayed a preponderance of local elements: for instance the syndicate of the C.F.R.A. (*Compagnie des chemins de fer sur route algériens*), with its leader 'Amara, the syndicate of urban sanitation workers. For that matter the C.G.T.U. disregarded its rival's departmental structure, and recognized only one regional, 'Algerian', union.

With the reorganization of membership in 1935, the C.G.T.U. split up once more into three Unions. In Algiers the old C.G.T.U. tendencies prevailed, while at Oran and Constantine reformists predominated.

[1] I owe several of the facts quoted in this paragraph to M. Angonin, of the C.G.T.   [2] Postes, Télégraphe et Téléphone.

Hence it was the Democratic union of Algiers, with its general secretary Fayet, that piloted the movement. We need to mention Muslim militants at Oran—'Allal Sa'dun and above all Taiyib Jaidir—who came from the Teachers' Union and, in general, followed the line of the S.F.I.O. (the Socialists: *Section française de l'Internationale Ouvrière*). The influence of the rival C.G.T. was not yet as great as it was to become after the war. But it had already spread beyond the cities. A militant Trade Unionist travelling through the Oran region would have found that, although the structure of agricultural employment was scarcely propitious for mass action, many workers were pinning their hopes to the Popular Front and the 'Cigiti'. Civic education was spreading, as well as class consciousness; and although it neglected, or rather skirted by, nationalist themes, and stressed social themes and the alliance between proletarians, it made a deep impact upon the masses. In the final analysis, this long-term education was the movement's main achievement.

In 1936, strikes broke out in agricultural regions where the working population was dense. Thus at 'Ain Temushent, in the heart of the Oran region,[1] the militant proletarians of Bani Saf took action. A Labour Exchange was set up in 1936. On 14 July of that year a great meeting was held, in which a mass of rural workers took part, secretly incited, it was said, by the Bashagha Bin Shiha. A few scuffles occurred between Socialists and Fascists; then all 'returned to order'.

Strikes multiplied in fruit- and vegetable-growing regions. Turbulent bands ranged the neighbourhood of Algiers. One such group was arrested in June near Fort de l'Eau, centre of the artichoke-growing region. The men were armed with bludgeons, vine-stakes and branches of mimosa.[2] Police reprisals were severe. Dr. Bendjelloul[3] complained to the Délégations Financières. Nothing was being done for the native, who formed the majority of the population. As Dr. Tamzali retorted to a *colon* delegate: 'I represent several thousand natives, whereas you represent only sixty big landowners.'[4] In Algeria at the end of June 1936 over 10,000 men were on strike. There was fierce rivalry when elections to the new municipal assemblies were held. The candidature of a Communist in the vicinity of Algiers aroused considerable controversy, which allowed him, rightly or wrongly, to indict the Administration's interference, and the hostility, the 'zoological'[5] hatred, he declared, shown to him by certain reactionaries. The word shows the degree of oratorical vehemence, at least, which the controversy reached.

---

[1] Cf. an unpublished study by Launais.
[2] *Écho d'Alger*, 16 June 1936.
[3] *Écho d'Alger*, 18 June 1936 and 23 June 1936.
[4] *Écho d'Alger*, 21 June 1936.
[5] *Lutte sociale*, 25 July 1936.

The same is true of Tunisia,[1] where the leading *colon* Vénèque attacked the Resident General himself, A. Guillon, who was guilty of allowing professional legal aid to the underprivileged and of applying social laws. The strike at Metlawi ended tragically, with sixteen dead and thirty-two wounded. Poverty brought thousands of unemployed into Tunis; their repression sometimes provoked street fighting, and a more or less spontaneous repetition of the deplorable Constantine incidents seemed likely. The Rassemblement Populaire, which celebrated its constitution on 14 June 1936 at Gambetta Park, worked to bring about reforms under cover of local socialist activities. Albert Bouzanquet, back from exile since September 1936, had resumed his place at the head of the C.G.T., where he formed a highly efficient team with Roberte Bigiaoui. The Unions demanded the establishment of collective contracts, the forty hour week, social relief, an unemployment fund, safety precautions and measures of hygiene, and extended powers for the conciliation board. 14 July gave the Left wing parties the opportunity for a fine gesture: 10,000 meals were provided for the destitute. Within a few weeks there occurred, in succession: a meeting of 1,500 commercial employees at the Labour Exchange; a carriers' strike; a meeting of those who used the Ariana train; a forty-minutes' strike in the Orosdiback establishment at Bizerta; and a general meeting of dockers.[2]

All these incidents within a single month illustrate the violent atmosphere in which protests and claims were made in Tunisia and in Algeria, and the same thing might be observed in Morocco.

Political Struggle

Needless to say, a nationalist strain mingled with the movement of social protest. The radical extremism of the French Left wing was eventually to be ousted by the claims of Maghribi patriots, for whom the restitution of their country was to supplant everything else.

Sa'id Hijji,[3] of Salé, edited *Al-Maghrib* from April 1937 onwards. The names of many future leaders appear in its pages. We read, in one, a number of protests against the Glawi's expulsion from Marrakesh of the poet Mukhtar al-Susi, an action ironically inconsistent with Berber policy, since this man was a whole-hearted Shleuh, an authentic champion of that civilization which hypocrites sought to protect from the ravages of Arabism and Islam, but which proclaimed itself to be Islamic and Arabic. Popular feeling ran high. At Fez, among the Seffarin, a nationalist neglected to salute the general, and was struck on his tarbush by a swagger-stick. The swagger-stick was a military emblem, the

---

[1] Once more I am indebted for these facts about Tunisia to the unpublished recollections of Dr. Cohen-Hadria, and to *Tunis socialiste*.
[2] Facts quoted from *Tunis socialiste*, June–July 1936.
[3] Facts quoted from Nos. 1, 2, 8 and 12 of this review.

tarbush a seditious one. The conflict of these symbols provoked serious controversies in the press. Meanwhile the nationalist movement made friendly advances to the Radical Congress, whose programme combined colonial liberalism with secularization.

The Left wing parties had not yet fallen out. The nationalist movement did not attack French sovereignty outright, it cultivated a progressive alibi and, moreover, played on a whole gamut of words. Arabic lends itself wonderfully to the use of synonyms which are fiery and yet polite,[1] to platonic incitement and incendiary generalization. Religion, literature and poetry provided rich substitutes for patriotism. At Marrakesh an association was founded to celebrate the Prophet's birthday; at Fez, the 'Scouts of 'Abd al-Mu'min.' Mingled with these we find more overt displays of opposition. To the great surprise of administrators, notabilities and heads of households, the adolescents of the city showed themselves capable, on such occasions, of braving Corsican policemen and Berber *mukhaznis*. On 16 May 1937, they celebrated the anniversary of the famous *dahir*. Instinctively applying the principles of bourgeois leadership, they cultivated the connection between these new themes of propaganda and the life of the city corporations. The working class of Fez was assiduously wooed. And while political protest was based on social and economic grievances, religious themes were not neglected: a classic opportunity was provided by the meeting at the Mosque for Friday's sermon.

The activity of political parties, to which I have already referred, displayed the same recrudescence, at this time, as in the parent state. For instance, here are the results of the elections in the major Algerian towns, relative to those of 1932:[2] the number of votes cast for the Communist party, in one sector of Algiers, rose from 177 to 3,294, in another sector from nought to 255, and in a third from nought to 200. At Oran, it rose from 720 to 3,200, from 140 to 3,330, from 212 to 1,850, and so on ... A journal had for many years been published in Algiers which had first been called *Demain*, Tomorrow, and since 1921, *La Lutte sociale*, The Social Struggle. A comparison between the various figures for this paper is extremely revealing. In 1920 it had been concerned almost exclusively with the affairs of Metropolitan France; it had touched on the native problem and the agrarian problem, but in a superficial and sketchy way. On the contrary *La Lutte Sociale*, from 1936 onwards, assumed an increasingly Muslim and Algerian tone. Its sales soared suddenly. The number of copies sold rose, in Oran in 1936, from 250 to 1,000; at Philippeville, from sixty to 150; in Algiers, from 1,300 to 2,000. And the issue of January 1936 differs widely from those of January

---

[1] Cf. J. Menaut, 'Les Élections aux Délégations financières,' *Afrique française*, 1925, pp. 78 ff.

[2] *Lutte sociale*, 15 Feb. 1926.

1920, in which a few wounded idealists expressed their thoughts, keeping their eyes turned on Metropolitan France and the U.S.S.R. Now is discussed on the front page, the fellah's destitution. In one issue we find portraits of Thaelmann and Bin 'Ali Bukhurt side by side. The latter came from Mazuna, a small city that had seen better days and was famous for its religious school. He had worked as secretary for a mixed commune; then his career was interrupted by political imprisonment. He was to play some slight part in the Muslim Congress in June. Another reporter signs himself al-Munadi, 'he who calls'. He pleads for a 'united Algerian Front', and offers friendship to the most irreconcilable politicians. The journal devotes a whole page to the struggle of Arab Brotherhoods in the Middle East. In the name of fraternity within the national struggle, it disregards the vast differences dividing Arabism from Communism. From June 1936 onwards, the title itself was printed in Arabic and in French. The two headlines were interlaced; 'The Social Struggle' is translated as *Al-Kifah al-ijtima'i*. The agreement is more than a matter of language.

In Tunisia we find the same tentative alliance. In 1936 and 1937, as we have seen, the regional committees of the Rassemblement Populaire tried to unite the S.F.I.O. and the Neo-Destour. The famous speech of Viénot, on 1 March 1937, over the Tunis radio, called forth sympathetic reactions from Dr. Materi and from Bourguiba. The latter, interviewed in Paris, was encouraging. A sort of united front seemed about to materialize, which might no doubt have led to positive constructiveness,[1] had not timidity unfortunately prevailed, in circumstances on which I cannot dwell here.

A Popular Front organization was also constituted in Morocco, on the initiative of the S.F.I.O. party. It stressed that 'the reasons for the profound discontent of the natives of Morocco spring from the economic exploitation of the masses for the benefit of financial oligarchies.' We see thus to what extent this protest movement, French in its essence and in its associations, concerned itself with purely native problems. This was a hopeful sign. Such syntheses, it is true, were not achieved without a number of ulterior motives. Moreover they affected not only the Left wing but sometimes, and in a more suspect fashion, the extreme Right Croix de Feu, the coalition movement, and the Parti Populaire Français. Underneath a whole network of occasional alliances and collusions we can discern the fundamental convergences which those rival brethren, nationalism and socialism, are sometimes willing to admit.

Ideological disputes form the substance of day-to-day reports, or draw substance from these. We may take at random one February day

---

[1] This emerges clearly from the texts collected by Bourguiba, *La Tunisie et la France*, pp. 77 ff. Cf. *Shihab*, May 1936, on the election of A. Guillon, which seemed to augur well.

in 1936, in Algeria. This is the picture drawn of it in the Opposition press.

At Constantine, a prize-giving ceremony at the Bin Badis school gives rise to a digression on Muslim religious reformism. In Algiers, the official distribution of figs to the needy, and a simultaneous police raid, suggest administrative ambivalence. At Hussein-Dey, the unemployed complain of a lack of support; and a bitter dispute arises between fruit exporters and the firms which have failed to load their boats. At Ténès, a scandal is revealed: where does the commune's money go? At Orléans-ville, people are urged to protest against the holding of a trial considered iniquitous and shameful: that of the rioters of Constantine. At Burj Bu Arrerij, a fellah commits suicide as a result of some extremely complicated adventures: his daughter-in-law was bitten, in his own home, by his dog, which presumably had rabies; so many administrative complications ensued that the wretched man preferred to kill himself, showing his over-scrupulous nature and a very serious change in collective psychology. At Ghardaia, we read of protests against the White Fathers' school; the Eucharistic Congress all over again! A *Sha'ush* (policeman) arrested a passer-by on a charge of drunkenness; apparently the latter was not drunk and had even refused to offer the virtuous official a drink. At Tlemsen, there are scandals in the municipal administration. At Constantine, police brutality and strikes in the local big store, the Globe. And so forth.[1]

Whatever the significance of these topical events, they bring out the intense liveliness of existence in the Maghrib. In this anecdotal context both sides mingle and conflict. Perhaps neither realized that the important fact was less the authenticity of these countless trivial details than the general movement they revealed. The combination of local protest with Left wing ideas reveals, in 1936–7, something hitherto hushed up. Humble people, living hidden in the crannies of this ancient land, unreconciled, protesting, in opposition to all the régimes that have succeeded one another there–the Colonial régime and those that preceded it, and perhaps those that may follow it some day–had shown themselves at last; and it is to the honour of the Popular Front that, for one brief moment, it gave utterance to their feelings.

When Marcel Peyrouton reached Rabat from Tunis, the opposition parties abstained from attending the ceremonies. In the spring of 1936 there was even an open clash. At the entry to Fort Lyautey, Socialist demonstrators came to blows with members of the P.S.F.[2] on the railway line. They hurled stones at one another, watched placidly by Moroccans, who observed that Europeans were no good at that particular game. This useful lesson was not forgotten. The Committee of Moroccan

---

[1] All these details are taken from one number of *La Lutte Sociale*, 15 Feb. 1936.   [2] Parti Social Français.

Action, from its office in the Rue Rahbat al-Kis at Fez, undertook a recruiting campaign. A vow of loyalty had to be taken. This was the pretext for which the authorities had been waiting to denounce the movement (10 April 1937). The unrest, however, did not die down. By an ironic coincidence, it was General Noguès, the Resident sent by the Popular Front, who had to repress it. At Meknes, in September 1937, a quarrel broke out over Bu Fekran.[1] This was a *wadi*, or river, part of which was used downstream by *colons*. The press protested violently that only a quarter of the supply was left for the Mosques and the Moorish baths: this was an infringement of the city's rights. For this was a recurrent theme; the city, insurgent against the authorities and threatened by obsolescence, constantly asserted its rights. The ensuing demonstration caused several deaths, and provoked even more violent uprisings at Fez, to which I have already referred. The army occupied the madina, and floggings were administered by the Boulmane *goum* (platoon of Moroccan soldiers under French command), at the very portal of the Qarawiyin. Reprisals involved the imprisonment of hundreds, the exile of many others; 'Allal al-Fasi was banished to Gabon, and thus acquired the title of *za'im* (leader). But, as we have seen, the unrest was not confined to the cities. It spread to several points of the Berber world—a new and significant phenomenon. Its influence extended even further: the Neo-Destour joined hands with the Moroccan Hizb. The ferment which resulted accounted in part, no doubt, for the unfortunate crescendo which culminated in the bloody incidents of 8 and 9 April at Tunis.

In Algeria, the new factor in the situation was the intermingling of French and Muslim movements. The opposition considered the belated, and reticent, trial of the Constantine rioters as a provocation. In fact, the conclusions of the trial were never made known. Several parties, more or less allies or rivals, united to commemorate the 'fortieth day' elapsed since the death of the Amir Khalid. A meeting organized by Shaikh Bin Badis for the 'Id al-Kabir was attended by three thousand demonstrators; another, run by the *Islahiya* of Oran, was banned. Even the Mozabites, forgathering in the Algerian mosque of Sidi Bin Nur in the Rue de Tanger, voiced their ancient demands, based on the pact of 1853 which had assured them certain privileges.

Algeria's Day[2]

I come now to the most important event: the meeting held in the hall of the Majestic Hotel at Bab el Oued on 7 June 1936. That week the Muslims of Algiers had celebrated the Prophet's birthday; groups of

[1] Cf. *Maghrib*, July 1937.
[2] Title borrowed from that of an article in *Shihab*, July 1936. It eloquently describes the enthusiasm of the crowds who participated.

them could be seen in the Rue de la Marine, drinking cups of mint tea in their favourite little cafés. At nightfall, Muslim families lit the traditional many-coloured candles–white, green and red–in the sanctuaries. Strains of the old Andalusian music which had been heard before the Europeans came, and was cherished by many, drifted everywhere throughout the Arab town. Crowds swarmed into the mosques, Sidi Abd al-Rahman or Sidi Mansur, or the mausoleum of Algiers' patron, Wali Dada.[1] On 5 June Léon Blum had formed his Government. His Minister of State was Maurice Viollette, well known in Algeria. Such was the atmosphere, local and general, at the time of the Congress.

Over 5,000 people attended the gathering.[2] As *al-Shihâb* put it, they poured in, 'leaving their tasks to follow their hopes.' Applause greeted the entry of leaders as different, as opposite as Dr. Bendjelloul, who owed his popularity to the events at Constantine in 1934, and the reformist shaikhs Bin Badis and al-'Uqbi. The meeting was opened by Dr. Tamzali, followed by Dr. Bendjelloul, with declarations of loyalty to France. The whole day recalls the States General of 1789. This Third Estate did not repudiate its connection with the parent state, but asserted its grievances. When we read these manifestoes today, we see that they refer chiefly to fundamental liberties. The atmosphere was consistently friendly to France, so much so that one press report about a speech in Arabic by M. Bushama naïvely comments: 'The translation was loudly acclaimed.' The Congress none the less appreciated, with a touch of awe-struck respect, the learned and flowery Arabic utterances of Shaikhs Bin Badis and Ibrahimi. Bin Badis attempted somewhat strangely to associate a movement that was essentially religious and Eastward-looking with the forces that he felt predominating at that time in France. 'When French liberty was sleeping,' he said, 'we kept silence. Liberty has revived in France, and we intend to follow it.' He was greeted with enthusiasm. A militant Communist, recently released, also won great applause. In short, a strange medley of tendencies found expression, between which there was no logical link save perhaps dissatisfaction with the existing state of things and the hope of a better future.

Under these conditions, what common ground could be found? The first motion demanded French citizenship without loss of personal status. Then followed a message of gratitude to the Socialist Congress; a plea for clemency to the Constantine rioters; a message of confidence in Maurice Viollette. The whole thing concluded, as was customary, with a banquet for a hundred guests at the Cercle du Progrès. When a few days later a popular demonstration was held in Algiers, the procession that marched from the Agha to the Place du Gouvernement

[1] *Écho d'Alger*, 3 June 1936.
[2] I refer to the reports provided by the *Écho d'Alger*, 8 June 1936, *La Lutte Sociale*, 7 June 1936, and *Shihab*; their attitudes are of course very different.

included a large number of veiled women, and displayed the unity, or at least the co-operation, of all sections of the working class, European and Muslim. A demonstrator hung a red sash round the equestrian statue of the Duc d'Orléans on the Place du Gouvernement—which would surely have delighted Victor Hugo!

Can one draw any definite conclusions from the deliberations of this latter-day *Tiers-État*? Of course one would have to look deeper, peer behind the scenes of the Congress and try to distinguish not only the pattern of tendencies but their level. Who knows whether more extreme attitudes might not already be discernible? The men who made the speeches and won the applause were all at least in their forties. I think, somewhere in the background, young men were listening in silence, whispering, questioning themselves, who were later to come into the public eye. The reactions of the Arabic press to the Congress were diverse. *La Voix Indigène*[1] stressed only the assertion of loyalty: it wrote that 'policy of assimilation has triumphed all along the line,' but mocked at certain orators such as Bendjelloul. It dealt severely with certain 'brazen sensualists, allied with so-called ascetics', the Western tendencies of some being as anathema as the Eastern tendencies of the others. 'Freemasons, atheists, people who deny the existence of God, congratulate the *"ulama"*, and the latter rave about the eloquence of the former.' In the Maghrib of that period, the use of the French language in oratory was still the privilege of an élite. Or again: 'Individuals who can scarcely earn a living, who have neglected the welfare of their families, take arbitrary responsibility for the interests of the native masses.' The remark was made by an opponent. But was he satisfied with the official state of things either? The murder of the mufti Mahmud Bindali, otherwise Kahhul, on 3 August 1936, under the arcades of the Rue de la Lyre, gave the police the opportunity to incriminate Shaikh Taiyib al-'Uqbi. Intrigues dragged on, but added to the tenseness of the atmosphere.

Even more important than the June demonstration was one which took place in the Municipal Stadium at Algiers on 2 August,[2] welcoming back the delegates that the Congress had sent to Paris. First a report of the mission was made by Dr. Bendjelloul, who was already being accused of over-moderation.[3] Missali, a militant decorated with the North

---

[1] 11 June 1936 and 16 July 1936.

[2] *Shihab*, Aug–Sept. 1936: 'Three days in a single month' referring to three important events: (1) the return of the Delegation sent to Paris; (2) the meeting at the Municipal Stadium, where Bin Badis improvised a *maqama*; (3) the arrest of al-'Uqbi, suspected of the murder of Kahhul. The number also mentions several outrages, inclusing attempted murder, against the '*Ulama*' at Constantine, Laghwat and Khenshela. The number of October 1936, p. 270, contains an article by Bashir Ibrahimi on the arrest of al-'Uqbi.

[3] Attacked in a violent article in *Shihab*: 'The Doctor's face unveiled'. According to *Shihab*, he lacked the qualities of a true *za'im*.

African star, dissociated himself from all the rest.[1] He urged the quest for independence. The moral demands of the *'Ulama'*, the electoral assimilationism of Ferhat Abbas, the concept of a 'nation in process of formation'[2] put forward by the Communists, were by no means inconsistent with this point of view, but they expressed it on other levels, at different rhythms, guided by a different set of symbols. The circumstances and the hidden side of all these events belong less to social history than to political history and to controversy between parties.

Relapse

Early in March 1937 Pierre Viénot, speaking over the Tunisian radio, had committed an outrage. He had dared to assert that the interests of individual Frenchmen were not always identical with those of France. This shockingly revolutionary remark insulted a symbol and a tradition. The conservative press reacted appropriately. And shortly afterwards the Government found itself pitted in a trial of strength against big business, on a specific issue.

Two investigators had been commissioned to pronounce on the revision of the clauses granted to the big licence-holders of public utilities. These clauses, which may have been justified in time of stress, now imposed an unnecessary burden on the Tunisian economy. The Resident General, Armand Guillon, referred to this in his speech to the Grand Conseil in November 1937.[3] And the representative of the Tunisians at this council, Sadiq Tlatli, stated in his reply that 'the Tunisian people note with deep satisfaction the promise of reform made by a qualified minister.' Guillon was promptly opposed by the vice-president of the Assembly, Antoine Gaudiani, who had just been elected almost unanimously. A veteran of Tunisian assemblies, having been re-elected regularly since 1927, he was a member of most important boards and businesses. As Director of *La Dépêche tunisienne* he had for some time, until the summer of 1937, had to deal tactfully with the representative of the Republic. But Viénot's sacrilege made him see red. His brief speech was a slap in the face for the Resident-General. 'Gentlemen, friends and constituents: I interpret your gesture as a wish to strengthen French positions in Tunisia, and not to let our legally allotted functions fall into obeyance.' These petty agro-colonial parliaments tended in fact to arrogate to themselves an increasing number of rights, claiming authority to debate the budget and, more or less, to legislate on the

---

[1] 'Pourquoi nous sommes contre le projet Viollette' (Why we are against the Viollette plan), *Al-Umma*, Jan. 1938.

[2] The phrase is Maurice Thorez's (1939).

[3] See the *Actes du Grand Conseil*, report of this meeting. In a report on the financial year 1936 (28 May 1937) the Crédit foncier d'Algérie et de Tunisie deplores the way in which events (i.e. social laws) are delaying recovery.

country's general interests. 'We realize with deep regret that our charter is no longer respected. Heavy burdens now weigh on the country's economy.' In fact Armand Guillon had revoked the licence of the Port of Gafsa on his own initiative. 'Such procedure, lacking due legal sanction, is all the more surprising since it occurs at a time when the field of public liberties is being extended';[1] an interpretation, *sui generis*, of the Popular Front. 'In any case we firmly intend to safeguard our independence.' The word *independence* was being widely used elsewhere, with a somewhat different meaning. Much discussion ensued; the task of the Committee of Arbitration already set up by Beylical decree on 21 September 1937 was to be an arduous one. The licence-holding firms protested. On 9 November they presented the Government with a memorandum from the Union Coloniale Française, later the Central Committee for Overseas France. The report of the Commission of Enquiry was mislaid three times in the files of the Civil Service. The Resident-General who had ordered the investigation, the minister who had dared to speak and to prescribe, were no longer there. The question of revision was never raised again until the end of the Protectorate: which was profitable for a few, disastrous for France, and instructive for the historian.

What Gaudiani did here was repeated by other members of the ruling class in Algeria and Morocco to paralyse the reforms of the Popular Front.

As we have seen, in Algeria Morinaud and his friends in the Senate had already, in 1935[2] rejected Viollette's proposals and passed Régnier's decree. The dilatory adjournment of the Blum-Viollette plan made the position even worse. For French citizenship without loss of personal status had become symbolic of all Algerian hopes. Confirming the views already described about the role then played by rural villages, French mayors replied to this surge of local life by a campaign of resignation. Their Congress, which met at Algiers on 8 February 1938, sealed the failure of the project. French policy had recoiled before this timid structural reform; it now had no alternative but to pursue, with ever more serious oscillations, the disastrous cycle of tactical concessions followed by repression.

In Morocco, where somewhat different conditions prevailed, the countryside remained largely untouched by political activity and maintained its allegiance to the Sultan. General Noguès, after the clashes at the end of 1937, combining his own personal skill with the old-established prestige of the Bureau Arabe, achieved superficial calm at

---

[1] Report of the Grand Conseil Tunisien, session of Nov.–Dec. 1937, pp. 234 ff.
[2] Cf. P.-E. Viard, 'Jeux sociaux et politiques en Algérie', *Questions nord-africaines*, 15 April 1938, and the pamphlet, which makes terrible reading today, published by the Federation of Algerian Mayors, *Les droits électoraux des indigènes algériens*, Algiers, 1938.

the cost of a few slight improvements. The problem was urgent nonetheless, and took concrete form with the exile of the principal leader. Here again an opportunity had been missed.

The end of the Popular Front closed an era of opportunism, risks and hopes. These two tense years ended in yet another postponement. The masses, their newly awakened consciousness further stimulated by inspiration from France, met with opposition from conservative forces: not so much from officials who might be talented or well-intentioned men, but from the supporters of an economic system: the *colon*, a colourful and loud-mouthed figure, often crippled with debts; the banker, remote, discreet, subtle, but in practice all-powerful; the concessionary, a man involved in private interests and public works . . .

Three protagonists. But the fourth? the native–where was he, or rather–for he was complacently exhibited from time to time–what part did he play in pulling the strings? And did the French authorities, who were responsible for arbitration, really practise it? On this point, let us avoid extreme assertions. Some rulers displayed undeniable clear-sightedness and generosity, skilfully playing off the three representatives of colonialism–the *colon*, the banker and the concessionary–against one another; and even backing against all three that awakening giant, the man of the Maghrib. Some were adept at instancing the requirements of native policy in order to control exorbitant appetites. They remind one of those street photographers of the time, who would set up a huge camera on a tripod and cover it with a black cloth, under which they manipulated mysterious objects. Several statesmen succeeded in taking advantage of the darkness, although not always for the benefit of the majority . . .

But in the last resort, whether through bad luck or weakness, through submission to pressure groups or involvement in collective impotence, the very men who saw how things stood did not act. They failed to build the inevitable future, while there was still time to do so.

CHAPTER XII

Respite

After severe conflicts, calm was restored. At what cost? That we know only too well.[1] The potential drama, however, did not clearly emerge from the apparent security of the whole. And this was not only the automatic result of repression. At that time, Franco-Maghrib relations seemed bound by a kind of spell. There was no racial hatred, nor even resentment. Maghribi intellectuals rejected any sort of xenophobia.[2] They knew that their strength lay in adaptation to what they were combating. Their denial was merely the counterpart of their hopes. Few questioned, or even discerned within themselves, the influence of long habit, of adherence to a certain culture, of the force of daily experience.[3]

Nationalism, in many cases, was identified with the trend towards modernism, in which, despite the interest taken in the Middle East, French influence still prevailed. In spite of anger and repression, and – already – of deaths unavenged, both parties sought to respect the terms of their pact. Violence, on either side, if sometimes intense, remained a political weapon. Moreover, in 1938, it had brought no solution. Everybody realized this. The champions still stood in the lists. By contrast with what was to come later, the situation at this time suggests a contest, not precluding friendly relations. Between the adversaries in a lawsuit which had been heard, if not judged, there existed strange and maybe immoral relations. Such ambiguities are characteristic of the

[1] This was the period described by Andrée Viollis in *Notre Tunisie*, an account of her visit to that country. She welcomes the fraternization of Shanik and Gaudiani (Feb. 1939), and reports interesting interviews with Dr. Materi (pp. 64 ff.) and with Bourguiba in prison (pp. 82 ff.).

[2] The political historian will, of course, have to distinguish shades of opinion, and to study, for instance, the role of Missali Hajj's Parti Populaire Algérien. Cf. for instance the journal *Al-Umma*, Mar. 1939.

[3] Did this psychological reassessment, often painful, which underlay many of the attitudes taken between 1945 and 1954, take place only as a result of the war? We shall not be able to tell until certain individual biographies have been written.

period and the place. But the fact is, that in spite of the floggings at Fez, the cruelties of Bordj le Boeuf, shootings at Tunis and banishment to Gabon, both sides stopped short within certain limits. *Hurma*, to use a Moroccan expression–self-respect and respect for the other person– remained largely intact.[1] Comparison with subsequent developments brings out these peculiar characteristics.

North Africa, in any case, was recovering an apparent euphoria. Relations between Muslim sovereigns and Residents-General were peaceful. In Algeria a great prefect, G. Le Beau, sought to maintain a balance between Muslims and Europeans, as skilfully and as inconclusively as he might have done between Left and Right wings in a French department. In Tunisia Armand Guillon retained the respect of the Neo-Destour, even while he repressed it. He was succeeded by Eirik Labonne, a prophetic economist who was also to make a good impression as Regent. In Morocco General Noguès succeeded in establishing friendly relations with Fez and with the 'Alawi ruler. When he had to go into exile in 1943, eye-witnesses saw Mohammed V go with him to his car and close its door with tears in his eyes: it was the end of an epoch.

Administrative equity, diplomatic tact and the Affaires Indigènes tradition seemed thus to unite, under these proconsuls, to bring to a peaceful close a period whose difficulties were eclipsed, in the eyes of all, by the dangers that seemed imminent. Meanwhile routine improvements went on; they were largely technical, and in any case solved nothing. True, a critical observer would not have been taken in by the almost total calm then prevailing in North Africa. He would realize that there were underlying future perils. Revolutionary and nationalistic attitudes, which had declared themselves in 1936, were only dormant. The cards were down. Basically, things were to go from bad to worse, even if they seemed to have calmed down on the surface. The issue had been clear in 1934–5, and France had refused to discuss it. When Daladier became head of the Government on 10 April 1938, the Popular Front era was closed for good and all. Many Maghribi hopes were involved with that great experiment of France and of mankind. Since then, things had come to a head.

Nevertheless the declaration of war in September 1939 brought touching evidence of what can only be called loyalty. This loyalty was to persist throughout France's terrible ordeal. There is nothing surprising about this, the Maghribi being a man with whom, to quote the British adage, 'you can safely go tiger-hunting'; he will not desert you when you are in the wild beast's clutches. France learned this by experience, and she should never have forgotten it.

[1] Witness, for instance, the courteous if not friendly relations that persisted between Armand Guillon and Bourguiba. It is said that Guillon saved Bourguiba from execution by over-zealous underlings . . .

'For the Native Peasant and Artisan'[1]

In Morocco the spring of 1939 was mild and promising. Fez inaugurated its fair. This differed somewhat from its predecessors, though these had paved the way for it. Only in 1938, indeed, had the fair acquired the characteristics which made it symptomatic of a new orientation. It was specifically devoted to the achievements of the Moroccan artisan. The President of the French Chamber of Commerce alluded to this in his speech, more emphatically than usual. These utterances, and this endeavour, obviously had Government encouragement behind them: and entrepreneurs had to concede support, although their direct interests were basically opposed to those of the artisan. Amongst these business men we find a few Muslims: al-Marnisi, head of the Moroccan Chamber of Commerce, the Sabti brothers, big exporters of cotton goods. Shanik and Bin 'Ammar had long been familiar figures in Tunis. Algiers had men like the Zuays, Tamzalis, Tiyyars. The Maghribi bourgeoisie seemed belatedly but increasingly to be identifying themselves with modern economic methods. They had established a stable relationship with French industrialists, banks and public authorities, which was profitable to them both as rich men and as hostages. Some of them meanwhile kept up an ambiguous friendship with nationalism. At Fez itself, where they were responsible for financing the opposition, one of them, Ahmad Mikwar, had the vital role of treasurer to the nationalist movement.

Yet tendencies resulting from the Popular Front inclined the Administration to favour the middle classes. This policy comprised a great deal of propaganda and a certain measure of democracy. Of course the administration continued to assist the big *colons*, who were closely akin to the big notables, the big marabouts and the big caïds, but it was not averse to helping the victims of colonial history: the artisan, partly ruined by the import of manufactured articles, the peasant, partly dispossessed, both of them deserving interest through their economic and social distress. Such a policy did not lack generosity; it could at all events be justified. The authorities did not dare carry it through. But almost from the start, it displayed touching results. It had a certain undoubted sincerity, for the sake of which its artfulness can be forgiven. It contrasted so favourably with traditional policy that it aroused the interest of such visitors as Pierre Viénot.

The 1939 fair, even more than its predecessor, marked a divorce from the old concept of native arts and crafts.[2] These had been a matter of

[1] To echo the title of an anonymous brochure (by Augustin Berque) published by the Minerva Press of Algiers, 1939.

[2] Cf. my article, 'Deux ans d'action artisanale à Fès', *Questions nord-africaines*, 25 June 1939. A similar reaction against the attitude to 'native art' is shown by Gabriel Audisio, *L'Art vivant*, special issue, 1938, p. 12.

concern for a long time: Prosper Ricard had tactfully supervised the revival of old techniques, while archaeologists, led by Henri Terrasse, and even municipal town-planners had fought resolutely for the respect of traditional styles. But these concepts, rightly based on aesthetic grounds, were powerless against the economic crisis. In spite of the profits drawn from the tourist trade, which concentrated on picturesque elements and Turkish influences, the craftsman in Morocco, Algeria and Tunis too frequently ended up as a prince's parasite. At best, a corner might be found for him in some administrative palace, such as the Batha palace, which housed a small group of coppersmiths and book-binders, and of miniaturists, whose tradition was gradually becoming obliterated. The best of these, the master craftsman, or *mu'allim* al-Hlu, a familiar figure in his stall in the Udayas, had just died. On the other hand, within the last year or so new ideas had sprung up in Fez. The artisan must be given his rightful place in the economic circuit of the country. Traditionally, a great Muslim city manufactures objects which it sells to Bedouin customers. Now the import trade (which had actually started long before the Protectorate) had cut off the city from its true function. Hence the deep distress of a population of artisans reckoned at over 50,000 in Fez alone.

Measures were therefore taken by politicians sharp enough to see the dangers that would result from the disappearance of this craftsman class and the consequent economic decay of the town. Three Credit Banks were established, and the old trades were put in touch with the standardizing bodies being set up all over Europe, through the intermediary of an Artisans' Bank. It was hoped to distribute their products in France, England and Italy, and even further afield.

A visitor to the fair would have noticed that some of the more important stands revealed a remarkable effort to apply new methods and ideas. The weavers, *derraza*, were the most severely threatened of all, through the import of cloth and cotton goods, They had not yet acquired the technique that had made medieval Flemish craftsmen famous. What they made would be bought only by the Bedouin in search of a *jellaba*: a coarse cloth, often beautiful in colour and in texture, but which could not attract a customer used to other fashions. And yet they now did their best to mix artificial silk with wool, to make a sort of tweed, to vary their colours according to the shades now fashionable with the younger generation, and to give their material enough consistency to hold a pleat. Their efforts were displayed in bundles of samples, and set out in a huge rosette. Lovers of the picturesque might be disappointed: Morocco—another sign of modern times—was abandoning the bright colours of the past in favour of the muted shades of industrial civilization. The silk-makers, *hrairiya*, were in even worse case. Their wares had long ago been supplanted, in furnishing materials for instance, by imported silks from Lyons. Nowadays they sold nothing but *seb-*

baniya, those richly-hued scarves still worn by peasant women from the mountains. As for the tanners, they had that very year risked a minor revolution, because one of them had experimented with eucalyptus bark from Mamora instead of the traditional tannins, *takaut* and *fernan*. Certain jurists from Qarawiyin had condemned these new methods as illicit. Like the weavers, however, the tanners had made an effort. They had refined their technique and revived ancient processes, such as the tanning of fine leathers with pigeon guano. They proudly exhibited dyed leathers, shagreen as fine as any from the industrial workshops of Mogador, and sturdy sheepskin. Even the makers of babouches, who, faced with competition from European shoes on the one hand and sandals on the other, could only hope for export to the African market, made resolute efforts towards the future. Their stand attracted considerable notice, for although threatened with unemployment they still retained their urban prestige. They had founded a small co-operative at Casablanca. The coppersmiths displayed various articles of nickel-silver and even, triumphantly, a pewter teapot moulded on the spot, thus betokening their earnest, if naïve, desire to vie with Manchester. Excitement, endeavour and hope were widespread; and as the guilds included many a poet-artisan, this whole-hearted enthusiasm found utterance in several volumes of *qasidas*.[1]

At about the same time[2] the Governor-General was travelling in Western Algeria, in the neighbourhood of Marnia. Here he visited experimental colonies for re-housing the peasantry, and was shown methods of popularizing and improving agricultural processes. Next he travelled through Nemours and Nedroma, still concerned with the well-being of peasant and artisan. Finally he reached Tlemsen, which closely resembled Fez and was threatened by the same decay. At a banquet for 150 guests that evening, one voice was raised in opposition. Maître 'Ali Talib shocked the assembled company by demanding the application of Viollette's project, which in 1939 still inspired local protest movements. Things ended peacefully, for Le Beau enjoyed people's confidence. And the fear of war, which was felt to be imminent, induced both sides to try and guarantee some sort of future.

Already at the Universal Exhibition in Paris, in 1937, the Algerian section had been largely devoted to craftmanship.[3] In 1939 an Exhibition

[1] Brochures, *I'lan al-sina'a al-fasiya bi-nahdatiha al-samiya*, 'The industry of Fez expresses its proud gratitude', and *Taraqqi al-sana'i al-fasiya*, 'Progress of Fez's industries'. These contain the work of several craftsman-poets who, like Hans Sachs, practise a popular, or even a learned, art while handling their knives or hammers. The relations between poetry, music, mysticism and the guilds on one hand, Qarawayin on the other, are traditionally extremely rich. The same is true of Tunis, Damascus and Cairo.

[2] *Afrique du Nord illustrée*, 20 June 1939.

[3] Official brochure published for the occasion, including an interesting study of Algerian carpet-making.

of Native Art was held in the Consular Palace at Algiers.[1] 1,738 articles were displayed; and presentation was made of a diploma, magnificently illustrated by the Barbaresque miniaturist Rasim, whose nostalgic and slightly precious art celebrated the glory of the dead and the consoling power of gardens in delicate lines and shimmering colours. More prosaically, the Native Providential Society of Tlemsen had turned to the mechanical manufacture of fabrics, thus competing with the import trade. The Administration's deliberate policy was one of resistance to the latter's offensive; since 1936 it had tried out some hundred experiments. It had set up, in combination with *colon* friendly societies, a Mutual Aid Society for Muslims, founded on a revival of the old S.I.P. (*Société Indigène de Prévoyance*). These co-operated henceforward with the activities of the Wheat Office. Between 1935 and 1937 their membership rose from 500,000 to 600,000. A Common Fund was set up at the summit, providing the 'driving-force.' These bodies, besides their traditional functions as providing credit and relief, concerned themselves with strengthening the position of the fellah and with organizing peasant life[2] according to a programme anticipated by Charles Lévy, financial delegate from Sétif;[3] it included the rehousing schemes at Marnia, La Sefia and Umm al-Buaghi, the extension of collective equipment centres, the institution of co-operative fig-drying plants in Kabylia, etc. Such modest organizations gave scope for individual initiative, and rendered real service so long as they were not vitiated by some human failing on the part of the local Administration. An effort to organize loans to the natives followed–at a distance, and very timidly–the example of *colon* lending societies. Possibilities of medium term borrowing thus became available, with the advantages and disadvantages suggested above.

Besides the training in craftsmanship carried on in the cities under the perceptive guidance of Prosper Ricard and Georges Marçais, there were interesting attempts at popular education. As North Africa was at that time being visited by an expert from the I.L.O., R. Marjolin, an expert on co-operatives, each Government felt bound to show a

[1] *Afrique du Nord illustrée*, 20 Nov. 1938.

[2] (Aug. Berque) *Pour le paysan et l'artisan indigènes*: cf. also the same writer's *Fellah algérien*, 1944; P. Berthault, *L'Évolution et l'Organisation de la paysannerie indigène en Algérie*, 1938–the *nec plus ultra* of a remarkable technique joined to big business paternalism.

[3] The name and policy of *paysanat* (spelt, in Algeria, *paysannat*) had been long familiar in official documents. Cf. for instance Morand's speech about Ch. Lévy's project, *Délégations Financières*, 1927, pp. 718 ff. But the work was only belatedly put in hand. This problem of organizing peasant life, of which Aug. Berque wrote in 1936 that 'we are barely beginning to glimpse it,' demanded a return to the country's essentially rural realities. Its promoters, in the process, opposed the 'orientalizing' trend in French policy towards the native, and thus the strategies then championed by Robert Montagne. But this rivalry of viewpoints is due to the separation between economic and social issues on the one hand, political issues on the other. In both cases obvious obstacles prevented success.

certain number of experiments. Besides the textile S.I.P.A. (*Société Indigène de Prévoyance Algérienne*) at Tlemsen, there was the *tassargal*[1] fishermen's co-operative on the coast of Agadir; that of the wood-cutters of Boulmane in the Middle Atlas; the collective sheepfolds founded at al-Hajib by a Civil Controller with a reputation for progressive views; in Tunisia, the co-operative of the potters of Nabeul (Nabil), and so on. The Resident himself travelled to Sminja to celebrate the twenty-fifth anniversary of its farm. At Dar al-Monastiri, in the madina of Tunis, he inaugurated an exhibition of carpets, ceramics and fabrics.[2] A Trade Week was organized in the suqs of Tunis; for the shopkeeper was threatened, equally with the peasant and the artisan.

As we can see, the aesthetic side of this achievement was only secondary, indispensable though it was to ensure commercial value in the world market for certain Maghribi articles, such as carpets. And what could the *Paysanat* do against the dispossession of the best lands? It is doubtful whether men like Charles Saumagne and Augustin Berque, who devoted themselves to these efforts, had any great illusions as to their success. At least they had the merit of conceiving and formulating, although with the timidity belonging to the period and to their office, a middle-class policy. It must be emphasized that certain clear-sighted observers realized that the policy of the notables, caïds and marabouts was doomed. This did not mean any drastic revision of the French régime. The funds it devoted to these improvements bear no comparison with the large-scale protectionism which benefited the *colon* and, indirectly, the European functionary. Now this inequality betrays more than injustice; it shows a failure in understanding. Help to the masses appeared, paradoxically, as a benevolent accessory to the patriotic and profitable effort undertaken by the Colonial system. The theory of gradualism,[3] precluding psychological conflict and decisive action, confined these efforts within the narrow circle of charitable paternalism, while the Maghrib was entering a revolutionary situation. It is doubtful whether more could have been done at that time, within the existing framework. The Colonial authorities denied any general scope to this well-intentioned reformism. They allowed it to achieve minor successes, encouraging to morale rather than positively effective, but they deprived it of any power over essential matters. No doubt at the time the record of achievements was not without influence on the zeal of individuals and the morality of administrative action; but only from a point of view which subsequent events were to invalidate.

[1] A kind of fish which the Shleuhs eat dried, and which is found in markets as far inland as Mauretania.

[2] *Afrique du Nord illustrée*, 20 April 1939.

[3] Which, after 1944, still divided the partisans of the S.I.P. from supporters of more revolutionary methods.

A Backward Glance

Did the régime realize that, like the Third Republic, it was doomed? In any case, its statesmen seemed deliberately to cultivate a legend that was already backward-looking. This explains the solemn tone of many occasions dedicated to the heroes of the past; and there were quite a number of these during these few months.

In August 1938 the painter Rochegrosse died in his splendid villa in the Chemin Beaurepaire, on the heights of Algiers; his large but uninspired paintings of the Maghrib bear much the same relation to Delacroix as a city square does to Nature. In the same year there died the administrator Jean Rigal (1883–1938), who knew and loved the Aurès region and planted many olive groves there, but who contrasted as sharply with his illustrious predecessors in the Bureau Arabe as his second-rate colleagues and successors did with himself. Khalifa Jallul died the following year. He had succeeded his father Lakhdar as governor of Laghwat; between them they had ruled there since 1952. He had retained the air of a gunman, a nomad chief, involved with the shifting strategies of transhumance. In this he contrasted with his chief rival for Governmental favour, Buaziz Bin Gana, lord of opulent palm-groves.[1] A statue of Lyautey was set up at Casablanca; a museum devoted to him at 'Ain Sefra.[2] Homage was thus paid to a well-tested myth; but increasingly the living factor was neglected in favour of the dead.

Decidedly, this period was fond of catafalques. Another old hero, General Nieger, attended the inauguration of the Saharan Museum of Wargla: broad surfaces of whitewashed walls, broken by pinnacles pointing to the skies. The style bears the name of Carbillet, who long exercised in these parts a beneficent but outmoded despotism.[3] Another famous figure of the inter-war epoch who now vanished from the scene was Mgr. Lemaître, Archbishop of Carthage,[4] who, as we have seen, organized that notorious Eucharistic Congress of 1930 at Tunis, which stirred up the nation's consciousness.

This sketch of the events of 1939 cannot conclude without mention of the Congress of Religious Brotherhoods.[5] On the invitation of the *zawiyas* of the Oran district, many heads of orders came together. We can see their portraits on the front page of magazines: elderly men for the most part, sitting four-square in armchairs that are almost thrones, clad in long robes, with their hands laid flat on comfortably-spread thighs, with biblical beards and portly figures which slander might

---

[1] Unpublished memoir of an administrator.
[2] *Afrique du Nord illustrée*, 20 Nov. 1938 and 20 Jan. 1939.
[3] *Afrique du Nord illustrée*, 20 Nov. 1938.
[4] *Afrique du Nord illustrée*, 1 June, 1939.
[5] *Afrique du Nord illustrée*, 20 June 1939.

attribute to primitive accumulation. At all events, these men of God forgathered. They exchanged many edifying remarks for the benefit of the public. And also, no doubt, behind the scenes and amongst themselves, many angry threats against the '*Ulama*' movement. To prove their up-to-dateness, they gave interviews. A Marabout from Toga told a journalist: 'Any reasonable person must look after his own interests.' The period ends with this commonsense adage, which sounds strangely on these lips. The zeal of the old Brotherhoods had been based on religious enthusiasm, but today, 'let the fellah concern himself with ploughing, the tradesman with business, the learned man with teaching and with his own conscience'. The learned man, '*alim*, was a word which had acquired a special colour since 1931. 'Let the marabout concern himself with the spiritual instruction of his disciples; let the official concern himself with his duties; and let whoever needs anything for himself or for his co-religionists make due request for it from the Superior Administration, through the intermediary of local authorities; he will find it the most profitable course.'

Thus the leading representatives of North African mysticism, like the official clergy, now preached a wholly secular morality.[1] The religious banner which they had assumed two generations previously, and which they had tried to withhold from the growing reformist movement in 1925, now passed to their adversaries; true, it had become imbued with secular values, but the values of the revolution were closer to religious faith than were those of conservatism.

Modernism and Incoherence

This conservatism styled itself realistic. Disregarding the ideas which were a driving force in the world and which, in its view, were ruining the Colonial régime, it argued in favour of particularism, of concern with detail. 'In politics as in administration you cannot be too down-to-earth.' Attempts to help the peasantry and the craftsmen were aimed at suppressing the unrest which was stirring in the masses. Governmental technique had meanwhile improved. It had even attained, under three proconsuls of unequal merit, a degree of efficiency as advanced as was possible under the circumstances of colonialism and its own obsolescence. A French administrative tradition became belatedly established in North Africa, and it did not lack distinguished practitioners.

Slowly but significantly the country was being modernized. In spite of the ruinous and ever-increasing discrepancy between economic and social developments, measures were taken which display a certain legislative wisdom. After 1935, the status of collective lands and forests was

---

[1] Aug. Berque, 'Les capteurs du divin: marabouts et ulémas', *Revue de la Méditerranée*, 1951, pp. 26–7. This passage, repeated by the Nationalist press, caused a scandal in official circles.

subjected to important regulations.[1] Some of these even imply the protection of native patrimony. The sale of land was forbidden in certain Moroccan tribes which had been unduly deprived. In Algeria, a stubborn policy was pursued concerning the great dams. In June 1938 and in December of the same year some of the leading financial delegates visited the dams of Ghrib and of the Wadi Fudda, which were nearing completion.[2] Not soon enough, incidentally, since the old dams were being gradually swamped. Techniques had improved. But some people had begun to say that it might have been better to avoid deforestation. On one of these occasions we note the presence of the engineer Martin, the author of proposals to which I have already referred.

One characteristic sign of modernization: the establishment of an automatic telephone exchange at Algiers in June 1938.[3] The radio stations of Algiers, Tunis and Rabat increased their range. We must stress this expansion of broadcasting, which concerned both Government action and the revival of the Arabic language; it is a phenomenon of capital importance. In April 1939, at roughly the same time as the Crafts Fair at Fez, was held the Trade Fair of Algiers,[4] remarkable for its abundance of apparatus: electrical equipment, refrigeration, and particularly agricultural machines, some of which were manufactured locally, such as deep ploughs for vineyards; which indicates the predominant agricultural trend. Unfortunately imported articles predominated among all this wealth, proving the weakness of local industrial production. The country was to suffer great hardship from this, when it was cut off from the parent state.

It is not only with regard to industry that the system reveals its weaknesses; it never solved the questions that had faced it at the outset: that of the 'complementary' relationship, in agriculture, of the Maghrib to Metropolitan France; that of the trans-Saharan regions; that of the efficient participation of natives in the running of their country. And this weakness, or incoherence, divided the French colonialists among themselves: settlers and administrators, vine-growers of Algeria and the Midi, agriculturists and bankers. Witness the debates of the Délégations Financières during 1937.[5] Certain claims were tentatively made by a minority of native delegates, Dr. Bendjelloul for instance. But in the report of Dr. Bordère, head of the Algerian financial commission, we read the following strange passage: 'Bankers are full of professional

[1] In Tunisia notably, where this 'progress', which moreover was ambiguous, has duly been analysed by J. Poncet.
[2] *Afrique du Nord illustrée*, 20 June 1938, 1 Dec. 1938.
[3] *Afrique du Nord illustree*, 1 June 1938. Algiers followed Blida (1930), Oran, Bel-Abbès, Mascara.
[4] *Afrique du Nord illustrée*, 1 April 1939.
[5] *Colons*' complaints against the Bank are not infrequent. Cf. H. Giron, 'Les bastilles modernes', *Vie tunisienne*, 19 Dec. 1933.

prejudice. They only consider their own private interests. The interest of the banks is to confuse State finance as much as possible, recommending the most complicated operations, so as to keep for themselves the arbitration fees.' Was a Left wing polemicist speaking? No; it was M. Leroy-Beaulieu, quoted by Dr. Bordère: 'Algeria realized in 1937 that the burden of its debt absorbed a third of its resources, over 500 million francs for 1,600,000 francs received in budgetary payment; it is colossal, it is almost impossible.' Now the Commission ascribes these excesses to the speculative rate at which most of these loans were placed in Algeria. The North African countries had no other source of capital, either at that time or today. And what is elsewhere got by a levy on savings, had here to be imported in the form of borrowings—we should say nowadays in the form of external assistance; this involved an interest of 9.5 to 10.5 per cent, a dangerously heavy rate. And thereby the authors of this remarkable document, a masterly analysis of the budget over 160 pages in length, propose to lower the borrowing rate, failing which Algeria is heading for disaster: 'she will remain crushed under the burden of charges imposed on her by the banks.' True, nobody actually mentions the Bank of Algeria, or the Mirabeau group, or the Union Parisienne, or any of those who placed the loans. But the criticism is aimed at them.

In the answer to this speech made by the Algerian director of Finance, a highly competent inspector of finance, no reference whatsoever is made to this part of the report. In this matter as in so many others, the crux was evaded. The régime now held its own less by domination than by interception and omission.

What Passed Unnoticed

Much of what was published at the time strikes one by its lack of foresight. Tunis, on 7 May 1937, enacted laws condemning the *gourbis* (hovels), thus stressing a phenomenon which, twenty years later, the municipality of Bilhawan had not yet finished liquidating. Morocco went one better, someone wrote in September 1938 that the *bidonvilles*, the shanty-towns, were about to disappear.[1] But were they more than symptomatic? True, the social ills of North Africa remained a *pons asinorum* in electoral speeches and administrative reports. The French Socialist Party, at its 1936 Congress, discussed the matter in great detail. But if economists were, at the time, in advance of politicians and, even more, of sociologists, let us see to what extent this the was case.

Two or three serious reviews, published in North Africa, were concerned with the question: the *Bulletin économique* (not yet *et social*), which had appeared in Morocco since 1933, and the *Supplément économique* of the review *Algéria*, published by the O.F.A.L.A.C. (*Office algérien de l'artisanat et du commerce*) from 1937 onwards. I have

[1] *Afrique du Nord illustrée*, 15 Sept. 1938.

frequently referred to the first of these publications; let us now examine the second. It is instructive to glance at these articles which, while singing the praises of a system, involuntarily pass judgment on it. Algeria, according to the prevailing doctrine, was dedicated to the expansion of modern (in her case, colonial) culture, which was to bring her new life, while her traditional culture was relegated to primitive backwaters.[1] A paradoxical reversal of the truth! Blinded by its omnipotence, the system made the rule appear the exception, and set the whole of native life on an inferior level. It even sought to eject traditional culture from its backwaters, by means of the technical agents of the S.I.P., who popularized aims without providing means, and without prospect of success; the village or urban moneylender, who alone profited by these new needs; and, worst of all, the forest ranger, who denounced the ancient common rights, pretexting havoc wrought by goats. With good reason, indeed, some alarm was felt at the deforestation of the land (June 1937). The blame for this was laid not on excessive mechanization, but on the survival of tribal agriculture.

During the past fifteen years or so, modern agriculture had benefited and indeed, to some extent, been kept alive by mechanization.[2] It had built up a coherent doctrine on this issue. The stock of equipment, which had grown inordinately large, had indeed collapsed after 1930. By 1935 it started to grow again. But everyone had learnt a lesson from the slump. Subsequent practices might provide interesting study for the technician. Almost everywhere classic methods of production were established, which had proved their worth in so far as the main crops were concerned. The technique of wine-making, by means of very complex operations such as sulphating, acidification and refrigeration, eventually produced well-balanced and healthy wines.[3] Agronomists, congratulating themselves on this, failed to observe that this skilled technique also led to concentration, and that cellars holding over 100,000 hectolitres were no longer the exception. This tendency was only apparently held in check by co-operation, which strengthened the local *cacique* at the expense of the small producer, and built up a whole organization, almost state-like in its majesty, for the benefit of the European agriculturist, while the native had to depend on the good offices of the S.I.P. and the Fonds Commun. Thus was formed a sort of Mutual Aid Society for wealthy whites, to the economic disadvantage of the native population. Some alarm might also have been felt at the stagnation of output.[4] In Algeria, no progress was made. The heaviest

---

[1] Isman, *Algéria*, no. 6, 1937.

[2] A. Bastey, *Algéria*, no. 29, 1939, perspicaciously notes that the mechanization which developed in Algeria after 1936 was 'undertaken in a wholly different spirit'.

[3] *Algéria*, no. 27, 1939.

[4] R. Bertrand, *Algéria*, no. 26, 1939. The author gives alarming figures. Cf. also Bessières, comparing European and native resources (ibid. Jan. 1939).

yield had been in 1913 and the figure for that year was never reached again. After the lean years between the two wars, there was indeed a certain revival, but the figures for 1938 were still far from those of 1914; sixteen million quintals, compared with well over twenty million before the war. What was the cause of the drop? The problem was vast. Some ascribed it to pauperization. In any case, it was due to the exhaustion of the land through over-strenuous methods of agriculture.

The most shocking injustice of all was in distribution. This was chiefly envisaged, as far as the Muslim masses were concerned, as a matter of wage-earning. To quote an authority, Professor Gaffiot:[1] 'Labour's position in Algeria is precarious, because it is in great demand. It is thus constantly in conflict with the business firms whose position it weakens. Capital on the contrary is in a favoured position because of its scarcity. Whence the excessive bank rate, and above all the excesses of usury, which it has not been possible to repress.' This analysis does not consider the huge phenomena which are so widely studied today, not only employment but also under-employment and unemployment: local economists were not advanced enough for that. It concludes with a comment whose optimism may strike us as hypocritical today, extolling 'the admirable regularity of the progress achieved by administrative care'. And in any case, thank Heaven, the native has 'great endurance', by reason of his religious faith.

The question once settled with reference to ethnology and theodicy, the chief, indeed the only problem that concerned the authorities was that of commercialization.[2] Now, thanks to mutual aid, thanks to the quota system and countless other causes—for there was nothing rational about this economic system—prices had risen again. In 1935 they had dropped by 25 per cent from those of 1930, the centenary year, which rightly or wrongly was considered typical. Now in May 1939 they rose again to 128 per cent. So that the war could be faced in a spirit of optimism . . .

When the review *Algéria* opened an investigation on the theme: 'Is Algeria a wealthy country?[3] it received characteristic answers. Gustave Mercier, to whom reference has already been made, combined every category of social superiority. He was a Financial Delegate, president of the Railways, former Commissary of the Centenary, son of an illustrious Mayor of Constantine, connected with a well-known financial group,

[1] Gaffiot, *Algéria*, no. 27, 1939.

[2] The OFALAC was created by a decree of 2 Mar. 1936, together with an Office du Commerce Extérieur and an Office Tunisien de Standardisation. The report of the Council of Administration of the Crédit Foncier d'Algérie et de Tunisie congratulates itself on the agricultural campaign of 1938–9 (16 May 1939).

[3] Cf. among others No. 29, July–Aug. 1939 and No. 30, Jan. 1940. Messerschmidt writes: 'We are somewhat afraid that the sons of these genuine builders may have forgotten the hard and magnificent efforts of their elders.'

an Arabic and Berber scholar. He was a cultured man, the author of notable studies on transformism, illustrating what he calls the 'ascensional dynamism' of life. Perhaps this is an intellectual expression of the optimism of his class. But what class was not aware that its triumph, in the North Africa of 1939, was illusory. Mercier's reply to *Algéria*'s questionnaire reflects the attitude of the colonial patriciate. 'The first source of wealth in any country is its manpower,' he tells us. But does not the vast majority of the population consist of backward natives? True, but they can perform considerable services. We are responsible for the great task of educating them, however. But note: technical and professional education, rather than mere instruction, is needed. This will of course increase production. Then follows a lucid statement on the arrested development of Algerian vines, the failures of cereal culture, and the drastic need for a water policy. This mixture of precise observation and error is ascribable to the system rather than to the man, who is an impressive figure.

In one of the editorials of this review I note a comment by M. Messerschmidt, one of the promoters of the co-operative movement in Algeria. He quotes a pamphlet by the nineteenth-century economist Frédéric Bastiat, who, in 1850, criticizing the loan of 50 million francs by Metropolitan France for Algerian colonization, had shocked his compatriots by asking them: 'What are you going to do with these fifty millions? Are we not following the shadow rather than the substance? Of course, the drained marshes, reclaimed lands, settlers' houses springing up in the waste land are all things that we can see. But what we do not see is the gradual dwindling, and failure to increase, of Metropolitan France's savings, from which this levy is taken.' In January 1940 this opinion was challenged by Messerschmidt,[1] the promoter of mutual aid in Algeria, art critic and sports writer, a typical member of the Colonial intelligentsia. He protests that Bastiat had been short-sighted, had failed to see the greatness of France and the vigour of her colony. Bastiat had indeed been mistaken; but so was his critic. The irony of history rejects them both together.

It is undoubtedly hard to distinguish the things that matter underneath the things that meet the eye. One can distinguish only what one is looking for. It is true that certain things, in the moral as well as in the physical order, are, like the sun and death, 'not to be looked at steadily'.

---

[1] Who had the merit of recognizing the danger of the *latifundia*, and the social change that had taken place in the ruling personnel.

Part 4

The Floating Island

I turned back, and perceived a vast
opaque body between me and the sun.

Gulliver's Travels, part III

CHAPTER XIII

Elementary Bases of Coexistence

O ne cannot write history without exploring the deeper levels below history. Many men came here, far from an older soil, from a more established way of life, from less direct adventures, in quest of something elementary.[1] For foreigners, but also for many of the land's original inhabitants, consciously or not, the Maghrib stood primarily for just that. 'A passionate continent,' François Bonjean has called it. But the most general passion of all was hunger.

Hunger

Colonizing a land meant, in the first place, getting food from it: plentifully for some, sparsely for others. All had come to seek sustenance from this African soil. For a few, this meant rich and delectable foodstuffs; but most were content if they could get their daily bread. Flat Arab girdle-cakes were made of barley, the two-pound loaf was of hard wheat.[2] In village ovens, when a pig was killed, they baked *fougasses* (Rabelais' *fouaces*, perhaps), a kind of sausage containing a large proportion of offal. These strong, spicy foods were washed down by a rough wine . . .

There were no refrigerators in the twenties; food soon went bad. There were no insecticides either, and left-overs were devoured by flies that disturbed one's siesta by day and mosquitoes that broke one's sleep at night. But mostly, man's appetite forestalled that of the parasites or the general decomposition of his food. People lived within that narrow margin which, in summer, separated the slaughter of an animal from its putrefaction. Dysentery, enteritis and typhoid wrought havoc among children, and above all killed the poor, while rich men and officials went

---

[1] Cf. for instance the fine description of ostrich-hunting by General Margueritte, *Les Chasses d'Algérie*, 1881, pp. 83 ff.

[2] The triumph of soft wheat and 'baking qualities' the export of 'strong wheat' are indicative of a profound transformation in the relations between European society and the Maghrib.

to Vichy every year for a cure. Thus the stability of the social order was maintained by a hierarchy of the bowels, which was naturally kinder to some than to others.

The terrible hunger which had driven immigrants from Sicily and the Balearic islands became repletion in the higher social reaches. Dyspeptic aristocrats rejected common fare, the coarse red wine, the fried and highly spiced foods. As an unwelcome duty, but a superb status symbol, envied and admired by all, they undertook that annual rite, the trip to France for a cure, on magnificently vulgar steamers.

In the saloons of the *Marsa II* or the *Manouba* there might sometimes be seen, among other members of the ruling class, a native chief. Duly supplied with money by his tribe, travelling by official request, combing a beard like Abraham's with a regal gesture, he would nonchalantly enjoy the attentions of the little group of high officials and young women who by chance (though not always by chance) travelled in his company. His fine woollen garments had a rich reek of grease, recalling their origin on the sheep's back; significantly, since the sheep, the Arab's own special animal, omnipresent in that patriarchal, waning world, providing the main dish at every feast, man's clothing, his wealth, his way of life, his ritual object, was one of the rewards promised to success in the Algerian adventure.

In the matter of food, wine and mutton were the predominant items. A brief scrutiny of various North African cuisines might allow one to distinguish, for instance, the 'Andalous' style of Fez[1] and Tunis, with its sumptuous pastries; a Nomadic style, as basic to all the rest as the rocky steppes and the alfalfa fields were to all other landscapes; Berber survivals, and small enclaves of Jewish cookery, formidably spiced.

The custom of eating, like communicants, from a common dish, leaving a 'surplus' remnant for *baraka* (grace), was being replaced in bourgeois families by the serving of portions in separate dishes at a high table.[2] This change, the history of which is worth tracing, had incalculable consequences. One should also study the persistence of certain dishes and methods of preparation, and their reappearance in new forms: an ethnographic investigation which is as yet beyond our scope.

Naturally, all the breeds of Europe contributed their recipes. Salted sardines, 'Spanish cutlets', chicken with rice, or *gaspachos*, were eaten

---

[1] Z. Guinaudeau, *Fès d'après sa cuisine.*

[2] This constitutes a revolution in Muslim family life: from communion to commensality, and thence to the bare fact of feeding oneself. Apart from cheap taverns for workmen or sailors, the opening of 'Arab restaurants' for bourgeois customers was a new and interesting phenomenon. In the thirties there was one at Rabat, in the Rue al-Gaza, and one at Algiers, Rue de Chartres: this was the *Restaurant égyptien* where notabilities from the interior of the country forgathered; described by R. Randau, *Sur le pavé d'Alger*, 1937, pp. 38 ff.

in the Oran district, with *muna* for dessert.[1] To the south-east of Algiers, Italian pasta were popular. Bouillabaisse, too, was relished. The parent state imposed its authority through French cookery, as well as through all other institutions. At the opposite extreme from its harmonious classicism, a native dish, *couscous*, which contained mutton, chicken, even fish on the Tunisian seaboard, won great popularity. Foreigners delighted in this tribute from the land they had tamed; *couscous* constituted the one factor that united everyone in North Africa. A *hadith* shows the Prophet healing Maghribi pilgrims, who had lost their way in the Hijaz, by means of a plate of *couscous*. The word, which is not explained in the Arabic dictionary, struck Westerners so early that we find it, barely deformed, in *Gargantua*. It made its way on to every European table.

To enliven this description let us turn to a cookery book, *Gastronomie africaine*,[2] a historic document, since it considers no dish too familiar or unworthy of notice. The names are amusing: we find a salad *à la Lyautey*, a ragout *à la Si Bouzaiz Bengana* (we have already encountered this *shaikh al-ʿArab*, a leading personality of the Biskra region). We read the extraordinary menu of the banquet offered by the Bashagha in his wonderful gardens. The menu is set out in two languages, providing instructive equivalences: *potage au blé vert Alya* (*shorba bel-frik*); *entrées*; *bouchées, cigares des Biban*; Tolga cabbage stuffed with rice (in Arabic simply *kefta*, meaning minced meat); gazelle from the plains with Saharan truffles (*rim bet-terfas*); prunes with Medina honey, and so forth. The list includes countless elements of local colour; the *chamelon des Arabes Cheraga, huwar ibel;* the *mouflon* (wild sheep) *Aurasien, sheftel auras*, and the lamb, *agneau pré-salé de Zaʿatcha*, of historic memory, which is a translation of *msewwer*, half a sheep, roasted.[3]

This is the splendid dish which forms an essential part of the caïd's hospitality, which is served to high officials on their visits or at outings of regional or sporting clubs, that peak of Maghribi gastronomy, popularly known as *meshwi*. The shrivelled carcass, the tiny scorched head, like a child's, have a suggestion of cruelty that provides 'local colour'. The sharp aromatic odour is wafted far around. Its preparation involves meticulous rites: the brazier has to be carefully

---

[1] This term, which I cannot explain, refers both to the cake that bears the name and to the spring festival where it is eaten *al fresco*. The custom belongs chiefly to the Oran region. It played an important part in the domestic life of the humbler classes and also in the relations between young men and girls. It involved moreover a sort of Paschal lustration of the neighbourhood of Oran: Santa Cruz, Cueva de l'Agua, etc. See a vivid passage in G. Audisio's *Héliotrope*, 1928, pp. 202 ff.

[2] By Léon Isnard, *Gastronomie africaine*, 1930. This may be the banquet referred to in *Le Cri de l'Algérie*, April 30 1927: 'Qui paie la diffa?'

[3] Alphonse Daudet in *Contes du Lundi* (impressions of a journey to Algeria in 1861-2) paints a 'gastronomic landscape' devoted to *couscous*.

watched, the spit turned, the meat basted with butter. Once cooked, it is exhibited like a trophy. The well-roasted flesh lies crackling on a copper or wooden platter, laid in the centre of the table or even sometimes at your feet, on a rush mat. Only the official from the Arab Bureau knows, like his nomadic fellow-guests, how to carry out the requisite ceremonial: how to pick up mouthfuls of meat lightly and as though casually, with three fingers of the right hand, how to masticate with pauses of meaningful silence, how to grope cunningly inside the carcass as if it were a mine from which the connoisseur suddenly brings out a triumphal morsel: the two kidneys embedded in fat.

But for most European diners this delicate feast becomes an orgy.[1] They tear off great slabs of crackling skin; they snatch at a whole leg, and cram handfuls into their mouths. The whole company seems intoxicated with meat. Combined with the fieriness of pungent soups and, sometimes, the effect of the wine served, according to an inflexible administrative custom, in sealed bottles, the meal provokes a primitive excitement which only the presence of a Prefect or a General restrains within the limits of decency. Discreetly, moreover, the Bashagha withdraws at dessert, probably to visit his wives. European ladies burst into loud laughter; a warm sense of complicity unites everybody, *rumis* and notables; the latter have enjoyed their feudal homage, the former renewed the friendship, through which the tensions of the Colonial situation are relaxed in hospitality for a while.

Meanwhile, trusted negro servants carry the remains into a neighbouring tent, where lesser notabilities—*jama'a* presidents, gendarmes, rich fellahs, representing the conquered country—repeat the performance at a lower level of dignity. A third group awaits the stripped carcasses. Everyone's appetite is keen; business matters and resentments alike are adjourned. Even the old men munch with toothless gums, laboriously chewing and eventually swallowing the gristly bits left them by their lords. Out of consideration for the harem, or for fear of fleas, the feast takes place in front of the chief's long dwelling, under a tent or a roof of leaves. Some distance away those natives who have not even been invited to the third or fourth service stand watching the ceremony.

If the winter was at all dry, or the spring wet, the harvest was ruined. In Morocco, when the Gharb did well the Haouz suffered from drought. And when the Haouz flourished, the Gharb was swamped. In the Mediterranean zone, many of the best lands had been taken over by the *colon*. Native property, which had become merely marginal, still hung on to the occasional fertile corner, but was chiefly found on the borders of the steppe, close to the 'dead lands'. A meagre field of barley or hard

[1] Described by R. Randau, *Le Professeur Martin* (edition illustrated by Ch. Brouty, p. 86) without irony, to depict the Europeans' effort to adapt themselves to their surroundings.

wheat was supposed to feed two families, the fellah's and that of his workman, the *khamis*—who was paid with one-fifth of the harvest. The poverty of farming techniques, the uncertainty of results, constantly exposed to climatic hazards, kept such a system in a perpetual state of bankruptcy. Basically, the only thing that maintained and perpetuated native agriculture was the fertility of the women, continually renewing these generations of lean peasants. The régime's economists had no difficulty in showing that the fellah owning less than about ten hectares (about what his yoke of oxen, *zuja* or *mashiya*, would plough in a year) would find it profitable to leave his plot of land and seek employment on a farm.[1] Profit, for the fellah, only began where wide open spaces were available, long stretches of fallow land, spacious pastures: in other words, where political power lay. Moreover, were things any different for the *colon?*

For this reason, few peasants were self-sufficient, or even managed to save anything. Except on the Atlantic seaboard of Morocco, where abundant rain moistened the rich plains of *tirs* (heavy soil) or *hamri* (red earth), they were only to be found among the few who, favoured geographically or socially, cultivated the olive, the fig tree or the palm tree. Most peasants grew cereals, and remained incurably poor. They had to eke out a livelihood in other ways; keeping sheep or goats wherever possible, seeking casual compensations everywhere, and thus retaining old habits of gleaning, hunting, and frequently of plunder. To that extent the fellah was still a Bedouin, and for all his sedentary way of life kept the evasive habits of the nomad.

Famine diets: wild artichokes, mallow stems, the almost poisonous tubercles of the *targhuda* or *bquqa*, prickly pears in season, barley edible roots, often provided his daily fare, supplementing the scarcely leavened girdle cake of barley or millet.[2] *Couscous* made of millet, coarse and black, had nothing in common with the luscious pale-golden heaps on the nobleman's table. For the poor man, meat of any sort was a feast, a gift from God, an adventure. He more or less suffered from hunger all the time. His tattered burnous barely concealed the leanness of his limbs. Recruiting boards, on medical inspection, rejected a large quota of youths as unfit. And of these bodies, whose muscles seemed to be

---

[1] They therefore conclude that settlement by Europeans is more profitable, over an equal area, for the native, than farming practised on his own account. Long controversies arose on this point in Algeria, notably with respect to vine-growing. Ch. Isnard reports some of these. At the period that interests us, the Civil Controller Mottes tried to prove the same thesis for the Mejerda valley, see *Bulletin de la Direction de l'Agriculture et de la Colonisation*, Tunis, 1925, no. 119. This learned humbug was founded on a truism: that mechanized agriculture is better than the use of animals. But it was not until 1944, with the Moroccan SMP, that anyone dared draw the conclusion that native agriculture itself should be mechanized.

[2] To which, ironically enough, an aphrodisiac effect is attributed.

wasting away, the virility of the men and the femininity of the women was strikingly accentuated, as though the species sought paradoxically to assert itself through these exhausted individuals. The sexual act was their final refuge. Popular wisdom was aware of this, when it declared that the *khamis'* wife was happier than the caïd's and that the Muslim was on the whole more virile than the European. The animals owned by this half-starved being: the howling dog, the lean donkey, the worn-out nag to which the language refused the generic name of 'horse',[1] like their master, enjoyed no regular pittance. The dog subsisted on filth and what he could plunder; the cattle on close-cropped vegetation or the thorny remains of an exhausted pasture. What might be the fellah's feelings when going past the notable's well-stocked stable, where the charger, his front feet shackled, stood peacefully savouring his barley; or along the path beside the *colon*'s field, where the ears of wheat were full of sweet ripening grain! The imagined savour of *frik* or *dshisha* would make his mouth water and torment his empty belly. Perhaps he did not yet feel hatred . . .

Children were born in profusion, from those nights when the couple were kept awake by hunger. They swarmed in the *mrah*,[2] with their swollen bellies, their beautiful eyes encrusted with flies. Their survival was a matter of chance; and yet for all that, or because of that, they were greatly cherished: they promised compensation to men's undying hope.

These almost timeless images and feelings take on a cruelly historic character through the vicissitudes of the period. I have already mentioned famine, and I shall have to do so again; for there were still famines in North Africa.[3] The first, in 1921, endangered economic recovery. The second, in 1937, added yet another difficulty to those which the Popular Front encountered in its timid attempts at reform. At that time, particularly in the south, men were dying like the beasts whose bones strewed the roads. And with their flocks they embarked wretchedly on the long trek northward. Municipal authorities, taking alarm, labelled these invading refugees 'vagabonds' and sent them back in lorry-loads to 'their original tribe'. Relief measures were undertaken which frequently showed zeal but which were naturally inadequate.

[1] In Moroccan dialect, '*aud*, a warhorse, is contrasted with *kaidar*, a lean nag, just as the *sloughi*, mongrel, is contrasted with the generic term for a dog.

[2] *Frik, dshisha, mrah*, respectively: 'grilled soft grain', 'gruel', 'space within a circle of tents', or by extension 'interior courtyard'.

[3] The distressing situation finds an echo even in the small colonial parliaments of Tunis, Rabat and Algiers, which were not tender-hearted by nature. In Tunisia, production and consumption of cereals dropped between 1921 and 1922, respectively, from 5,628 to 1,548 and from 2,587 to 1,820 thousand quintals. The total production of cereals in Morocco dropped from 28,000 to 15,000 thousand quintals between 1934 and 1935.

Heart-rending sights were to be seen all along the roads–an old woman from the Moroccan Haouz picking up grains of barley out of the dirt, and crushing them between two stones to make a sort of pap for an emaciated baby. It was at this time that a young journalist named Albert Camus gave a tragic description of the misery in Kabylia.[1] And at Algiers the old journalist Mallebay[2] published his *Science de gueule*. An appalling inequality divided the rulers from the ruled, or, more summarily, those who were satisfied from those who were starving.

Sexual Desire

The walls were covered with obscene graffiti. The physical and moral world was divided between male and female. The constant reference to notions of activity or passivity in describing people, situations or behaviour illustrated the exuberance of the masculine symbol. At the very time when human beings were dying of hunger, they were also dying of sexual desire; and not always metaphorically. Their historic experiences and their economic conflict intensified their traditional sexual ardour,[3] which reflects an elementary force, an attitude to life, and a challenge. It also serves as an immediate moral principle.

Every Moroccan chief kept his band of dancing girls, his *shaikhat* who were artists, of course, and whose art was inordinately valued even when they were past their prime. A caïd from the Gharb once made one of them ford the river Wargha in full spate. In the ensuing fluster, the girl declared with loud shrieks that she had lost her bracelets, those heavy bangles of twisted silver or gold which are sometimes picturesquely called '*asir s-sabun*, 'ropes of washing'. They were worth a large sum, which the feudal lord could not supply on his own. He therefore called on his subjects; no tax was ever more readily paid. Several years later, after the caïd's death, the tribe related his exploit as being worthy of Antar. Sometimes things went further, to the point of murder; in the Hodna in 1932, it was said, the son of a noble family, for love of an Ouled (Aulad) Nail girl, slew his rival and, with his terrible *busa'adi* (Saharan knife) wrenched out his teeth . . .

The law courts tell many tales of mutual passion. The North African sought compensation in this. And the European emulated him, accepting the distribution of labour which gave power, money and instruction to one side, masculine privilege and summary jurisdiction to the other. Moreover, European youths, becoming increasingly integrated in the country's life, did not intend to be left behind. As students in Paris in the

[1] His articles in *Alger républicain* were republished in *Actuelles III*.

[2] Former editor of *Annales africaines*, and author of interesting memoirs the last volume of which has unfortunately not appeared, as far as I know.

[3] M. Seklani boldly describes the Maghribi male as *homo eroticus*, in 'La fécondité dans les pays arabes', *Population*, no. 5, 1960.

thirties they were at one with their Muslim fellows on this point; both were distinguished from the Metropolitan French comrades and even from their Middle Eastern ones by their deliberate and systematic sexuality. Violently opposed on political issues, having already split up their student associations, they were at one over their tastes in food and their attitude to love.

In the Maghrib, land of the Ram, sexual desire was all-pervasive, exacerbated by contention and privation. An ethnic rather than a moral prohibition kept the Muslim woman from the newcomers. The colonial subject made it emphatically clear that on this issue he would not yield, seeing in his womankind his last hope of autonomy and hence of survival. Now the beauty of these women appeals to Mediterranean as well as to Eastern taste. The Algerian woman, veiled in white, looks like a white amphora with billowing folds at its base; the Bedouin woman, on the contrary, uncovers her face and much else beside; sometimes her garment, split down the side from armpit to ankle, reveals a golden-brown and seductive body.

No doubt in the city slums, as the troops began to roll in, the Maghribi woman, whose world was falling apart, would disobey her nation's taboos. No doubt, too, in remote regions, Aurès, Ouled Nail, Haouz, Middle Atlas, ancient rites sanctioned the gift of her body to the stranger. And of course, more personal relationships were sometimes established. As far as one can tell, their significance is great; their story has not yet been told, and never will be. In such cases, the triumph of sexual union is more than a psychological one.

Apart from such rare instances, relations were only possible on the horrible fringes of the two worlds. The Casbah of Algiers combined African brutality with the prostitution of Marseilles. With its shadowy and squalid cul-de-sacs, seductive and yet blatant, it spread over the upper part of the town. For all its hideousness, it inspired descriptions by Louis Bertrand and Lucienne Favre,[1] and a romantic film, *Pépé le Moko* (1935). Each town had its special district, set apart for the purpose, to which peasant women flocked in defiance of the rules. Sometimes such a district had architectural value, such as Busbir at Casablanca, the first and for a long time the only Maghribi attempt at housing for the native population! At Fez, Maulay 'Abdallah echoed with the screech of huge hydraulic wheels, and the sultan's palace submitted to its propinquity with a truly regal indulgence, which also betrayed colonial decadence. Tourists, visiting artists and writers, Gide himself, visited the Ouled Nail street in Bu Sa'ada.

But there were limits beneath which the prostitute would not sink. According to a familiar Western pattern, she kept to the conventions of

---

[1] *Tout l'inconnu de la Kasba d'Alger*, by Lucienne Favre; *Nuits d'Alger*, by the academician Louis Bertrand (1930), written in a pompous yet vulgar style.

patriotism or at least of xenophobia. Not only did she reject certain Western habits, but she would also reject the foreigner's advances. At Tunis, segregation was the rule in the brothel, Muslim women being kept for Muslims; Jewish and other Mediterranean prostitutes for foreigners. For obvious requirements of law and order, the police allotted certain days to legionaries, others to *tirailleurs*, etc.; for any infringement of the rule soon degenerated into a free fight. Prostitution, far from being anarchical, thus provided an illustration of the civic order. Theorists may see in it the result of colonization, as in Europe the result of capitalism. But in North Africa at that time it fulfilled a more important function than in Europe. A physical outlet, a ritual outrage, it confirmed and protected the established order. Revels where sexual pleasure was combined with dancing, loud singing, and indulgence in anisette, beer and *kif* formed part of the general order of things. The tempestuous, though controlled, current of life in the Maghribi haunts of vice acted as a form of irrigation; the virtue of private citizens was protected, certain wild impulses were exorcized and certain taboos laid aside for a while.

But corruption spread beyond the reassuring bounds of the Busbirs. The poverty which led to the sale of daughters, the frequency of repudiation in marriage, and procuration drove many women to more clandestine practices. Not only in the special districts, the military brothels and the reserved streets, unlawful sexual indulgence became widespread. The *hejjala*[1] of Morocco, the *azriya*[2] of the Aurès were too often reduced to trading their bodies. Then there arose subtle interconnections between tradition and innovation, between the collective and the individual. For prostitution represented one form among many of the individualism arising from the destruction of old ways and standards. By a strange conjunction between age-old licentiousness and modern vice, the orgiastic rites of the Maghrib mingled with the debauchery of Parisian low-life; the same evolution of personality, the same psychological upheaval to which the people of North Africa were being led by other, more respectable ways, and under the banner of progress.

But we may disregard such disturbing similarities. In the last analysis, the solution was a poor one: this kind of sex led nowhere, remaining, by definition, sterile. The excitement born of inter-racial contact should have culminated in a bacchanalian frenzy, in one of those 'nights of madness' during which, it is said, certain populations periodically intermingle. Nothing of the sort took place. Prostitution and pederasty functioned only on the rejected fringes of ethnically separate societies; beyond which, the two groups could no more achieve unity through

[1] Divorced woman.
[2] Divorced woman or widow, living in a state of sexual emancipation.

love than they could merge politically. There was no intermarriage;[1] there were not even any bastards. Physical exclusiveness was maintained almost absolutely, despite a century of colonization. Each side protected itself against the other. Islam brandished its anathemas; Europe stressed the results of inequality. One side threatened damnation, the other misalliance. For a European could not consider marrying an Arab Berber girl, however desirable, even if her law had sanctioned it; marriage, on the other hand, was possible between a Maghribi male and a European woman, if he had managed to win her—a prize for the relatively small group of workers and intellectuals seeking promotion or expatriation. Illicit relations, which in other countries and analogous situations involved such wide demographic and moral consequences, here remained sterile.[2] This barrenness, this self-segregation of the two masses lasted throughout the whole colonial period. In the end, the two ethnic groups formed themselves racially intact beneath a superficial uniformity due to daily contact and the cumulative influence of their surroundings.

A strange contradiction: in a land where sexual desire was rife, the impulse of the two groups towards one another was interrupted, the elements remained dissociated. The human mortar with which the ruined city might have been built failed to set. On one side, the minority's fear of being absorbed by the majority, the competitive presence of European womanhood, that jealous guardian of controversial values—racial pride, bourgeois convention. On the other side, a withholding of the essential, a prudent guarding of the last stronghold: part of the basic pattern of Arab behaviour. North Africa was thus the country of frustrated impulses[3]. Cut off from one another, at the very moment when an embrace might have ended their strife, the two antagonists sought and discovered explanations for this mutual fiasco. One of these was syphilis,[4] the importance of which became exaggerated to the proportions of a myth. Thus the European's fear of contagion frustrated the Muslim's sexual revenge, but at the same time kept the Muslim out of his reach.

The Muslim, moreover, rejecting both the myth and the reality of infection, gloried in his compensatory energy. He sought in proud progenitiveness—frequent sexual activity, abundance of offspring—a revenge for the humiliations inflicted on him, to which he had added the supreme humiliation of submitting to them. The conquest of French womanhood being, at the time we are considering, a matter of individual enterprise and rarely successful, the Muslim remained unsatisfied. He

---

[1] Cf. D.-H. Marchand, and others: *Le mariage mixte franco-musulman,* Algiers. The substance is meagre, the commentary arid.

[2] With a few exceptions.

[3] I shall refer again to this apparent paradox.

[4] Cf. pp. 90 ff. A recent Tunisian estimate wavers between 13 and 25 per cent *Dépêche tunisienne,* 19 May 1961). Better not commit oneself!

could forgive himself for many other defeats: in the professional field, for instance, where his attitude was one of arrogant insouciance. But he suffered, even more than from the injustice of his position, from the impotence of his desire. Now in the twenties, fashion had liberated young women, in North Africa as in the parent state, from many conventional restraints. Their bodies were revealed by their clothing, displayed on beaches, stimulated by dancing. The sight of some of these, at those moments of intense African heat when sexual excitement is irresistible, had become a delight and a torment. It sometimes happened that some important public figure, swathed in his burnous, had to leave the official table hurriedly because he could no longer endure the sight of some buxom lady in a low-cut dress.

What are we to say about the younger generation, particularly about those who, from 1925 or 1930 onwards, at school or college, were friendly with girl students and were sometimes accepted by them? Almost everywhere, at this period, the Maghribi man sought to conquer that forbidden creature, the European woman, unfamiliar and hitherto unattainable, so different in her ways, dress and mind from his own women, to whose position he longed to reduce her; she summed up the whole of his frustrated vehemence. From his lost lands, from his shattered hierarchies, from his forfeited values, all his sense of deprivation and resentment rose up to concentrate on her image. And while he desired her, and might have hated and insulted her, or even violated and killed her–as sometimes happened–he nevertheless respected her.

For countless unspoken or overt reasons, there was solidarity as well as tension within this society. The harshness of repression was not the only factor that controlled the violence of men's instincts. Moral models, common to a large extent to both native and foreigner, arose from the self-check imposed on desire. But the native found them harder to follow because of the curbing of his impulse towards a femininity whose various aspects were embodied in the Frenchwoman: her civilizing influence, her touching weaknesses, and that hope of understanding which braved all interdicts. For in this masculine world, France, although armed with brutal powers and oppressive authority, wore a feminine aspect[1] in the eyes of the Maghribi male, and conquered though he was, he longed to conquer her.

Fear

The harshness of the operations involved in the conquest of Algeria over more than two generations, the brief but cruel explosions which

---

[1] The simile is used in an article signed Ezzedine Cherif ('Izz al-Din Sharif), in *La Voix du Tunisien*. But one has only to consider the postage stamps, the busts of the Republic, etc.

more recently, during the first world war, had occurred at Lambèse and elsewhere, the violence of tribal resistance in Morocco, the appearance of a new form of violence–street fighting–all suggest the idea of a country submitting with fury in its heart. Events subsequent to the second world war only strengthen this view. It is therefore plausible, and in conformity with one interpretation of things, to argue from such evidence that the Maghrib accepted foreign domination only under direct constraint, and this would have been quite natural.

Nevertheless, the sociologist, inevitably less respectful of moral arguments and reluctant to interpret any historic fact in absolute fashion, restores diversity to this vast space, this long chronology[1] and this wide range of situations. He cannot answer the question whether these subjugated men accepted French domination or merely endured it, and how, and at the cost of what tensions, without taking into account a multiplicity of cases and a variation in time, which are themselves connected with the vicissitudes of the conflict between the two sides for the appropriation of signs and of things.

In the first part of this book I endeavoured to consider this conflict from two historical points of view: the transformation of the setting, and the evolution of social meanings. But could one not go even further? Since the colonial power at that time presumed on its legitimacy, dominating everyday life and the customary course of events, could one not measure its repressive force by the efforts made to shake off the superimposed order? The assessment of the repressive organization would provide, in this respect, indubitable evidence. We should of course have to distinguish between the actual personnel of the occupying power[2] and those agents who collaborated in any way towards the maintenance of law and order: *mukhaznis*, *ojaks*, militiamen, policemen, etc. Secondly, a rough idea might be got from the crime figures shown by legal statistics,[3] discriminating as far as possible between crimes of

---

[1] The period under consideration covers the half-century roughly dividing the end of rural uprisings in Algeria from the birth of urban nationalism, as M. Lacheraf has shown, cf. 'Le patriotisme rural en Algérie', *Esprit*, Mar. 1955. Cf. also his earlier article, April 1954.

[2] On 1 Mar. 1938, the total strength of the army consisted of 73,307 for Algeria (2,099 officers), 51,326 for Morocco (2,102 officers) and 29,562 for Tunisia (818 officers). Out of these, the number of Frenchmen was respectively 19,500, 11,700 and 7,724. On 1 July 1939, the army of French North Africa consisted of 46,000 Frenchmen, 16,000 foreigners, and 85,000 natives: total 147,000. The number of Muslims engaged under the French flag varied, between 1935 and 1939, around 20,000 per annum. (Information provided by the department of history of the Army.) At the time of the Armistice, there were less than thirty thousand men in the whole of North Africa, which evidently contrasts with the period subsequent to 1954!

[3] Thus, according to the *Annuaire statistique de l'Algérie*, the number of attacks by natives on Europeans was 11,151, in 1935; among those guilty of offences, there were 17,691 Europeans and 70,726 Muslims, i.e. relatively *fewer* Muslims; 5,831 *infractions à l'indigénat* (infringement of rules governing the

honour, passion or revenge and the more brutal sort. Political detentions would provide another kind of data, psychologically very different from the first, but which could be combined with the first in an assessment of the forces which, in one way or another, rose up against the existing order[1]. The graph thus drawn, each element of which should be interpreted in relation to the structural or conjunctural tendencies, would have to be compared with the same graphs drawn for similar countries in the Islamo-Mediterranean zone, colonial (Egypt, Syria) or non-colonial (Andalusia, Sicily). From this we should doubtless discover exact data about the characteristics of repression in North Africa, and local reaction to it in the form of violent, illegal or refractory behaviour.

But such research has not been undertaken nor even, so far, conceived of, to my knowledge. Moreover, although it might provide us with precise details, it is questionable whether it would account for the specific conditions of the system. Its particular character was its aspiration towards normality, regularity and even ordinariness. Political repression, in any case intermittent, stopped far short of the horrors it has since perpetrated.[2] Judiciary repression had, we believe, no particular criminality to subdue. Such observations, if confirmed, would direct research towards those less sensational elements and more subtle planes where pressure and protest were exerted; and therein lies the truth of the problem.

The period here considered was in fact noted for its claims to civil peace. This was established immediately after tribal resistance had been quelled, and was now so firmly grounded that the types of violence which from time to time preoccupied the authorities and alarmed public opinion were those familiar in civilized countries: waves of banditry, demonstrations which might lead to street fighting, strikes, a few political assassinations (some of them contrived). The fact that these outbreaks terrified the subjects or beneficiaries of the 'French peace' shows that they were still rare, and contrary to the usual course of things.

native population); tens of thousands of offences against forest rights. This simple enquiry suggests possible ways of clarifying the question.

[1] V. Demontès, *L'Algérie économique*, 1923, vol. III (cf. p. 137, no. 9, bibliography), estimates at 11,4/00,000 the proportion of criminal cases from 1903 to 1906, twice as many as in France. Cf. also E. Norès, *L'oeuvre de la France en Algérie, la justice*, 1931, pp. 284 ff. on offences peculiar to Algeria. But the archaic character of the interpretation casts doubt on the facts quoted.

[2] Hence the innovation represented by the Régnier Decree of 30 Mar. 1935, and the importance I attribute to it, cf. p. 257. With respect to repression, it constitutes a backward step, since the institution of political offences reverses a process, which was well under way, of liquidation of exceptional judiciary procedure (cf. Larcher et Rectenwald, *Traité historique, théorique et pratique des juridictions repressives musulmanes*, Algiers 1931). It was promptly applied at Jijelli (cass. crim. 20 Jan. 1938, *Revue algérienne, tunisienne et marocaine de législation et de jurisprudence*, 1938, II, 113, from an unpublished study by J.-P. Charnay).

A régime can be defined by the relations it establishes between the habitual and the exceptional.[1]

It is true that this calm was jeopardized by the fear of insurrection, or at least of spasmodic acts of revenge, which the white population immediately ascribed to the 'fanaticism' or 'evil instincts' of the other side. The 'revolt of the Arab', the isolated outrage usually with a religious motivation, which broke out here and there, as though to discharge some latent anger, were a continual source of anxiety even to the most tranquil and self-confident citizens. Literature reflects these feelings; the sense of being a permanent minority in the countryside, of having once committed excesses, of having incurred the resentment and wounded the pride of that Other who was the whole country and its people, became a characteristic feature of the European in North Africa. From time to time, it was confirmed by real dangers. In 1916, in some market of Southern Oran, the conscription which had recently been imposed provoked certain disorders. Women shrieked, and men looked threatening; objects which might be weapons were produced from some neighbouring marabout; some Spanish labourers, watching the scene from a distance, cut their animals' traces and fled at top speed towards the town, where the administrator, a melancholy soul, talked of putting women to death and then committing suicide. When in 1925, in Northern Morocco, Abd el-Krim captured French advanced posts, won over several recently subdued tribes and for a while threatened Taza, panic spread. At Fez itself, public figures kept their children away from school. The 'Rifans' year', 'am al-Rifi, was to remain famous for the sudden fright it gave to the already established order, in excess of its actual importance.

The *colons* unfailingly alleged the insecurity of their position, and spoke of rebelliousness or even of insurrection. They raised this issue in Algeria after the reforms of 1919; they did so again at the time of the centenary, under the Popular Front, indeed every time it was proposed to make the system less harsh. Dubious as their arguments may appear, they do illustrate certain objective features in the situation. North Africa at this period consolidated some people's profit and intensified the poverty of others, emphasizing hierarchies as imperturbably as if they believed in themselves. But the whole set-up lived under an indefinable threat. Rival explanations, seeking to describe, in retrospect, the atmosphere then reigning in North Africa, will have to take this specific anxiety into account. Whether or not the colonial order had imposed itself by violence (a point which statistics can settle), it did not free men's hearts from apprehension. A sense of precariousness, the

[1] This was also Viollette's opinion, concerning Algeria: *L'Algérie vivra-t-elle?* 1931, p. 405. Dr. Fanon's interpretations, *Les damnés de la terre*, 1961, pp. 40 ff., seem more valid for other historic milieux.

dread of an imminent settling of accounts which might lead to bloodshed, whetted men's appetites, sharpening their desire for gain and pleasure. The very prosperity enjoyed by a few made them more apprehensive of what was in store, not through any social scruple but from fear of being called to account. Few Europeans in the Maghrib, rich or poor, and few of the wealthier Muslims, were immune from this anxiety.

Such a feeling was the counterpart of the latent rebellion of the Muslim majority, which still persisted under their surface acceptance, even when this took the form of active co-operation. The important element here was something lying beyond the reach of clear consciousness or moral qualification, or even of political aspiration. In the relations which grew up on the fringe of the two societies, where contact existed—friendship between schoolboys or fellow soldiers, loyalty between men or even between groups of men—something subsisted which was neither religious reticence nor impotent anger nor watchful violence. Was it not simply the vigil of history?

Injustice

This diffused apprehension found an echo in certain apparently contradictory attitudes in the people of the Maghrib.

In the slums of Algerian towns, aggressiveness concealed and compensated for submission. The policemen who paraded in pairs through the narrow streets of the Casbah dealt out lashes before words, and nobody had yet dared to protest. But altercation flourished at Belcourt and on the beaches of Bab el Oued. Here the natives expressed their impatience in insults and bravado.[1] No doubt this was merely an outlet for their misery, but it kept up, at the lowest level, the picturesque interracial tension.

On the other hand a courteous dignity, hostile or distant, characterized most attitudes in the interior of the country. In Morocco, in the newly developed zones, an imperturbable solemnity redeemed the most painful situations. The European who ventured there, in a civilian capacity, was not respected, but considered in terms of the troubles he might bring you. Naturally, a *modus vivendi* was eventually established wherever men worked together in farms or markets: surly familiarity on the one hand, unreliable and sometimes equivocal familiarity on the other. 'Partnerships', *suhba*, were formed, which ranged from mistrust to camaraderie by way of business relations. 'Don't make enemies among the *colons*,' seems to have been the motto of the caïd and the rich fellah, similar in this respect to their leader the *hakim*, the administrator, whose

[1] Whence the characteristic frequency of interracial insults. Cf. in the interesting *Dictionnaire illustré de la Tunisie* by P. Lambert (1912), p. 61, the definition of *bicot*: 'A contemptuous term for an Arab, used by the French populace in Africa, who are sometimes anti-Arab without knowing why.' The study of such terms has not been made. Cf. my article on interracial relations in North Africa, *Bulletin international des Sciences sociales*, 1961.

prestige could never have protected him from a petition signed by the clients of the *cantine*. In some official statements the foreigner was tactfully described as a 'guest',[1] so long as he remained in a minority, or even a 'bringer of culture' (the term *mu'ammir*, applied to the *colon*). Hatred and admiring curiosity towards the intruder thus tended to fade away, while a whole gamut of attitudes was displayed, from unfriendly reserve to good-natured complicity, without ever departing from a general background of protest.

Fear, at the period we are concerned with, and particularly as the civilian régime gained control, was no longer fear for one's life, one's children or one's honour. True, such feelings persisted in regions where the *barud*, armed conflict, was still going on, such as the forward marches of Morocco until 1934. 'Pacification' had cost many lives here, since 1912.[2] But it was finally considered to be established over the whole stretch of territory between Mogador and Gabès, and between In-Salah and Algiers. From now on, other apprehensions came into play. These varied in intensity and in the manner of their expression according to whether some form of legality *à la française* had been attained. The latter enjoyed the prestige due to the merits of a magistracy which was still immune from the corrupt habits of petty officials or police brutality, yet public opinion was justifiably suspicious of specialized institutions, particularly when these were exceptional ones.

Once the heroic age of the Bureau Arabe was past, wherever the administration's technique lagged behind the development of social habits – which was the case throughout the civil zone, particularly in the neighbourhood of large centres – the Maghribi suffered simultaneously from the anonymous power of bureaucracy and the arbitrary power of individuals. Through a basic defect in the administrative machine, the more specialized the institution, the more it diverged from the French norm, the greater were the dangers of discretionary rule, with its usual attendant train of injustice and peculation. Not that personal merit did not count here, or that the masses did not benefit, here and there, by the rough justice and speedy decisions of some patriarchal judge or some upright *hakim*. But inevitably individual greatness is rarer than individual weakness. And moreover, apart from any question of personality, there comes a time, there are regions, in the development of a colony where such greatness is ineffective. The *shikaya*[3] was a living force in the Southern territories, in the primitive

[1] A term used, by a curious coincidence, to designate the free *hospes* of the Gallo-Roman tenant. Every society needs conciliatory euphemisms as well as 'cathartic' insults.

[2] These operations cost the French army 25,000 dead. By how much should this be multiplied to estimate Moroccan losses?

[3] A sort of informal praetorian justice, common to the system of personal chiefdoms and the Bureau Arabe in the Maghrib.

regions of Morocco or Tunisia, but practically nowhere else. Wherever tribal custom and natural right no longer functioned, while French law was not yet fully applied, there reigned an intermediary zone where regularity was too often merely mechanical, where abuses were rife, while primitive violence reigned side by side with European formalism.

We only have to study the Opposition press of the time,[1] read between the lines of the legal reports, or note the countless anecdotes, too often founded on truth, to imagine, without any partisan exaggeration, what the existence of the underdog may have been at that time. Tahar Sfar's memoirs[2] provide some illuminating stories. True, he makes use of them for ethical denunciations in which the positive investigator cannot follow him. This state of things cannot be explained by human wickedness or original sin; it reflects a failure in understanding, due to the colonial phenomenon. And on the other hand, an institutional discordance which exposes the native to two sorts of abuse, because it places him at the meeting-point of two systems, the one national but decrepit, the other efficient but alienating. His lands are not safe from the Machiavellian schemes of the broker; his wife, if she is attractive, is not safe from those of the moneyed men. The anxiety he feels about the safety of his family and his property is enhanced by resentment against the sharks of his own race, as avid to devour him as is the foreigner. No doubt there are judges and administrators, some of whom are respected; but their entourage is so unfriendly, their information so inadequate, they are armoured by such a carapace of procedures![3] And apart from these, there is no hope of relief, save in complicity.

If then the anxiety of the colonizer is chiefly moral or even instinctive, that of the subject is only too frequently based on everyday experience. No doubt his specific resentment against the overlord, the administrator, the forest ranger, the usurer, the riparian proprietor, the man of law, the pimp recruiting women for the brothels, the sharp-shooter on leave, and so forth, also included feelings of xenophobic honour, if it did not anticipate the concept of nationalism. It usually compromised with all this, as it did with the tangible necessities of the context. This compromise naturally changed in scope and in character according to how long

---

[1] *Passim*, in *La Voix du Tunisien* for instance. Cf. 19 Jan. 1932 (a European foreman tortures a workman: he is discharged, whereas a sexual attempt made by a Tunisian is punished by two years' jail. The journalist comments: 'Accused by a Frenchman, a Tunisian cannot fail to be guilty.' *Voix indigène*, 15 May 1930. Etc., etc.). The Ligue des Droits de l'Homme, the revolutionary parties, and certain philanthropists constantly denounced this sort of injustice. Thus V. Spielmann, author of many pamphlets on Algeria, *Le Centenaire au point de vue indigène*, 1930; Jean Mélia, *Le triste sort des indigènes d'Algérie*, etc.

[2] *Journal d'un exilé*, pp. 32 ff.

[3] The examination undertaken at my request by J.-P. Charnay of the Muslim cases quoted by *La Revue Algérienne* brings out the irrelevance of jurisprudence in this field, which itself reveals a certain failure of justice.

the situation had existed, and the territorial, social or mental *milieu*. It was inevitably a heavy burden on the just instincts of the population and the just aspirations of the individual. But the Maghrib of the inter war period was neither the Maghrib of the conquest nor that of the nationalist uprising. We must avoid anachronistic comparisons. At that time, radical protest was made only by the primitive warrior class, itself obsolescent, or by the bourgeois intelligentsia—the two extremes of Maghribi social types. Moreover, thorough-going exploitation was seldom revealed. Owing to the antiquity of the system and the specific nature of Franco-Maghrib relations, both the repression endured and the deliberate tension between groups were a matter for internal, or inward, jurisdiction—and this implies both their specific condition in the present and their freedom to construct the history of tomorrow: a strictly conditional liberty!

CHAPTER XIV

Types and Situations of the Time

A bundant material is available for anyone wishing to extend to the Maghrib of the interwar period the *Historic Iconography* which the late Gabriel Esquer had restricted to Algeria under the French conquest. Newsreels, private films, family photographs, collections of caricatures, annuals, illustrations from the daily press, and particularly such magazines as *L'Afrique du Nord illustrée*[1] enable us to reconstitute the look of the period. Glancing through these documents, we see marriage groups – brides escorted by sleek-headed pages. Here are tough little boxers showing off their muscles in preparation for their exhibition matches against visiting champions; Marcel Cerdan was to be one of their number. (The whole country worshipped physical strength; sports enthusiasts adopted El Ouafy (al-Wafi), who had won glory for France at the Olympic games in 1929. In such cases, racial differences were forgotten). Other pictures show Bastille Day parades, led by the *nuba* of sharp-shooters with its mascot, the ram; and in a very different style, the young Sultan of Morocco posing for the ceremony of the *hedya*,[2] very slim and pale, clad in his hieratic *jellaba* and shaded by his parasol. Governors and Residents, resplendent in gold braid, stand surrounded by their brilliant escorts of officers and Arab chiefs. Next we see the essential substructure of all the rest: photographs of dams, cornfields and orchards. The posters produced for the centenary all, almost without exception, exalt a topical symbol: the good *colon* with his good Arab.[3] Postage stamps, some of which, particularly those from Morocco, are very fine, illustrate the same theme. On a lower level, postcards showing 'views' of sites or monuments reflect the incongruous

---

[1] Published by J. Carbonel, who was connected in various ways with the firm of Bastide-Jourdan, established in the Place du Gouvernement soon after the capture of Algiers.

[2] *hedya*: the Moroccan chiefs' annual act of homage to the Sultan, on the occasion of canonic festivals.

[3] Described at length by G. Mercier in *Le Centenaire*.

conjunction of Orientalism and provincial homeliness; while those that show 'scenes and types' reduce to a picturesque or vulgar folklore such elements of independent life as the Maghrib still retained: its useless aspect, no doubt, but one which still attracted customers.

Returning to the pictures of those in power: they deserve a closer scrutiny, as they throng to a reception at the Summer Palace, for these are the masters of the hour, not indeed those who move behind the scenes and pull the strings, who provided subsidies, buy and re-sell, but those who officiate, who appear at ceremonies and parades. To begin with, the native 'notables', who well deserve their name. The 'spiritual' leaders, not the personnel of the mosques, mediocre figures despised both by their superiors and by their disillusioned flock, but others, 'rich, corrupt and triumphant', with swaggering gait, large appetites and easy morals, all wearing gold-embroidered turbans ostensibly brought back from pilgrimages, the Tunisian *kashta*. Others combine European and native dress, jackets and particularly waistcoats adorned with heavy watch chains, together with impressively billowing trousers, the *serwal*. The *Élus* have definitely adopted striped trousers; but most of them still wear the *tarbush*, since their electorate might disapprove of hats. On the French side, here are the dignitaries from the parent state. They have not all the senatorial manner of Lucien Saint, or Marcel Peyrouton's vigour, or the biting shrewdness of Noguès. Their attitudes and expressions are unconvincing; they are almost as depressing as those portraits of Second Empire soldiers, whose subsequent defeat one cannot forget. More lively, more vigorous, equally responsible are the managers of the colonial system.[1] Tough, crafty fellows, combining the ruthlessness of the North African with the wiliness of local politicians, they have a burly truculence which is fascinating; they seem to belong to a new race. And they are well aware of it. Almost invariably the mayor who accompanies a visiting minister of the French Government makes great play of his four-square toughness, his somewhat equivocal frankness. Brawny, full of vitality, exaggerating the physical appearance of a French farmer in a way that would be touching if we did not know it to be costly, he deliberately displays red cheeks, a broad-brimmed hat and a drooping moustache. This applies to men like Cuttoli, Morinaud, the late M. de Carnières, d'Aucouturier, and many others. Finally, their womenfolk: in Algeria, the local type definitely predominates; elsewhere, in Tunis, particularly at Rabat, society ladies display, in their dress and manner, a Metropolitan style that is only slightly overdone. But at the receptions in the Summer Palace, or tea-parties at the Oriental Hotel, the Algerian woman is in the majority. A dark and buxom beauty, embodying the ideal of the local photographer who has snapped her or the journalist who publishes her picture, she illustrates the pattern of the period, with her semi-Latin, semi-African grace and her somewhat exaggerated, yet

[1] Cf. H. Kleiss's caricatures, *Les Assemblées algériennes*, Algiers 1934.

quite Parisian elegance; she charms the manager in his leisure hours, and rewards the ambitions of the aspiring dignitary or of his son, who, after competing for the University stakes, has moved on to some liberal profession.

All these conquerors, and many more, forgathered at the reception held on 3 July 1930, in a Barbaresque villa of El Biar, known as the Villa du Traité.[1] Their faces and attitudes, as well as their biographies and their ideas, bear witness to a world which has now vanished, but which then thought itself established for ever.

'Companions of the Garden'

It was in 1934–5 that, if my interpretation is correct, the Maghrib crossed a decisive threshold. Shortly before that date a local writer had portrayed the principal characters at the very point when the pattern was about to change. R. Randau, who had returned to Algiers from French West Africa in 1933, was disturbed about the problem which was on everyone's mind, that of 'citizenship without loss of personal status,' in other words of assimilation combined with preservation. I have already referred to this project, shortly afterwards popularized under the name of the 'Projet Blum-Viollette'. As we know, the French Government, instigated by the ruling class of North Africa, was to reject this urgent, though respectful, appeal, and with it, many prospects for the future. Randau published, in collaboration with the Algerian writer 'Abd al-Qadir Fikri (the pseudonym of that Hajj Hammu who had made a speech at the Sidi Ferrush ceremony) a fictitious dialogue entitled *The Companions of the Garden*.[2]

The characters represent the Algerian world of that time. A European intellectual, visiting the South, corresponds with a Muslim friend in Algiers, one of the *évolués* as they say. The figures that surround them include: an old warrior chief, out of sympathy with his time, the Bashagha Bu Hamra; the marabout Ma'ammar, hostile to reformist aspirations, which threaten to affect his income; a *colon* of the pioneer breed, now out of date since he speaks Arabic; a financial delegate named Sidi 'Ali, deeply preoccupied by problems of mutual credit and business success; then, in Algiers, one Dr. Buzid, a self-made man of humble origin; a touching old schoolteacher, product of secular education; Sidi Lakhdar, an eloquent reformer, in whom we recognize Shaikh Taiyib al-'Uqbi. The book, moreover, closes with a conversation between Robert Randau and the Shaikh. We must also meet Sidi Lasfar, 'the Yellow One', a hypocritical and rapacious mufti; Mlle Jeanne, an outspoken woman lawyer; and finally young 'Isa, president

---

[1] Acquired by the Bashagha Bin Shiha, and placed by him at the disposal of the State.

[2] Algiers 1933.

of the Students' Association, such bodies having begun to play their part since 1930–he may perhaps be Ferhat Abbas.

The Egyptian actress Fatma Rushdi[1] had just scored a triumphant success in Algiers. An old believer asked her the embarassing question: 'Why have you given up wearing your veil?' To which she replied: 'A woman's true veil consists in her virtue.' Which took the wind out of the questioner's sails! Meanwhile traditionalist circles in Algiers were still worrying about the representation of the human form in photography, and objecting to the broadcasting of the Qur'an over the radio. But reformists retorted conclusively that Baghdad had just dedicated an equestrian statue to Feisal. A strange argument, indeed; the Maghrib had suffered so much from the isolation imposed by French rule that it took the Middle East as its pattern. As a matter of fact, traditionalist culture in all its forms was collapsing in Algeria. Educated men were scarce; and for some time past the craftsmen of the Casbah had begun to disappear–those exquisite jewellers, those workers in ivory who produced such beautiful daggers had now ceased to exist, except for tourists. Musical taste itself had declined, and now subsisted only in an almost unrecognized folklore. On the other hand new ways of life were beginning, timidly, to emerge. Algerian society was shocked by a wedding party recently held in a brasserie at Deux-Moulins. The bride and bridegroom, belonging to two leading families, had danced with their guests. However, at the end of the party, the ladies put on their veils again.[2]

This is what the period was like, with its hopes, its setbacks and its disturbances. Certain timid attempts at settling and housing the peasantry were made. According to official experience, when decent homes were provided for Arabo-Berbers they camped out with their animals in the courtyard. In fact, the administration built a few makeshift, Potemkin-type villages. The fellah was reluctant to settle in these. It had not yet been realized that the external characteristics of any society correspond to one another, and that it is impossible to alter the elements of a whole without altering all its correlations. For this reason, many reforms failed for over a hundred years. The failure, indeed, was not confined to Algeria, nor even to the Islamo-Mediterranean world. It was the common lot of those who were not yet known as 'basic educators'. So much so that in Tunis at that time, political reformers were afraid of social reformers, and everybody was shocked by the ideas of Tahar al-Haddad, without seeing that his syndicalism and feminism

---

[1] Her visit and that of the film *Unshudat al-fu'ad* (Song of the heart), 1932, met with strong disapproval from the authorities.

[2] In 1936, a son of the Bin Gana family married a Muslim girl from the Algiers bourgeoisie, a high school graduate. During all her stay at Biksra she had to submit to the rules of the gyneceum. (Unpublished note by an administrator.)

ought to form part of a single whole with the nationalist movement. In Algiers, as I have said, our 'companions' were chiefly concerned with Viollette's ideas, with the nascent '*Ulama*' movement and the articles recently published in the *Jeune Algérién*.

The book thus has the merit of reconstructing an élite of the period, more bourgeois than aristocratic in spirit, and more moderate than extremist; that is the least one can say. The 'companions' are well-educated people, almost too well educated. Their garden is a walled one; the Maghribi countryside stretches out all around it, and the Maghribi soil lies underneath it.

The Man at the Base

Underneath? Once more, we must return to the fellah, without seeking to reduce him to a single type. And yet there are features common to the Dukkala ploughman and the planter of Sfax which make his evolution one of the themes of this story. Behind the major conflicts of the period, we must picture the peasant and his world, dissatisfied, embittered, rapacious and hopeful. He clings tenaciously to every crack in the system, and builds his life there. His attitudes vary between subservience and non-compliance, from disinterestedness to greed. Innumerable studies and biographies are needed, masses of small facts must be collected—which hitherto have tempted nobody—to gauge the full importance of this figure, humbler and more obscure but more significant than many others. Peasant life was affected by the economic and moral systems, and by politics, as much as it affected them. It was in fact the substructure of everything else in the Maghrib. It was concerned not only with the evolution of the relations of production: the decline of the sharecropping system, and of the system of remunerating herdsmen by a share of the animals born, and the gradual replacement of these methods by the payment of wages,[1] or the evolution of religious attitudes, for instance the decrease in the prestige of marabouts and brotherhoods—but with other phenomena, common enough indeed but of tremendous consequence: the use of chairs and tables,[2] of plates, the initiation into the mysteries of official forms, the preference for sedentary dwellings over tents, the spread of new foods, new ways of dress, behaviour and speech. And nobody, at the time, kept a systematic note of all this, which was so essential.

This peasant was still a pawn rather than an agent in what was going on. But everyone was frightened of his silent strength. Resistance had cost him terrible losses, which he seemed to have forgotten, or of which he never spoke. Perhaps he was waiting, or perhaps he was reluctant to yield to the temptation of the modern world, of which the foreigner

[1] A fundamental subject which has been insufficiently explored.
[2] To evade legal distraint Algerians also invested in high metal beds.

offered him so meagre a share. So much has been written about him, his superstitions, his primitiveness, that we almost lose sight of him as a historic human being, under the weight of accumulated learning and of action, both equally concerned to treat him as mere building material. Now the real problem was just the opposite: to find out from him what of his latent power still survived, and what mutations and substitutions were needed to bring about its ultimate resurgence, maybe in the unexpected form of an industrial worker. Here again, the novelty of the task is baffling. I hope that implicitly my story will reveal the gigantic adventure which is even now taking place.

For the moment I wish only to stress three aspects, because they are revealed by first-hand documents.

The first comes from a profound observer of Northern Morocco, who has lived there uninterruptedly from 1911 to the present day.[1] Recalling his memories to compare the picture of the Moroccan labourer at two periods as distinct as those preceding the first and the second world wars, he writes to me as follows:

My 1912 picture is that of a tall, thin, nonchalant man. On his head he wore a *rezza* (a calico band swathed round his skull), on his body a *qmija* (a piece of light-weight material folded in two, with an opening for his head and with the sides sewn together to within eight inches of the top to allow the arms to come through). He rarely wore trousers, but always a belt of rope or leather. As soon as autumn drew near with its cold and damp he would put on his *jellaba*, made of coarsely woven wool, thick and greyish in colour, almost waterproof owing to the goat hairs or strands of wool. The hood with which he covered his head in rainy weather also served to store his food. His shoes consisted of rectangular pieces of untanned ox-hide, with which he surrounded the soles of his feet. The hairy side was outermost. The leather edges, bound with laces made of palm fibre, hugged the foot and were fastened at the ankle; the whole thing formed a convenient kind of leather sabot.

His work consisted of driving animals, donkeys, oxen or horses, yoked in pairs by a bent branch of hard olive wood, to which was bound a piece of metal, fastened with a metal ring and wooden wedges, which made it easier to scrape and lift the surface of the earth after the rains had fallen. He would hold the instrument in one hand, the whip and the reins with the other. The area under cultivation generally comprised five or six teams, often belonging to the same owner, supervised by a *muqaddim*. Other labourers, associates or small landowners, worked on their own property or on collective farmlands.

When you went past these groups of workers in the countryside, generally on horseback, in the autumn or spring, you were given a friendly welcome. If you made the slightest effort to talk, the labourers

[1] My friend Émile Biarnay, to whom I wish to express my gratitude.

would stop working. They would gather together and talk, their curiosity aroused. Then one of them would draw from his hood a piece of unleavened bread made of wheat, barley or millet, which he unceremoniously offered to the stranger, even if the latter were European. *Hak reghif; sherrek t-ta'am.* You would accept his offer: *Baraka'llah u fik; Rebbi ikhlef'.* You had made acquaintance; you were friends. Before leaving him you could say to him (here followed a few proverbs) to which he would sometimes reply with a smile: *Jat, ma krehnash; ma jat-sh, ma tkeserna-sh,* 'if the harvest comes, so much the better; if it doesn't, we shall not be any worse off.'

Thirty years later, about 1940:

In the field, we met other labourers. They bore no resemblance to those of old. On his head the new peasant sometimes wore a *rezza,* or else a close-fitting cap, *tagya,* or a peaked cap. On his body, a ready-made shirt with sleeves. A pair of trousers bought in the market, or from a pedlar—the latter did not exist formerly; he bought his stock from tradesmen at Suq al-Arba' or Kenitra, who renewed theirs from the wholesale merchants on the Mediuna road (Casablanca), who in their turn received them in large bales.

A jacket, often bearing letters indicating its origin. A worn pair of trousers, whose pockets were frequently turned out in the hopes of finding some forgotten object. Shoes of coarse leather, which fitted more or less.

He sometimes drove a metal plough, but to his chagrin he could not replace or tighten the screws for lack of an adjustable spanner.

He was clothed indeed, but no longer by the same tradesmen. He earned more money, but he had just as little left.

When you talked to him, he was less forthcoming, less curious, more indifferent. If you greeted him in Arabic he would reply *bonjour* in French. Instead of offering you bread, he asked you for a cigarette, or wanted to know the time.

True enough; the immemorial was now disturbed by its initiation into time.

The second document comes from a former Civil Controller in Tunisia. He gives a vivid picture of those petty leaders who emerged from the masses and whose proliferation, after a certain date, might seem like spontaneous generation if it had not, on the contrary, reflected the resurgence of long buried forces.

In 1934 I was stationed at X . . . My boss learned that the number of cells of the Destour party had strangely increased in a completely isolated region that could only be reached with difficulty along bad roads, and where no Frenchman lived or owned lands: the Blad Regeb. This was due to a little old man, without property or apparent prestige, who wore a white beard like a shaikh's. He could scarcely read or write. But his eyes glittered with inner fire, which seemed to consume him. His least remarks were always uttered in a vehement tone of mystic exaltation. There was something slightly mischievous about him. It all formed a curious mixture. Later, in the district of Suq al-Arba', I met other individuals of the same type, almost always old men, who were efficient leaders of the crowd in rural areas. I have the impression that the Party has neglected them since the achievement of independence.

To go back to our friend, the authorities were beginning to worry about his influence. My boss, who was a broad-minded man with a sense of humour, had nicknamed him 'the Lion of Regeb'. Then came repression under Peyrouton, and the order to break up the cells. This operation gave rise to a kind of expiatory ceremony. We went to the spot in question. And there, close to a *hanut* (stall or room) lost in the middle of this vast steppe, the caïd had gathered together the 'culprits', those who held Party cards, the Lion at their head, in the presence of all the shaikhs and a large crowd summoned thither for its edification. The cards were publicly burned. The caïd, an insignificant person, an alcoholic and a dishonest judge, admonished the sinners. Meanwhile the Lion stood silent. But on his face, with its extraordinarily mobile features, one could read all the emotions that he was trying to repress: anger, sarcasm, irony and contempt . . .

And was that time to which the peasant had gained access to be the Time of Contempt?

The third document, taken from Algeria's history, illustrates the role of the marabouts, inseparable at that time from rural life.

In 1794, in the neighbourhood of Mostaganem, was born in the Mejaher tribe the future Shaikh Muhammad al-Snusi (Sanusi), who died at Jaghbub in 1859, and whose descendant King Idris is the present ruler of Libya, by the grace of God and of Great Britain. In 1796, in the same tribe, was born one of his cousins, Sharif bin Takkûk,[1] who, on his return from Fez to Algeria after the occupation, founded there in 1859 a Sanusi *zawiya*, Bugirat, near Lhillil. He died there in 1890, having endured political internment. His son and successor Ahmad, who had returned from Jaghbub in 1893, was also interned by the French. On his death in 1924, he was succeeded by Shaikh 'Abd al-Qadir bin Takkuk. Meanwhile the Administration had become favourably inclined towards the *zawiya*. This change took place about 1914. The seditious movement of the Bani Shugran was in fact checked, thanks to the Shaikh, on the outskirts of the commune. During the food shortage of 1920 the *zawiya* sheltered a number of destitutes, presumably to its advantage in this world and the next.

[1] Unpublished note by the administrator Freychet.

These developments illustrate the rule that maraboutism, beyond a certain stage, ceases to express or rather to reveal the secret forces of Maghribi society. Whereas it became wealthy and 'loyalist', other champions arose. They were sometimes recruited, in traditional fashion, from the same family. While Shaikh 'Abd al-Qadir bin Takkûk served France and made use of her, his cousins the Latrush fought against him, challenged his investiture and finally supported the dissidence of one of his brothers (1931). This rivalry assumed electoral form. The two rival systems contested for the nomination of caïds and aghas, for decorations and credits. Shaikh 'Abd al-Qadir himself was crippled with debts. 'A great lord, extremely domineering and proud, and much favoured by the Administration,' he found no suitor noble enough for his daughters. As he had thrown in his lot with the French, the rival branch supported the opposition movement.

But while these hostile brethren, under successive régimes, went on challenging one another's claims, other 'signs' appeared on the horizon. From 1931 onwards the influence of the *'Ulama'* pervaded rural areas, appealing to Islamic tradition. Their moral reforms mobilized national resistance forces and thus paradoxically fulfilled the same function as the maraboutism which, after an interval of perhaps one generation, it had supplanted. The present crisis provoked a new substitution, in which political disagreements predominated unquestionably over religious controversy. Only through later developments is it possible to tell whether, in the Mostaganem region or elsewhere, the shift of emphasis from religion corresponded to an enduring evolution in the minds of the peasantry, and whether the new symbols that influenced it were entirely of another order.

The Business Man

In the twenties, Claude Farrère visited Morocco, and wishing to extol Lyautey's achievement, portrayed in a novel[1] some of the more picturesque figures of that time.

The noble figure of a pioneer officer is contrasted with that of a business man. We meet the latter returning by boat from France to Morocco, in conversation—soon to take an amorous turn—with a French lady, on the deck at night. The business man, who has retained all his youthful energy, pours out his heart. He is a self-made man. He began as a caravan leader, even before the establishment of the Protectorate. One of his colleagues' most profitable methods was to take back baskets-full of camels' ears, to show their employer that the caravan had met with disaster and that many animals would have to be replaced. In this and

---

[1] *Les hommes nouveaux*, which received a glowing review by Ladreit de Lacharrière. Such men were characteristic of the Lyautey period: not only business men but also technicians such as J. Delure, who began as a workman.

other ways this enterprising business man made good. 'From 1910 to 1912 I bought camels and mules, sold them, bought more. I travelled on all the roads of Morocco. In 1910 I had five thousand francs; in 1912 I had three thousand!' Transport was a vital factor in the process of penetration, so that building up his own fortune became a patriotic duty: 'The old *bled* had to be changed into a civilized country at one blow!' Now civilized countries 'can be bought and sold at so much the square yard.' So then, 'in 1914 I made twelve thousand francs. I had acquired a few shops here and there, at Casa and Fez' (shops which happened to coincide with town planners' development schemes—people have to help one another!) 'I'd sold a bit of everything: canned goods, meat, bread, wine, flour, linen, cloth, all the necessities of life. Finally I became a trader in lands. I had done well by myself, and I'd done well by the Empire.' And the French lady, who has high principles, sighs: 'You did the right thing.' Nevertheless she asks him: 'How did you happen to stay in Morocco while others were at war?' For all through the war he was increasing his original capital by 200 or 300 per cent.

True, this man had often risked his life on the highways and in the slums of Morocco, as fearless as he was tireless. He remained a man of the people, part Cévenol outlaw, part Mediterranean tough and part American gangster. Loud-mouthed, greedy and randy, strong-featured, zestful at work and in pursuit of pleasure, he went about in baggy corduroy trousers over heavy boots, with a gorgeous zouave belt under a waistcoat with buttons missing. By way of apéritif he liked pernod, or even coarse red wine. Throughout the twenties he could often be seen at the Hotel Excelsior in Casablanca, in session with kindred spirits. It was of such men that the Marshal was thinking when he made his famous remark, that one could not build a country with the winners of good conduct prizes. He was a pioneer, a kind of Caliban. In him were mingled the vices and aptitudes of both races. Naturally, he spoke Arabic, and his Moroccan craftiness was strengthened by a typically Western stubbornness. He was law-abiding, or at least he knew how to keep within the law as far as possible, and was even more adept at buying the goodwill of anyone who might get in his way . . .

Such a man might end up as a big *colon*, a powerful entrepreneur, a rich landowner, a magnate in transport or mines, director of a chain of newspapers or vice-president of a large municipality. He would become an important figure, almost an honourable one, who dined with the Resident-General and married his daughter into the nobility. By the thirties he would have been decorated with the Legion of Honour and thus absolved from certain of his youthful sins. With age he would have lost much of his vehemence, but also many of his aptitudes. A good stroke of business was now no longer something achieved by energy and cunning but by bargaining in offices. The Arab world, whose perils and

whose fascination influenced his youth so powerfully, had now paradoxically disappeared from his calculations. He now saw it as consisting
of types to be made use of, without terror or glamour: workmen, bus
passengers, obsequious notables, not yet competitors or even consumers.

The third stage would show our man, forgetful of his youth, aspiring
only to the enjoyment of power. He wants nothing more from Morocco
than a pretext for his speculations. He had completely lost sight of the
reality of the country. He himself is no more than an *assignat*, which can
now be justly criticized for the crudity of its aspect.

This species of men, risen from the people, grew rarer as North Africa
grew older, which happened rapidly under the colonial régime. Nobody
has studied their careers, nor what part they played in the real working
of the machine, allowance being made for differences of period and
region. The fact is that beside this tough, truculent man of affairs, there
were others of a more discreet type who wielded real power. Nobody
denounced these save the Communists. Public opinion only concerned
itself with them when feelings ran high, immediately after the first or
second world wars for instance, or during the Popular Front period.[1]
Even today, in a way that is strangely naïve, anti-colonialism is readier to
attack local personalities, because they are more colourful, than those
who coldly manipulate capital, and who are unfortunately more active
than ever in the affairs of Metropolitan France, even in those of the
liberated countries. The *colons*, however, knew better. Their periodical
attacks on the bank, which they obeyed but loathed, showed a clearer understanding of the relative positions, in the economic hierarchy, of the
animator and the mere executive, whether business man or client. It is
clear, as many passages in this book bear witness, that they took their
revenge in local affairs, in terms of power and profit and of psychological
suggestion. But behind them, and far above them, loomed the shadowy
figure of the financier. He was seldom resident in North Africa; his
activities kept him in Paris for most of the time. He knew how to fix
himself up locally with friends and collaborators, not drawn exclusively
from among his business managers and acquaintances. Through the
solidarity that reigned between members of the Government and international capitalism, he was frequently associated with the proconsul and
his officials. The part played by the financier in the creation and destruction of the colonial system was a considerable one.

Consider, for example, the role of the Hersent group in connection
with the little port of Fedala[2], which was devoted to the export of petrol-
eum. The promoter of the group, Georges Hersent, had created the
whole thing. He had obtained a concession for building and exploitation

[1] Cf. for instance the brochure *Maroc, voici tes maîtres*, published by La Libre
Pensée, 1937.
[2] 'A typical example of French colonization in Morocco,' said M. Peyrouton,
Itinéraire de Casablanca à Tunis, 1922, p. 33.

as early as 1913. Thereafter, of course, he bought land cheap, at about 5 francs the square metre perhaps; twenty years later it was worth 150 to 300 francs. His nephews kept up the business. They exploited, in addition to the port of Fedala, huge harbour enterprises at Casablanca, Safi, Bizerta and Lisbon, and even as far afield as Rosario in the Argentine. In 1937 they were granted credits on a large scale, on Swiss capital. 100,000 shares of a managing and profit-sharing land-holding were distributed among the shareholders. And at least twenty-five firms could be mentioned which, already, came under the control of the group.

But this was a small concern compared with those actuated by the Morocco State Bank, itself dependent on the Banque de Paris et des Pays-Bas. This is a typical example of those enterprises which, dealing with every sort of commodity from the lead of Zellija to the phosphates of Southern Tunisia, by way of the iron of Mukta al-Hadid, and with every activity from imports to lighting, not forgetting transport nor, of course, the purchase and sale of 'property', dispense investments, administer energy, introduce techniques and thus pursue wealth through the agency of human beings. I have already mentioned Laurent-Atthalin. The history of Morocco, although it finds a place for far smaller figures, has tactfully omitted him. I am not concerned with analysing his activities – which only a specialist could do – nor with passing judgment on an achievement which naturally invites controversy. I am only interested here in the figure of this hero of the *grande bourgeoisie*, a former student of the Polytechnique, and *maître des requêtes* in the State Council.

'Of medium height, slender, with a sallow complexion and the black eyes of a magician,' he is thus described by one of his former collaborators, extolling the abilities and style of this immensely powerful figure. By means of the Compagnie Générale des Colonies, he was influential in every sphere of the French empire. In Morocco he was behind the State Bank, the Tobacco companies, the Tangier-Fez railway, the Compagnie Générale; he inspired the research projects into hydroelectric power, he 'combined' railway companies, and by his influence on the magnate Epinat he coordinated motor transport; he eased the colonists' debts by arranging for the State Bank to participate in the Caisse Fédérale; and so forth.

Power of this type, like some vast vegetative growth, tends to stifle anything extraneous to itself. This monopoly was in fact exercised with a consistency unknown in Algeria and still more in Tunisia. It was presumably oppressive by nature and ruinous in the long run, and it undoubtedly weighed inordinately on French policy in North Africa. Only the colonial situation, like any other human situation, cannot be considered solely in economic terms: neither the individual nor the group can be reduced to the laws that determine them. The Lyautey period was certainly the most inspiring moment in France's colonial history, since the Egyptian expedition. And yet it would not be false to consider Atthalin as the counterpart, in the financial world, of the great Marshal, and the latter as the legendary representative of capitalist enterprise. The correctness of both these statements illustrates the ambiguity of individual talent and, so to speak, the *redundancy* of the human element.

The Left Wing

A section of Left wing opinion had, at the time, put forward a critical interpretation of Lyauteyism, in a polemical context and with attitudes which provide us with a new subject of observation. Just as we have recognized in the business man at various levels one of the leading spirits of the time, his counter-type, the Left-winger, also presents an interesting figure. Just as among the men of the Maghrib, after a certain date, the restoration of local vitality went hand in hand with the growth of nationalist feeling, so among the French, the existence of parties corresponded to a passionate involvement of social conscience with ideology. But only Left wing parties deserve mention here. Not that the others, such as the Croix de Feu in 1935, were lacking in vitality. But they were far from expressing so significantly certain problems and certain attitudes. For neither the traditional Right wing, nor Fascism, replaced what was then called the *esprit colon*, or equalled it in interpreting the aspiration of the privileged elements. It did not indeed function as an active party, like its opponents on the Left. For Socialism, as well as providing a framework for co-operation and action, offered analyses and tackled problems, and its hypotheses had a considerable influence on Muslim opinion.

Tunis-socialiste,[1] originally a weekly, appeared daily from 1924 to 1934, a time of relative freedom for the Press in Tunisia. It was during this period—which corresponds, curiously enough, with the phase of economic recession—the only Socialist daily in non-Metropolitan France. Its suspension by Peyrouton in 1934 coincides with the repression endured by the Neo-Destour, to whom the paper had frequently offered 'rights of asylum'. It revived at the time of the Popular Front, but collapsed again after the grave events of 1938. Its lively contacts with the world around it ensured it plenty of advertisements: we read in its pages praise of Sidi Da'ud's *butarg*, a kind of vermouth, 'the Socialist's apéritif', of a certain dentist, and of the monumental mason Bu Khubza. Such traits of local colour appear side by side with elaborate doctrinal arguments, with the ruthless commentaries of Duran-Angliviel (*La fenêtre ouverte*) or Cohen-Hadria (*Pointes de feu*). Thus for many years an attempt was carried on to provide honest information, justice

[1] The complete files of which I was able to consult, thanks to Dr. Cohen-Hadria.

and education. And although it did not offer unconditional support to the nationalist movement, indeed had its moments of disagreement and controversy with it, the contribution of this paper and the movement of ideas and activities which it reflects, on the intellectual, political and syndicalist planes, is even today considered of value by the Tunisians.

La Lutte sociale,[1] in Algiers, was an organ of the Communist party. Immediately after the first world war, Communism was very active in Algiers and also in Tunis, where militants such as Louzon and Finidori had some influence on local elements. After a phase of collapse due to repression, the movement revived at the time of the Rif affair. Cachin made a vigorous attack in the Chamber against the granting of military credits, and demanded consideration for the peace offers initiated by the British journalist Gordon Canning.[2] The themes of national liberation and of social revolution were here united; but this unity was to suffer setbacks.

At Bizerta a little clandestine journal called Bu Shkara, 'the man with the wallet' (i.e. the capitalist), distributed tracts, together with those of the North African Star, which had its seat in Paris. But the Communist party dissociated itself from the latter group. True, it asserted its unfailing sympathy with colonial efforts towards emancipation, but it denied any connection with these organizations. Hence there developed all sorts of actions, reactions and interactions, which aroused police interest, and with whose complexities the present study is not concerned.

One point that must be stressed, however, is the inevitable reaction of the local authorities. Even supposedly democratic or progressive Residents, men like Steeg or Viollette, struck back as hard as the rest. France had decided to deal firmly with Abd el-Krim. In 1926 the Ujda talks proved abortive. There was a public scandal about an agency for deserters at Casablanca, involving Carette-Bouvet, editor of the Cri Marocain. Many people were convicted.

One would like to go beyond this jumble of events, which it is not easy to clarify, and to envisage a general picture. I shall confine myself to tracing, from first-hand information, the evolution of attitudes towards Moroccan emancipation.[3]

On 26 September 1925 a branch of the S.F.I.O. (French section of the Workers' International) was formed at Marrakesh. 'Instinctively, the French population of Morocco, accustomed to clear thinking and de-

[1] Cf. Afrique française, 1920, pp. 20 ff.

[2] Renseignements coloniaux, 1926, pp. 20 ff; cf. Renseignements coloniaux, 1928, p. 652, 'La propagande communiste en Afrique du Nord'. This review frequently reverts to the same subject. Cf. for instance. Afrique française, 1928, p. 98, L'écume du Maroc français '.

[3] I owe much of the (unpublished) information in the following paragraph to an old militant democrat of Rabat, Arthur Biau.

cisive action in business affairs, has given its approval, in part at any rate, to the re-establishment of a logical order of things,'[1] that proposed by Socialism which, by means of that very logic, applied to basic matters, 'will assert its influence over our sound and vigorous youth.' In 1928 a prospector from the Belgian Company of Ougree-Marihee discovered coal at Jerada. The Socialist Party, denouncing the anarchic speculation which was rife in this industry, demanded that it should be nationalized, as the phosphates industry had been. The B.R.P.M. (*Bureau de recherches et de participations minières*) of Eirik Labonne, to which I have already referred, cut through these contradictory petitions. This was too much for the Trusts, and the initiator faced defeat once again. At about the same date, and in much the same spirit, the association of Public Services published a brochure recommending State monopoly of motor fuel. It denounced the dangers of single crop-husbandry, protested against the inadequacy of the S.I.P.'s (*Sociétés indigènes de prévoyance*), and asked for the institution of a Wheat Office.

In this, these progressive civil servants, from whom the Left wing was almost exclusively drawn, showed themselves possessed of foresight. But an element of somewhat equivocal uncertainty hampered the actions of the movement. What about the future of the colony as such? What about the permanence, or on the other hand of a possible easing, of the relations between France and the local population? On such points, most of these Left wing movements show hesitation. True, at that time men's understanding of the situation, indeed the situation itself, had not reached the point at which clearcut solutions could be envisaged. Already in 1926, at the Interfederal Socialist Congress of North Africa, held in France,[2] the Tunisian section had published a pamphlet in which we read: 'The Socialist Party does not seek to use the colonies as a field for socialist experiment; it merely claims for them a social status inspired by that of Metropolitan France; it seeks to enable the local populations to achieve their own evolution, and to put them *as far as possible* (my italics) on the same level as the population of the parent state . . .' Finally, it shows extreme consideration for its mandators, officials of the lower and middle grades. And its resolution, passed on 4 April 1926 admits that 'colonization is in itself legitimate.' The most that can be sought is social equality. Social and political ideals are thus, quite wrongly, opposed to one another.

Consequently there was much uncertainty in the relations between the Moroccan S.F.I.O. and the nascent nationalist movement. The paper *Maroc Socialiste*[3] attacked the review *Maghreb*, whose leading spirit was

[1] *Cri du Maroc*, 26 Sept. 1925.
[2] Cf. *Renseignements coloniaux*, 1926, p. 103.
[3] Le Nabec, delegate from the Third College, in *Maroc socialiste*, 5 May 1934. *Le Progrès de Fès* takes up the cudgels for Dr. Christiani, who had been personally attacked by *Maghreb*.

R.-J. Longuet. 'We do not want the Moroccan workers to be sacrificed to the appetites of a few young bourgeois.' Was this clearsightedness, or an excuse? The leaders of the party considered that 'freeing a nation does not necessarily mean freeing its proletariat. Only when those fundamental liberties have been gained will the problem arise of orientating the colony towards an international community.' *Maghreb* retorted that the French militants in Morocco were suffering from the distorted viewpoint of colonialism. Correspondingly, North African nationalism sought its allies elsewhere than among the Metropolitan Left wing, which stood accused of Jacobin assimilationism. But it is only fair to point out that Moroccan S.F.I.O. courageously protested against the ban on *Maghreb*.[1]

I come now to Moroccan Socialism's more positive achievement, its denunciation of scandals and its constant battle for the respect of human rights. It devoted a monograph, the first of its kind perhaps, to the deplorable shanty-town of Rabat, the Duwar Dum,[2] pointing out that workers' pay there did not exceed 3 francs per day under private employers and varied between 3·50 and 5 francs in municipal undertakings. In this dispossessed suburb, the *sha'ush* became the aristocrat. Small tradesmen, humble retailers, with a capital of one to four hundred francs, made 1·50 to 3 francs per day. How could a budget be built up on such minimal resources? Now philanthropists were urging economy on wretches who lived below the economic level! The authors try to estimate the indispensable expenditure on food. For four people, this comes to about three francs, excluding *couscous*, poultry or condiments. A man in this plight earns just enough to keep him alive.

Protest occasionally resulted in dangerous tension with the Government. In February 1934, the Socialist delegates of the Third College left the Council's session.[3] Their motion, a daring one for the time, protested against a system of administration which not only did not practise, or allow to be practised, any control over authority, but substituted for this what was locally known as 'authority to control'. On this point they came into conflict with those members of the ruling class who controlled the daily Press (the 'Mas chain'). In 1938 the Casablanca section, exasperated by this opposition, put forward a motion, one passage in which reveals all the ambiguity of French Left wing thought in a colonial country: Socialism in Morocco must avoid two equally fatal perils, 'on the one hand, to abstain from the struggle for national emancipation, under pretext of defending the social demands

---

[1] *Le Populaire marocain*, 29 June 1933.

[2] Study by L. Paye and Baron published in the *Bulletin économique du Maroc*, then in *L'Écho du Maroc*, 11 and 12 Aug. 1936. *La République* (8 Mar. 1935) deplores the housing situation in Morocco.

[3] The conflict arose about the demand for an eight-hour day and for higher wages (agricultural labourers worked 14 hours for 2 francs 50 a day, declared Maître de Carbuccia, S.F.I.O. delegate from Meknès).

of the masses exclusively, would be to play into the imperialists' hands; on the other, to abstain from defending the social demands of the masses under pretext of fighting exclusively for national liberation would be to play into the hands of the Moroccan bourgeoisie.' The dilemma was put thus in 1938, and needless to say, heralded others far more violent, whose solution is unfortunately still to be found at the time of writing.

The difficulty of the conflict was due not only to the historic conditions by which the French Socialist derived certain benefits, moral and material, from the colonial situation. It resided fundamentally in the complexity of the latter. European domination merely reflected, and to a certain extent usurped, the expansion of technical culture. Now this expansion brought with it social and mental relations historically in advance of the civilizations which it affected. This incontestable fact overruled every other aspect, in the early stages of the situation. The so-called 'civilizing' character of colonization resulted not only from its direct achievements but still more from the reactions it aroused in the native population. Nationalism was in many respects one of these reactions. Socialism, aware of the subtle intermixture of positive and negative, could only base its choice, as between national and social ideals, on an analysis of local conditions and customs, on considerations of method and of timing. Now we are well aware today that the nationalist ideal was bound to prevail, at least provisionally, over any other, in countries seeking emancipation. Already at that time it had won the support, not of all but of the majority of Maghribi leaders. One can scarcely blame European socialists for not having had the same intuition. Bred in the French Jacobin tradition, they were saved from chauvinism only by an internationalism itself in advance of nationalist aspirations. Even today, many 'liberals', breaking away from imperialistic egoism, do so by identifying themselves with 'the Other', which implies failing to recognize his difference.[1]

The 'Little Men'

This is not the only discovery, as embarrassing in practice as it is stimulating to theory, resulting from decolonization. One of the surprises of the present period is the attachment to the colonial status shown by people whom one would have expected to be indifferent to it. Civil servants, clerks, humble European tradesmen, had no connection with the play of monopolies nor with capitalist investment, except in so far as they suffered from these; in a different way from the native, but almost as

[1] In connection with the ideological controversy between socialism and nationalism one should quote the important discussion that took place at Tunis in 1932, on the occasion of André Philip's visit. Cf. the unpublished *Souvenirs* of Dr. Cohen-Hadria; *Voix du Tunisien*, 23 April 1932. Such controversies, followed by reconciliations, lasted throughout the colonial era.

shockingly. They had no share in the responsibilities of rule nor in the joys of action. They were thus devoid of any sort of colonial ethos. And yet they fell into line with the attitude of the ruling class, by a process shrewdly described by A.-P. Lentin.[1] This presents the analyst with a difficult problem. This large social group, whose average income was less than that they would have enjoyed in Metropolitan France, contradicted their objective role by their feelings, and their economic situation by the way they behaved. The fact that they benefited indirectly from belonging to the preponderant race, that for lack of technical accomplishment or wealth they prided themselves on their origins, that they drifted into a sort of racial prejudice although they could by no means be considered as 'exploiters', has often been demonstrated, in depressing analyses, with a wealth of reasons which would have been more convincing if they had come earlier. With the hindsight due to facts, we can indeed recognize today, in certain attitudes of the twenties and thirties, the germ of others which would have amazed us at the time. What could be more legitimate than the 'colonial third',[2] or the vitality of regionalist feelings? But already at that time the opposition of Tunisian nationalism to the plethora of civil servants and their demands, for instance, or to the solidarity of Corsican employees in certain jobs, went far beyond the specific occasion, to anticipate the problem of the *petits blancs*.

Any arguments based on such a viewpoint would be anachronistic. Not only did the 'little men', at that time, feel themselves in opposition to the 'big men', but they often took up native causes, played an active role in Left wing parties, put liberal theses into practice. In certain towns it was they who elected progressive councils, upheld the Popular Front in its day, demanded and eventually won, on the pretext of representing the consumer, the establishment of a 'Third College' in the Moroccan Council of Government.[3] They were responsible for strongly pro-Muslim motions. They eventually secured the gratitude, or the tolerance, of the Trade Union movement for Maghribi workers.[4] Above all they

---

[1] *Cahiers internationaux*, 1957, no. 77 ff; *Faim et soif*, July–Aug. 1961 ('Le drame de Bab el Oued').

[2] In so far as it was considered as a supplementary compensation for expatriation. It is ironical that such 'advantages', granted by international services of technical assistance, aroused no protestation. In such cases, of course, they weighed less directly on local budgets . . .

[3] Cf. *Renseignements coloniaux*, 1926, p. 542. The Third College was set up by a decree of the Resident, 13 Oct. 1926. With regard to the first election to the Third College, see *Afrique française*, 1927, p. 260; it deplores the intrusion of politics into the presumably apolitical problems of Morocco. At the Council of the Moroccan Government, the defence of the small peasant was only undertaken by the Third College. Cf. for instance the report of Arensdorff on the *paysanat* (proposals for the peasants' welfare), at the session of 28 June 1938.

[4] In Tunisia, with Manceron (1933). In Morocco, under Noguès (the Bonnet decrees which, since they excluded Moroccans from unions, was often criticized from 1943 onwards).

constituted the crowd, that crowd which gradually concentrated in the large sea-coast towns, overflowed from the outskirts into the fashionable districts, and indulged in tumultuous demonstrations which were not, at the time, those of the extreme Right. On the contrary, they claimed to be democratic and pro-Muslim, and were recognized as such by the Maghrib.

True, through competing with natives for authority over workmen or in the lower grades of the administration, and through the conflict of mores in unsegregated suburbs, this group had acquired a petty bourgeois rather than a working-class mentality. In North Africa Europeans, even when poor, were 'working class' only by procuration. But many people of the Maghrib were taken in by this, as were these Europeans. They were recruited partly from the rejects of the colonial adventure: failed tradesmen, settlers of the pre-vineyard era, dispossessed by later developments; and partly from non-French Mediterranean people, frantically seeking assimilation to all things French. Most of these, whether they remained aliens or acquired the privileged status, intervened only indirectly in public affairs. We are struck, when we read the list of members of the Assemblies, to find that they are almost invariably of French origin. Names implying Italian, Spanish or Maltese descent[1] become numerous only much later. The same is true of the Administrative Councils; while the lists of scholarly successes often show a young Muslim beating the sons of naturalized Frenchmen.

Tensions grew markedly among these second-class citizens. Each took pride in his own achievements, in imitation of French models. For there was severe competition between them for trifling profits, petty honours, and comfortable settlements. Each accused the other of stealing 'the Frenchman's bread' or the 'Arab's bread' as the case might be. This rivalry, which did not constitute emulation, could lead only to race hatred. Its culminating point was reached in connection with the total assimilation of the Jews, which provoked aggressive bitterness among the Muslims.

For this large group of European origin or status sought primarily to be integrated into the French system. It was impelled by a savage vitality. While rigidly hierarchized in its economic strata and its functions, it became increasingly unified by a melting-pot process which gave it an awareness of its interests and a pride in its distinctive characteristics. These were not mere folklore, but in folklore they find self-awareness and vivid expression: 'Hernandez is a highly-strung creature, in whom are found all the qualities and defects of the *homo mediterraneus*. He feels obscurely that he is the more or less legitimate descendant of three ancient divinities: the Sea, the Sun and, to some extent, Jupiter.'

---

[1] Whose representatives were deeply concerned, until quite recently, to establish their *integration* with France. Cf. for instance the importance ascribed to this problem by Demontès.

From the sea he gets his versatility, 'the ideal of serenity...and the love of violence. The sun has given him a zest for life conducive to optimism but not precluding indolence. Jupiter has given him pride . . . For our Hernandez is the complete mythical Frenchman.'[1]

Hernandez does not express himself much in the press. In the *Écho d'Oran*, for instance, he appears only at errand-boy level. In all this he is treated as an object rather than as a subject, somewhat like the fellah to whom he feels, and above all believes, himself to be fundamentally opposed. On the other hand he respects the 'gentlemen'[2] who, privileged by their origins ('Frenchmen from France'), their merit (ex-soldiers, retired N.C.O.'s), or their learning (schoolteachers), provide the link within the same district or the same business concern, between his inarticulate though loud-mouthed group and the lower strata of Authority. He sometimes gets on to the Municipal Council, or gets his delegates on to it: for instance the Abbé Lambert, who became Mayor of Oran, and whose photographs were said to be used as amulets for men on fishing expeditions, or for women against difficult pregnancies.[3]

Lower grade officials, particularly where bureaucracy made them proliferate, as in Tunisia and Morocco, constituted a relatively important body. They fostered a certain vein of opposition which often coincided with that of the Left, although it was never identical with it. The *Cri Marocain* concerned itself with personalities and complaints. Its attacks though sometimes of questionable integrity, are frequently amusing and even pertinent. Sometimes it ridicules a high official, who, doubtless in quest of statistics, pays a visit to the famous Busbir.[4] Sometimes it attacks the Banque de Paris et des Pays-Bas.[5] It comments, not without perspicacity: 'Not many years have elapsed since the French population of Morocco first became aware of its own social reality. To begin with it formed merely a sort of appendix to the central power': a definition

[1] Jean Olivieri, 'Plaidoyer pour la famille Hernandez', *Monde*, 25 Feb. 1960. Other articles by Jean Cohen, 'La grande peur des petits blancs', ibid., by André Bénichoux, 'Plaidoyer pour les Français d'Algérie', ibid. Also, with a different emphasis, but in a brilliant and often profound fashion, the books of A. Memmi, *Portrait du colonisateur*; J. Pélegri, *Les oliviers de la justice*; and particularly P. Nora, *Les Français d'Algérie*. See my article on interracial relations in North Africa, in the *Bulletin international des sciences sociales*, 1961.

[2] For instance the municipal bureaucrat who, under the pseudonym of H. de l'Olnaie published a curious pamphlet, *Vingt jours rentier*, 1929.

[3] Contemptuously described by Augustin Bernard, *Renseignements coloniaux*, 1935, p. 3.

[4] The 'reserved' (or brothel) district of Casablanca, named after one 'M. Prosper' of the heroic era. Cf. *Cri du Maroc*, 19 Sept. 1925. There were at that time 300 'priestesses' at Busbir. In the same number we find attacks on 'Mazagan's rapaciousness' with reference to an obscure affair about pawnbrokers' terms, and against the civil controller of Suq al-Arba', who had built himself a luxurious office.

[5] Ibid. 14 May 1923: the cover depicts an enormous octopus, with the inscription: 'And if there's only one left, I want that.'

which is quite valid for the early years of Morocco, but becomes increasingly inaccurate as that population acquired its own distinct characteristics.[1] The *Cri du Maroc* was, needless to say, not a democratic organ; we find it protesting against a railway strike.[2] However, it traces an ironical portrait of those Government officials, well-informed, disdainful, dressed in the latest French fashion, who looked down on the business men of Casablanca; the latter indeed paid them back in other ways.[3] The useful function of this sort of paper was to uncover scandals; it attacked not only petty tradesmen, but powerful flour millers or the market gardeners of Mazagan. It aimed at creating an association to keep down the cost of living in Casablanca.

Apart from these ambitions, it exercised a certain educative role. Not that it was invariably in the right; but it started certain eddies in local life. In this respect, it contributed something new to the country. For there had hitherto been no means of expression for the underprivileged in the Maghrib. Almost to our own day, too many obstacles intervened to stifle their voice. The press of the *petits blancs*, on the contrary, opened the way for a national press. By raising scandals, it contributed to creating history.

The part played by the life of their neighbourhoods and of their societies in rousing these humble and forgotten elements into activity has been insufficiently studied. The local patriotism of the Maarif section of Casablanca is paralleled by the pride of Bab el-Oued in the twenties, and the story-telling humour of the suburbs of Bone. And one might well study those regional groups in which Corsicans, Lorrains or Gascons forgathered to recall their native land and conquer their new land! One of the distinguishing characteristics of North African life is the bond that existed between these emigrants and their home province. At the time of the centenary, the Association of Landais, Béarnais and Basques was proud to count among its members the Governor-General, the Director of Native Affairs and the famous tenor Cazenave, who had retired to practise the goldsmith's trade in Algiers. The Corsicans, so much abused by the Neo-Destour, welcomed their great compatriot Pietri when his duties brought him to Tunis.[4] In 1937 those of Morocco published a sumptuous pamphlet[5] decorated with photographs and caricatures. There is something touching about these pages, which include biographies of great public servants such as Dr. Christiani, the apostle of medicine at Fez, Pietri, Lyautey's director of finance, of whom I have already spoken, and other more modest figures. One such, to take a random example, was born in 1868 and came to Morocco in 1912 as

---

[1] Ibid., 30 Mar. 1926. [2] Ibid., 30 Mar. 1926.
[3] Ibid., 23 Jan. 1926, 'Le R'bati de toujours.'
[4] *Dépêche tunisienne*, 9 Sept. 1934.
[5] *Les Corses au Maroc*, kindly supplied by M. Casamatta.

accountant to the civil engineers. In 1913 he formed a Committee for District Defence in Casablanca, then a young city; he worked to provide sewers for the new town, and he created a district significantly called *Quartier de la Liberté*. Then he set up a 'Veterans' Association', presided over war charities and aid to ex-servicemen, and was active in promoting the Victory Monument. To be complete, the study should also consider ex-servicemen's associations, with whose activities local elements some-times co-operated; sporting societies, and from the thirties onward the Maghrib Boy Scout movement.

But on this point, as on so many others, we shall have to wait for future research.

Daily Life

History is not the sum but the living synthesis of all these movements. This is why the energy of any particular one may have no effect on the course of the whole, if it fails to understand the way things are going. The period witnessed endless waste of human material. This could not have been seen or foreseen. For a very long time the French authorities had a sense of profound connivance with what was happening. They felt favoured by fortune. On the contrary, those who opposed them had to overcome doubt and weakness, to which some succumbed: these con-stituted the lost generation, the 'heedless youth', *shabab ghafil*, of which Sa'id Hijji wrote so impressively.[1] The task of the historian is to estimate the weight and significance of men and things, through and in spite of successive situations. But in relation to what? He cannot, of course, base his judgment on current events, which provide *an* explanation but not *the* explanation of earlier situations. The observer, the contemporary, lacking a sufficiently sensitive method, could not—except through the intuition of individuals or groups—see things in their true perspective. They could only explain them, illusorily, in terms of what they ex-perienced, what they saw and what they were. The autonomous and specific character of the moment, and its more strictly historical reality, reside in this very uncertainty: a fascinating conflict between the necessary and the possible . . .

But while the false truth which thus emerges, uncertainly, from day-to-day events baffles as much as it fosters the quest for meanings and causes, it does enable us to distinguish those things that are sympto-matic and functional from those that are not. This implies a concrete approach, which is not the least of our guarantees. Although the types I have sketched may well seem to be identical in everyday life with many others of secondary or negligible importance, and to be distinguished from these only by 'values' imperceptible at the time, we should grasp

[1] Cf. p. 376.

the living essence of history if we could interpret what happened on a single day[1] in one of the three countries of the Maghrib.

Let us therefore reconstruct, with the help of a Tunisian newspaper, this medley of facts, this confusion of silhouettes. A *colon* has had his donkey stolen. A *béchariste* (a professional go-between) puts him on the track of the thief, who, 'like a proper Zlass, stoutly denies everything'. (The eternal Bedouin is here contrasted with the sedentary farmer, in a tension aggravated by the colonial situation.) But the Civil Controller is particularly concerned with the security of official *colons* in the Jebel Mansur. (Surely, if this required such close watch, it is due to a notorious failure of the Service des Domaines.) Then we read of the usual worries about excessive drought or excessive rain. People have been stung by scorpions (an exotic element which constitutes one of the land's defences). Pilgrims back from Mecca are welcomed home (Islamic rites are more than ever a symbol of permanence). Hail has ravaged the plantations of Enfida (a reminder of traditional colonial problems). Safur treats its new railway workers to a drink. Hammamet arrests a malefactor (from insecurity we move to repression . . .) Gafsa says goodbye to its retiring caïd, Si Ahmad Longo (but what is a caïd?) The Remounting Commission reviews some 350 horses, belonging to the aforementioned Zlass tribe (good horsemen, but wholly unadapted to the new agricultural order). Kebili celebrates the return of the *hajj*, pilgrims from Mecca. Krib expects a fine crop of almonds. The fields of Massicault are threatened by an invasion of sparrows: a *twiza* of (more or less) voluntary beaters is organized. (Sparrows play an important part in this ecological context. The authorities concerned are rural, although colonial. The question is, who benefits by the immemorial system of mutual aid of which they occasionally make use . . .) Etc., etc.

Many realities, from the lowliest to the most important, might be revealed by such a survey. The incidents here reproduced bring out several figures of the time and of the country, in all their homely detail. But naturally the relations between them–whether reciprocity, or neutrality, or coexistence, or mere coincidence–are brought out more sharply by the economic or political events which account for their propinquity, whether in contrast or in harmony. We have here the beginnings of a classification. For the mere succession of situations, which are never identical, is continually modifying the balance of forces and the hierarchies of significance. The Residents-General no longer have to deal with M. de Carnières, a colourful pioneer, but with his inferior successor Antoine Gaudiani, who is above all a business man rather than a *colon*; the leadership has passed from one category to another. Some important Director of Public Works, on leave in the private sector,

[1] 1 May 1934, according to *La Dépêche tunisienne*.

expresses approval for big concessionary enterprise as opposed to colonization. Such peaceful or violent shifts, alliances, controversies reflect the
evolution of man's relations with the march of things.

The dominant figure in Algeria is perhaps less that of the great
Governor than that of the great *colon*, who initiates undertakings and,
so to speak, catalyses various interests; Charles Munck for example,
with his tobacco co-operatives at Bone, in which the fellahs joined
readily. At the other end of North Africa, Morocco was one huge firm,
the boss of which was perhaps not the man one might have expected.
One day the President of the Casablanca Chamber of Commerce dared
to tell the Marshal: 'Hitherto you have been the military leader. Now it's
time to be realistic.' Lyautey tells us that from that day he lost all his
illusions.[1] The historian knows what the business man meant by 'realistic'. Maurice Viollette, and later Armand Guillon, fell victims to the
same vested interests. On the other hand, the authorities joined hands
with them in a common, and almost constant, excommunication of the
Left wing. During the same period, Rober-Raynaud, an official journalist, denounced the influence of Moscow on 'the intellectual with a
tarnished reputation, the pretentious clerk, the idiot pure and simple, the
neurotic bureaucrat, and a handful of women whose hysteria impels
them to self-sacrifice.'[2] Such are the characteristics ascribed, in certain
quarters, to the liberals of Rabat, Algiers and Tunis. Chaignaud knew
something about that. So did Duran-Angliviel, on whom devolved the
inspiring but thankless task of representing democracy single-handed
in the Tunisian Grand Council. We find him involved in a revealing
controversy, over co-operation with Islam, with a writer in *Tunisie
française*: 'Show me a single example of progress made by the fellah,'
challenges the *colon*. 'The workers on this farm, with barley at 48 francs,
work five days a week; if barley were at 25 francs they'd work no more
than two. You say they are pariahs, but they are pariahs of their own
free will.'[3]

A typological study of this period, having grasped the significance of
these types and situations, to which one should add many more, might
regroup the observations made in this chapter, and here and there in
previous chapters, to form antithetical pairs: the rulers and the masses;
the *colon* and the fellah; archaicism and modernization in rural life;
developments that look towards Europe and those that look eastward.
These contrasts, which are by no means symmetrical and cover only

---

[1] *Afrique française*, 1924, p. 46.

[2] *Renseignements coloniaux*, 1925, pp. 41 ff.

[3] *Tunisie française*, 4 July 1936. Malcor, in a controversy with Duran-Angliviel,
relates his misfortunes as a 'social' *colon* at al-Aura. The cruel phrase is Marti-
nier's, writing in the same paper (11 July 1936) about Tunisian *gourbis* (shanties,
slums).

part of reality, vary with the passing of time. The man of the Central Service, the bureaucrat cut off from the Muslim mass, contrasts ever more strongly with the men of the Bureau Arabe. The latter, more or less loyal to the tribal system, tends to sink into anachronism as other forces come to power. The business man and the engineer are more radically opposed to him than the *colon*, who indeed may be 'big' or 'small'–the difference is considerable. Broadly speaking, those who play an active part, or at least who can recognize their personal influence on the course of events in the country, whatever their rank in the hierarchy or their income level, are opposed by the growing crowd of common folk. These count only by their mass. But just because their existence is more important than their function, who knows whether they do not constitute, in this colonial society, the essence of Europeanism? Only this was not recognized until much later on.

As against those, natives or aliens, who put up with the state of things, good or bad, others fought against it, others again rejected and evaded it. The latter, searchers for beauty and lovers of sensation, initiators of hypotheses or merely pursuers of an elusive future, collaborated subtly with the militant element to provide guiding signs. Their role is not always obvious. Public opinion could always distinguish between the ruling class and the little men, the rich and the poor, conformists and the opposition, yes-men and malcontents. But it did not always grant these outsiders the place they deserved. Now such anxious questioners, whether escapist or militant, reflected or stimulated, or helped to stimulate, the movement of their avid and brutal society. But their role, at that period, remained unobserved, like other phenomena which, expressed by a word, a face or an idea, interrupt the most powerful continuities.

CHAPTER XV

The Flavour of Life at the Time

As we thus reconstruct everyday life in the Maghrib, we are led from the study of particular figures to that of a *presence*; by this means the past is restored to us, not as a 'preparation' for our own time, but as an autonomous process of becoming. And the difficulty of reconstructing, in our own day, the existence of the Maghrib in the inter-war period is not only due to the variety and complexity which were to be expected from a system which mingled together some fifteen million men. It is due to subsequent events which the historian cannot pretend to have forgotten. But what place are we to allot them? If we stress their imminence, we are merely 'prophesying about the past'. Now the past cannot be reduced to mere antecedence. It lived on its own account. It must therefore be considered in its own right. Only on that condition can research find in it 'what it had not perceived, and recognize it, and sometimes show how the past reappears, transformed, in the future.'[1] In North Africa, moreover, the long interconnected sequence of events left room for men's freedom of action. They *were* that freedom. They concealed forces which were not discerned by specialists or politicians, and neither by the Government nor by the opposition, since the discord was being lived through rather than analysed. But where people's powers of reflection and foresight were baffled and impotent in the inter-war period, the immediate state of things told the truth. We must therefore look to the concrete facts of the period, in the midst of its actual happenings, to give us the relations between situations and their meanings, between events and the future.

A Human Gaze

A historical situation is revealed by the look in people's eyes. Naturally this was the case in the Maghrib. In its cities at that time, most women wore the veil. Only their eyes glittered, and one was left to guess at

[1] Henri Lefebvre, *Voies nouvelles*, June 1959, p. 22.

the hidden face, the separate world. Those eyes expressed a silent hope, which was answered by a call from men's eyes. In these exchanged glances there was not only a reciprocity, the admission of a co-presence, but other messages. Woman's appeal to what she hoped for, as against what she had: a certain failure to communicate between the sexes: the mutual obsession of two races. For the European was a party to this exchange. He could read in the eyes of the men, as in those of the women, his historic condition in the Maghrib. A minor character in a novel by Sartre, driving through Marrakesh in a cab during the false mobilization of 1938, is bewildered and overwhelmed by the challenge in those eyes.[1]

Violence gleams in them, or cunning: a secretive attitude at any rate. As Fromentin admirably observed, 'they are huge and dark, with warm transient gleams; as the crowd thins away, those black pupils dilate till the whole eyeball is filled with them; there remains barely one lit spot at the outer corner of the eyelid, a blood-red speck at the inner corner. These eyes look like two black holes in a silent mask, through which the soul at certain moments, which one can anticipate, reveals itself by fiery flashes.'[2] A latent, explosive force. A drawing by Chassériau, entitled 'An Arab', is reproduced in *Une Année dans le Sahel*. It shows a muffled figure with a triangular face, transfixing you with a terrible gaze.[3] One has the same impression from the painting that shows the Great Caïd of the Harakta tribe, 'Ali Ba Ahmad, visiting Paris for an Imperial fête in the sixties. Théophile Gautier, too, felt the power of those 'terrible, gentle eyes, melancholy and yet fiery, which seem turned inward and yet pierce you through';[4] an artist's impressions, but they tell us a great deal. The European is always struck by that keen glance, which reveals not only the animal vigour of a lover or a warrior, but the contemplation of an inner and a future world, a sense of presence or of emptiness, a denial which is an affirmation. Religious fervour, still widespread at the time, carried this significant quality to its highest point. About 1920, an Algerian novel described the failure of an uprising led by a Marabout. The rebel is conquered. The victors, speaking in the *lingua franca*, declare: 'I went into the hut. I didn't look at Musa face to face, because he's a magician and he would bewilder me. They pierced him from behind. As Musa tumbled over to the ground they made us turn our heads away, so as not to meet the evil eye.'[5]

There is something worse than an injurious look: a look withheld, or falsified. Remember the inexpressive gaze of Tunisian beys in their

---

[1] *Le Sursis*, 4th ed. p. 45.

[2] Fromentin, *Un été dans le Sahara*, 1930, p. 153.

[3] No. 4884 in the Cabinet du Louvre. Cf. also nos. 24384, 24442 (five heads), 24410, 25447, etc.

[4] Th. Gautier, *La Presse*, 18 Mar. 1845. Gautier himself vividly describes 'that melancholy, like the sun's, and that sadness, like the sky's, which give such poetry to every Oriental eye', *Loin de Paris*, 1865, p. 78.

[5] R. Randau, *Cassard le Berbère*, J. Carbonel, p. 181.

official portraits. Or again the use of dark glasses which, from 1935 onwards in North Africa, as indeed throughout the Arab East, proclaims hostility, repudiation.

In one of Camus's last stories, the insignificant hero, a *petit blanc* touting samples of cloth round Southern villages such as Laghwat, has put down his suitcase for a moment. Now 'from the other end of the square a tall Arab lean but sinewy, wearing a sky-blue burnous, was approaching ... Only the tarbush round which his turban was wound distinguished him from those French officers of the Affaires Indigènes whom Janine had sometimes admired. He came forward steadily towards them, but seemed to be looking beyond them, while he slowly took off one of his gloves, "Well," said Marcel, shrugging his shoulders, "he surely thinks he's a general!" Yes, they had that haughty air in these parts, but this one was really going too far. Although the whole square around them was empty, he walked straight towards the case of samples, without seeing it, without seeing them. Then the distance between them dwindled rapidly, and the Arab was almost on top of them, when Marcel suddenly seized the handle of his case and drew it back. The other passed by, without seeming to have noticed anything, and walked on in the same way towards the ramparts. Janine looked at her husband; he had a hangdog look. "They think they can do anything nowadays," he said ...'[1]

We might also draw up a catalogue of European glances. It would be a series of individual figures and situations. If we could collect a wide enough range of such evidence, we should have probed fairly deeply into the inner history of the period. Men's looks, in fact, imply the formation of disruption of a social pattern, the movements that run through it, the impression made on individuals and groups; for each man reads in the other's eyes what he means to the other, and this constitutes their common destiny.

If, through the interrelations between the ephemeral and the constant, between particular individuals and anonymous forces, something as intangible as a look—which cannot be defined except by the artist or the poet—can tell us so much about a period, the same is true of other forms of contact.

Under the general title of 'cultural conflicts'[2] French thinkers in the thirties studied this problem. René Maunier investigated 'contacts'. *L'Afrique française* anxiously scrutinized the mutual relations of the two national groups. But few people, from the collector of sociological traits

[1] *L'Exil et le Royaume.*

[2] 'Psychologism' played a considerable part in this, and pluralism appeared as the *nec plus ultra* of comprehension. Cf. G. Hardy, 'Psychologie avant tout', *Outre-Mer*, 1st term, 1934. Besides Hardy one should mention E.-F. Gautier, R. Maunier, etc.

to the Colonial journalist, suspected that an existential surface of history was involved. This was not merely a question of the exchange of influences,[1] but of a reciprocity. Acting at different levels and in different ways, in the most ordinary or the loftiest aspects of human conduct–eating, speaking, loving, thinking–and expressed by men's glances, in the most fugitive moments of experience, this gave these groups their structure and their historic individuality.

The Picaresque and the Decadent

Imagine a young schoolmaster, recently come from France to take up a post at the Lycée at Bône, round about 1930, making his way to the harbour, along the Cours Bertagna. The town at that time numbered 50,000 inhabitants, half of them Europeans and half Muslims, which implies a considerable disproportion of forces. It was a busy port. In 1928 it took in 3,700 vessels with a total burden of 4,100,000 tons, carrying 700,000 tons of merchandise. The visitor would admire the phosphate works, with their rubber conveyor-belts, which swallowed up such huge quantities of material. 250 tons per hour, they said. He could wander over vast terraces, admiring the achievement of France's civil engineers or of her Empire, a newly fashionable theme. But this favourable impression would soon be painfully cancelled out by what he heard around him: an extraordinary concert–or rather cacophony–of voices, including every language of the Western Mediterranean–Arabic, Kabyle, French, Italian, Spanish, Maltese, plus a number of dialects and patois[2]–all spoken with a strong local accent.

These voices did not merely mingle in conversation or in talk about work, they deliberately uttered insults. And these insults are well worth studying. Hitherto sociologists and students of dialect have neglected them. But if we listen to them properly, and know how to interpret them, they can tell us a great deal! They consist for the most part of casting aspersions on the opponent's ancestry or his conjugal happiness. The first theme belongs to a society which is still partly genealogical. The insult most frequently uttered is a curse on your father, your relatives, your 'dead'. The second is derived from a mingling of eroticism and commerce. This time it is not your system of relationships which is called in question, but the virtue of your wife or your sister. Of course people may come to blows about such insults, but it all depends on the tone in which they are uttered. Sometimes the speaker, if he accuses you of trading your wife's favours, shows a certain appreciation of your

[1] Hard as it is to assess in depth the influence undergone by the Maghribis, we are even more baffled when it comes to measuring that which they exerted on the European. Analytical psychology, as well as social psychology, will no doubt discover subtle traits of adaptation such as those referred to by G. Jung, with regard to North America, in *Problèmes de l'âme moderne*, 1961, pp. 61 ff.

[2] These gave rise to the literary genre known as 'Algerianism'.

343

talents in that direction, and the expression that stigmatizes your birth may imply a tinge of envy.

For the attitude which this society, prompted by a shrewd instinct, adopts towards the bastard or the pimp is not always one of condemnation. It may on the contrary be complimentary, in which case the imputation is acknowledged not with a vengeful blow but with a knowing wink. Our observer, if he has made a certain progress in his understanding of the *milieu*, is struck by its intermingling of altercation and abuse, mutual loathing and complicity, even, sometimes, of crude sympathy.

This picaresque or baroque element is only the reverse of certain shocking characteristics. But it is stimulating and amusing. Those who are familiar with it become so fond of it that it becomes not only part of their folklore but almost their favourite national characteristic.[1] The texture of life is not only composite–which is not surprising–but a patchwork made up of rags and tatters, full of solemn rents and ridiculous ornaments. The aesthete in quest of beautiful sounds and colours, scenes and styles, feels deeply wounded. He takes refuge in those regions from which he imagines such discords to be absent: for instance,[2] in the bay of Hammamet at Bu Sa'ada, in the upper districts of Fez, such as Duh. He does not realize that he is himself out of harmony with the setting and that wherever he goes, he takes with him the disparateness he had tried to evade.

In short, throughout the length and breadth of the Maghrib between the two wars, and despite the beauty of certain types, certain images, nothing was clear-cut. Delacroix and Fromentin would not have recognized it. No doubt something of their Maghrib still existed in some dark corner of a madina such as Fez, or in the steppes where horsemen still galloped through the esparto grass. Painters and travellers, driven ever further afield, could still rediscover a certain vein of purity. But the impure predominated as the fusion took place between old and new, between alien and native.

Advancing Europe carried before it a heterogeneous moraine of utensils, dress, ways of speech and behaviour.[3] In many cities, the old

---

[1] This became a literary genre. Cf. Brua, *Fables bônoises.*

[2] Frequented by André Gide and many others . . .

[3] Many observers have described these violent contrasts, especially in Algeria, and the picturesque or deplorable effect resulting from them according to the writer's interpretation. Already Alphonse Daudet, during the Second Empire, had sensitively perceived and rendered the true character of this ailing society, influenced no doubt by Fromentin and even Feydeau but chiefly by the evidence of his own anguished sensibility, of a sort that Loti paraded a generation later. The evidence of Frenchmen might be supplemented by that of foreign visitors, unfriendly perhaps but clear-sighted: such as Broadley ('Urabi's advocate), Doughty or Sykes, travelling in Tunisia or Algeria. Many Englishmen frequented Algiers at this period. It would be interesting to explore their reactions.

districts were done for; confined, crushed and denatured, they existed only as reserves of dubious reputation: casbahs, the haunt of society's dregs, thieves and prostitutes. Meanwhile, as the new districts supplanted one another, those that were beaten in the competition were invaded by a motley mob, predominantly of Mediterranean origin. Sinister or ludicrous figures thronged these areas, where influences clashed or mingled, but the compelling power of sunlight, of the land, of the contest nevertheless sharpened men's zest for life.[1] What became of the old, the weak and the sick? Nobody cared. The avidity of hunger and thirst; the common impulse towards gain, sanctioned by the system; the excitement of desire; victory for some but discomfiture for the majority, while none remained unaltered; many appetites with little restraint, profit for some through the ruin of others; all this vehemence, spurred on by a sense of risk, barely curbed by the civil law, but brought back sharply when necessary to the requirements of the *imperium*, and governed meanwhile by obedience to French models, which served it instead of structure—clung fiercely to life and crushed whatever was not itself, whatever differed from itself, or whatever part of itself failed or weakened.

One needs to be romantically naïve or shrewdly indulgent to let oneself be taken in by certain gestures. Descendants of the 'great families', many of which only date back a couple of generations, were encouraged by official favour and the enthusiasm of important visitors to display traits recalling their past: a noble physical appearance, skill on horseback, princely hospitality—all so much publicity, and rarely given gratis. And all this was already so debased and insincere! The Algerian nobility had gone steadily downhill since the Second Empire. True, it still knew how to sweep majestically through the waiting-rooms of the Bureau des Affaires Indigènes. But its function was no longer that of the true feudal lord, adjudicator, representative and apex of the tribe. With few exceptions,[2] it consisted solely of official dignitaries and debt-ridden opportunists.

The decadence of their style of living reflects that of their function. Even at Laghwat, the home of the Agha Jallul bin Lakhdar, a typical nobleman, was furnished in European style: 'The *salon*, long and narrow like all Moorish rooms, had at either end a commonplace suite of furniture in gilt wood and damask silk, one crimson and the other blue. Fine carpets and cheap Oriental knicknacks were the only local note in contrast with this banality.'[3] As for the inferior nobles, their ungrateful

---

[1] G. Audisio admirably conveys the picturesque, but somewhat sinister, aspects of Algiers, with touches that remind one of Goya: *Jeunesse de la Méditerranée*, 1935, p. 109.

[2] At this period, Bin Gana of Biskra and Jallul bin Lakhdar of Laghwat were still lords in the full sense of the word, owing feudal allegiance to the French Republic rather than being its subjects. The term 'protectorate' has been used of them by a well-informed observer.

[3] Marie-Anne de Bovet, *L'Algérie*.

guests, who insisted on drinking wine with their roast mutton, often describe with roars of laughter a ragout served in a chamber-pot, or the swarm of lice on the splendid carpets. In fact the growing ugliness and vulgarity of the setting, the deterioration of a magnificence which now rang false, brought out more strongly the disorder that reigned in manners, language and thought.

Among the ruling families in Tunis, at the Court itself, we notice disturbing phenomena of prodigality and corruption. In Morocco the sharifs, whom the Sultan delegated as khalifas in certain Imperial towns, gave a very poor impression of the monarchy. When we turn to the great caïds, we witness an even worse state of things.[1] Nearly all the noble chiefs at that period were crippled with unsavoury debts, and their methods of retrieving their fortune were even more suspect. Side by side with gestures that display nobility and breeding and that could still impress visiting writers such as the Tharaud brothers, Pierre Mille and Henri Bordeaux, we note acts of petty meanness, vices devoid of any grandeur. True, modernization on a small scale was taking place. But it was often misleading. In the summer of 1932 one of these great chiefs, dining alone with a European guest, made a great show of being Westernized. His French was perfect. He combined the elegance of his race, the Biblical appearance that would delight a painter, and recollections of the 'Latin quarter'. They dined on a terrace outside the house. A door was pushed open; the host gave a shout: 'Stay inside!' He wanted to prevent his wife, a Frenchwoman, from showing herself. At about the same period, also in Algeria, a petty caïd, who had studied at the *madrasa* and represented the democratic stratum of his class, took his guest along with him to visit a notable scion of a once great family. At the end of the meal he wrapped up a leg of mutton in a newspaper (probably the *Mubashir*) and carried it carefully home for his supper. Two parallel outrages, so to speak: one against modernity, the other against tradition.

If these privileged members of society displayed such demoralization, resulting from the evolution of things, the humbler products of the same evolution could boast no greater refinement. Among the urban petty bourgeoisie or the middle-grade peasants, who were impressed in spite of everything by technical innovations, a shabby, hybrid way of living prevailed. Carelessness in dress, the too frequent neglect of the ritual care of the body, vulgarity in manner and speech, grew worse as one descended in the social scale. Now there was practically no transition between the middle class, petty tradesmen produced by the decomposition of society or subsisting on the crumbs of authority, and the working

[1] On this decadence see Augustin Berque, 'Esquisse d'une histoire de la seigneurie algérienne', *Revue de la Méditerranée*, nos. 29 and 30, 1949. On the family in question, see Manuel Bugeja, 'Les Ben Ferhat', *Bulletin de la Société de géographie d'Alger*, 1916.

class. All descriptions of this period, based indeed chiefly on urban documents, stress the extreme poverty, the filthy, verminous and disintegrated condition of the crowds. Two striking phrases, *Aulad Blasa*, *Bani Ramases*, describe this new section of humanity, which ought to have been a source of shame to those who made use of it.

These cynical victims of a vast social upheaval sometimes sank to the lowest depths of all. Old men begged; girls sold themselves; young men, having worked as errand boys, bootblacks, odd-job men, ended up as *yaouleds*. Artists brought this new picaresque element into fashion; Herzig caricatured the children, the wretched, quickly-corrupted street urchins; visitors to picture galleries contemplated such figures with good-humoured contempt. Types, races and classes were thus displayed for the indulgent amusement of the higher strata; the process continues right into the top levels of preponderant society, so that only the French senior civil servants or the biggest *colons* could laugh at themselves if they felt like it, whereas everybody made fun of the degradation of those below them. A new type of literature sprang up, based on *yaouled* talk and ways; the ground-floor level of a hierarchy of satire, in which Mediterranean slang provides the mezzanine.

Maghribi Sarcasm

In fact, ways of speech reveal and characterize the various groups. Several of these existed, formed by a process of decomposition, or combination, or manifold transitions between the two poles consisting of Qur'anic Arabic on the one hand and literary French on the other. The latter enjoyed official dignity. It prevailed wherever major questions of power, culture or economy were involved. But it was spoken with a strong accent, even by the French themselves. The Qur'anic language still conveyed its own special values, even enhancing them by contrast, but only dialects were in use in everyday life. In the lower strata of the population the two idioms were degraded into slang, patois, forms of lingua franca influenced by Spanish, Italian or Maltese. From these, Musette derived a literary genre whose interest has been stressed by Gabriel Audisio. The Tunis radio scored a huge success with one M. Martin, whom some took for a Jew, others for an inhabitant of Bône, others again for a converted Muslim. He could assume any of these characters at will with astonishing skill. Kaddour bin Nitram – his pseudonym – 'made himself the interpreter of the languages and street cries of Tunis: the dialect of the Maltese coachman, the Corsican policeman, the civil servant from Languedoc, the Jewish tradesman, the ex-tirailleur turned alcoholic, the city slicker singing to his guitar, with a flower behind his ear, and merchants of every sort, and beggars of every sort. According to the reckoning, fifteen languages or patois at least!'[1]

[1] Cf. *IBLA*, 1941.

Sarcasm mingles with joviality. With an ambiguous complexity that is typically Mediterranean, this good humour conceals a not unselfconscious avidity. The few who enjoyed success knew that it was precarious; they chose to laugh, while taking their revenge for its precariousness by making gibes at the underdog. The poor became sardonic, by way of excuse for their own weakness. Louis Bertrand declares with satisfaction that the sons of Pépète disdainfully reject syndicalism.[1] He is wrong, in fact; but there was indeed an element of self-repudiation in the behaviour and attitudes of the downtrodden. The French authorities had to reckon with this characteristic. They acquired accomplices, rather than collaborators; they acted neither as overlords nor as employers, but frankly as exploiters. Anyone who professed loyalty to the 'civilizing mission' talked of in the books would cut himself off from the society of those who possessed things and who acted; worse still, he would disappoint those whom he wanted to help!

As the future was to show only too clearly, grave consequences were to spring from this attitude. For the time being it conferred a harsh vibration, a sense of latent cruelty on events and attitudes and words. Among these ardent, zestful people even desire had lost its frankness, laughter its brightness, speech its directness. Passion became devious, reality was afraid of itself. Sincerity grew cunning or sarcastic. A kind of dull film disguised the keenness of men's gaze, the alertness of their behaviour. Lofty feelings, disinterested loyalties, any kind of nobility, speech itself had to assume vulgarity in order to 'pass'. Even men's hearts spoke in lingua franca. But it was a self-conscious, self-critical jargon, a kind of double or triple talk; for vulgarity itself was insincere, *de mauvaise foi* in Sartre's sense. Each man used irony against others and against himself. And when employed by nationalist writers, this irony assumed savage polemical qualities. When exchanged between members of the ruling race, it suggested that of the haruspex. But it mostly vented itself in obscenities. It coloured most conversations between members of the exploited class and, more significantly, between them and their exploiters. Hence the peculiar mocking tone heard everywhere in the tramways of Algiers, on the quays of Bône or Bizerta. It was not without a certain attraction; it certainly helped people to go on living. But it expressed denial rather than hope; it betrayed a phenomenal falsity which the moralist may perhaps ascribe to injustice.

Stimulation and Reserves

The whole of this society, whether indulging in insincere and ignoble compromise or revealing, by its discords, its basic resentment and anger, seems to be alternately or simultaneously turbid and distorted. I am

---

[1] Preface to 1920 edition of *Pépète et Balthasar*.

referring to certain concepts of contemporary thought; J. P. Sartre[1] has described the 'viscosity' of certain phenomena, which constitute suspect contact between the world and oneself, between the Other and oneself. They are semi-liquefied, as it were. The fusion which they imply deprives the elements in question of their essential character. It even precludes any successful dialogue between them. Things seem falsely clear or falsely opaque; their opacity lacks force, their clarity lacks meaning. This is the case with certain aspects of the colonial process, which life in North Africa disguised and yet revealed. Lévi-Strauss,[2] making a comparison between certain Indian tribes of South America, notes that certain characteristics have no 'justification', are not functional to the life of the tribe but contrary to it, atypical. They do not lead you to any essential reality but represent a borrowing, a contamination. The ethnographer might find it illuminating to distinguish in any society the elements of 'distortion', the discords that reveal 'the unmistakable stamp of the event'.

The Maghrib, during the inter-war period, gives one the impression of a flow of half-solidified lava. On its surface we distinguish scoria and roughnesses, but vitreous portions too. Is not this always the case with a situation arising out of fundamental conflicts and exchanges? We should be able to discriminate, from studying the superficial level, between what truly expresses history, what contradicts it and what eludes it. Maghribi life shows us these alternations of rough and smooth elements. And in so far as it was colonial it was more deeply affected by them than the life of any other country. For, to keep up our image, the changes, the metamorphisms (to use a favourite term of E.-F. Gautier's) brought about there by colonization go deeper, involve more diverse elements. History is being made partly through external constraint. The role of incoherence is therefore not only revealing but creative. One might say, in Hegelian terms, that it proclaims a positive negativity. The disparate factors in the Maghrib, its picturesqueness and its irony, its 'turbidity' and its 'distortion', illustrate both adulteration and fertility. The harsh contrasts, the slippery elisions we discern in it manifest an intense conflict between destruction and re-creation.

But if the country and its people thus seem to have been entirely activated in terms of colonization, were there not some zones safeguarded from that activity? What was the extent of these metamorphisms, which found expression in collusion or in altercation? In what measure did the historic movement proceed from them, by action or by reaction, directly or indirectly, and in what measure, on the contrary, did it proceed from the zones that were immune?[3] In Moroccan marriage contracts we find

---

[1] *L'Être et le Néant*, pp. 700 ff.   [2] *Anthropologie structurale*, 1958, p. 132.

[3] We need not consider here the theoretical implications of this problem. Cf. my article: 'Colonisation-décolonisation, comment les définir?' *Cahiers internationaux*, no. 128, 1961.

a significant expression: the bride is described as the *masuna*, the 'protected one'. Similarly, were there not layers in the life of the period, individual or collective psychologies, institutions, which were protected and which pursued their stubborn existence untouched by historic processes; which may indeed have been responsible for the future? This is a serious question.

Maghribi Inhibition

When the historian's attention, or the contemporary's awareness, turn from the social or psychological summits of the Maghrib to its lower levels, they meet with resistance as though from the increasing density of some fluid. Within the system, no single element understands those elements that lie beneath it; if it does understand them it is afraid of them. There comes a time, there are circumstances when the tatterdemalion stops clowning and the social reject becomes a menace. From the serene sanctuaries of profit, legality and rational explanation we reach the haunts of irregularity, insecurity and uneasiness. In the social scale, this represents the level of the *petits blancs* and the Muslim neo-bourgeoisie. Lower still, darkness, anger and contagion. Here we find the obscure agitation of the 'dangerous, fanatical and syphilitic' multitude, barely restrained by tabus and bludgeons. We have reached those zones of the collective being which correspond, in the individual, to the terrifying regions of the unconscious.[1] To speak in psychoanalytical terms the native–foundation of the whole society, and latent menace–was the *id* of French Algeria.

From the patriarchal chief, the *amghar*, with his armour of traditions, to the Fort-National schoolmaster, product of secular education, the Berber-speaking people displayed a vast range of experience, which included a considerable part of conscious behaviour, of collective and individual choice. To a certain extent, they made as much use of traditional rejections as of modernistic compromise.

The same elasticity was shown by those who spoke Arabic. They displayed a wide gamut of types, from the Biblical nomads of the South to the 'Andalusian' bourgeois of Fez or Tunis. Many sons, deserting the faith of their fathers, sought to combine loyalty to things Eastern with adherence to French ways and culture. But official policy was as wrong to boast of this 'assimilation' as was the university in its insistence on the opposite traits of traditionalism or primitivism. Both forgot the individual for whom these extremes contended, or whom they affected. For under this threat to its identity the whole of the Maghrib seems to have changed in order to remain itself, and to safeguard its essential unity

---

[1] Again the 'grotto' theme.

by indefatigable diversity.[1] To safeguard it, or at least to try and do so; and the attempt was by no means always successful. But success or failure can only be assessed in relation to the country's continuity and its unity.

Both of these, in general, eluded the foreigner, and particularly the colonist. Western power divides; that is its system. It analyses; that is its mental habit. This wide variety of figures and ways of speech, of reactions to the impact of the West, misled it even while it exploited them. Naïve despite its cunning, deceived while trying to deceive, the Western power dwelt on differences which it reconciled by its actions. According to its basic fiction, everything started with itself; determined to abolish the past, it indiscriminately included in that past the mediocrities of the pre-colonial era and the glories of Islamic classicism. Ungrateful towards the former, which enabled it to triumph, it rejected or misunderstood the latter, which might have given it the opportunity for a humanist reconciliation. Whereas its interest and its merit would have lain in entering the mainstream of North African life, and without foreseeing that some day this might be the only solution for it, it ignored or interrupted that mainstream. Or at least it tried to do so. Although in essence a historic phenomenon, it claimed to be absolute, and believed itself to be final. In such excesses it contained the seeds of its own ruin. But its power to actuate remained immense. And since it derived support simultaneously from industrial civilization and from the prestige of a universalist culture, there was no element, in such countries and among such peoples as came under its sway, that it failed to affect and modify, directly or indirectly, positively or negatively; none, or almost none . . .[2]

This preponderance, this ubiquity contrasted with its weakness. The régime which the Colonial power imposed on the people of the Maghrib, and asserted forcibly whenever necessary in spite of France's more liberal inclinations, required a power which it no longer had. Not only because it was losing touch with those realities that contained the germ of the future, but because it assumed the dangerous role of a spearhead relative to the parent state. Between its dynamic force and the lassitude, or maturity, or goodwill of 'French Frenchmen' there reigned a contrast of which it was proud, but which in the long run proved its undoing.

The position of the colonials was illogical. They felt Algerian as opposed to the French, but French as opposed to the Arabs.[3] In this lay their pride, but also their secret flaw. They were building the future in a blind alley. Did they know it? In any case, they had to contend with

---

[1] In certain respects, the Maghrib reacted against European action by simulating diversity, while French authority reacted against the unity of the resistance it met with by the use of diversifying analysis and action.

[2] But that 'almost' can cover everything.

[3] All the handbooks of public law reproduced this ambivalence in the chapter headed 'The Algerian Legislator'.

their own weaknesses; their superficial swagger concealed watchful uneasiness, their unconstraint was a bluff, their energy an effort of will. They disguised nervousness behind a show of brutality. Heirs to an ancient tradition, they assumed a youthful vitality which they did not feel. In fact, they became contemporaries of the pastoral folk they had dispossessed; these could appeal to their Biblical ancestry to safeguard their future. Our colonial sought to imitate them, quoting St. Augustine where the other quoted Muhammad. His truculence had something exhausted about it. Consider his village, with its central square, its bandstand and its plane-trees, the *cantine* where everybody, Muslims included, forgathered to drink anis and play cards. Family privacy, moral conformism, the conventions of the institutional set-up were in paradoxical contradiction to both the virtues and the vices of such a way of life. Its virtue was adventurousness; but it had grown staid. Self-imposed tabus repressed the sexual urge which might have completed the cycle of colonization by general interbreeding.

The system was only held together at the cost of a sharp struggle, and thus of a terrible waste. And primarily, for the colonist, a waste of oneself. One always hoped to cut one's losses at someone else's expense; but one never got away without some mutilation of body or soul. What was left was 'better than nothing'.[1] One would make it up somehow. And so avidity became mealy-mouthed, passion was watered down, fertility dropped, pride dried up, vitality contradicted itself. It was inevitable. This retrenchment was secured mainly at the expense of others. Self-imposed conformity was imposed even more strictly on the native crowd, whose impulses must be curbed. For oneself, it meant turning over a new leaf; for the native it meant mutilation. Thus the rebellion that threatened among the repressed and downtrodden was controlled, or at any rate eluded. The system demanded toughness from its boys and chastity from its girls,[2] profit from its efforts, the elimination of useless elements[3] – including the noble and gracious things of life – and constant watchfulness, as in old Bugeaud's days. Because basically, and although fear was never admitted, the colonials dreaded the upsurge of savage forces, that basic revival which would mean the end of privilege.

For the men of the Maghrib, the reverse was true. Their reality was superior to their status. They were emerging from a long sleep. For many years, indeed, native society had been in the grip of a slowing-down; entirely focused on the religious antithesis: Islam versus Christianity,

---

[1] *Mieux que rien* is a common Algerian phrase.

[2] It would be cruel, but quite correct, to show the relationship between colonial puritanism and the native's prostitution. In this connection, Faulkner and R. Wright have provided a key to the understanding of certain aspects of the Maghrib.

[3] 'They want to identify the useful and the true', R. Randau, *Annales africaines*, 15 Jan. 1935.

law versus chaos, it had drifted into that indifference which takes hold of men and groups who fail to keep up with the movements of the world.[1] The influence of the Brotherhoods often corresponded, as I have said, to this kind of attitude. Even movements of opposition took refuge then in sterile metaphysics. This was the criticism levelled at the Old Destour, from 1934 onwards, by the Neo-Destour. With the progress of nationalism, henceforward, resistance assumed more appropriate forms.

What are the signs of a crisis? The increased sale of newspapers; unusual police activity; the sight of housewives hoarding provisions and small boys carrying stones on to the terraces. One might also refer to statistical observations, such as the frequency of certain words in the press. But we should take speech into account; now we know nothing about what was being said in homes and streets. So we recognize a crisis chiefly through its incidents. Anything may happen; murder, sometimes. But sometimes, too, the crowd restrains its violence. Unconsciously repressed, it breaks out in individual acts, in excitement over sport, in sexuality. We are not adequately equipped to grasp all these aspects, to sum them up and interpret their meaning. Stability or instability, crisis or lull do not suffice to define legality or lawlessness, but reveal an alternation of increasingly violent shocks, so violent that it was eventually to shatter everything.

Things Endured, Things Accepted, Things Protected

This alteration also affected certain immemorial Muslim attitudes. They seemed to deploy their forces around the refuge provided for them by faith, by secrecy, by unintelligibility: a grotto harbouring the strength of the race, to quote the allegory of *Nedjma*.[2] Deployed or withdrawing, according to their external fortune, they pause before that pattern of projecting and receding points, that star-shaped polygon which is a major theme of Arabic art.

But their offensive genius met with a challenge from the colonial situation. Not only was its impulse checked by the adversaries' ruthless ventures, but these increasingly penetrated it. With their ideas, as well as their material objects, they threatened that inner sanctuary from which the Muslim spirit drew its strength and to which it withdrew to gain

[1] Fromentin had expressed this admirably in *Une année dans le Sahel* (Plon, 1930): 'Since they cannot exterminate us, they put up with us; since they cannot escape us, they avoid us. Their principle, their maxim, their method is to keep silent, to disappear as much as possible and make us forget them' (p. 21). They ask 'for very little . . . for the integrity and tranquility of their last refuge' (p. 19).

[2] By Kateb Yacine. Cf. my dialogue with Kateb Yacine and Duvignaud on 'Les mystères du polygone étoilé', *Afrique-Action*, 26 June 1961. I have set forth these views in an article: 'Sur un motif ornemental arabe', in the *Mélanges Taha Hussein*, Cairo.

fresh strength. All the mental and social patterns of the people of the Maghrib became distorted. Not only did they endure invasion, they displayed acceptance. We have frequently noticed the influence of French models, and each time we have been baffled by their ambiguity. Alternately or simultaneously oppressive and stimulating, beneficial and disastrous, they served not only as agents for a domination both material and moral, but also for ultimate enfranchisement, not merely political but total. This is true of everything that concerns culture and historic values; few among the leaders of Maghribi emancipation failed to be inspired directly by French models; and their indirect influence was even greater. But they also had an inhibiting, restrictive action. Common, in part, to both colonizers and colonized, they proved perhaps the latter's most effective weapon against the former. For good or evil, deliberately or not, they were put into practice. It was through them that the system was held together, more surely than by any form of police or military coercion[1].

Meanwhile besides this receptivity, the Muslim was displaying other attitudes, springing from more spontaneous sources, from zones—geographical, social or mental—that were still more or less intact. To consider only the moral plane, there was for instance the faith from which he drew his strength, the language that set him apart, the family ethic to which he clung, not for its own sake but to safeguard his identity.

A second image might be introduced here to supplement that of the star-shaped polygon. Imagine a series of screens interposed, by this protected and yet deeply threatened being, between the outside world and himself. Several of these—psychological, linguistic etc.—serve him as mediators with the world. He needs them in order both to absorb and to repel external interference. This meanwhile advances further, crosses the language barrier, reaches inward to the most secret zones: morality, taste, even the very heart itself. For the acquisition of an alien culture, not only in the realm of customs and language but in that of attitudes, divided the man of the Maghrib in the depths of his being, causing the feeling of alienation, of alteration, which was to explode one day with terrifying force.

Nowhere perhaps in the colonial world were situations in such violent contrast with the character of the races involved. A ruler grown weary, liberal by tradition, is led to exercise increasingly intolerable pressure. A subject of vigorous and aggressive character is forced to yield and almost to absorb the other's will, or at any rate his presence. The situation is a strange one, with so much mutual interaction between two partners who stand locked in conflict. Remaining hopelessly themselves, they undo and remake one another.

[1] Kipling, who should know, described as *emprise morale* (with reference to Algeria) what I have called the influence of *models*. Cf. *Souvenirs of France*, 1933.

The fact that in the Maghrib at that time the characteristics of the two nations contradicted themselves, that their virtues acted in reverse, and that the victor's cry of triumph rang false, gives us a suggestive indication. The depth of contact between the two, the breadth of its implications, are doubtless responsible for the complex and denatured character of these figures, these attitudes, these scenes. French rule was not simple. It worked by good and evil methods. Taking advantage of the inequalities created by technique, which were in its favour, it employed threats, but it also worked by means of seduction. It practised contradictory spells, and the natives' reaction to these was itself contradictory. They unresistingly paid the price for a long-term technical apprenticeship. They rebelled, openly or otherwise, against exploitation and injustice. But they almost invariably subscribed to France's cultural values. The story of their independence was thus to a large extent bound up with the 'lessons' they learned from these.[1]

Clearly the Maghribi response was not a simple one. It implied ambiguities, some of which were inherent in the colonial system, while others, more serious, sprang from the fact that in this struggle there were not only hostile forces to be repelled but desirable values to be accepted. Now some of these, in the long run, affected the object which was being fought for. Resistance to an aggressor, however insidious or brutal, would have been a simple matter. But there were other aspects of the adversary, things to be forgiven, admired or loved.[2] And that was what stirred men's deepest feelings.

[1] Until the introduction, or reintroduction, of more 'indigenous' standards. Hence the major interest of the development of social sciences in these countries.
[2] Anti-French attitudes, among the Arabs at least, are influenced by this ambivalence. But disappointment (or hope) have merely whetted their anger.

CHAPTER XVI

Expression and Meaning

Deep down, the order that prevailed in the Maghrib concealed a battle. Behind its façade of technical equipment, of institutions and profits, the country was, physically and morally, in dire distress. Thought and action made no contact with its essential truth. Its least gestures were instinct with life, and yet that life remained unexpressed. All felt it, but none could grasp it. Even artists failed; some clung to the ancient Semitic belief that 'God shall enlarge Japheth',[1] while others, more numerous, extolled the modernism which was supplanting tradition in the land and in its ways.[2] Such themes as 'the Arab hostess',[3] 'French heroism' and the 'Latin fusion' had their rival exponents. One man, stirred by the truculence of the present, impugned the permanence of traditional values; others reacted in the opposite way. Countless theses and interpretations split up what was essentially one. The Arab-Berber population indeed, claimed to represent that lost unity; yet this unity was contaminated and interrupted. What they said was of less value than what they did, and still less than what they were.

The only authentic factor in the Maghrib of that time was the impotence in expressing themselves, expressing anything, that afflicted people and things. Not because the reality was something manifold, shifting and uneven; for that is the case everywhere; but in virtue of a characteristic which a single painter has conveyed—the greyness that results from the intensity of colours, and that mingling, or profanation, that takes place between all the categories of one's being, leading one, as Baudelaire said, from some rare perfume, suggestive of a haunt of vice, to 'the unplumbed limbo of sadness'.[4]

[1] Genesis ix, 27.
[2] A theory expounded at length by Louis Bertrand in the preface to *Notre Afrique*, 1925.
[3] A theme illustrated by Victor Hugo in *Les Orientales* and revived, in a somewhat fanciful manner, by Léon Roches in *Trente ans à travers l'Islam*, 1884, vol. 1, p. 358. This seems to be one of the archetypes of French reactions to the East.
[4] Baudelaire, speaking of Delacroix, *Curiosités esthétiques*, Crepet, p. 120.

Recourse to the Maze

Consider once again that 'star-shaped polygon' which represents not only the basic structure of Arab behaviour but an intense and secret historic reality. The outer periphery is a ring of acute angles; the centre of the star is an inner space, seat of 'the concrete impersonal',[1] shrine of a nothingness that may perhaps be everything: source of aggressive sallies followed by withdrawals, when the Arab's being takes refuge within mazes where his pursuer is lost, but where he himself is led by some guiding thread towards what is essential.

Sometimes this revulsion from a world profaned is paradoxically combined with political activity, or at least with an interest in the transformations of the Arab East. People believe, or pretend to believe, that these provide an orthodox version of progress, conciliating the world of Abraham with that of the machine. It then becomes possible to extol simultaneously, as the *Taqwim al-Mansur* did, the victory of the Ghazi and the dignity of the kalifate.[2] In 1925 the same organ, whose editor Taufiq al-Madani had just visited Paris, sketched a piquant comparison between the virtues and vices of East and West,[3] concluding, with satisfaction, that the East had the superior merit of spirituality.

The last dazzling display of old-style rhetoric still delighted many men of the 1920 generation. For these, the merits of Arabic writing were due to its sacred archetype, the Qur'an. They did not see that the literature handed down to them was adorned with the decadent elegance of academicism. The anthologies offer plentiful samples of these old-time men of letters, ranging from the aristocratic *fqih*, swathed in his burnous enjoying the scents of his garden, to a group of Tunisian writers more varied and more skilful,[4] belonging to an already old-established renascence: Mustafa Agha, Shadli Khaznadar, Kabbadi,[5] and others.

The protests of the devout, the deliberate archaicism of rhetorical writers, the horror of innovation, were all forms of evasion. These attitudes grew rarer in the thirties, surviving only in a few isolated figures. But their social foundation remained secure. They corresponded, in the field of behaviour, to the intimate withdrawal of Muslim family life, centred round the marriage bond, which remained about the only thing untouched by colonization. If the nationalists accepted this, although believing in it less and less, it was because they felt it to be a

[1] Kateb Yacine's expression.

[2] Tunis, 1923, p. 168.

[3] Ibid, 1925–6, pp. 93 ff.

[4] Zahiri for Algeria, 'Abbas Qabbaj for Morocco, Zin al-'Abidin al-Snusi for Tunisia. The last-named, who is still writing, has been of great significance.

[5] On the two former, see the anthologies above mentioned. On Kabbadi, see the special number of *al-Fikr*, Tunis, 1961.

refuge.[1] The veil of their womankind was their last fortress. The segregation of dwellings, the special character of customs, the insistence on remaining 'different' as a symbol of lost liberty, the recourse to sexual excesses, even to drugs or, in other cases, to violence, were all ways of saying NO to the world that threatened them; of return to those protected places, that shrine within the polygon that still guarded their inner life. A soul, a race thus took refuge within the cavern where, in Kateb Yacine's allegory *Nedjma*, a strange figure dwells, one steeped in the ancestral Bedouin heritage. From this shrine they would be able to rise again. And the past, by means of which 'all these things would be added unto them', survived in the old districts of the cities and in men's hearts, as involved and mysterious as a maze.

Protective Screens

But life drove them out of these refuges. How could they avoid communication, temporal involvement, the new relationships that explain one to oneself? The unintelligibility which had served to protect them quickly became illogicality, which is unforgiving. The illiteracy of the masses, the obscurantism of those in power: these, henceforward, were the things to be combated. 'Clarify!' demanded Ahmad Huhu in the columns of the newspaper *Basa'ir*,[2] Military service, emigration to Metropolitan France, the modernization of the economy required and diffused a sort of French which was no longer the rifleman's jargon but the industrial worker's slang. This new linguistic field served to reflect the shafts of the adversary–in both senses of the word, throwing them back and yet reproducing them. It provided a ground for the seeds of culture; and it was of such paramount interest that much of the Maghribi vitality was absorbed by it. To get outside oneself, even at the price of abandoning or destroying part of oneself: to go forward to meet the Other, and against the Other; this impulse of collective psychology now prevailed over everything else. Towards 1930, in Algeria, this authentic movement, encouraged furthermore by the legal fiction of assimilation, reached such strength that the authorities seriously envisaged the disappearance of Arabic.

This was the more noticeable because a jealous scholarship, a kind of cultural Malthusianism concurrently held back the expansion of the French language, realized by European opinion to be dangerous. For French confers on those who speak it 'a weapon which is redoubtable through its explosive quality, and whose power is enhanced by its irre-

---

[1] This was expressed, a good deal later, by Frantz Fanon, *An. V de la Révolution algérienne*, 1959, pp. 13 ff. Shadli Khairallah, in his controversy with the Socialists in 1932, had written: 'Leave our women alone' (*Voix du Tunisien*, 8 Aug. 1932).

[2] *Ma'a himar al-Hakim*, Constantine, 1933, p. 10.

verent and revolutionary spirit.'[1] And that is why each week Tunis received seven to eight tons of French publications.[2] The nationalist movement, in controversy and argument, made deliberate use of the French language. Articles in Destour papers, passages in the *Jeune Algérien* or the Moroccan *Plan of Reforms* pay touching homage to its lucid and liberating qualities. On the other hand, the authorities shed no tears over the illiteracy of the masses. They counted on time to 'remedy this situation', which would take 'at least two more generations'.[3] Education tended, although inconsistently and somewhat shamefacedly, towards so-called vocational training,[4] which would provide foremen and loyal servants.

But if France as represented by her institutions too often lagged behind revolutionary France,[5] it was still more hostile to the revival of Arabic. The North African Conference of 1929 had recommended an enquiry on the diffusion of the Qur'anic idiom. In May 1930, at the Délégations Financières, the administration turned down a resolution on the teaching of Arabic in primary schools. In his alarming report on bilingualism, *diglossie*,[6] William Marçais began by setting forth the difficulties which the Arabic language, owing to its sententious and gnomic character, experienced before becoming an instrument of medieval culture; first by borrowing from Syrian grammarians and Greek philosophers, as in our own day by borrowing from Europe. In this process Arabic, according to Marçais, increased its ambiguity rather than its precision. His criticisms, well-founded in respect of grammatical analysis, are less so in the field of social dynamism; languages are things but are also tendencies. It seems that this great Arabic scholar, at that period, underestimated the forces of transformation and adaptation. His conclusion was that written Arabic had 'suffered a setback in Tunisia and in Algeria'. He even envisages a disappearance of Arabic dialects in the more or less distant future. This severe report did not go unnoticed. In December 1931, in fact, a Congress took place in Tunis at which many Muslims were present. These included such men

[1] Shadli Khairallah, *Voix du Tunisien*, April 26 1932.

[2] *Dépêche tunisienne*, 20, 24 Sept. 1934. The demand for *Le Canard Enchaîné* increased tenfold in a year!

[3] G. Mercier, *Le Centenaire*, 1931, vol. II, p. 70.

[4] There were frequent controversies about this. Thus Muhammad Bourguiba attacked J. Despois on the subject of Sadiqi, *Voix du Tunisien*, 18 Feb. 1932 ff. Shadli Khairallah attacked the ideas of G. Hardy, ibid., 8 Mar. 1932.

[5] In 1937, Tunisia had sent 200 students to France and granted 95 baccalaureates, plus 5 *brevets supérieurs*. Algeria had only 50 baccalaureates plus 6 University diplomas. Morocco, in ten years, produced a single licentiate in law. This situation met with frequent criticism in the nationalist press. Cf. particularly *Risalet al-Maghrib*, 'ta'tikh al-talaba al-magharība bi-Fransa', 1 Dec. 1942, an interesting historical survey.

[6] *L'Enseignement public*, Dec. 1930, pp. 401 ff; Jan. 1931, pp. 20 ff; Feb., pp. 121 ff. The report is discussed at length in *al-Nadim*.

as Busha'ib Dukkali, who introduced Muslim reformism into Morocco; Hajjwi, of Morocco, considered an enlightened modernist at the time; 'Abd al-Haiy al-Kittani, an erudite student of tradition; Maulay 'Abd al-Rahman bin Zaidan, the historian of Meknes. And Tunisians, among whom all the most highly educated families of the Zaituna were represented–the Nifer, the Bin 'Ashur, the Mrad, the Ka'ak, and others of the linguistic élite. The Arab press[1] campaigned fiercely against Marçais's presidency. The protest spread to include an intelligentsia which had long been French-speaking, but which saw in Classical Arabic a symbol of resistance.

During the thirties this symbol acquired a historic character. What hardly anyone realized was the constitution of a new linguistic field, derived from ancient Arabic but destined for new tasks. The language sought to escape from what might be called its anthropological reservation, and to vie with French as an instrument of historic struggle. Nevertheless its strength did not lie in its success as a means of information and communication, as its supporters believed, but in its aggressive symbolism. In this the Maghrib followed the example of the Middle East. And yet this revival, *nahda*, was already old-established in Tunisia, where the Khalduniya (the Tunisian Cultural Association) had been militant since the beginning of the century.[2] It was newer in Algeria and in Morocco, where no such tradition existed, and where official teaching was oriented, for obvious practical reasons but also with a certain astuteness, towards the use of dialect. The latter tendency was even stronger at the Institute of Rabat,[3] where R. Blachère fought manfully in support of the Classical traditions of the East.

In any case, in Algeria too Arabic emerged from the seclusion of the Mosque and attempted to fit in with the modern world. The Algerian society *Al-Shabiba* proclaimed, through its president, that 'we must revive simultaneously our language, our religion and our country.'[4] We recognize the theme of Shaikh Bin Badis. He had already founded, in 1929, his *Jam'iyat al-tarbiya* at Constantine. The school founded by certain Algerian bourgeois such as Bin Smaya and the Damarji, under the direction of Shaikh 'Umar Sma'il, was its rival politically but worked towards the same cultural restoration. The movement grew and proliferated. In Oran we find the free *madrasa* of Zahiri Taiyib, another at Saint-Denis-du-Sig in the very middle of the settlers' zone. By the end

---

[1] *Zahra*, 2 Dec. 1931. [2] Cf. p. 201.

[3] The systematic transcription of Arabic into diacritic signs, the preponderance given to the study of dialects, are characteristic of the school of Rabat, in contrast with that of Algiers, where Fagnan and R. Basset distinguished themselves and where Bin Cheneb (Bin Shanab) is still teaching.

[4] On the theme that the Press is the voice of the people. Cf. *Shihab*, Nov. 1930, pp. 607 ff. A North African conference (cf. *Afrique française*, 1929, p. 124) piously enquired into the causes of the neglect of Classical Arabic in schools and presented a report on the subject . . .

of 1931 there were a score of such establishments: three times that number by 1935, and with these were associated, by 1938, some 150 cultural clubs or organizations.[1] At the same period the review *Al-Shihab* championed the historic role of spoken Arabic. As well as doctrinaires and polemicists, its contributors included a genuine poet, Hammu al-'Id.[2]

Languages

Whether French or Arabic, the speech of North Africans was seldom natural. How could it be? Most of them had had to abandon their mother tongue, Arabic or Berber, on the threshold of school or profession. Where races were divorced and customs confused, language acted as an obligatory mediator. For after all, one has to communicate in practical life. But bilingualism became increasingly rare among Europeans. It tended to disappear the further one moved from pioneering times and regions. The use of interpreters, as official intermediaries, became widespread, obliterating diversity, levelling differences. Then came the time when this, too, was abandoned. Interpreters disappeared from the offices of the Governor-General and from those of the Residents' technical advisers: only those who spoke French were admitted there. A great part of real life was thus left silent.

The languages themselves—French, Arabic, Berber and accessorily Spanish,—Italian and Maltese—were never spoken in their pure form. Each, in fact, was cut off from the others, and from being a springboard for communication became a dividing wall. Except, of course, for the French *koine* (lingua franca); but this was stratified in hierarchical levels, almost in regional dialects, as Arabic had been, to a more serious extent. People might sometimes 'talk like a mosque', but only on solemn occasions, almost only in prayer. On the contrary all North Africans aspired to the use of administrative French, the language that would open doors and ease procedures. And then their voices, their intonations, their gestures, almost their whole personalities would change. The rest of the time they would speak some sort of jargon, either separately or in complicity with one another. A schoolboy from Metropolitan France would jabber a nasal jargon which his Kabyle schoolfellow would echo. Both, in class, would imitate the teacher's idiom: a French which was functional to the point of absurdity. At home both would talk some sort of patois or dialect, more or less related to its French, Arabic or Berber sources. Grammatical correctness was so alien to people's way of life that it was considered insincere, affected, domineering, although it was derived from models whose attraction and authority were felt by all.

[1] Unpublished study by Augustin Berque.
[2] S. Bencheneb, *Mohammad al-'Id Hammu 'Ali, Documents algériens*, cultural series, 1946, no. 7.

Good Arabic, good French were to be found only in Mecca and in Paris; in other words, nowhere at all. What they had in common, on the other hand, was their accent.[1] It assumed, strangely enough, the same characteristics in French as in Arabic (slurring of long syllables, loss of resonance of vowels, a guttural and nasal intonation). But this way of speaking, which the necessities of the system tended to impose on everyone, did not spring from a pure source, and it resulted not in unity, but merely in compromise.

Of course there were common levels of exchange: (1) official French, from the police report to the classical authors taught at school; (2) the French spoken in business, in everyday affairs, which every Muslim who hoped to get on economically or socially had to acquire; (3) the French of workshops, harbours and barracks, spoken with a strong Mediterranean twang, full of Arab and Maltese expressions; (4) lower still, the lingua franca of various trades, as used between road-menders and stone-breakers, or the prostitute and her client, or the housewife and her charwoman.

But these were purely pragmatical levels. Their extension corresponded to that of the *francité*, the Frenchness which imposed a position and a function within a certain order on the whole of North African life at that time. But this means of communication was poor. Its deficiencies reveal one of the defects of the system, which was to authorize no fundamental exchange, only forms of collusion.[2] Nobody remained unaffected by such collusion. If the nationalist movement discerned the explosive values, indeed the values pure and simple, of classical French, the *colon* underwent an adaptation which brought him nearer to his Muslim neighbours than to his fellow Frenchmen. But his contact with the former remained superficial. And in their case, although such contact involved their whole being, its expression remained limited. Clear-sighted observers such as E.-F. Gautier were unaware of its repercussions. This revolt of the inner depths was a silent one. Or else it spoke in terms of self-interest or politics, which limited its scope severely. It was thus subject to much censure, the worst being self-inflicted[3]. One of the reasons, or characteristics, of this was the necessity, imposed on all rebels, of linguistic substitution–of official French, or of classical Arabic, for the maternal dialect. And each of the two parties, admitting only what was essential, remained locked within itself.

[1] 'Thick and muddy', but lively and energetic, according to Montherlant, *Il y a encore des paradis*, Algiers, 1935.

[2] The interlocutors, being thus placed at different levels and different stages of culture, *pitch* their voices differently. Cf. the 'toneless' voice so characteristic of the Shleuhs, and on the contrary the deep, harsh bass of Arabs from the Sahara. It is true that Maghrib sociology has not yet reached these refinements–or rudiments–of observation . . .

[3] Whence, by way of compensation, its exuberance at times of political crisis.

The difficulty of communication did more than merely add to the obstacles to clear-sightedness and sincerity set up by a system that seems deliberately evasive. The dispersion and the mediocre quality of the languages reflect a society which has failed to formulate itself, because it has failed to *see* itself or to *will* itself: shuffling and prevaricating, stopping in all things midway between the Other and itself, making a virtue of opacity. This opacity protected the various groups from one another; it had the same effect between individuals, possibly between the two sexes. The attitudes of both natives and Europeans had a quality of deadness; they lacked all transparency or resonance. Despite kinships and propinquity, they were totally devoid of Middle Eastern effusiveness or Meridional spontaneity. Restrained vehemence, self-critical toughness, cold sarcasm, passions wildly felt but cunningly exploited; how hard it is to describe this special quality in all the manifold forms it assumed! It not only affected speech and behaviour; it can also be recognized in a typically Maghribi form of sexuality, at once excessive and conformist . . .

This blend of excess and conformism is characteristic. The violence and truth of people's innermost feelings was prudently repressed, for fear of breaking the fragile framework which held the whole thing together after a fashion. Through legal sanctions, but also through acquired habits, language, self-interest, feelings, fashion, this fear came to dominate French, Muslims and neo-Latins, for contrary reasons but at the same time. Through coercion, but even more through convention or attraction, this kind of common norm acted as a premature brake on over-violent impulses. The colonial Maghrib thus took shelter against external and internal perils. But it lost some of its vitality. In order to subsist, it refused to fulfil itself, rejecting at the same time self-expression and history. For the Maghrib revolution was to consist of making speech spring from its innermost being.[1]

The Arts

What is true of human behaviour is equally true of art. I said at the outset of this chapter that its testimony was to a large extent contradictory. This assertion must now be qualified.

Like all ancient civilizations, the Maghribi cities had a system of meanings which persisted wherever modern times had not brought about the ruin of their Madinas. They thus retained, among other things, their old music called 'Andalusian' in Morocco,[2] and in Tunis subtly connected

[1] *'Ilm l-krusha*, 'the learning of the bowels', thus, in the Atlas, they describe poetic inspiration . . .

[2] On this point the reader is referred to the huge study by the Baron d'Erlanger, continued by Mannubi Snusi. They both attended the Congress of Eastern Music at Cairo (1938).

with the traditional study of sounds and colours. The taming of singing birds, whose melodies practised ears delighted in distinguishing, and a hagiology propitious to contemplative enthusiasm, linked pleasure with piety and instrumental refinement with popular warmth of feeling. In this sort of music the choice of *genre* is bound up with the emotional content to be expressed. Like Turkish or Persian music, it connects the expression of idea or feeling with the choice of sequence or mode, not as in our own music with the free construction of rhythms and sounds. It is as it were hieroglyphic where our music is alphabetical. Mustafa Sfar, one of the greatest experts, so it is said, had drawn up a table showing the correspondence of the different modes with the activities of life, the 'mansions' of the year, the hours of prayer. It was he who, late in 1934, founded the association called Rashidiya in Tunis, in order to emulate the musical effort of Algeria and also to combat the growth of Western-ized music in the manner of 'Abd al-Wahhab. He noted down old melodies hitherto jealously guarded by virtuosi. He thus brought them out of the esoteric sphere into that of popular education. His attempt prospered. In our own day this music has won wide audiences among the younger generation.It is significant that it should enjoy such a revival at a time when all North African society has taken a vital new turn.

The significance of the symptom escaped observers, particularly administrators, at the time. It is true that their attention was focused on quite different problems in which, according to an alternative which is familiar to ourselves, academicism conflicted with modernity. For most people, Algeria is represented by the 'Algerian Suites' of Saint-Saëns, who died at Algiers in 1921. Only specialists, such as the Baron d'Erlanger in Tunisia, Alexis Chottin in Morocco, J. Rouanet and par-ticularly Léon Barbès in Algeria, took an interest in the evolution of local music.[1]

And yet where else can we read as certainly the message of a people divided not so much between East and West as between two versions, the 'Western' and 'Eastern' versions of itself? The decadence of national music in Algiers was a deplorable fact; true, amateurs gave so-called 'Arab' festivals, but these were for the most part merely survivals. An instrumentalist might call himself 'the last performer on the *rabab*', another (the *mu'allim* Sasi) 'the seal', *khatim*, i.e. the last, of the mando-linists. We are a long way from the great executants of the preceding generation, Mnemmech, Menzino, Sfindja.[2] When a tradition degener-ates into nostalgic folklore, or on the other hand into a pastime to amuse tourists, it is indeed dangerously impaired. The taking over by the Administration of the craft of carpet-making confirms this deca-

---

[1] A Congress of Eastern Music was held at Fez in 1939, following that at Cairo.

[2] *Presse Libre*, 27 May 1930.

dence. Although this action was a charitable one and its achievement in some ways remarkable,[1] it represents an ominous supersession. The carpet-weavers, like the coppersmiths and leather-workers, left to themselves, were lapsing into decadence. They could only be saved, to some extent, by being taken over by the State, and adulterated in the process.

In Tunis, in Algiers,[2] the earliest theatrical ventures were promising, and introduced people of real talent, such as the tenor Mahieddine (Muhyi al-Din) or the impresario Ksentini. The songs they offered mostly consisted of whining plaints or trivial parodies: an outrage not only to the city's culture but to the modern spirit striving for expression amid all this turmoil and adulteration. This is true not only of the Arab 'saynète'. *La Famille Hernandez* recently scored some success in Paris; it marks the climax of a genre which had been flourishing for a long time on Algiers radio, with the comedian Janot's *Carnaval du tirailleur, Mustapha revient de Paris*,[3] etc. I have already referred to Kaddour ben Nitram; many other attempts could be cited.

Was this 'Algerianism'? Robert Randau, even before 1914, had appealed for a development of 'Algerianism' in literature.[4] His example is not very convincing. True, it is possible that some day there might emerge from this mixture of races 'a colour intense and pure, from this hybrid version of the French language a form of speech as different from academic French as American is from English.'[5] For the time being, this 'Algerian' style meant complete lack of style. In literature, as in the plastic arts, the theatre, music and song, caricature reflected a misshapen reality. But being self-satisfied and lacking any spirit of innovation, it remained unconstructive. Respectful and farcical, it failed to make use of colonial irony, but eluded it.

The same is true, in the field of painting, of the so-called realism which 'proletarianizes' the picturesqueness of the painters of old. The hackneyed theme of burning light and broad stony spaces has its parallel in the theme of filthy back streets, low taverns and prostitution. Did this sort of orientalism, which no longer even admitted to the name, fail through some vice inherent in the genre, or for lack of genius? In spite of some honest efforts, few of the 'Abd al-Tif group are on a level, not indeed with Fromentin and still less with Delacroix, but with the tragic psychological studies of Chassériau, the ethnography of Dehodencq, the historic accuracy of Guillaumet. 'Orientalism' confessed itself finished as

---

[1] To which many exhibitions bear witness. Cf. Aug. Berque, *Les Arts indigènes algériens*, Algiers, 1934; important studies by G. Marçais, Prosper Ricard and others; and a practical attempt to launch the rescued, or renovated, carpets of the Maghrib on the foreign market.

[2] S. Bencheneb, 'Le théâtre arabe d'Alger', *Rev. africaine*, 1935, pp. 72 ff. Unpublished thesis by Farid Ghazi.

[3] *Presse libre*, 29 June 1930.   [4] *Les Algérianistes*, Paris, Sansot, 1911.

[5] As sought today by Henri Kréa.

early as 1875,[1] which marks a striking coincidence with the advent of the *colon*. The valuable research undertaken since 1900 by Marquet, Launois, etc. was of aesthetic rather than of analytical interest. Only Dinet, so profoundly aware of a conflict which he experienced within his own soul, can touch us by his loving attention to Algerian humanity. But he remains an anecdotal artist in a conventional tradition. Nothing brings out more clearly the distinction between art which is truthful expression and art which is profoundly significant than the overpowering contrast between Dinet and Delacroix. The few days which the latter spent in North Africa are more important, in the pictorial expression of a land and its people, than all that has been done there, since, for over a century. And this did not happen by chance. Delacroix, impelled by his romantic genius and his revolutionary fervour, sought in Africa a truth that was both local and universal, while his successors, even Fromentin, looked with eyes that were no longer disinterested at this alienated and dependent land.

In one of the centenary volumes, that devoted by V. Barrucand to the 'Orientalist' painters, we find an accurate comment—even though swathed in prudent phraseology—on that failure to feel. Algeria 'is not merely a wine-cellar and a granary.' Most of these painters confuse Orientalism with brilliancy of colour, and humanism with a caricatured realism. There is no hope for Algerian art unless it breaks the shackles of mediocrity, self-interest and prudence, and moves boldly forward so that its progress is 'proportionate to its desires'.[2]

The Rupture

The historic development of Arabic, the choice of French by the Maghribi nationalist movement, were bold ventures, in a world in travail, which one must not expect to find invariably successful. The language of *al-Shihab* is too often harsh and scholastic. Bin Badis, a stirring orator, was less at his ease as a writer. A man like Makki Nasiri, who has studied in Cairo, wrote with greater fluency. The merit of these lies elsewhere: in their instrument, and in the significance of their gesture. The use of Arabic as a modern weapon, the use of French as a means of transposing, almost recreating, oneself. Neither process had an aesthetic motive. In spite of achievements to which I have referred, the form lagged behind the content and above all behind the significance of these writings. Our own period, which has at last witnessed a great French literary movement in North Africa, due almost entirely to North Africans, does not fully appreciate the immense amount of work, and no doubt also of wasted effort, involved during a whole generation to make

[1] J. Alazard, *L'Orient dans la peinture française*, 1930, p. 68.
[2] *L'Algérie chez les peintres orientalistes*, 1930. The most sincere work written by the editor (and contaminator) of Isabelle Eberhardt.

such an achievement possible.[1] I am not thinking of the depersonalization recently complained of by Malik Haddad, for this use of the French language, far from being a result of colonization, was a deliberate choice, a gesture of opposition; but of what had to be sacrificed in order to establish a form of expression, French or Arabic, voluntarily subject to the aesthetic criteria of Paris or Cairo. Was not academicism a danger in both cases? And was not the development of French or Arabic style achieved at the cost of some mutilation? No doubt more subtle evolutions would have to take place before this artistic form could rehabilitate things hitherto trivial or suspect, and tactfully ignored: popular poetry, Arab or Kabyle, for instance, or the melting-pot of demotic French, in short all that hardy, cross-bred reality which is the essence of North Africa. I do not of course refer to the folklore picturesqueness or to the so-called naturalism which were only too rife during this period, but to the authentic inspiration latent in certain Shleuh poems published by Justinard in the review *Aguedal,* and in Jean Amrouche's *Chants Berbères de Kabylie.*

Certainly nothing of the sort is to be found in the collection *Notre Afrique,* published with a preface by Louis Bertrand in 1925.[2] It includes a story by Abdel-Kader ('Abd al-Qadir) Fikri, author of the 'first Algerian novel', *Zohra* (1926). This is journalism, at best sincere, at worst dishonest, in any case superficial. North African literature may, it is true, be more important through what it says than by the way in which it says, or does not say, things: its choice of language, the confusion of its form, its inhibitions. The same is true in politics. If the entire Maghrib, from 1930 onward, resounded with a quarrel about definitions, the interest of the latter resided elsewhere than in their conscious formulation or their legal arguments. That is why, despite their faults of inadequacy or inconsistency, they are capable of expressing a rupture.

Within the 'developed' sectors, whose extent was constantly increasing, the French establishment now gave up that close connection with native realities which it had maintained for so long. There had been a tacit sense of continuity, a concept of undividedness; the abandonment of these kept pace with the progress of self-consciousness, of questioning, of anxiety. At the same time both parties abdicated a major part of the nameless relations resulting from their long cohabitation. These

---

[1] S. Bencheneb, 'La littérature contemporaine en Afrique du Nord', *Cahiers du Sud,* 1947, pp. 248 ff; *al-lugha al-'arabiya wal-adab al 'arabi fi'l-Jaza'ir, Al-Adib,* Beirut, Jan. 1954.

[2] At least he includes a Muslim for the sake of appearances. This is not the case in most of these collections. Thus the anthology entitled *Méditerranée nouvelle,* which appeared in Tunis in 1937, includes not one single Tunisian, with all due respect to its promoter A. Pellegrin.

relations subsisted only in the more archaic borderlands. At other times and among other people, as well as in other places (for these borderlands were not only geographical, but psychological) they broke apart. Tentative efforts to establish coexistence in North Africa were doomed. The authorities were torn in contrary directions. The wish for regularity and assimilation, after the model of the parent state, implied begging the question; but a pluralistic aestheticism was no more satisfactory. Ought they to have recourse to the psychological approach, which claimed the authority of Lyautey, or the economic approach, which already inspired the technocrats? These versions of a single fact–the Franco-Maghrib rift–worked against one another, and all together against the evil they sought to combat.

As for the Muslims, if they feared for Islam it was because they felt the threat to the unitary bases of their moral and social being. The reformism appealed to by the most enlightened believers only purified religion by substituting historic tensions for religious tension. Wherever new light was shed, it revealed inequality and depersonalization. These aggravated one another, but their respective remedies–mastery of adaptation, maintenance of authenticity–contradicted one another. The growth of self-knowledge brings separation, division. The political movement which sought to denounce injustice and propose solutions represented primarily rupture with the Other and with oneself. History disrupts humanity before restoring it.

Naturally, history directed these men in apparently contrary directions: Abbas towards assimilation, Bin Badis towards its opposite; the Neo-Destour indicting the Old for backward-looking opportunism, and the latter accusing the former of compromising on principles and of exaggeration in action. Moroccan nationalism oscillated at that time between two leaderships, one Western and even Socialist in tendency, the other inclining towards Pan-Islamism and Pan-Arabism. All these divisions illustrate the uncertainty of the Maghrib's future, torn between Europe and the Middle East. They undoubtedly reveal more than mere discord between men and tendencies. But they only set forth, in the form of divergent ideologies, the ambiguity inherent in the very being of the Maghrib. And thus the most significant leaders were those who were most ambiguous; which means, in tactical terms, those most capable of sudden reversals or double-edged actions. Terminologies were less important than attitudes. Reciprocally, these, taken all together, bear reference to a common situation. When religious reformers called the Marabouts hypocritical reactionaries, or the latter accused the former of irreligion, they reveal the parallel perplexity of Islam at grips with the modern world. If Arab and French tendencies were in conflict between and within groups and individuals, this shows the vacillation of the Maghribi being between two systems. And while some saw salvation in a return to primitive purity, and others in iconoclastic modernism, they were all seeking to save the same collective being, and perhaps the same future, by different methods.

The European faces the same conflict, but his alternatives are scantier because he is less deeply committed. One effect of the Colonial system was, paradoxically, to free a growing mass of Europeans from contact with the local mass, and from preoccupation with the real problems. The Frenchmen tended to become absorbed, moreover, in the political controversies of the parent state. These did not fit North African situations. However sharp and direct the conflict between Left and Right wing, it did not exactly correspond to the basic confrontations of North Africa. This is so true that when serious situations arose, such quarrels would be set aside, and all would unite–apart from a praise-worthy handful of liberals–against the Muslim. That point had not yet been reached. But already the dominant race had cut itself off from the world it had sought to exclude. The egocentric dispute within which it confined itself made it–despite appearances–a minority, perhaps already an alien, in respect to that nation which so imperatively had to be formed. Only nobody suspected this.

The Great Reversal

Cult, or rejection, of the past? This is the title of a novel about conversion, published a long time after it was written by the historian Mukhtar al-Susi.[1] I should incline to date it between 1925 and 1930, like most of the phenomena hitherto considered in this chapter. The narrator has three brothers, one mystical and wealthy, the second a shabby, corrupt shopkeeper, the third a lawyer, divorced from a European wife; the four of them represent aspects of the traditional type, now disintegrated. A piety at variance with the times, a Europeanism at variance with the country, and an anti-social deprivation, are all three contrasted with the middle-of-the-road position of the fourth brother, an honourable man, a good Muslim and a good Moroccan, concerned with finding reasonable ways of adaptation. The hero seeks to redeem the brother whom the West has led astray. Hence an exchange of letters, a sort of psychological novel highly revealing about the conflicts within Maghribi families and individual souls at that period.

The time had long since passed when the citizens of Islam, represented by the 'Ulama' of Fez, would play homage to the great mystical houses, as they did at the time of Ma' al-'Ainin. Later generations show a striking evolution. The young men of the thirties, belonging to the oldest and noblest families of Morocco, led the modernist movement. Men like 'Allal al-Fasi, Bil Hasan al-Wazzani, Brahim Kittani, Makki Nasiri or Rashid Darqawi have personally experienced this change of gear. Because, quite apart from political events, and the growing if not

[1] 'Baina'l-jumud wal-juhud', in Da'wat al-haqq, 1957.

universal influence of French culture, or at least of Western life, they sought to adapt themselves to the Middle-Eastern emancipation movement. In the august *Khizana* of Qarawiyin, the masters sadly observed that their students, particularly the young men of Fez, read only Egyptian reviews. They actually *read*, which was a terrible revolution! The old chants sung by rote, *hifz*, were being replaced by *mutala'a*–reading to oneself.[1] This was a sort of profanation. An incomplete one however, for this younger generation, standing between two wars and between two worlds, had not yet repudiated its childhood idols. It thus considered with almost religious awe the development of Syria and particularly that of Egypt, as communicated to it through the intermediary of the *Hilal*.

The *Salafiya* movement, which Henri Laoust was then studying in Cairo,[2] provided these adolescents, who combined in an enthusiastic syncretism religious anxiety and national resentment, with a pious alibi. Its ambiguity served it well. Here and there, indeed, old believers denounced its weaknesses; true, their attacks were inspired by a narrow ritualism, and thus their battle was lost in advance. But restricted as they were by literalism, they foresaw that their adversaries' advocacy of reason and moderation would slacken religious tension and eventually weaken the sense of transcendancy. But they did not know how to say it; their attack was feeble. The reformists, who also had the advantage of eloquence, ridiculed them. In so doing, however, they did not go beyond certain limits. They themselves broached certain problems, such as the feminine question, with infinite precautions. This became clear at the time of the quarrel provoked by Haddad's book.[3]

Wherein lay progress, wherein reaction? In the sphere of conscience, the Socialists were quite right to condemn the conservatism prudently preached by the Old Destour. But in so far as this prudence concerned one of the last defences of the Muslim, and so to speak one of the last fields in which he could exercise his sovereignty, it must be considered, objectively, as more progressive than its opponents. On the other hand, once emancipation was in sight, and still more once it had been achieved, it would be 'barbarous' to defend the wearing of the veil, or polygamy . . .

When the Tunisian Land Office (*Service foncier*) passed its law protecting the 'occupiers', it injured those wealthy citizens, mostly members of the upper bourgeoisie, who were heirs by transmission of the *habus*; their protest eventually secured the abrogation of the decree by Marcel Peyrouton, which was scarcely a good sign. Meanwhile Bahri Giga, one of the subtlest of intellectuals, had attacked this 'class struggle legislation' and even praised the peaceful existence of the tenant farmer, living

---

[1] I noted this at the time in an article written for the *Annales d'histoire économique et sociale*, 'Dans le Maroc nouveau, la vie d'une université islamique', 1937.

[2] His article in the *Revue des Études islamiques* excited great interest.

[3] Cf. p. 102.

'under the generous and beneficent aegis of the *zawiyas*'.[1] This decree, for all its equivocal character, had beneficial results when applied by liberals such as Henri de Montéty. But it attacked the economic basis of the Destour, which at the time was indistinguishable from the old Tunisian bourgeoisie. The apparently reactionary protest was thus justified in the long run. Would it be so on a still longer view?

All these things represent conflicts between levels of significance[2] and also illustrate radical changes imprinted on these by the course of history.

In Algeria, the one of the three North African countries where European impact was most strongly felt, these conflicts and uncertainties reached their highest point. Shaikhs al-'Uqbi and Bin Badis defended, as an inviolable fortress, an individuality which they proclaimed to be Islamic and even Arab. They thus opposed the assimilationism of Ferhat 'Abbas, who, as we have seen, was equally staunch in his insistence on 'status'. And from 1936 onward a third cry was heard, the demand for independence. Which of the three formulae, which were interconnected rather than true rivals, corresponded most closely to the profound wishes of the community, the nature of things and the opportunity of the moment? One has the impression that doctrinal opposition was prepared to compromise on grounds of fact. It implied as much sometimes to the Popular Front, which, as is well known, turned a deaf ear. The quarrel of levels of significance here touches on politics, but this unfortunately makes it none the clearer . . .

Haddad, an occasional versifier, had dared to exclaim: 'Enough! The Arabs are content to be anything and everything, they rest on the virtue of their ancestors, they have thus destroyed within themselves their forces of renewal, they have destroyed one another in the service of their hatreds, while their own learning illuminated others and their sign, their significance, retreated . . .'[3]

This revolutionary message was also that of a great Tunisian poet at this period. Shabbi, in about 1930, returned to his native Jerid. Then began for him what his biographers call 'the era of disasters', *nakabat*.

He lost his father; a cruel blow, for this father was his deeply respected guide. He married; but we are told nothing about this marriage, even in the recent number of the review *al-Fikr* devoted to the poet. There are thus in his life many episodes, or rather many elements, about which we are ignorant. Finally he died, from what cause we do not know, in 1934, about the same time as Tahar al-Haddad.

---

[1] *Action tunisienne*, 2 Nov. 1932.

[2] This is reflected in Shabbi's lecture on the Arabs' poetic imagination. Cf. *al-'Alam al-adabi*, by Snusi, 1930. *Al-Shihab* echoes the lecture, Mar. 1930, p. 125.

[3] Abu'l-Qasim Karru, *al-Tahir al-Haddad*, p. 45.

In this poet the 'will to live', *Iradat al-hayat,* had something of the pantheistic inspiration of Walt Whitman. His poetry thus goes far beyond the traditional *hamasa.*[1] He speaks of his hope: 'If the people seek life one day, fate will perforce answer them, the night will perforce fade away, and the oak tree perforce be broken.'[2] Then he amplifies his theme, associating this dynamic force with nature and, as ever, abjuring the past: 'I curse the man who does not evolve with time; he is content with the life of a stone. See the universe, so full of life; it loves life and despises the dead, however great they were' (*mahma kabura*). The accent is a revolutionary one. 'When souls aspire to life, fate is forced to answer them.'

But in the case of Shabbi, how did fate reply? On this point, listen to his poem on the unappreciated prophet: *al-Nabi al-Majhul.* ('Prophet': Jubran had written thus, thus was Schehadé to write; the longing of the Islamo-Mediterranean world for mighty voices that would denounce the evils of the present and dominate the future through their incantations.) 'O my people, why am I not a woodcutter? I would rush at the trees with my axe! Why am I not like the torrents which in their course destroy tombs, one after the other!'

Or again: 'All that feels the light, all that creeps on the earth or flies above it, birds, flowers, scents, springs, waving branches, oceans, caverns, mountain peaks, volcanoes, valleys, deserts, light, shade, darkness, seasons, clouds, thunder, snow, vanishing mists, hurricane and fertile rains, catechism, religion, vision, sensation, silence and song; all of it lives in my heart, freely like the children of eternity, forever fresh and enchanted.'

A little further on a melancholy poem on his father: *I 'tiraf,* Confession. A feeling of robust tenderness links this innovator with the preceding generation. 'I did not think, O my father, that after your death I could still remain thirsty for life, could drink intoxication from its stream, could go back into the world with a heart yearning for delights and songs.' Life prevails over pain. 'Truly, the son of Adam in the very depths of his soul is the slave of life, which inserts itself within his faith.' And this appeal to unconditional life, this impulse towards nature, towards the freshness and the copious force of what is new, puts Shabbi in the direct line of the great Mediterranean poets.

Shabbi, Haddad: two unequal figures, indeed, but who are at one in their common challenge of traditional things. The unappreciated poet and the unappreciated reformer withdrew from the struggle in about 1930, betrayed by their people and persecuted by the authorities. The precocity of their message kept from them those who should best have

---

[1] *hamasa*: collection of ancient Arabic poems in the epic genre.

[2] I follow, somewhat freely, the translation by Ahmad Guedira (Qadira) (Seghers, 1959), comparing it with the Arabic text of the *Aghani'l-hayat.* One of the first 'discoverers' of Shabbi was al-Mahidi, *al-Afkar,* 1 Dec. 1936.

understood it, that section of their own people who remained deaf to them, and among the French those who should have welcomed in their writing the shattering of a Maghrib too narrowly restricted, and the consequent upsurge of that which, in a new Maghrib, might best respond to France. A dialogue was thus lost. It would have gone beyond political controversy, since Haddad and Shabbi touched something deeper. The lyricism of the one, the revolutionary impulse of the other—for Haddad, as we have seen, sought not only the emancipation of woman but that of the working man–expressed a variation on the relations between man, woman, nature and technique. Both of them, starting from the most traditional culture, that of theologians and scholiasts, came to reject its obsolete elements. And the experience of both, starting from the colonial system, without which they would have been inconceivable, covers a splendid range of feeling and of action. It opens on to a future which is not only that of their nation but of humanity. And it speaks its wise advice not only to the North Africans of 1930, but to those of the future.

The Return of Ibn Khaldun

Apart from any question of political morality, no message from French learning or literature had such aptness in North Africa at the time. There was nothing immature about these; but their testimony was neither spontaneous nor critical enough. The often outstanding merit of the authors is unquestionable; so is the remarkable excellence of their techniques, although the discipline which concerns us most here, namely sociology, denied its object not indeed all human dignity, but any historic existence.[1]

Among the scholars, of whom many were my masters and my friends, I shall confine myself to discussing one, the most talented of all. Of E.-F. Gautier's epoch-making books two chiefly, *Les Siècles Obscurs du Maghreb* and *Moeurs et coutumes des musulmans* have won acceptance for a typology in which East and West are indefinitely counterbalanced: the 'biological' system of the one, the 'local' or 'topographical' system of the other; the tribe on the one hand, the village on the other. Here we

---

[1] 'In the land of the Berbers, however attentively one studies human events, everything remains somewhat drab, monotonous, lacking in relief. However one strives to rise above the facts, one fails to discover those broad and luminous historic landscapes that Renan so powerfully described in his studies of the East, when he showed us, as from the summit of a high mountain, the vast currents of civilization flowing in from every direction. On the contrary we discover here, for the most part, only an inextricable tangle of dried-up ravines, a dusty heap of insignificant incidents which depress the spirit and seem irreducible to any logical classification' (R. Montagne, 'La vie politique des Berbères', *Renseignements coloniaux*, Aug. 1931). Nothing is more illustrative of the difference between two generations of researchers, corresponding to the progress of reality itself, than the contrast between such a viewpoint and that of the present work.

find the visual antithesis between the society of transhumants and the settlers' centre which grows at its expense and devours it. But Gautier did not perceive the transformations which, at the very time he was writing, were shifting the alternative. It could now be considered in economic and social terms, no longer racial but in certain respects national. Henceforward the contrast lay between the activation of forms resulting from colonization–towns, villages, working-class suburbs above all–and the bureaucracy of a self-satisfied, bourgeoisified system; between landless pauperism and a dispossessing landlord class; above all, between present and future. And when the ingenious professor scrutinizes the past, the only conclusion he draws from Ibn Khaldun's message–although he does so with some profundity–is an admission of powerlessness, almost an abdication. Now Ibn Khaldun had noted, and had condemned in unforgettable terms, the settling of nomads in a country of orchards, and hence the collapse of a society of Islamo-Mediterranean sedentaries. But in fact Ibn Khaldun's true place is elsewhere; he was a man of the Renaissance, out of his setting. His life, a long story of ambition and failure, was spent not in Florence but in an already besieged and despairing Granada, a Middle East overrun by Mongols, a Maghrib dominated by its tribes. His criticism, as 'prospective', one might say, as that of Machiavelli, formed no school. Five hundred years after him, the French geographer reads in his work only the story of failure, not the promise of revival.

Gautier's analysis thus reaches a deadlock common to his time. In his system, two possible futures seem unalterably determined: that of the North Africans' Maghrib, doomed to economic precariousness and social stagnation, and that of the European settlers' Maghrib, doomed to exploit the weaknesses of others and to foster their divisions. Such was in fact the situation at the time. It could not but arouse anxiety. Seeking to become totally and enduringly rooted in this Maghribi land, the French system postulated the incorporation of its citizens in the Maghrib. But in what form, in what direction, at what cost?

The same hesitancy, reflecting the same contradiction, can be seen in the work of an essayist and novelist to whose testimony I have frequently referred: Robert Randau. It is an important and unduly neglected achievement. True, his study of Algerian life, seen through the eyes of an explorer rather than a *colon*'s, has not found an appropriate style. It, too, stops half-way. Randau, in spite of his gifts of observation and feeling, was himself a victim of that failure to express things, or to express oneself, which seems to me one of the characteristics of the *milieu*, and his writing, for all its violence and rhetoric, remains unconvincing. The North African French sought a means of self-expression and failed, even in the case of their most important witness, because the system denied them, and denied itself, a language.

Last Literary Openings

Arab broadcasting did not develop in Tunisia until after 1938. But then it made amazing strides. Its review, *Thuraya*, ('The Pleiades'), became an organ of great literary significance. The man who speaks over the radio differs from the old-fashioned man of letters, proudly concerned with unusual words and assonances. He is pressed for time; he learns to improvise on his subject, *maudu'*, within specified limits. He seeks collaboration from every genre: music and declamation, prose and poetry, dissertation and the drama. He thus aims at an aesthetic totality which had been dreamed of, though never clearly envisaged. The new human voice, whose volume could be regulated with such wonderful ease, revived a power that had been lost: the spoken word, reinstated in its old dignity, over and above the prestige of the printed word, which despite the recent spread of printing had not completely lost its esoteric character. The new voice, even when it spoke in classical style, could be felt, if not wholly understood. To quote an Arab poem:

> *I did not understand the meaning, but my heart was grieved by it, and I understood its grief.*[1]

It carried the major themes of its time into men's homes, and even into women's hearts. The type of humanity which it served to express was different not only from the earlier generation which I have described, but also from the pioneer generation of the 1925–30 era. The latter, who figure in the last pages of the anthologies of Qabbaj and Snusi, deserve to be considered more closely, as they were at the time by observers as friendly as François Bonjean and Émile Dermenghem. They studied at the Lycée Français, but they were alert to developments in the Arab East.[2] While fervently seeking to absorb all that was best in French culture, they discovered, with equal fervour, that at times they detested France. 'Ali Bilhawan set his pupils the following subject for an essay: 'What do you feel when you see a European in Tunis?'[3] A social sense, fostered by the decay of the old groups, gave rise to numerous clubs and associations. The younger generation was aware of itself as a social class. It terrified its elders. In the national library of Tunis, it read nothing but romantic literature, except for Gustave Lebon's book on Arab civilization. It eagerly scanned the pages of illustrated magazines from Cairo. Its attitude towards the Arab East was rather too much influenced by that of the Orientalists, or again consisted merely in reversing the

---

[1] Lines quoted by Fadil bin 'Ashur, *al-Haraka al-adabiya*, pp. 181 ff. This admirably distinguishes values of expression from values of meaning . . .

[2] P. Letellier, 'Le jeune Tunisien', *Ibla*, 1937. The journal *al-Nadim*, of Tunis, devoted a special number (1932) to the literary revival. *Al-Shihab* itself examined the 'malady of the young', May 1931, p. 213 and *passim*.

[3] According to one of his pupils.

attitudes of Colonialists. In these effusions, not everything is of positive
value. An unfriendly critic might justly denounce their impulsiveness,
their derivative character. These young writers were in too much of a
hurry, and they took merely the outer shell, rather than the deep meaning, of the cultures that surrounded them, whether French or Arabic.
But could they have done any better?

Already, several years previously, Shabbi had written to his friend
Hliwi: 'I want to live, but for what? With my heart shattered against the
stones of life, *sukhur al-hayat*; with my unhappy consciousness; a life
spent wandering round obscure tomorrows . . .'[1] And another forerunner
of so many later developments, a Moroccan youth who, emaciated and
bitter-eyed, left the aristocratic twilight of the Fez madina and the
mazes of theology to pursue the great themes of the *risorgimento*:

'As soon as I had completed my fifteenth year, and while I was still
at play and intoxicated with the pleasures of life, I was possessed by a
lofty thought, by a spirit of recusancy. My people are unhappy. They
have found no path towards what they desire. For their sake I gave up
my life's pastimes, I could swallow neither food nor drink . . . I no longer
knew sleep . . . I was prey to a devouring fire . . .'[2]

Once again, however, political disquiet merely revealed deeper
conflicts. A young Moroccan yearns for a 'revolution of reason', *thaurat
al-'aql*,[3] just as Chateaubriand had once appealed to the 'longed-for
storms'. In the same review[4] Sa'id Hijji, who was to die prematurely in
1942, protests that 'we look in vain through the Arabic dictionary to
find an epithet that can describe this younger generation of ours. I can
find only *ghafl*: 'heedless' youth, youth that lacks 'a sign'. We recall
Rimbaud's

> *Oisive jeunesse*
> *à tout asservie,*
> *Par délicatesse*
> *j'ai perdu ma vie.*

These young Moroccans, too, were wasting their lives away. And
Sa'id Hijji, reproaches them for it with touching sincerity. No doubt
political activity appeared to some of them as the only way out. But
others were to have recourse to drugs, or to suicide. The unfortunate
al-Qurri was to die in prison: *zughbi*, his friends in Fez called him,
'doomed to misfortune' from childhood onwards. A number of Tunisian
writers, proud of their desperate Bohemianism, forgathered at the

[1] Letter from Shabbi to Hliwi, *Afkar*, 1 Nov. 1936.

[2] 'Allal al-Fasi, in the collection by Qabbaj, *al-Adab al-'arabi fi'l-Maghrib
al-Aqsa*, vol. II, 1929, pp. 2 ff.

[3] *Al-Thaqafa al-Maghribiya*, 12 May 1938. The article is by 'Abdallah
Ibrahim, future president of the Council. On the 'malady of youth', *Shibab*,
May 1930.

[4] Ibid, 26 April 1938.

'Madmen's Club'. One of these, at least, had talent: Du'aji, who has surprised the present generation by his uncanny foresight.[1]

These examples, indeed, are taken from the intelligentsia. The crowd,
which might have recognized in them its own secret distress, concealed its
uneasiness behind coarse laughter. The popular bard al-Smawi criticizes
the young man of the new Iron Age: 'This generation has acquired a sad
reputation! Always on its high horse, always picking holes, never saying
yes to anything. You see a boat unfurling velvet sails, but it's sure to be
carrying horrible black coal.'[2]

No doubt these brief and scattered expressions of feeling did not, save
in the case of Shabbi, lead to any great literary work. The sacrificed
generation, which so tragically recorded the failure of its elders, was to
turn to action rather than fiction in order to recover its balance. Even so
it was, at the time, severely restricted by an order which it did not merely
endure but to some extent endorsed. For Arabic-speaking intellectuals
were more keenly aware than anyone else of the attraction, as well as
the danger, of imported culture. Imported though it was, it had its own
intrinsic merits. In order to resist it one must understand, and so love it.
If there was antagonism between opposing parties, there was equally
a conflict, or contradiction, within each of them which is characteristic
of the Colonial problem. For the influence of France was felt more
through the dissatisfaction it created than through what it actually gave.
France thus created its most effective political opponents. But the contradiction was equally bitter for those enemies who were too closely
involved. The intelligentsia, won over to the values they were combating,
daringly took their stand mid-way between France and the Maghrib.
Then, repudiated by both sides, they gave way to doubts and lamenta-
tions. Such is the sad lesson of an era of struggle! Hostility, inspired by
deep-rooted resentment, does not preclude sympathy for your adversary;
while your own country, for which you suffer and may even die, rejects
the prophetic image of itself that you offer it.

Correlative to the development of written Arabic, but unconnected
with it, a great French-North African style grew up at that time. The
reign of the 'Algerianists' came to a close without bequeathing to the
country which they felt rather than understood either a Kipling, a Zola
or a Durrell. The gaps in their aesthetic achievement reveal the defeat
of their reality. They reflect, in spite of themselves, what was barren and
limited in their period. But before being repudiated by history, they
were rejected by the literary movement of the parent state. Once again
the baroque, picturesque and picaresque elements stood condemned.

[1] Taufiq Bakkar, 'al-Du'aji', al-Tajdid, Tunis, no. 5-6, 1961, p. 76. Cf. Farid
Ghazi, 'La littérature tunisienne contemporaine', Orient, no. 12.
[2] Ibla, 1939, pp. 78 ff.

Through the Algerian Camus, an effort towards an unattainable purity was pursued. Many social elements contributed towards this paradoxical 'francisation'. With the progress of broadcasting, of mass communication, of air transport, the Maghrib was losing its provincial character; and also, to some extent, its individuality. It was no longer possible for an artist, a man of letters or a teacher to make a great career in the Maghrib solely by means of the Maghrib. This had both good and evil effects. Good, since inspiration was no longer confined to the colonial confrontation; evil, since North African anguish and anger took their place in French literary jurisprudence, and were thus ennobled, at the cost of being expurgated.[1]

The number of galleries grew; museums were enriched. The growing cult of the gramophone and of concert-going made people familiar with symphonic music. Grenier and Hytier at the Faculty of Algiers, Guibert in Tunis, Bosco at Rabat spoke in a universal language which perhaps paid too little attention to the concrete things of the Maghrib. New young magazines, such as *Mythra, Fontaine, Mirages, Les Cahiers de Barbarie* and *Aguedal* correspond closely to the *Nouvelle Revue Française* or, even more, to the *Cahiers du Sud*.

But the Maghrib was too remote, or else too close; transplanted into great French writing, it could survive only by means of sublimation. Whoever lived within its shores soon felt the need to emigrate from them. Past a certain stage, Maghribi literature had to choose between literary truth at the cost of local authenticity, or the reverse.

To a certain extent, indeed, talent can raise a writer above such a contradiction. True literature can be achieved without a factual accuracy which is perhaps better neglected; of this we find sufficient proof in Gabriel Audisio, a Mediterranean writer who cannot forget Africa, and whose fiery inspiration is undying.[2] Jean Amrouche, whose *Chants Berbères* I have already quoted, prophetically sketches the outlaw, smoking his cigarette on the mountain top, with the bitter tang of the oleander on his lips.[3] Among the rising generation, Emmanuel Roblès, J. Roy, R.-J. Clot, J. Senac, and the most illustrious of them all, Albert Camus, we hear the clear egotistic voice of youth, haunting Tipaza and the small bars of Bab el-Oued.

But meanwhile a younger generation of a different sort, stronger through knowing the adversary and having suffered more, was already preparing its literary message, within the mazes of the mountain and of

[1] The influence of French 'models' on Camus was so strong that *qua* moralist he by-passed the problem of his generation and his native province, and *qua* novelist he only admitted the Maghrib into his work after subjecting it to much elaboration, and consequent mutilation.

[2] G. Audisio has also undertaken to write the history of this section of French literature, and I am indebted to him for many useful suggestions.

[3] J. Amrouche, *Chants berbères de Kabylie*, 1938.

the mind. A message, or a battle? The Casbah of Algiers is itself a maze. 'This usurped strength, which discovers itself and transforms any attempt at escape into an exile, this strength through suffering, is what impels militants into action from the very threshold of their childhood, often in defence of a refuge from which there is no way out. For the condemned man going to his death, this crepitating white night blots out everything, covers everything, to infinity. This is indeed the inextricable plenitude of the "star-shaped polygon", where the inner void dies out like a camp fire, all forms abolished. Peace be to its ashes.'[2]

[1] Kateb Yacine, at the end of our conversation, reported in *Afrique-Action*, 26 June 1961.

Part 5

The Maghrib: Past and Future

CHAPTER XVII

'France, In these Lands, was Unaware...'

F rance, in these lands, was unaware of her own mortality. So too, were the men of the Maghrib. Now, less than twenty years after the last developments described in this book, great changes have occurred, posing a new set of problems and implicating all the continuous traditions of this section of the world. And even more tremendous changes are looming ahead.

The emergence of new nations from the maturity of an empire ought not to have been considered by France, or by those who had broken free from her, as her defeat. But circumstances which are still only too much present dramatized the birth of these nations. Between two such antagonists, this was inevitable. Both the French and the Arabs consider any battle as a judgment of God. Victory in 1918 had seemed to justify France's privileges, whereas in fact it intensified her duties. Forty years after, the cessation of Colonial power inverted these legendary moralities. For the men of the Maghrib, the era that was their freedom's prehistory was seen, by a strange paradox, as that unremitting hell depicted by many Frenchmen. France, as is her custom, pronounces an ethical judgment on any period concluding with a catastrophe, or an apparent catastrophe. Only, in opportune contrast with other phases of her history which ended equally disastrously–the Second Empire, the Third Republic–she was able in this case to ascribe part of her responsibilities to someone else. It was thus her local agents, administrators, *colons* and *petits blancs*, who bore the blame, rather than France herself. Thus their villainy freed her from her remorse, which in its turn served to justify the loss she had suffered. Now the accusations, even the condemnations which must be made in this case, have nothing to do with masochism, the quest for alibis, or the transference of passions.

In the present work, I have constantly abstained from facile anachronistic judgments in considering the things and the people of an epoch that is past.[1] And yet the conclusion, twenty years later, enables us to see things in perspective. No doubt the general direction of history did not exclude other eventualities. But this was what actually happened. It was thus enough to preserve, in telling the story, an awareness of possibilities, as in a tragedy whose end is known to everyone, author and spectators, but in which all the same the action is held suspended between the fate decided by the gods and man's free will. In a study concerned with distinguishing the degrees of significance of events and things, we thus held a guiding thread. Writing after the event, we were able to analyse or rather to unfold what, to those living through it, appeared undivided. The flavour of life at that time, which people felt but could not explain, revealed its historic content long afterwards. It is only today that we can understand why so much initiative failed, why so much good-will and talent were expended fruitlessly. For the Colonial hypothesis has shown itself to be sterile in the long run, and as wasteful of the colonizers' faculties as of the lives of those colonized.

Finally, it is only by seeing things from this distance that we can allot responsibilities. Now we know unquestionably that the reformers' view was the right one, although it did not go far enough; that the 'agitators' were wiser than 'right-minded people', that conservatism was in the wrong, not only in preventing new developments but in liquidating actual achievements. When the *colon* mayors resigned sensationally in order to interrupt consideration of the Blum-Viollette project, they assumed a terrible responsibility not only towards the future of the Maghrib but towards France's heritage. They shared it with those Parliaments and governments that upheld their excesses, and buried that project of reform as they buried that of the Franco-Syrian and Franco-Lebanese treaties. France, at any rate political France, thus lost one of her great opportunities of modern times.

It was admirable that a newcomer from Alicante or a young Kabyle from the mountains should both be able to claim their share in French culture. In the contemporary process which reduces the diversities of the planet to a handful of major types, France played an honourable part. The British Empire appeared better endowed for successful transactions than for fundamental actions. American influence had not yet asserted its force. Spain seemed a 'small nation'. China was still colonial. Little was known about the ethnographic humanism of the Soviet Union in Asia. France seemed to surpass all these world-shapers by the boldness of her promises. And now, through weakness and avarice, she abandoned her mission. To have set up the colonization of the Maghrib as a symbol of her achievement, to have favoured it above other factors which were more valid or merely more viable, to have failed to

[1] On this point I agree with the salutary comments of Ch.-A. Julien in his preface to P. Nora's interesting book, *Les Français d'Algérie*, 1961.

revise pernicious decisions when the time came, and to have misunderstood or persecuted those who championed such revision, all this showed singular blindness on the part of France.

It would obviously be possible to allot responsibilities even more precisely, to the point of mentioning groups and individuals; but a deeper study of these things leads one to implicate, as this book has repeatedly done, the system itself within which groups and individuals function. I do not mean by this to make vague accusations against the colonial régime, but in a less sentimental and more historical fashion, an indictment of the position in which it placed Metropolitan France in relation to the Europeans and Muslims of the Maghrib.

The parent state, confirmed by the long history of its power, made even greater by the successful outcome of the Great War, seemed to justify its title of 'Metropolis'. Not so much the 'mother' implied by etymology as a dominating father, to whom his children looked for care as much as they dreaded his anger. A voracious father, to whom volunteers and conscripts sacrificed their flesh unsparingly, as many campaigns bore witness; but who reigned protected by his myth, exalted by his civilizing role, while others, far beneath him, carried out their tasks of exploitation and administration. His proconsuls played the part of mere gamekeepers, while business men and *colons* were his humble investment-agents; meanwhile his majesty was cleared of all blame for the excesses committed in its name. Local authorities were contrasted with those of the parent state; subjects felt that 'Frenchmen from France' would always put things right. This meant losing sight of the colonial relationship, which consisted, as far as the parent state was concerned, in draining the result of men's labour and the land's fertility towards Administrative Councils, and transforming them into financial values. But it also involved discovering the French nation's true character, which, though most frequently distorted by those who ruled in its name, would break out from time to time in generous outbursts, and which survived, always recognizable, in its thinkers and revolutionaries.

In any case, true or false, this was the image of France which dominated all the disputes of the time from afar. Some subjects endured, others accepted it. All, more or less, both accepted and endured it. The system, despite the use of coercion, was not merely a matter of penalties and rewards. It also imposed itself from within. The variety of situations gave rise to this strange sense of Metropolitan France as a father-figure, to which Islam, though still unconquered in men's hearts, offered no real competition. For although the men of the Maghrib still turned to religion for symbols of their resistance, and looked to the Arab East for archetypes and true images of themselves, they had more or less taken France into their inner lives. Not only through language, behaviour, fashion, literature, imitation, adherence, but also and perhaps chiefly through rebellion, those 'models' which we have repeatedly pin-pointed through this story ensured the authority of the usurping father-figure, even though this led men eventually to emancipate themselves from that authority. But the man of the Maghrib was aware of a constantly aggravated contrast between the France he desired and the France he knew by experience, in a word between the ideal and the reality of France.

Now the latter, naturally, differed widely from the former, and no-where as much as in the Colonial relationship. The University, the French press, the inspiring intercourse between young North African patriots and the Left wing intelligentsia, the whole marvellous story told by the books and landscapes and monuments of France, were increasingly in contrast with the shabby realities of Colonial life. Students and workers, consciously or not, experienced this discrepancy in their own lives and spread bitter resentment of it. Many a young Algerian, proudly aware of his hard-won culture, would protest, when faced with the crude barbarism of certain Frenchmen, that he was the truer representative of France. And if his fellows in Tunisia and Morocco did not share this passionate urge towards assimilation, at least he shared with them an admiration for civilized values and a bitter hatred of those who enjoyed privilege by right of their civil status. But in practice the latter predominated over those whose actions might be inspired by the ideals of the parent state. It was thus foreseeable that any total revolt would some day reject both that reality which was guilty of prevailing over the ideal, and that ideal which was guilty of failing to make itself obeyed. The day would come when the tension between the two would become intolerable; in other words, when the growing influence of French models, among them those of the Revolution and the Resistance, would have lost all plausible connection with the colonial situation. And then, as other hitherto repressed or down-trodden forces emerged, offended Arabism would unite with disappointed pro-French sympathies to produce a terrible explosion.

In 1939 this was still a fair way off. The authority of France was protected by the achievements of secular education, by its military prestige, its democracy which was still respected, the heritage of 1789, and a position in the world which was still sound. But the inner sympathy with one France and the anger against another France, the idealization of the one and the indictment of the other, intensified awareness of France's guilt. The Frenchman's existence was more real, for the man of the Maghrib, than that of any other colonizer for any subject race. Was this France's opportunity, or her misfortune?

The power of these models was equally felt by the Europeans of North Africa. They paid their racial tribute as courageously, if not as meritoriously, as the native Africans. At least two-thirds of them were foreigners by blood; but they freely paid the price for access to what they considered a superior form of citizenship. They implanted a new race on Maghribi soil, guilty of disregarding its predecessors on that soil, yet energetic and ardent. Intellectually they remained neophytes. Their literature, whether restricted to regional picturesqueness or aiming at universalité, was in either case dominated by Parisian standards.[1] The same submission can be observed in their language and in their customs.

If this partial community of ideals between natives and Europeans led to nothing lastingly constructive, it was because they were at cross purposes. Each expected the same ruler to act in opposite ways. The Europeans tried to confirm their preponderance with the help of France; the Muslims sought to shake off that domination. For the former, France stood guarantee for the established situation; while the latter expected her to make reparation. The system, consciously or not, made use of this discord. Official France mistakenly encouraged these rival interpretations. Between herself and the two North African populations on the one hand and between these two populations on the other, existed an equivocal relationship. In exchange for an unconditional allegiance which was to prove ruinous for both parties in the long run, the parent state granted the North African Europeans *carte blanche* to exploit the country, limited perhaps by humanitarian or technical considerations but not at all by any feeling for the other party's nationhood. The future development of that other nation, which had been clearly claimed as early as the thirties, and even boldly planned for by Maghribi and French reformers, was obstructed by the French with postponements or deliberate refusals, even by repression. Thus the beneficiaries of the régime were encouraged to dig themselves in, preserving their own advantages on the basis of a French domination increasingly contrary to the whole trend of French history. In fact the system proved more oppressive— both subjectively and objectively—at the end of the period than at the beginning.

The result was not only that it aroused furious resentment, but that human elements whose chief virtue had been audacity became rigid in their conservatism. The sons or successors of pioneers grew wholly bourgeois. On almost every plane, they were not merely content to frustrate the progress of things to their own advantage. They did worse; they frustrated their own progress, in the cultural and economic spheres, in the broader social and moral fields. Outwardly sovereign, this power stopped short of self-fulfilment. Was it through lack of energy, through demographic weakness? One could argue about the reasons, but the fact is undeniable. Under its apparent prosperity, ardour and exactness, French North Africa seemed to falter and give up from the thirties onwards. Such a view may seem paradoxical. Rising nationalism felt

[1] It is interesting to note that the *Robert* Dictionary, successor to *Littré*, originated from Algeria.

itself to be struggling against total submersion. In appearance, this may have been the case. But actually the reverse was true. The dwindling vitality of the Europeans implied a more genuine menace. If it had declined, it was because it had stopped short in the very process that constituted its right and its destiny: its impulse towards the land and people of the Maghrib.

French domination had gone beyond straightforward mercantile control from the start. It had sought to implant itself, to appropriate to itself these people and their land. It could only do this by also adapting itself to them. For reasons of which many escape us, and which include the increasingly devious use of the parent state's authority, it ceased, after a certain point, to keep up the effort. The period of financial enrichment and political concentration that followed the organization of the colony in 1900 is broadly coincident with this process. Defeat could be foreseen, in the long run; not as yet political defeat but, more seriously, anthropological failure. The dominant race did not look forward to any creative future in which it would assume responsibility, even in its own interests, for the destiny of this land. It became set in the *status quo* of conservatism and exploitation. It thus competed with the mass of the native population, to whom it made no serious offer of future prospects. Excluding any future for the Other, it jeopardized its own future. While subscribing to the doctrine of Metropolitan centralism to an excessive degree, it made use of this to defend its own privileges indefinitely. And in doing so it debased and disqualified that doctrine.

Thus rejecting all chances of assimilation, by which I mean not the absorption of the Maghrib into the parent state's identity but the disinterested expansion of French values in the Maghrib, the French colonial drifted apart from Metropolitan France, towards whom he felt increasingly alien. More dangerously, he was cutting himself off from the life of the people around him, of whose existence he grew less and less aware, whereas they were increasingly aware of his. Whether indeed by intellectual attraction or by colonial resentment, the Frenchman appeared to the native as essentially *someone who is there*; the result was a moral enrichment, to which the harshness of experience contributed no less than the benefits of education. But this sense of presence was no longer reciprocal. In the inter-war period, the native had become increasingly the concern of specialists. His real nature interested only revolutionaries and researchers, or a few survivors from the pioneer generation; not even, always, the Arabic scholar! For the European, who, or rather what, was 'the native'? A menace, an uncertain quantity, something to be made use of or at best to be taken care of.

Whatever conclusion one comes to about the basic hypothesis of the system–and I have already stressed the futility of eleventh-hour moralizing–one cannot but fail to recognize the worsening effect of such relationships even in their original position. They eliminated all chances of discussion among the three parties involved.

Such a system entails dangerous weakness, or, if you like, immorality. From 1919, and still more from 1930 onwards, its end was felt to be inevitable. True, when the second world war broke out, the threat was still in abeyance. The chronological framework of this book is too limited to include the whole of a story which should by rights have started at the beginning of the century (an all-important date for Algeria) and ended with the Sétif rising of 1945. But any framework would have been arbitrary. Within the limits of the one I have chosen, no irremediable tensions were felt. At all events, they were not decisively formulated. The opposition almost always acted by proxy and through synonymies. Even before the 1914 war it had shifted from the ground of elementary revolt or metaphysical rejection to that of a contest, which implied an exchange. Moderate attitudes visibly prevailed over extreme attitudes, a *modus vivendi* over uncompromisingness. France controlled the ordinary affairs of life. True, at the opposite poles of violence – that of the subject and that of the colonizer – the antagonism persisted. To the image of the oppressor, who tainted whatever he touched, corresponded that of the inferior fit only to provide manual labour, cannon fodder and building material. But in everyday life such incongruities were discreetly repressed. On the surface of events and of behaviour, ambiguity reigned.

I have therefore dwelt not on the mutual challenge of incompatible ideas, the contest between rival theses, but on the relation that grew up between them, the modifications and, finally, the social being that arose from their intercourse. This was a reaction against so many studies which, by insisting too much on first data, distort the secondary reality which is derived from these. Such reality is nowhere seen better than in the Maghrib between the two wars, which is characterized by mutual conditioning, almost general adulteration, and ambiguity. The colonial phenomenon, which consists of destroying and remaking, is here to be found in the very heart of people and things.

Even when, on the occasion of a conflict, the ambiguity is resolved into such antitheses as revolt versus conservation, resistance versus repression, the opposition remains more formal than real. To deny the clear-cut character of the issues does not mean lessening the sharpness of the conflict; on the contrary. Although it drew much of its strength from a sense of kinship with the Middle East, the nationalist movement was based to a large extent on what it was fighting. Independence was already claimed as the ultimate goal, and envisaged as the very negation of colonialism; but however keenly both parties strove within this negation, they would achieve nothing until they had left it behind. If they derived part of their substance from forces anterior or exterior to colonialism, they derived another part from its positive character. And neither in the present nor in the future will anything emerge from the confusion–no accurate ideas, no efficient achievement–save by dint of separating the positive from the negative aspects of colonialism.

It is true that in the end history simplifies everything. From the tangle of elements a trend emerges. And this was already apparent by 1930. Certain clear-sighted minds had recognized it then. The downfall of the system was immanent in its apogee. This was not the result of any nemesis. The accumulation of the same factors, the same urges, resulted in effects contrary to those it had produced hitherto. The Maghribi nation arose out of the colonial triumph. Perhaps we could even fix the date of this reversal: 1934–5. After this date, which appears to me as a threshold, a logical node, the key to a pattern, an almost total change is apparent. The same ambiguity of life is still evident, but it points in a new direction. While the struggle progressed, its object had shifted. Nationalist claims now implied a maturer Westernism in the way of life, a maturer reason in religion: the opposite of everything the old Maghrib had fought for.[1] The colonial powers, while mastering the State, lost contact with the land in which they had sought to implant themselves. Their self-interest lost them the advantage of the cultural values spread by France, which had served to arm their expansion, and which now armed those in revolt against it; while the nationalists, by their choice of rationality, took over the cultural task from the enfeebled colonizer.

Thus each side was fighting for something which it was not, or was no longer. And both contributed to the advent of something which nobody as yet imagined. Nobody? The feeling of certain groups, the intuition of certain individuals led them to put in hand this great upheaval, even if they did not clearly conceive it. The ideas and facts that kept most faithfully to this process gained much of their strength from it. It inspired men and things, giving wholeness to separate elements and resolving situations. It combined in a common direction, continuously or by fits and starts, the most diverse impulses of Maghribi life: the impact of material and abstract energies on a land, the response made to them by that land, competition between moral codes and the progress of consciousness.

The propagation of industrial culture had assumed, in this country, as in many others, the oppressive form of imperialism. The *colon*, as an economic and social type, had prevailed over all others, and had carried this encroachment of form over content, so to speak, to intolerable extremes. French domination, selfish in its use and reticent in its communication of progress, did nevertheless bring two worlds and two

---

[1] Cf. the Arabic proverb quoted by *al-Shihab*, Oct. 1930, p. 578: '*idha wasala al-shai' ila haddihi, raja'a ila diddihi*', the thing having reached its end, turns into its contrary'.

systems into contact with one another. It carried with it a whole host of things and ideas. Its voluntary educative efforts, and more broadly the spread of its literature and its way of life, intensified by the reactions this provoked, constituted its most positive and least contested contribution. Now this process did not only involve the two partners at a particular stage of their development. We should be misjudging the special character of the Franco-Maghribi situation if we neglected the factors that gave it such powerful resonances.

For the drama represented centuries-old conflicts, far exceeding the importance of the colonial situation. The Frenchman, in the eyes of the Maghrib, stood for Byzantium, *Rumi*, while the Levant recognized in him the Frank, or *Franj*. To the Arab peoples, France represented Hellenism, and also the power of Rome at its harshest. At the period we are studying, North Africans over the whole southern face of the Mediterranean, from the Western Protectorate to the Eastern Mandate, from the Atlantic to the river Taurus, saw in France the embodiment of almost all the roles in which West fought East during so many centuries,[1] under forms as diverse as the Roman Empire, the spread of Turkish power, the Crusades, maritime rivalry, Mediterranean trade, and finally colonial imperialism. The conflict between colonizer and colonized had a significance beyond their mutual relationship, because of all these memories and echoes. It had become the conflict between two permanent heroes, two classic figures of the ancient world. Thus it had a symbolic meaning exceeding that of any other imperialist venture. To find another example of such confrontation we should no doubt have to go back to the days of Muslim Spain. But in the present case, it was the Arabs who were striving to reconquer their own. In this respect the Maghrib seems an Andalusia in reverse.

At the very least, an association of ideas which this study cannot disregard caused the people of the Maghrib to identify the expansion of industrial civilization with that of Mediterranean Christianity. Hence, as we have seen, the legitimate but in fact disproportionate fears aroused by the Eucharistic Congress of Carthage or the *dahir* of 1930. Moreover the Maghrib in the twenties was peopled to a large extent by Old Believers, for whom a system based on temporal determinism was nothing but a form of *ishrak*;[2] whence the vehemence and astonished horror of their resistance to it. In the culture spread, willingly or not, by the French, and which claimed to have both practical and ethical aspects, they saw the culmination of the ascendancy of material things, of bondage to objects. They would have to do much violence to themselves, or descend to many compromises, before willingly accepting this culture. They

---

[1] Of which British policy in the Levant took full advantage.

[2] Literally, 'polytheistic association' of other beings with God. The mystery of the Trinity, according to N. Berdiaeff, 'is orientated towards the world', *Dialectique existentielle du divin et de l'humain*, 1947, p. 62.

certainly did not do so without mental reservations, nor, at first, without utilitarian aims. Such an alteration affected their most respected traditions. In the era of colonization, as in the days of Byzantium, traditional Islam was characterized by its rejection of whatever interfered with immediate experience, whatever interposed itself between God and his creatures. It accused Satan of 'stealing' (*yastariq*)[1] the secrets of that dialogue. But there were many beings and things whose interception was to be feared. The Prophet condemned any form of priesthood. Instituted religion must be answerable only to its originator. In our own day, Islam condemns colonial alienation not only because of its injustice but because it stifles man's impulse towards the divine and eternal under a layer of interests and procedures.

Thus all those things whereby the new Maghrib was being built up: the growth of foreign enterprise, the evolution of law and jurisprudence, increased acquisitions, and above all capitalist accumulation, were essentially abhorrent to Islam. Against that process of construction, at once reifying and reified, armed with the material and moral weapons of modernity—analysis which breaks things up, synthesis which distorts them—Islam could only react, so long as it had not learned to use these weapons, by recourse to the strength it had always possessed: that by which, fourteen centuries earlier, the proud nudity of the Arab had defied the complex richness of Heraclius.[2] Thus it opposed colonization by appealing to primal forces: virility, patriarchal pride, belief. Undoubtedly these forces, during the early stages, must have had to shelter in the protective shadow of a mountain cave, unless it were in the depths of the unconscious, and that thus the appeal to autochthonous energies sometimes took the form of a descent into hell . . .

For a long time the Muslim could only resist these developments, of which he was the instrument as well as the object at stake, by his indefatigable appeal to his *usul*—his sources, his principles, his origins. He thus exalted the fundamental as opposed to the historic. But meanwhile he had become increasingly possessed of the objects, languages and weapons of his adversary. He quickly put these to the test. Success, like failure, only led him to a more assiduous study of other lessons. This acquisitive resistance is the stage at which we find him at the outset of our story, and we leave him having in many respects assimilated—through secular Westernization, or through Islamic modernism—even more of these weapons, these languages, these objects. The fact that his adopting them had not yet enabled him to make a full recovery of his own, that he still only partially belonged to history, that in other words his modernity was acquired rather than fully assumed, endured rather than deliberately chosen—created many difficulties for him. Torn be-

[1] *Qur'an*, XV, 18.
[2] *Hadith*, tr. Houdas and Marçais, vol. II, LVI, ch. 102, p. 327; ed. 1345, vol. II, part 4, p.54.

tween fact and faith,[1] he compromised them both and contaminated them more than he conciliated them. As faith was still powerful within him, a modernity imbued with the contribution of the alien, and with his own struggle against that alien, seemed to him a renunciation of that faith. Those parts of society or of the individual which were unaffected either by that contribution or by that struggle suffered from neglect, even more than the rest suffered from usurpation. To the Maghrib, its own contemporary history appears primarily as heresy. Experiencing denaturation, the Maghrib fights back with its old weapon – purism, return to the sources, the quest for the fundamental. It upholds intransigence, as against acceptance; Arabism, as against *francité*; insurrection, as against compromise – the insurrection of the heart, if not that of the nation.

It was not the least of France's errors or misfortunes in the Maghrib, at that time, not to have satisfied or surmounted these demands. Or rather to have found no common conclusion for the twofold process which, motivating the two parties individually, and both of them reciprocally, drove them further apart as the matter of their quarrel increased. For the Maghrib was growing physically while its soul was thus being rent asunder. Colonial accumulation intensified until it led to its own destruction. National attitudes hardened to the point of total mutual rejection. Instead of purifying what had been achieved, the system accentuated contradictions. How can one wonder that at the end the Maghrib felt itself compelled to follow its historic course single-mindedly, even at the cost of bloodshed?

Now since the beginning of time this land of discord, *eris*, and of desire, *eros*,[2] has been a scene of encounter and of strife. Agreements have been as cruel as conflicts, and conflicts as fertile as agreements. Whatever is created here has been contended for by the fiercest forces, but at the same time it has been warmed by the glow from rival fires. Thus Muslim civilization and Graeco-Latin civilization united on the Western Mediterranean in three lands: Spain, Sicily and North Africa. To consider the latter alone, one might say that from the very beginning, its destiny has made it the prey alternately of East and West:[3] Carthage, then Rome and Byzantium, Islam and then France, and now an Arabo-Berber reconquest. This gave rise to great suffering, as is only too well known. But history contains within itself its remedy and perhaps its pardon. Man's hope disregards implacable straight lines. We may hope, therefore. But for what?

[1] Here the problem of the Maghrib is akin to that of the Arab East, as I have tried to define it in a recent book.

[2] Recalling presocratic philosophy.

[3] I need hardly say that my 'West' is that of the Industrial Revolution, and that this East–West parallel is limited to historic developments, having nothing in common with the disturbing suggestions of Denis de Rougemont . . .

The time has not yet come for an epilogue about the issue and consequences of a conflict which threatens to spread far beyond its geographical, human and logical limits. The Islamo-Mediterranean debate of which this book has tried to portray one phase, of considerable importance no doubt through its challenge and of moving interest to our own hearts, was a somewhat limited one, in space and time, and was visibly becoming more so. The colonial system, which had come from overseas, wanted paradoxically to cut off this land from its horizons, including the French horizon. And for this reason it ended up as a parody of itself. It liquidated, in rigid diagrams, the possibilities of development it had itself opened out. On the other hand, the problems it posed opened on to wider problems, more familiar in our time: is the world to become socialist? Will man regain his totality by means of and in spite of technique? Will emancipated nations provide their own hypothesis of humanity? Colonial history touched such questions only in an indirect and negative fashion. It therefore came to an end because of its unfitness as well as its anachronism. Nations who discarded it achieved nothing, if they did no more than discard it. For through emancipation they only attained access to even harder problems. This inclines one to fear as well as to hope. Finally, more general risks are involved in the extension of their problem sought by these nations and our own. The Franco-Maghribi conflict, even seen in its widest form, may disappear in a planet-wide conflagration which would transform the existence of the human beings involved and the nature of the object at stake. The conjectures I shall venture to make will thus depend on the assumption that the setting and substance of the conflict remain identifiable.

With this qualification, I do not believe that the Latin element introduced into North Africa during the colonial era will vanish from it. But it will have lost more than its political power. More profoundly, it will have failed–largely through its own fault–to give direction to the transformations it had itself inaugurated. In its effort to appropriate a race and a land, it should seek to adapt itself to them, rather than them to itself. At that price, resuming, within legitimate bounds, its impulse towards that race and that land, it might still continue to diffuse its own values, and might take part in fresh syntheses.

An empire may break up into independent nations, but this does not mean that the people of the Maghrib will revert to an earlier stage of their own existence. To ensure their future, they had to sacrifice much of their pre-colonial even more than their colonial past. They thus find themselves, like their brothers in the Middle East, absorbed by that dispute between the authentic and the effective which undoubtedly constitutes the profoundest debate in which they have been involved since their conversion to Islam. For this reason, according to one ancient interpretation of the term *jihad*, holy war, their fight is not so much against the Other as against themselves–against a certain aspect of themselves. And it is in this sense, too, that the sub-title of this book may be understood.[1]

Success in this task, and in the twofold struggle that it implies, would open up a wonderful future for the southern shores of the Mediterranean. Let us avert our eyes from the terrible events of today. At the close of a study of a Maghrib that is past, we should look to the Maghrib of the future. No doubt, like France, it has many obstacles to surmount, many risks to face. We are still burdened, as were the French and the people of the Maghrib of the inter-war period, by inheritances and habits some of which threaten to prove fatal. But we are no longer in the time when Catholic kings, violating their sworn word, drove the Moors from the land they had liberated. While history is being made, nothing is inexpiable. Or rather everything can be repaired, because everything has got to be rebuilt. The nations, faced with tasks of such gravity, have something better to do than to indulge in nostalgia and revenge. If this is true, the Maghrib of tomorrow, born of the Maghrib of yesterday, will cease to harbour eternal dreams of reconquest. It will reconcile upon its soil former enemies, now become brothers, and the Andalusia twice lost will become for both of them an Andalusia regained.

---

[1] *Jihad*, the 'holy war', is above all an inner conflict of the soul, an attempt at self-mastery. So the commentator al-Qasimi, Cairo edition, vol. XII, p. 4384, discussing the *Qur'an*, XXII, 18, speaks of *jihad al-nafs*.

Glossary of Arabic Words and Expressions and Local Terms*

W̲e have collected here, for the benefit of the non-specialist reader, the Arabic, Berber and other words, expressions and local terms used or mentioned in this book, accompanying them with a rough translation, valid for their context and necessarily arbitrary. They are given here in italics – in transliteration. A circumflex (^) denotes a long vowel, an apostrophe (') the glottal stop, and an inverted apostrophe (') the laryngeal fricative. Consonants with dots beneath them (ḍ, ṭ, ṣ, ẓ) are emphatic.

abendu: olive-trees in joint ownership
adab, pl. *âdâb*: literature, belles-lettres
'âdil: clerk of the court, *qâḍî's* witness
adrar (Berber): highlands
âfâqîyûn: coming in from the country
agurram, pl. *igurramen* (Berber): marabout, man of God
'ainuh l-khaḍra: green eye, denoting a ladies' man
ajyâl, sing. *jîl*: generations, age-groups
'âlî d-drîba: guest-room, upper chamber (Tunis)
'âlim, pl. *ulamâ'*: man of learning, Muslim teacher
'âm ṣâba: good harvest year
'âm esh-sherr: year of scarcity, dearth
Amazigh, pl. *Imazighen* (Berber): native of the Middle Atlas
amghar (Berber): Berber chief
amîn: master of a guild (Tunisia)
'âmir: reclaimed land (opposite to *ghâmir*)
anflûs (Berber): dignitary with communal responsibilities, formerly religious
'arḍ kabîra: rich soil, cornfield
'arsh, pl. *'urûsh*: tribe, tribal land
'aṣîda: kind of gruel

* The French or local form of a classical word is given in brackets.

396

'aṣîr ṣ-ṣâbûn: (lit. ropes of washing) thick coiled gold or silver bracelets (South Morocco)

'aṭṭâr: grocer

'attûr: tailless (Tunisian Sahil)

'aûd: horse

azaghar (Berber): plain, lowland

'azîb: princely domain (Morocco)

âzrîya: divorced woman or widow, sometimes living in sexual freedom (Aurès)

baladî (*beldî*) town-dweller, sedentary as opposed to nomadic, a local man

bâmya: a kind of mallow

bâna: calm (with reference to the sea) (Tunisian Sahil)

banadesh: Tunisian pastry

baraka: blessing, intangible quality possessed by holy men

barâtel: arcades (Tunis)

barrânî: stranger, outsider

barûd: combat, war

basapân: marzipan (Tunisia)

bâsh: south-westerly wind, sirocco (Tunisian Sahil) (see *shîlî*)

bash 'âdil: *qâḍî's* senior clerk

béchariste: intermediary between thief and victim

belgha: oriental slipper

bendir: tabor

beylik: state, government (Tunisia)

l'bîrô 'arab: Arab bureau (local French administration)

bît d-drîba: janitor's quarters at hall entrance (Tunis)

blaighîya: (guild of) makers of men's slippers

bqûqa: kind of tubercle

bṣal Far 'ûn: sea-onion, sea-scilla

bsîsa: kind of gruel

bundâf: coarse material (Fez)

bûrî: mullet

burj (*bordj*): small fort

bûsa 'âdî: Saharan knife

caïd: see *qâ'id*

cantine: kind of club, café, where people gather to chat, drink and gamble

dâhir: Sultan's decree (Morocco)

ḍahrâwî: northerly wind

dallâl: public crier

dâr: house

dâr qshûr: (lit.) 'house of (on the) crust'
darjîya: ladder (Sahil)
darr jîya: 'come and milk me' (Sahil)
dasâ'is: intrigues, snares
debbâgha: (guild of) tanners
dehs: alluvium, rich clay soil (Morocco)
derrâza: weavers
dhû murû'a: man of honour and esteem (literary)
diffa: big reception, feast where a sheep is usually roasted
dîn: religion
drâzât: weaving (in a wider sense: workroom (Fez))
drej u-ktef: decorative stonework (Tunis)
drîba: vestibule
dshisha: gruel
dukkâna: bench outside house (Tunisia)

fallâh (fellah): peasant
faqîh (fqîh): jurist-theologian, scholar
fehhâm: coal merchant
fernân: green bark of an oak-tree, tannin
fiqhî: lawyers' slang
fliyû: marjoram
foggâra: underground waterway (South Morocco)
frîk: roasted soft grain
funduq (fondaq): inn with inner courtyard

garrûs: dace, sea-perch
gern jdi: kind of wild artichoke
ghâba: olive forest
ghadb: anger
ghâmir: land lying beyond the perimeter of a reclaimed area (opposite to 'âmir)
gnâwîya: kind of mallow (Tunis)
goum: company of Moroccan soldiers, colonial troops in French army
guish: military tribe; the land allotted to it
guitoune: tent

habûs: pious foundation (in the Near East: *waqf*)
hadâr: town-dwellers
hâdhâ dyaul-râ: 'he is one of ours' (Morocco)
hâdhâ uld famîlya: 'he is of good (or noble) birth'
hadîth: Prophet's sayings, Muslim tradition
hâjj: person who has accomplished the pilgrimage
hâkim: governor (in the colonial administration)

ḥall liyâ: 'take me'
ḥallîya: pastry
ḥamâsa: anthology of ancient Arabic poetry
ḥamrî: red land
ḥanût: shop, room
ḥanût s-sahhâra: saloon for musical soirées
ḥara: ghetto (Tunis, Fez . . .)
ḥarâm: prohibited
ḥarîka: town quarter (Tunis)
ḥarka: small armed band
ḥarmel: rue (medicinal herb)
ḥashîsh: hashish
hedya: annual courtesy visit of Moroccan chiefs to the Sultan
hejjâla: divorced woman (Morocco)
henshîr: landed estate (Tunisia)
ḥifẓ: learning the Qur'an by heart
ḥirâf: trades, guilds
ḥizb: party
hrâirîya: silk-makers (Fez)
ḥûḍ: earth shaped into a basin at base of tree for irrigation
ḥûma: quarter
ḥurm: holy enclosure
ḥurma: self-respect, respect towards others (Morocco)
ḥuwâr: young camel's meat (dish)

'ilm l-krûsha: learning of the bowels (poetic inspiration)
imâm: leader of prayers in a mosque
inzâl: perpetual lease over a *ḥabûs* (Tunisia)
ishrâk: polytheistic association
istaraqa: to steal
isti 'lâmât: information (bureau)
istiqlâl: independence
itkellem bel-fiqhî: 'he speaks lawyers' slang'

jabalî (jeblî): north-westerly wind
jadîd: new, modern
jaish (jîsh): army
jaiyid: pl. *jiyâd*: man of rank (Algeria)
jamâ'a: tribal council
jdâm: kind of leprosy
jellâba: man's cloak with hood and sleeves
jifa: beast, dead or killed, that has not been canonically slaughtered (Morocco)
jihâd: holy war
jininâr: a general (slang)

jlâlbîya: (guild of) makers of fine fabrics
jnân l-bḥer: country house

Ka'ba: black cube-shaped building in Mecca, the centre of the Islamic world
kâhyalik: jurisdiction of deputy *caïd*
kaidâr: nag
kefta: minced meat
kerkûr: a pile of stones, cairn
khaḍḍar: greengrocer
Khaldûnîya: cultural association in Tunis
khalîfa: local representative of the Sultan (Morocco)
khâmis: sharecropper, tenant who receives a fifth share of the produce as salary
khâtim: seal
khbîza: kind of cake
khelwa: cell
kherrâza: (guild of) slipper-makers
khubbeyza: mallow
khuṭba: Friday sermon
kîf: Indian hemp
kîmîya: chemistry, alchemy
klâ: to eat (dialect)
ksâd: slump
kshûk: kiosk on top of house
kurdunîya: (guild of) shoemakers
kusksi, kuskus, kuskusu: couscous, North African dish

la krîz yâ khûyà: 'it is the crisis, brother!' (slang)
lâ ta 'taqed wa lâ tantaqed: 'don't believe, but don't criticize'
laṭîf: special form of public prayers in mosques
lebbâṭa: (guild of) leather-workers
liff: clan, faction

ma'allem: master craftsman
ma'allem shkairî: (lit.) 'satchel man', employer in tanning industry, a kind of entrepreneur
madîna: Muslim (section of a) town
madrasa (medersa): higher school of law and theology
mahdî: leader of a millenarian movement
maida: table
mâjen: disused well
majlis (medjlis): assembly council
majlis al-baladi: municipal council
majlis al-'urf: special council under the presidency of the Shaikh al-madina (Tunis)

makhzen: government (Morocco)
maktûb: (lit.) what is written, fate
manḍâ: pay-clerk
mandîl: duster, cloth
maqṣûra: small rear-chamber (Tunis)
marsâ: port
mâshîya: yoke of oxen
maṣûna: protected one (said of a Moroccan bride)
maudû': subject
mauqif (*mûqef*): station, place where labour is hired (Fez)
mausim: fair held in honour of a patron saint (Morocco)
meshwî (*mechoui*): roast mutton
medsher: village (Morocco, Jebala)
meḥrath meknâsî: primitive plough made of a bent wooden branch and a metal blade
merja: coastal swamp
merryût: marrubium
mesqât: impluvium (Tunisian Sahil)
mestaraq: kind of barn (Cap Bon)
miḥrâb: direction of Mecca marked by a niche in a mosque
mishwâr (*mechwar*): inner promenade ground in Sultan's palace (Morocco), name of a public square in Tlemsen
miskîn (*meskine*): destitute, poor
mrâḥ: open space surrounded by tents, inner courtyard
msâkhrîya: (guild of) makers of women's slippers (Fez)
mṣewwer: half a roasted sheep
mu'adhdhin: the one who calls people to prayer, muezzin
mu'allaqa: room on first floor above the 'patio'
mu'ammir: settler (bringer of culture)
mudda'î: plaintiff
mugran: confluence of two rivers
muḥarrik: (lit.) mover, district warden, janitor, gatesman (Tunis)
muḥtasib: legal officer in Fez, arts and crafts inspector (of Andalusian origin)
mukhaznî: militia man attached to local administration (Morocco)
mukhifîya: urn, jar
mujâhidûn: participants in a holy war against the infidels
mulk: private property (land)
muna: cake made in Oran to be eaten out of doors
muqaddim: overseer, local agent of a religious brotherhood
muṭâla'a: reading to oneself (as opposed to recitation)
mu'tamidîya: chief town of nine districts, *shaikhats*, forming an administrative unit (Tunisia)
mu'tamid: delegate
muẓâhara: street demonstration

nahḍa: revival, awakening
nakabât: disasters
nefra: brawl (Algeria).
niẓâm: organization, curriculum
ntâ' jeddûh: 'in the manner of his grandfather' (Tunisia).
nûba: musical band, musical suite
nuwâr: 'flowers' (term used with reference to syphilis)

ojak: troop (Turkish word used in Tunisia)

qâ'a: room on the first floor above the 'patio' (Tunis)
qabîla (kabyle) pl. *qabâ'il*: tribe, canton
qadîm: ancient
qâ'id (caïd): tribal chief, government agent
qal'a: fortress, eagle's nest
qandîl: candle, lantern
qaṣba (casbah): fortress, the Muslim section of a town
qaṣida: poem, ode
qbû: room opened out of a wall, sitting-room
qmija: kind of shirt
qorrîṣa: kind of bitter lettuce
qubba: small funerary monument surmounted by a dome

rabâb: kind of violin
rabât: suburb (Tunis)
raffaḍa (raffeẓ): to resist with weapons
râqda: fallow
Ramaḍân: annual month of fasting
rezza: calico headband
rfîṣ tûnsî: mixture of crushed dates and semolina (delicacy from southern Algeria)
rîm bet-terfas: gazelle with truffles (dish)
rodd bâlek: 'careful!'
Rûmi: Christian

sabâṭ: vaulted passage (Tunis)
ṣadâq: dowry
ṣaff: league, kabyle clan
ṣâḥib, pl. *aṣḥâb*: companion, partner
sbisrîya: chemist's shop (Tunis)
sebbânîya: silk neckerchief
sedra: wild jujube tree
seffârîn: brass-workers
sefnârîya: wild carrot
selq: wild spinach

sha'b: the people
shabâb ghâfil: 'heedless youth' (literary)
shabîba: young people
shaikh: elder, wise man (general term of respect)
shaikh al-madîna: town-government representative, title among the
  Bin Gâna (Biskra)
shaikhat: women singers, usually of easy virtue
shalamush: kind of double fork (Tunisia)
shandaqûra (Berber): *ajuga viva* (plant)
sharbîya: earthen jar (Sahil)
sharqî (*cherqî*): easterly wind
sharr bîya: 'have pity on me'
shâ'ûsh (*chaouch*): orderly, guard, porter, constable
shebka: esparto net on back of a beast of burden
sheftel auras: mutton from the region of Aurès (dish)
sherbîl: woman's embroidered slipper
shikâya: court of arbitration held in open market
shîlî: south-westerly wind, sirocco
shluq: south-easterly wind
shorba bel-frîk: wheat soup
shwaishîya: makers of *shishîyas*, red felt skull-caps
sîba: dissidence
ṣîla: princely munificence
skâken: knives
smawî: north-easterly wind
ṣûfî: Muslim mystic
ṣuḥba: kin, partnerships
ṣukhûr al-ḥayât: 'the stones of life' (literary)
sûq: open air-market, small street occupied by artisans
sûqî: dealer in fats, cheese, salt, etc.
ṣwâr: sing. *ṣûra*: silver bracelets

ṭaba': decorative design on women's slippers
tabaṣṣur: circumspection
ṭabya, pl. *ṭwâbi*: ridge of soil separating fields
ṭagya: close-fitting cap
tâjir: (lit.) dealer, merchant; also settler
takaut: tannin
ṭâlib, pl. *ṭalaba*: student
tallghûda: cardoon (kind of artichoke)
taqbilt: Shleuh canton (Morocco)
targhûda: kind of tubercle
tassargal: kind of fish eaten dry by the Shleuh (Morocco)
taṭauwu': free choice
taṭwîf: circumambulation

403

t-bârek Allâh: 'God bless you'
temmâr: fruit-seller
tertîb: tax on agricultural produce in Morocco
thadderth: small fortress where grain is stocked (Aurès)
thaura: revolution
thaurat al-'aql: mental revolt
tifef: mushroom, kind of sow-thistle
timijja: mint
tirs: rich soil (Morocco)
tqarriṭa: woman's neckerchief
tshemmesh: to bask in the sun
tufik: Kabyle grouping
turba: dome-shaped funerary monument (Tunisia)
twiza: collective labour

uffâda: amber-scented syrup
'ûra: privy parts
uṣûl: bases, origins

wa'da: annual feast
wâdi (oued): river bed seasonally filled with water
wâ'iẓ: preacher
wakîl (oukil): representative, the defence counsel in a Muslim court
waqf: see *ḥabûs*
waṭanî: national, nationalist

za'îm: chief, leader
zâwiya: (*ṣûfî* centre or monastery) religious centre
zenqa: small street
zidhûm: sweet onion
zughbî: ill-starred
zuqu: pine-flavoured gruel
ztâwer: history, 'intrigue' (Moroccan dialect)
zûja: plough drawn by two animals

Index of Names

405

Index of Places

Index of Tribal Groups and Families

Index of Authors, Periodicals, etc.

415

General Index

419